Publishing Digital Video

Second Edition

Jan Ozer

AP Professional
AP Professional is a division of Academic Press

Boston   San Diego   New York
London   Sydney   Tokyo   Toronto

United Kingdom Edition published by
ACADEMIC PRESS LIMITED
24-28 Oval Road, London NW1 7DX

ISBN 0-12-531942-8

Printed in the United States of America
97 98 99 00 CP 9 8 7 6 5 4 3 2 1

For Dr. Barb
Four down, one to go.

Contents

Chapter 3   Windows Development Environment   35

Chapter 4   Streaming Multimedia   59

Chapter 5   Streaming Audio Technologies   81

Chapter 6   Tour de Codec   113

Chapter 14   Low-End MPEG Compression Tools   467

Chapter 15   MPEG-2 Technology   521

Acknowledgments

I recently had the honor of attending Max Cleland's inauguration as U.S. Senator in Washington, D.C. A triple amputee from the Vietnam War, Max's achievements are truly inspirational, and the ceremony was joyous and uplifting and filled with love.

One unanticipated but hardly surprising benefit was walking away with a colloquialism to start this acknowledgment. In retrospect, it's hard to imagine attending any political inauguration, much less that of a *southern* senator, without taking away some pithy words of wisdom.

Quoting Georgia Gov. Zell Miller, Max began his comments by saying, "If you see a turtle on the top of a fence post, you pretty much know that it didn't get there by itself." Truer words were never spoken, especially in relation to this book.

This book has been a work in progress since the completion of the last book. I owe several individuals and organizations extreme debts of gratitude for helping me through this period.

I learned what I know about the art of benchmark testing at *PC Magazine*, where editors Brian Nadel, Tom Mace, David Lidsky, and Jamie Bsales consistently pushed the editorial envelope, providing the discipline and rigor to bring order to the chaotic worlds of digital video, graphics, and Internet multimedia. Working in the labs with the likes of Jeff Mace, Jay Munro, Jon Hill, Don Labriola, Jim Karney, and Linda and Erik Von Scwebber was a consistent pleasure and constant learning experience.

David R. Guenette, editor of *EMedia Professional* (formerly *CD-ROM Professional*), edited more than his share of my overly voluminous writing, provided consistent support, emotional and otherwise, and even picked up a tab or two after some particularly "reflective" evenings in richly paneled hotel bars. Abigail Crane of *Computer Shopper* funded most of my early learning curve into streaming audio and video technologies, and Elaine Elliot and Rivka Tadjer also pointed me in new directions.

In truth, working with these folks was like Hanukkah all year round, getting new presents at every turn and being paid to play with them. Most days around Doceo, it doesn't seem like "work" at all.

Writing a book, for better or worse, always feels like work, and this one wouldn't have been finished without the help of several friends and co-workers closer to home. Michelle Weiss, my indefatigable coordinator, was many times the eyes, ears, and stopwatch on this project, providing a fresh and objective viewpoint and much more concentration than I could bring to bear. Erika Jolly also found herself impaneled on the Doceo jury, providing an oft-necessary deciding vote on the still image, video, and audio tests that we performed.

Lisa Torres-Rosen, Michelle's mom, not only served Doceo jury duty but also was the star of the video benchmarking the new Sony DV technology. Thank goodness for that—we all needed a fresh face in our test videos, and I'm sure you readers do, too.

Reed McMillan of Splash Productions produced the greatly enhanced CD-ROM in the back of the book, with David Buonomo of Blue Atlas Productions writing most of the code. Largely through their efforts, the CD-ROM has grown from a static container of video files to a vital component of this living book.

This book has particularly benefited from contributions made by other organizations, large and small. In 1993, GTE Visnet graciously donated the benchmark clips for Doceo's Video Compression Sampler, many also used in this book. Intel has provided a range of support for our testing activities and IBM has been continually gracious with access to their labs, equipment, and technicians. Mindspring, Inc., our friendly neighborhood ISP, provided much advice and access to their server, even after going nationwide. Other companies that provided products for testing or test beds include Adaptec, Adobe, Asymetrix, ATI, CompCore, CeQuadrat, Data Translations, Diamond, Duck Corporation, FAST, FutureTel, Horizons Technology, Matrox, MediaMatics, Microsoft, miro, RAD Game Tools, Sony, Truevision, Ulead, and Xing.

Special thanks to Chris Ewald and Cathy and Sherry Manning of Triad Interactive for supplying a Washington, D.C., home base, tons of editorial direction and several test clips. Thanks also to Phil Davis of Chicago's Imagination Pilots, who contributed the critical test clip and sidebar describing real-world video overlay. Thanks to the crew at Four Palms for many clips used for MPEG-1 testing.

I owe many thanks to my colleagues in the digital video field, particularly Jeff Sauer at *NewMedia Magazine*, who created the benchmark tape used to test MPEG-1 products. Both Jeff and *DV Magazine*'s Richard Popko gladly shared their testing experiences, validating some results and letting me know when to push harder, providing much-needed feedback on the bleeding edge.

I'd also like to thank *Computer Gaming World*'s Jill Anderson, *DV Magazine*'s Heidi Carson, the Gartner Group's William Caffery, Four Palms' Ken Santucci, Steve Griffin of the IAT, Ted Greenwald of Interactivity, David Duberman of the *Daily Spectrum*, *PC World*'s Mike Desmond, Jerry McFaul of SIGCAT, Pat Tracey, and Charlie White. Thanks for taking my calls, thanks for helping out.

I appreciate the patience and support shown by AP Professional during the course of this project. Special thanks to Julie Champagne, the warm voice at the end of the phone, and the shock absorber for the inevitable bumps between author and publisher. Well done.

Lest this section outpace the book, we'll end here, mindful that while there are almost certainly some names forgotten, no contribution was unappreciated.

Preface

"I don't think we're in Kansas anymore, Toto."
Dorothy to Toto, *Wizard of Oz*
"Duh."
Toto to Dorothy (cut during final editing)

Video developers aren't in Kansas anymore, either. In 1994, if you could produce high-quality Indeo files for 2X CD-ROM distribution, you could write your own ticket in any multimedia publisher or in-house training department. While it's still important today, you also need to know about MPEG-1, which presents a totally different spectrum of issues. Since you're the "multimedia person," you'll also find yourself dealing with questions about streaming audio and video on the World Wide Web. A working knowledge of DVD and MPEG-2 round out the resume of the video professional on the rise.

While initially a challenging but fairly one-dimensional occupation, publishing digital video today is about distributing video assets over a multitude of delivery mediums and target platforms. Mediums range from floppy (potentially) to CD-ROM, Internet, and DVD. Target platforms start with 486/33 computers and top out with MMX-enabled, 200-MHz Pentiums, and Pentium Pros.

Publishing digital video is about working with new tools like digital video cameras and "Firewire-based" capture cards, video editors that provide virtually unlimited creative flexibility, and new encoders that compress audio and video down to previously unthinkable bandwidths. Ah yes, and working in Windows 95 or NT rather than Windows 3.x—all of which means a much broader knowledge base and expanding range of skill sets. So, as you've probably guessed, these are the issues we'll be dealing with in the book.

HI THERE!

Thanks for buying this book, or, lest I sound presumptuous, thanks for picking me up in a bookstore and scanning through the pages to see if you want to buy. Now that I've got you for a moment, I'd like to share my vision of the book with you.

Our goals are relatively simple. First and foremost, assuming you have the basic tool set—camera, capture card, and video editor—our goal is to help you learn how to use them to their fullest capabilities to produce the best possible quality video most efficiently.

If you don't have the tools, we show you how to invest your money wisely, to spend where it delivers additional value and to save where it doesn't. Oh yeah, we show you how to install the tools as well. If you're exploring new markets like streaming audio and video for Internet delivery, we demonstrate what's currently possible with demonstration clips, cutting away the voluminous Internet hype and let you see for yourself what can be done at 28.8 kbps.

Our teaching theory is also relatively simple. Some folks enjoy understanding the theories that lie under the techniques, the "whys" under the "hows." Others just want to get the job done as quickly as possible, or efficiently delegate work to coworkers. Our goal is to serve both requirements.

Detailed Procedures and Theory

For those who just want to get the job done, we've included detailed procedures that you use throughout the video production process, customized for specific applications. Wondering which audio values to use when capturing for Indeo video interactive? Got you covered! How about the resolution and frame rate for a software MPEG-1 encoder, nonlinear editing, or even for Internet delivery? Same story—step by step we illustrate the controls and specific values that you should use for all four applications. Also new are animated screencams that help you locate critical menu commands.

For those looking to perfect the art, we've included tons of theory on a range of topics, from compression to editing to digital cameras, all supported by comparative videos. For up close and personal analysis, we've included the latest version of VCS Play, Doceo's dual-screen video display.

If we say that BetaSP produces better quality than SVHS, you can load comparative videos side by side and see for yourself. Ditto for techniques like precompression filtering, video transitions, and alternate key frame interval settings.

The CD-ROM also contains each chapter in Adobe Acrobat format. If you choose to read that way, you can view videos and screencams from within Acrobat, instantly seeing the points made in the text.

A "Living" Book

We're living on Internet time now, which means that technology books can become dated before they hit the shelves. Sad, especially for the author, but a fact of life.

In this regard, the CD-ROM contains information and sample files that couldn't make it into the book. For example, Intel released the Intel Smart Video Recorder III (ISVR3) late in the production cycle, and we couldn't review the product along with the rest. But the CD-ROM contains sample files from the ISVR3 so you can compare for yourself. Ditto for modifications made by Data Translations for their Broadway product, and for RealAudio 3.0 from Progressive Networks.

Looking forward, we know that Corel will soon introduce a video editor to compete with Premiere, and that Macromedia is planning to do the same. Optibase and FutureTel have announced sub-$2,000 real-time MPEG-1 encoding cards, and FutureTel an MPEG-1 video editor. Matrox will soon ship Rainbow Runner, a video capture daughtercard for their Mystique graphics card.

For all these products, and all others that affect the digital video landscape, our goal is to apply the relevant test suite used in the book to update our features tables and make this new information available on our Web site (www.doceo.com) and/or via updated CD-ROMs. Not all information will be free—hey, a boy's gotta eat—and reader response will ultimately dictate how long we continue. But our goal is to create a living book, which keeps you up to date long after you make the initial purchase.

So, buy the book because the current content is of immediate use to you. When you install the CD-ROM, you can register via e-mail, and let us know whether to advise you of future updates. Check www.doceo.com every now and then and we'll let you know which product reviews are coming down the pike.

CHAPTER OVERVIEW

All chapters are fairly modular, so you can jump in anywhere without losing synch. Each chapter starts with a brief description of the contents and most end with a summary, so you should be able to tell quickly whether the information is immediately relevant.

Now a quick chapter-by-chapter overview.

Theory and Overview

Chapter 1   Introduction to Digital Video   What's the big deal about digital video? Everything! It's all huge. Here we'll overview the capture and playback process, and you'll see why digital video eats kilobytes for breakfast, megabytes for lunch, and gigabytes for dinner. Better order your new hard drive now.

Chapter 2   Introduction to Video Compression   This chapter describes how compression works, not just for the propeller heads and compression junkies (like me), but for everyone working with digital video. You'll learn how to film for compression and how compression options we'll use later impact video quality and display rate.

Chapter 3   Windows Development Environment   When you develop video under Windows, you're on Microsoft's playground. Good thing, too, since before Microsoft launched Video for Windows in 1992, the playground was confusing and populated by largely incompatible products used in highly specialized vertical markets. Not surprisingly, no consumer or even corporate mass market existed. Now Video for Windows has been upstaged by ActiveMovie. Read all about it here.

The Internet

Chapter 4   Streaming Multimedia   Without question, the most significant new medium for transmitting information is the Internet—how did we ever live without it? Very few digital products of any kind, in-house or commercial, reference or entertainment, are developed without some vision for using the Net for marketing or data distribution. Get up to speed fast on new concepts and technologies like streaming audio, video, electronic documents, and VRML.

Chapter 5   Streaming Audio Technologies   Streaming audio technologies like TrueSpeech, RealAudio, and StreamWorks have made big noise on the Web. Play multiple samples to hear for yourself how they compare in terms of quality. Learn when you can safely use free technologies like TrueSpeech and when it's better to have a server-based product like RealAudio.

Operation

Chapter 6   Tour de Codec   Here we look at both streaming video technologies and CD-ROM–based technologies including MPEG-1. See which streaming video technology *really* delivers the low-bandwidth goods and how Indeo video interactive (IVI) stacks up against MPEG-1. Speaking of IVI, Intel incorporated more options than Carter has pills—learn how to configure your video file for maximum quality and playback performance.

Chapter 7   Analog/Digital Video   You've got a five-figure budget burning a hole in your pocket and want to buy tools that deliver optimum quality to the final compressed video. Analog video comes in many flavors, each with a different price tag, and digital video technologies like Sony's DV Format are also entering the picture. Does investing in quality at the front end create better video? You'll see for yourself in this chapter.

Chapter 8   Capture Karma   What features should you look for in a video capture card? Which current card gives you the most bang for your capture buck? We compare FAST's AV/Master, miro's DC30, Truevision's Bravado, and Digital Video Arts' WakeBoard. On the CD-ROM is the Intel Smart Video Recorder III, which costs hundreds less than all four others. Find out which delivers the best video quality for capture for compression (Cinepak/MPEG-1), streaming Internet delivery (VDO), and nonlinear editing.

Chapter 9   Surviving Your Capture Board Installation   Installing a capture card in a Windows 3.1x system involved a familiar but very inefficient technique called plug and pray. Windows 95, along with Intel and a bunch of happily compliant vendors, brought about a new paradigm, plug and play. Never in the history of computing has one consonant made such a difference. Still, around every bend there's a banana peel that can cost you days of debugging. Learn how to identify and avoid them here.

Capture, Preprocessing, and Compression

Chapter 10   Video Capture   Video capture is the first step in the digital process. Here's where you select frame rate, resolution, and other video characteristics. This chapter presents statistics and sample videos to aid your selection and describes how to maximize capture quality. Step by step, we also describe the software controls and hardware links needed to capture in both step frame mode and real time. We address four distinct scenarios: capture for nonlinear editing and capture for MPEG-1 encoding, streaming Internet, and traditional software-only codecs like Indeo video interactive.

Chapter 11   Video Editing   Now that your video is on disk, it's time to get it ready for compression. Programs like Premiere and MediaStudio offer a range of options like titling, transitions, and special effects. They also compress to Indeo and other formats with more or less efficiency. Learn which does which functions best, and when VidEdit does it better. See where Premiere does the absolute best job and when a program costing hundreds less does just as well.

Chapter 12   Video for Windows Compression Controls   The chapter we've been waiting for—finally ready to compress! Here we apply compression theory to select the right compression technology and parameters and produce the highest quality video file.

MPEG-1/MPEG-2

Chapter 13   MPEG-1: Overview   MPEG-1 has made the transition from hardware to software codec, and now should be considered in virtually all linear playback video applications. This chapter presents a high-level view of the MPEG-1 landscape, covering encoding and decoding options.

Chapter 14   Low-End MPEG Compression Tools   When is an $89 MPEG-1 encoder better than a $75,000 MPEG-1 encoder? When you don't have $75,000, of course. Here we cover six low-end MPEG-1 encoders costing $89 to

$1,500, analyzing comparative video quality, playback display rate, and compatibility. Several options are real winners, but others can cause more problems than they solve.

Chapter 15 MPEG-2 Technology   DVD is the next "must have" technology in the digital video arena, and MPEG-2 is the video compression technology that makes it happen. Learn what MPEG-2 and DVD have to offer, and when you need to factor these new technologies into your development plans.

What We Don't Cover

We still don't cover Macintosh technologies, making the book of marginal value for those working on the Mac or PowerMac. Our editing chapter focuses more on the basics than how to make your movies look like *Independence Day* or *Jurassic Park*. We also don't cover the programming side, so if you're looking for low-level advice on how to integrate videos into Visual C++ or Asymetrix ToolBook, you're in the wrong place.

I'll end the beginning with a story. I was on a press tour years ago, visiting *InfoWorld* to meet with a technical analyst and reporter. I was chatting with the analyst before the reporter arrived, and had just given her a book written by the president of my company on an obscure branch of geometry.

When the reporter came in, the analyst raved about the book and asked the reporter if she, too, wanted a copy. The reporter looked at the title and said, "No—why don't you just read it and tell me how it ends."

I hope you'll want to read this one and see for yourself.

About the CD-ROM

The CD-ROM should be considered an integral part of the book. It is arranged in subdirectories by chapter name, using the chap_x naming convention. Most of the videos referred to in the book are included in their respective chapter by figure number. For example, Fig12_12.avi would be the source of Figure 12.12 in the book.

The CD-ROM contains some materials that aren't referenced in the book simply because of time constraints for the book. When this happens, we'll let you know via notations on the PDF file for that chapter.

The printed page cannot completely and accurately represent the video, so we urge you to follow along. The video camera icon (see icon at left) indicates when a video is present.

Install the CD-ROM by running setup.exe from the root of the CD-ROM. Please read the readme.txt file in the root of the CD-ROM before installing to catch up on any last-minute program changes.

When you install the CD-ROM, you'll be asked to register by e-mail and whether we should let you know when we add new data to the CD-ROM. Coming soon are reviews of low-cost MPEG-1 encoders from Optibase and FutureTel, a look at Corel's new video editor, a round up of Firewire capture cards from miro, FAST, and DPS, and many other tidbits.

We hope you'll join our efforts to make this a living book. While not all information will be free, it will keep you abreast of the latest tools and technologies that affect your ability to efficiently produce digital video for all distribution mediums.

VCS PLAY

VCS Play is Doceo's dual-screen video playback application that you can run by double-clicking on the VCS icon in the Publishing Digital Video Group. The program lets you compare MPEG, AVI, and MOV videos side by side, identifying the codec used to compress the file and the comparative bandwidth (Figure CD.1). You can also play the file and measure the display rate and create a histogram of the file's streaming bandwidth.

As we describe in the book, all video files are named after their respective figures, so fig12_5.avi is the video file from which we captured Figure 12.5.

You can use VCS Play on any video file, either from the CD-ROM or from any other source.

Figure CD.1   The new, 32-bit version of VCS Play with the cool, dual-screen display.

Your version is a fully functioning version of the program except that *the book CD-ROM needs to be in the CD-ROM drive to load the program.* Once the program loads, you can remove the CD-ROM and play any video from any source.

The full version of VCS Play retails (on a CD-ROM with lots of other stuff) for $50 or more, depending on content. You can upgrade to the full retail version that doesn't require the CD-ROM for a mere $25 if we can download a new executable to you, or $35 if we have to send you a diskette (includes shipping and handling).

If the VCS icon doesn't show up in your Publishing Digital Video group, you can install the program by running setup.exe in the VCS subdirectory on the CD-ROM. You can also load the program by clicking Start > Programs > VCS32 > VCS32.

Briefly, to play a file, press the yellow file folder located on the lower left-hand side of both screens. Play the file using the VCR-like controls just below the image. Here are some quick commands to try to get familiar with the program.

(a) With a video loaded, place your mouse cursor anywhere on the video and press the left mouse key, zooming into the video. Use the right mouse button to return to a 1X view.

(b) Touch the "eye" icon, taking you into the video file statistics screen. Note the details provided. The "ear" tab takes you to audio statistics.

(c) The "monitor" tab lets you play the video in different resolutions, while the magnifying glass, shown in the right-hand side of Figure CD.1, is the frame profile. Note that we can now tell you whether the frames are intra, bidirectional, or predicted frames when working with an MPEG-1 file, a cool new feature.

(d) The final tab—not really sure what the icon represents—contains new ActiveMovie performance statistics. Hit F1 to learn what they mean.

Those of you who have used the program before might notice that report printing is gone as a feature. This didn't seem particularly important to most users; if you think it's a necessary feature send us e-mail (jan@doceo.com), and we'll consider putting it back in.

ADOBE ACROBAT

Adobe Acrobat Reader is a viewer for electronic documents in Adobe's Acrobat format, also known as PDF files for their file extension, .PDF, which stands for Portable Document Format. A copy of the reader should be installed during the setup procedure.

All book chapters are included on disk in PDF format. If you read the book on screen, you can play most videos captured as screen shots by simply clicking on each figure's caption. Within each PDF file, you'll also have the ability to search for text strings.

Load the table of contents by loading contents.pdf from the root of the CD-ROM, which contains hyperlinks to each chapter. Each chapter subdirectory (e.g., \chap_1) also contains the PDF file for that chapter, which you can load directly.

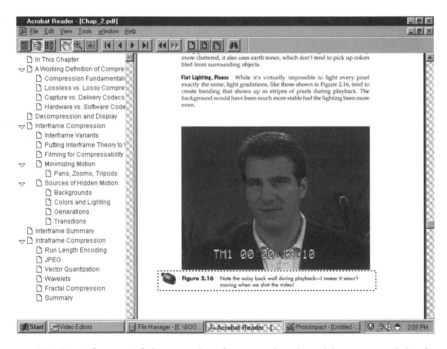

Figure CD.2   Files in Adobe Acrobat format. The dotted line around the figure caption indicates that you can click the caption and play the video.

The Acrobat Reader has an array of display options. We've created a table of contents for all files so you can touch the section you want to read and jump directly there. All chapters should be in their most readable position with the table of contents showing (Figure CD.2). You can change this easily by using either the menu controls or icons located above the page.

You can run Acrobat by double-clicking on the Reader icon in the Publishing Digital Video Group or by clicking Start > Programs > Adobe Acrobat > Acrobat Reader 3.0. If for some reason the Acrobat doesn't install during CD-ROM setup, you can install the reader by double-clicking on setup.exe in the acroread subdirectory.

I encourage you to spend some time experimenting with the Reader's many features. Acrobat is a great way to publish documents on both CD-ROM and the Web, and we're glad to include it. For more information on Acrobat, check out www.adobe.com.

Chapter 1

Introduction to Digital Video

IN THIS CHAPTER

The term *digital video* refers to video playing on a computer in digital format. It does not include analog video playing through a special add-in card or animation. This section covers two topics. First, we'll briefly describe the capture process, in which video and sound are converted from analog to digital format. This topic is covered in detail in Chapter 7. Then we'll discuss the storage and bandwidth problems this conversion creates.

Concepts covered in this chapter are used throughout the book, and a working knowledge is essential to your understanding of future chapters. More important, we'll define many of the acronyms, slang, and technojargon used in and around video and multimedia.

WHAT IS VIDEO?

Video is a stream of data composed of discrete frames, usually including both audio and pictures. Television signals in the United States have 30 discrete frames per second, while European stations broadcast 25 frames per second. Most movies are filmed and played back at 24 frames per second.

All images start out in *analog* form, whether captured on film or on videotape. For me, analog was always a pretty confusing term. Definitions like "the representation of information by variable physical quantities such as the size of electrical voltages—voltages which are analogous to the original data" just didn't compute.

The term finally started to make sense when an engineer took his finger and drew a curvy sine wave like that shown in Figure 1.1. Analog is a naturally continuous signal, with breadth and depth. There are no pixels or other fixed boundaries, no precise values. The signal is virtually infinitely magnifiable, which lets you take a 1-inch slide and blow it up to billboard size without loss of quality or pixelation.

In contrast, computers are *digital* devices that process all information as zeros and ones. A picture on your computer isn't continuous. It's a collection of pixels, each with a precise value, usually defined as some blend of red, green, and blue. If you blow a computer picture up to billboard size you still have the same number of pixels—they're just bigger. So your billboard ends up looking like those huge screens at stadiums that look great from far away but resemble color connect-o-dot drawings from close up.

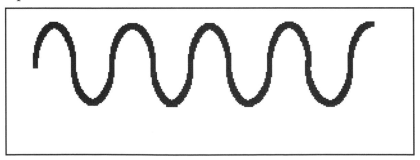

Figure 1.1   Analog sine wave.

When you convert video from analog to digital format, or *digitize* the video, you take in the analog signal, divide it into discrete pixels, and assign a precise value to each pixel. In the old days of 2- and 4-bit graphics cards and monitors that displayed only 16 different colors, pictures looked awful. There just weren't enough colors to simulate the analog event.

Today's 24-bit video cards offer over 16 million colors, more than enough to fool the eye into believing that the digital video shown on the screen is actually a continuous analog event. But we're getting ahead of ourselves. Let's look at the hardware.

Video Capture—Overview

OK. You've got some analog footage to digitize. Maybe some clips from your latest annual meeting, customer testimonials, or maybe just some home movies. The first thing you need is an *analog source* to input the analog video signal into the computer. Generally, any device that can feed a signal to a television can be your analog source. VHS and laserdisc do just fine.

Then you need a *capture card* or *frame grabber,* which is a printed circuit card installed in your computer. As a point of reference, capture cards that operate at 30 frames per second are called "real-time" capture cards. Most capture cards come with software that controls the capture process. For example, when working on the Windows platform, the software is usually either Adobe Premiere, Ulead MediaStudio, or some other similar program.

Most analog devices feed 30 frames per second into the computer at resolution of 640×480 pixels, the standard for broadcast television. Most video captured for compression and playback is captured at a resolution of 320×240, and often the frame rate is dropped to 15, 20, or 24 frames per second. So the capture card's first task is to shrink the video to the target resolution and drop frames to reach the target frame rate. These processes are both forms of *scaling*, in which the characteristics of the analog signal are scaled back for use on the digital platform.

After scaling, the card digitizes the video by dividing the frame into pixels and assigning a digital value to each pixel. This process is shown in Figure 1.2.

 Video You can view a live demonstration of this process by double-clicking on CAPTURE.AVI in the Chap_1 subdirectory.

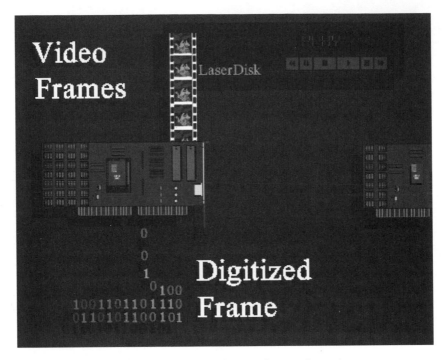

Figure 1.2 Capture board digitizing frames from a laserdisc.

Most capture cards don't digitize audio, so you'll also need a sound card, another printed circuit card installed in your computer. Like the capture card, the sound card takes in the analog audio signal and assigns a digital value to specified points in the audio stream (see Figure 1.3).

When video and audio are captured on separate devices, the software that ships with the capture card combines the two digital streams into one synchronized file. On the Windows platform, combined audio/video files are usually .AVI files, which stands for audio/video interleaved, the Video for Windows standard formulated by Microsoft back in 1991.

Bandwidth Defined

The term *bandwidth* is used in two ways. First, it is a measure of a device's *capacity*, or ability to move information to or from a device, system, or subsystem, normally measured in quantities of data per second. CD-ROMs are usually measured in kilobytes per second (KB/s) with an old single-

Figure 1.3   Sound board digitizing from a laserdisc.

spin CD-ROM drive capable of transferring 150 KB/s. Newer drives are typically measured comparatively to single-spin drives, with a 2X drive capable of 300 KB/s, a 4X drive capable of 600 KB/s, and so on.

Note that traditional communications equipment like modems, ISDN, and T-1 lines is measured in kilo*bits* per second (kbps), rather than kilo*bytes* (KB/s). This means a 28.8 kbps modem, virtually the fastest you can get, produces only about 3.6 KB/s, roughly 41 times *slower* than a now obsolete single-spin CD-ROM drive. ISDN, at 128 kbps or 16 KB/s, is about nine times slower than the same CD-ROM drive. As we'll see, this makes the Internet extremely inhospitable to multimedia formats.

Bandwidth is also used to describe the data flow necessary to support a process like video playback. A 30-second video file that is 4.5 megabytes (MB) in size has a bandwidth of 150 KB/s, because data must be transferred at that rate to play the file without interruption. This usage is a measure of requirement, and when used in this manner, bandwidth is used inter-changeably with the term *data rate*.

As you would expect, problems occur when a process' data rate exceeds the bandwidth capacities of any system component. It's useful to experience this agony firsthand, early in the learning cycle, because it is so fundamental to everything we'll be doing. So saddle up Windows Explorer/File Manager, click your way over to the Chap_1 subdirectory, and double-click on meetingf.avi. This should load Media Player and attempt to play the file (Figure 1.4).

This raw file has a bandwidth requirement of 3.5 MB/s, fatter than the capacity of even the fastest CD-ROM drive. When you play the file, you'll notice brief bursts of audio and video playback, followed by much longer periods without activity.

In our little experiment, the video file's bandwidth *requirement* is exceeding your CD-ROM's bandwidth *capacity*. Any time this dynamic occurs,

Figure 1.4   When video file bandwidth exceeds system capacity, bad things happen.

whether from CD-ROM or from the Internet, bad things are bound to happen.

Since the data rate of raw digital video exceeds the transfer capacities of almost all computer system components, bandwidth is an issue that must be addressed early and often in the video capture and creation process.

Video Bandwidth

Let's analyze the bandwidth of a video file. Assume the captured file has a resolution of 320×240, which means that there are 76,800 pixels in each frame. Each raw pixel represents one byte of data.

We captured the video at 24 bits color depth, so it takes 24 bits or three bytes of data to describe the color of every pixel. As we discussed, the high color depth is necessary to simulate all of the colors in the original analog video. However, it also means that each video frame, uncompressed, is about 230 KB in size.

We captured the video at 15 frames per second. That translates to about 3.45 MB of data per second, or over 212 MB per minute. In one hour you'd accumulate about 12 gigabytes of data. Probably a bit more than you have on your hard drive, wouldn't you say?

	Per Frame	*Per Second*	*Per Minute*	*Per Hour*
Uncompressed bandwidth	230.4 KB	3.46 MB	207 MB	12.41 GB

It also exceeds the transfer bandwidth of most computer system peripherals. Quad-spin CD-ROM drives transfer about 600 KB/s, less than a fifth of what's required. PCI bus computers can handle the load, but you need a pretty exotic hard drive to get close to sustaining 3.45 MB/s transfers, not to mention that you could store only five minutes on a one gigabyte drive. So even after scaling video resolution from 640×480 to 320×240, and cutting the frame rate in half, our uncompressed video is still too large to store economically and impossible to access in real time.

That's where video compression comes in. For without compression, there would be no digital video.

SUMMARY

1. Digital video is video playing on your computer in digital format, not analog video playing through a special adapter.
2. Video is originally filmed in analog format, a naturally continuous signal with breadth and depth. When video is digitized, or converted to digital format, precise color values are assigned to fixed points, or pixels, in the analog stream. This allows the digital computer to represent an essentially analog event.
3. Digitization requires both video and audio capture facilities and an analog source to feed the video stream into the computer. During capture, video is often reduced in frame rate, resolution, or both, in a process called scaling. Capture software like Adobe Premiere controls the process, including audio/video synchronization.
4. Bandwidth has two meanings. The first is a measure of device capacity or ability to move information to or from a device, system, or subsystem. For example, a single-spin CD-ROM drive can transfer only 150 KB/s into the computer and accordingly has a bandwidth of 150 KB/s.

   The second meaning refers to the data flow necessary to support a process like video playback. For a example, a 30-second video file approximately 4.5 MB in size has an average bandwidth of approximately 150 KB/s. When used in this manner, bandwidth is used interchangeably with the term data rate.
5. To play smoothly from any source, whether Internet or CD-ROM, the file requirement must be less than the capacity of the device or communications link, or smooth playback will be interrupted.
6. Even after scaling from full to quarter screen, raw video has a bandwidth of over 6.9 MB/s, well above that of the fastest CD-ROM. For this reason, compression, in one of its many flavors, is absolutely essential to digital video.

Chapter

Introduction to Video Compression

IN THIS CHAPTER

Video compression is the science of the impossible. As we've seen, without compression, most computers can't supply the data, much less decompress and display at 15 frames per second.

The currency of the impossible is the trade-off. Technologies trade off screen resolution for file size, color depth for frame rate, and video quality for data rate. All to deliver a steadily improving but still less than dazzling video stream.

This section starts by defining compression, then moves to the decompression and display process. This will help you appreciate how much work goes into playing digital video files. Then we'll study the two main elements of video compression, interframe and intraframe compression.

One of the most often asked questions is why cheap television sets outperform Pentium computer systems respecting video playback—in essence, why analog video is superior to its digital counterpart. Well, we've narrowed the gap since the first book, but the TV still has a little on even the most advanced system. We'll address that herein.

Finally, the classic compression trade-off is video quality for bandwidth, and as file size approaches CD-ROM rates some loss in quality is inevitable. However, video compression works extremely well in some cases and very poorly in others. Understanding the compression mechanics presented in this chapter will help you work with compression—not against it—and help you produce higher quality compressed video.

A WORKING DEFINITION OF COMPRESSION

As we've seen, uncompressed video is a sequence of frames containing pixels. Video compression is a process whereby a collection of algorithms and techniques replaces the original pixel-related information with more compact mathematical descriptions (Figure 2.1).

Decompression is the reverse process of decoding the mathematical descriptions back to pixels for ultimate display (Figure 2.2). At its best, video compression is transparent, or invisible to the end user. Video consumers—the end users actually watching the video—don't want compression, they want video. So the true measure of a compression technology is how little you notice its presence, or how effectively it can reduce video data rates without adversely effecting video quality.

COMPRESSION FUNDAMENTALS

Video compression utilizes two basic compression techniques, interframe compression, or compression between frames, and intraframe compression, which occurs within individual frames. We'll cover both topics in detail in a few moments.

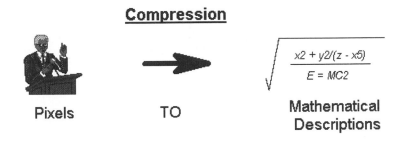

Figure 2.1   Definition of compression.

A few other points. First, the techniques and algorithms used during compression transform a video frame from a collection of dumb pixels to a set of instructions used by the decompressor to recreate the original pixels. So when we talk about a frame "telling" the decompressor what to do, you'll know what we mean.

Second, compression doesn't change the number of frames in the video. During scaling, you may drop the frame rate from 30 frames per second to 15. However, once you submit a video to the compressor the frame count doesn't change. Even during interframe compression, wherein frames "borrow" information from other frames, each frame contains its own separate description.

Third, while all codecs use intraframe compression, not all use interframe. For example, early versions of TrueMotionS from Duck Corporation and Horizons Technology do not use interframe techniques, though Duck released a version with interframe compression in mid-1996.

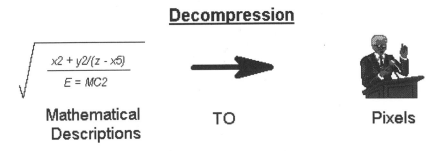

Figure 2.2   Definition of decompression.

Finally, you can't buy interframe compression from one vendor and intraframe from another. You buy one product from one vendor that takes in digitized video and produces compressed files. The same with decompression, which is always dedicated to one compression technology. This compression/decompression combo is commonly referred to as a codec.

Lossless vs. Lossy Compression

One of the most fundamental concepts in compression is the difference between lossless and lossy compression. Lossless compression techniques create compressed files that decompress into *exactly* the same file as the original, bit for bit. Lossless compression is typically used for EXE and data files where any change in digital makeup makes the file useless. Lossless compression is used by products like STAC and DoubleSpace to transparently expand hard drive capacity and by products like PKZIP to pack more data onto floppy drives for delivery or storage.

In general terms, lossless compression techniques identify and utilize patterns within files to describe the content more efficiently. This works quite well for files with significant redundancy, like database or spreadsheet files. As a whole, however, these techniques typically yield only about 2:1 compression, which barely dents uncompressed video files.

Lossy compression, used primarily on still image and video files, creates compressed files that decompress into images that look similar to the original but are different in digital makeup. This "loss" enables such techniques to deliver from 30:1 to 50:1 compression.

Run an EXE file through a lossy compressor and you've got serious problems. However, in a 24-bit image file, a few changed pixels or altered shades is virtually unnoticeable. This is especially true in video, where your eye has to spot defects in 1/15 of a second.

Lossy Compression—Example   Figure 2.3 is a 180 kilobyte TIF file. Figure 2.4 was compressed to about 4 KB using a lossy compression technique called JPEG. At about 45:1 compression, JPEG was over 22 times more effective than most lossless techniques. Even upon close scrutiny, it's almost impossible to tell the images apart.

You might be thinking—4 KB per frame, 15 fps, that's a bandwidth of 60 KB/s and the video looks great. What's the problem? We'll just use JPEG.

Well, unfortunately, it doesn't work that way. JPEG implementations can decompress and display a file very quickly, often in under a second on

Figure 2.3   Original file—180 KB.   **Figure 2.4**   JPEG file—4 KB.

Pentium class machines. However, video requires at least *15 frames per second*. Whereas still image codecs can focus on quality at the lowest possible file size, video codecs must be concerned with quality and *display rate*, or the rate at which frames decompress and display. Otherwise, they would produce video that looked like fast, high-quality slide shows with audio.

For this reason, video codecs aren't the sequential operation of lossy still image codecs, they're built from the start to provide the optimal balance between display rate, video quality, and bandwidth.

All relevant capture and delivery codecs are lossy technologies—it's the only way to achieve the required compression. By both definition and operation, this translates to loss in quality, which is the first reason that digital video doesn't look as good as analog video. The second reason relates to the cumbersome nature of the decompression and display process. We'll get there in a moment, after we explore two other definitions worth addressing early.

Capture vs. Delivery Codecs

It's helpful to make an early distinction between "capture" codecs and "delivery" codecs, though the line is not 100 percent clear. Capture codecs are used in capture cards to compress video before storing it to disk and usually are implemented through dedicated codec chips or chipsets. If you've looked at capture cards, you may have heard of Motion JPEG, the most popular capture codec, used in systems ranging from $500 capture cards to $100,000 AVID editing suites.

Motion JPEG is a high-bandwidth, high-quality codec that uses intra-frame techniques only. While you might capture with Motion JPEG for editing and subsequent compression with a delivery codec, you would never ship a CD-ROM containing Motion JPEG video, since the bandwidth would be too high and all your customers would need special chipsets in their computers to decode the video.

Delivery codecs are used to compress video after capture and editing. Here the focus is on achieving target bandwidths like 2X CD-ROM rates while maintaining as much quality as possible, and for this reason, most delivery codecs use both interframe and intraframe techniques. Popular delivery codecs include Indeo, Cinepak, and increasingly MPEG on CD-ROM and codecs like VDO and Vivo on the Internet.

The line between capture and delivery codecs blurs in two instances. First, Intel's Smart Video Recorder, one of the most successful capture cards in the mid-1990s, uses Indeo as the "capture" codec, but during capture compresses only with intraframe techniques. In most instances, developers recompressed the video using interframe and intraframe before delivering the video on CD-ROM.

The second instance is MPEG. Many products capture and compress to final MPEG format in one step, including a pretty hot board from Darim we'll look at in Chapter 8. Note that you would *never* use these products to capture video for subsequent editing or compression, only for MPEG-1 compression.

Hardware vs. Software Codecs

Capture vs. delivery codecs isn't the distinction that MPEG blurs—it also virtually obliterated the distinction between hardware and software codecs.

Ah, the world was a simple place back in 1994. Software codecs like Indeo and Cinepak could play on any computer that could load a Video for Windows or QuickTime runtime, actually performing acceptably well on 486/66 computers and the brand new Pentiums.

In the other corner stood MPEG, the monolith, with shockingly good video quality but one vast ball and chain—you needed a specialized card in your computer to play the video back. Although they were cheap, they never worked particularly well and MPEG playback cards, despite the hype, never really caught on.

Then, as Pentiums accelerated into the 100s, graphics architectures became more streamlined, and graphics cards more powerful, three companies discovered that you could play back MPEG files without special hardware. Today, on a Pentium 133 you can actually achieve close to 30 fps from a CD-ROM, a remarkable achievement when viewed from where we stood in 1994.

Unfortunately, MPEG still has some thorns and hasn't quite taken the world over yet, but in many markets it may not be long. Still, when we talk of "software-only" codecs, we are typically referring to Indeo, Cinepak, and TrueMotionS, as well as the low-bandwidth ranks of Vivo, VDO, and CoolTalk. Except now we say "traditional" software-only codecs.

Decompression and Display

Video decompression and display has become increasingly efficient over the past two years, but it's still a far cry from the simplicity of painting analog signals down a TV monitor. Understanding this process helps you appreciate why video still chokes most computers. It's also critical to understanding subtle differences between codecs and how innovations like the PCI bus and video coprocessors accelerate video performance.

To illustrate this process, we've recruited some real specialists. Our first helper is Mikey, who represents your computer's host processor. Since we're running in Windows, that means he's either a 386, 486, or Pentium. Mikey's a painter, which is pretty appropriate given the amount of painting done during video playback.

Vinnie represents your video processor. As you probably know, every video card has its own processor. Vinnie's role in digital video has traditionally been very small, but it's growing rapidly, and he'll be a major player in the near future.

Video You can view a live demonstration of this process by double-clicking on PBACKBAS.AVI in the Chap_2 subdirectory.

Retrieval   The first step is retrieving the compressed data stream into main memory, which is typically performed by the host central processing unit, or CPU. Here the data is being retrieved from a CD-ROM. As shown in Table 2.1, this simple transfer requires a surprising amount of processor overhead.

Figure 2.5   Step 1—data retrieval.

Note that retrieval from a CD-ROM takes almost twice the CPU overhead. As we'll see, that can mean that video plays faster from a hard drive than from a CD-ROM.

Table 2.1   CPU overhead required to retrieve data at 150 KB/s. Tests performed on an 80486 computer with VLB bus with 8 MB RAM.

	Hard Drive	*CD-ROM*
150 KB/s transfer	11.1%	21.10 %

Decompression   After the video is in main memory, the CPU converts the mathematical descriptions contained in the frames back to pixels to start the display process. Since 1995, the CPU has been sharing the load, since most advanced graphics cards serve as "video coprocessors," accepting partially decompressed video and completing the job.

Figure 2.6   Step 2—decompression.

Still, as processors get faster, codec developers assume more decompression power and create advanced codecs to deliver higher quality video at 30 frames per second (fps) as opposed to 15. The average codec has gotten that much more difficult to decompress, and codecs like Indeo video interactive or MPEG (with software-only decode) make today's Pentium 90s perform like yesterday's 486/33 computers struggling to decompress 15 fps Cinepak files. With software-based MPEG-2 on the immediate horizon, it's reasonable to assume that your CPU will be struggling to keep up with video decompression and display well into the next century.

Transfer to Graphics Card   Since 1995, Intel and particularly Microsoft have worked hard to make video playback more efficient by eliminating the need to work within Windows Graphics Device Interface. Prior to these efforts, all standard video codecs had to convert each frame to Windows Device Independent Bitmaps (DIBs) and place it in a memory buffer for transfer to the graphics board. Although wasteful in terms of processor power, this mechanism allowed applications to work with all graphics cards without writing specific drivers. The unfortunate side effect is that it slowed video playback to a crawl.

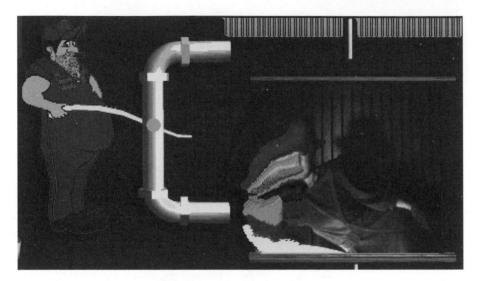

Figure 2.7   Step 3—transfer to video memory.

Keep in mind that the same processor that is struggling to retrieve the data from the CD-ROM and decompress in main memory is also in charge of moving the decompressed data, now seven or eight times its original size, through the bus to the graphics card. Talk about no rest for the weary!

Paint to Video Memory   At this point the video processor takes over, painting the video to video memory and converting the data back to analog format for display.

This time- and CPU cycle-consuming process all relates back to the fact that video is an analog format that digital computers can only simulate, never operate in its native form. In contrast, your television takes in an analog signal and transfers it to the picture tube. No decompressions, constricted bus transfers, or file conversions. Small wonder a $200 television can outperform your Pentium when it comes to video.

INTERFRAME COMPRESSION

Interframe compression uses a system of key and delta frames to eliminate redundant information between frames. Key frames store an entire frame while delta, or difference, frames record only interframe changes.

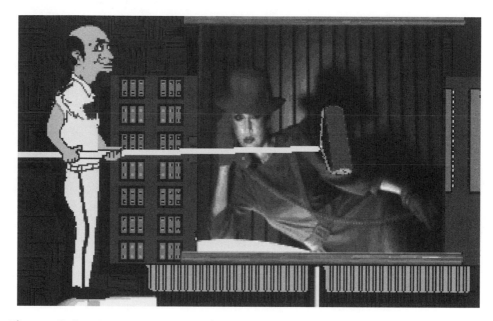

Figure 2.8   Step 4—paint to video memory.

Key frames, or reference frames, are not compressed at this stage. Instead, they're included in the compressed stream in their entirety to serve as a reference source for delta frames. Delta frames contain only pixels that are different from either the key frame or the immediately preceding delta frame, whichever frame they reference during compression.

During decompression, delta frames look back to their respective reference frame to fill in missing information.

Here's how it works mechanically. Figure 2.9, or frame 13857, is the key frame, and frame 13859, shown in Figure 2.10, is the delta frame. The frames are two apart because the video sequence from which they were taken was captured and compressed at 15 frames per second. Both frames are divided into blocks of pixels. The delta frames are compared, block by block, with their respective key frames. Blocks that match are discarded. Blocks that don't match are saved, as shown in Figure 2.11, and subsequently compressed during intraframe compression.

During decompression, key frames are carried forward to help construct delta frames. In essence, during decompression the delta frame tells the codec, "I'm just like the key frame except for these pixels." Or, in our

Figure 2.9   The key frame.   **Figure 2.10**   The delta frame.

example, change the numbers, adjust for some minor face movement, and use the rest from the key frame. The decompressor makes the changes and converts the frame to a Windows DIB for transfer to the video card.

   Video You can view a live demonstration of this process by double-clicking on INTERFRA.AVI in the chap_2 subdirectory.

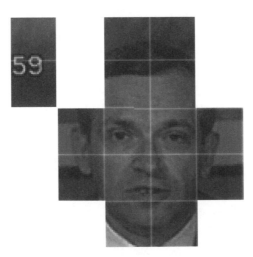

Figure 2.11   Delta frame with interframe redundancies removed.

Interframe Variants

Different compression techniques use different sequences of key and delta frames. Most Video for Windows codecs, for example, calculate interframe differences between sequential delta frames during compression. In this scheme, shown in Figure 2.12, only the first delta frame relates back to the key frame; the rest relate back to the immediately preceding delta frame. In other schemes, all delta frames relate back to the key frame.

As shown in Figure 2.13, MPEG gives us three kinds of frames, I or intraframe, which corresponds to the key frame; P or predictive frame, which roughly corresponds to the delta frame, and B or bidirectionally interpolated frames, which look for redundancies in both the immediately preceding and immediately succeeding I or P frames.

Not surprisingly, the B frames give MPEG its punch, since you double your chances of finding redundancies that fuel interframe compression. For this reason, Intel added B frames to Indeo video interactive, introduced in late 1995.

Whatever the scheme, all intraframe compression techniques derive their effectiveness from interframe redundancy. Low motion sequences like the "talking head" shown in Figure 2.11 have a high degree of *inter*frame redundancy, which limits the amount of *intraframe* compression required to reduce the video to the target bandwidth.

All relevant intraframe techniques are lossy in nature. When there's less data to compress there's less loss in quality. During playback of low motion sequences, less decompression is required, which reduces the load on the host CPU and boosts the display rate, increasing perceived video quality.

Interframe motion is the enemy of interframe compression, decreasing both video quality and display rate. Let's see just how badly.

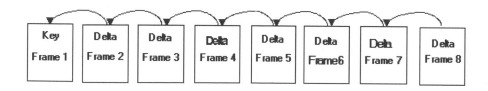

Figure 2.12   Delta/key frame sequence for typical Video for Windows codec.

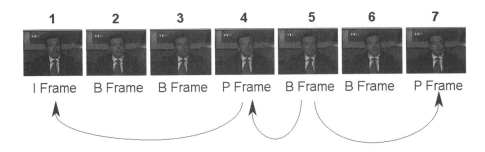

Figure 2.13   The I, P, and B frame sequence, especially the B frames, give MPEG its compression punch.

Figure 2.14 is a raw frame from a high motion sequence. Figure 2.15 is the same frame, compressed to 150 KB/s with Video 1, the same codec that produced the high-quality talking head image shown earlier in the chapter. As you can see, quality dropped dramatically and the motion video is practically unusable. Not only did quality suffer, the display rate for the second video was three frames per second slower than the first.

As you may have guessed, Video 1 is not our first choice for compressing high motion sequences. However, although the effects may not be as severe, motion degrades the video quality of all codecs.

Figure 2.14   High-motion sequence, uncompressed.   **Figure 2.15**   Same frame, compressed.

Putting Interframe Theory to Work

As we've seen, the degree of interframe compression significantly affects how well a video sequence will compress. If your video doesn't compress well, it won't look good, especially when compressing to a fixed bandwidth.

Many common analog film techniques cripple interframe compression. For example, panning, or moving the camera slowly across a field or object, changes every pixel every frame. Similarly, zooming, either closer to or farther away from the subject, also changes every pixel every frame.

When simply converting analog assets to digital format, you don't have a lot of input into how to film for compressibility. However, when starting from scratch, you can take steps to improve compressed video quality without dramatically affecting the perceived artistic quality of the video. They generally fall into two categories—minimizing motion and avoiding hidden motion.

Minimizing Motion

Pans   What can I say? Pans are bad business for video compression, but there's often no other way to provide perspective. If you have to pan, do it slowly, to give the codec a chance to adjust. Fast pans are almost impossible to compress well, and the general blurriness provides a great canvas to show off the large chunky blocks that often appear.

Zooms   Same deal with zooms, except that with zooms you generally have an alternative—a fast cut to a close-up or long-distance shot. Although cuts involve extreme interframe change, they're over quickly and you can take steps—like placing a key frame at a scene change—to minimize their effect.

Tripods   Filming without a tripod often introduces motion that's imperceptible in the analog world but extremely damaging to digital video. Prior to one COMDEX in Atlanta, I borrowed some footage from a buddy who worked with Deion Sanders' show on TBS. One sequence that looked great on the VCR was Deion interviewing Barry Bonds. However, the scene compressed very poorly. When we closely examined the original footage, we noticed that the video shifted one or two pixels up and down virtually every frame, and later learned that the show was shot with a hand-held camera. If you're serious about getting good results, use a tripod whenever possible.

Many of you will find this advice too restrictive, as I've heard at seminars and classes over the years. One comment from SoftBank, a seminar for computer-based training executives, presents the issue well. After briefly describing the points listed above, one attendee raised his hand and said, "You're eliminating all the fun effects that make video interesting—which is why we use video in the first place. If all we wanted to use was static talking heads, who needs it?"

His question came very late in the seminar and caught me off guard, so I didn't really have a smooth answer. But after some reflection, here's what I think.

The state of the art in digital video is the state of the art—it's what it is. Several codecs can compress high motion sequences and deliver good quality at reasonable data rates, so most video shots are possible. However, interframe motion stresses compression; it's a fact. And arty pans and zooms and other extraneous motion will detract from video quality.

The best approach is to analyze which motion is critical to delivering the intended message of the video. Then try to minimize all others. This lets you deliver your true message with the highest possible quality video.

Sources of Hidden Motion

Clean Subjects and Backgrounds   All analog video, no matter how clean, contains a shimmering-like quality that codecs see as interframe motion. Veteran camera professionals know that pinstriped shirts turn to mush on camera, as does complex wallpaper. Capturing and compressing these types of sequences only makes it worse.

Make your subjects dress in relatively simple clothing—paisleys and madras, checked shirts, and tight pinstripes are all out. Avoid highly saturated colors like bright reds, greens, and blues that typically distort codecs. Avoid complex wallpaper and paneling, and if you see venetian blinds in the background, run—don't walk—to another location.

Clutter Is Good   Codecs seem to abhor a clear background, turning a clean gray wall into a swirling mass of motion. Motion artifacts are more clearly visible on a plain background, so using a more busy approach is better. Figure 2.16 is me, shot in the studio against a clear gray wall. Figure 2.17 is our talking head shot, with a more cluttered background. Play both files, concentrating on the background wall, and you'll see what I mean.

Color-ific   It also seems that a gray flat background is probably the worst background for filming for compression. It's not a primary color and it tends to absorb and highlight colors from surrounding objects. In various captures and compressions we saw pink and green appear in the gray, often many pixels from the source of the color. Note that Figure 2.17 is not only more cluttered, it also uses earth tones, which don't tend to pick up colors bled from surrounding objects.

Flat Lighting, Please   While it's virtually impossible to light every pixel exactly the same, light gradations, like those shown in Figure 2.16, tend to create banding that shows up as stripes of pixels during playback. The background would have been much more stable had the lighting been more even.

Figure 2.16   Note the noisy back wall during playback—I swear it wasn't moving when we shot the video!

Generations   Each time you copy or "dub" a tape, you create another generation, which, like a photocopy of a photocopy, is a bit more degraded. This isn't a problem, of course, when using a digital analog formats like D-1 or Digital BetaCAM, or when you edit digital video files on a computer. However, traditional analog editing suites have to dub for most transitions, titles, or special effects, creating three or four generations for even the simplest editing.

These dubs create noise that is manifested as artifacts and increased background noise after compression. For one of our first projects, we shot our studio video with BetaSP, mastered to 1-inch format transitions, and then copied the master to BetaSP for capture. To test how much degradation occurred by the third generation, we captured the same frame from both the original and third-generation BetaSP tape. Figure 2.18 shows the results.

 Figure 2.17   Here the noise is much less obvious because it's contained by the boundaries in the background. Clutter is good!

Overall, the changes are subtle and not very apparent on the printed page. We've included the original BMP file on the CD-ROM, which is a bit more revealing. If you play the videos themselves (Fig2_18l.avi and Fig2_18r.avi) you'll see that the original tape produced less background noise, greater facial contrast, fewer artifacts, and generally clearer color. Producers seeking the absolute highest quality either edit digitally or dub as few times as possible.

Transitions   Transitions are the bridge between two video sequences, and the type of transition used has a dramatic effect on video quality, covered in detail in Chapter 11. In general, transitions that hide one video while revealing another, like simple wipes, are very easy to compress. In contrast, transitions that push one video in and the other out operate like a fast pan, creating high motion and artifacts. Artistic dissolves and fades create similar problems.

Figure 2.18   Each video generation degrades video quality. Compare video captured from the original with video captured from the third generation.

It also goes without saying that proper lighting and similar techniques are also critical to capturing high-quality analog footage. What makes multimedia so difficult is that most of the tasks are new—you not only have to have a great idea, you have to be a script writer, cameraman, director, editor, creative director, and often the star as well. Then you have to digitize it, code it, package it, and sell it. If you're investing tens of thousands of dollars in a project, you probably should invest a couple of grand on a photographer and director—at least the first time out.

Interframe Summary

A few closing comments about interframe compression. First, when comparing codecs, remember that even minor differences in interframe motion can dramatically affect performance. So when you look at demos, be sure to notice the amount of motion. Better yet, use identical test clips. Finally, never judge a technology solely by its talking head performance, especially if you'll be working with moderate action scenes. As we saw in Figure 2.15, the ability to produce high-quality low motion sequences doesn't automatically translate into the ability to produce high-quality action sequences.

INTRAFRAME COMPRESSION

Intraframe compression is performed solely with reference to information within a frame. It's performed on pixels in delta frames that remain after interframe compression and on key frames.

While intraframe techniques are often the most hyped, overall codec performance relates more to interframe efficiency than intraframe. For this reason, we'll provide only brief descriptions of the intraframe technologies and focus the bulk of our attention on the individual codecs.

Run Length Encoding

Run length encoding, or RLE, is a simple lossless technique originally designed for data compression and later modified for facsimile. RLE essentially encodes "runs" of different pixel lengths.

Imagine that this page was divided into 2200 lines and 1700 columns, or 200 dots per inch for the 9.25-inch height and 7.5-inch width. This is the maximum resolution of group III facsimile. Look at the blank line immediately above this paragraph. You could describe the line as 1700 discrete white pixels, which would take about 1700 bytes of data. Alternatively, using RLE, you could define the pixels as one run of 1700 white pixels, which would be much more efficient.

Most 24-bit real-world videos, however, don't have long runs of identically colored pixels. Although RLE works well in the black-and-white facsimile world, it's an extremely inefficient mechanism for video.

JPEG

JPEG stands for the Joint Photographic Experts Group. JPEG still image compression technology has been adopted as a standard by two international standards organizations, the CCITT and ISO, and is the most prevalent technology. JPEG operates through the following three-step process.

Step one is the encoding mode, where the data is converted into frequency space for the discrete cosign transform (DCT) analysis. DCT starts by dividing the image into 8×8 macro blocks like those shown in Figure 2.19, then converts the colors and pixels into frequency space by describing each block in terms of the number of color shifts (frequency) and the extent of the change (amplitudes).

Because most natural images are relatively smooth, the changes that occur most often, or high-frequency changes, have low amplitude values, meaning that the change is minor. In other words, images have many subtle shifts among similar colors but few dramatic shifts between very different colors.

In the next JPEG stage, quantization, amplitude values are categorized by frequency and averaged. This is the lossy stage because the original values are permanently discarded. However, because most of the picture is categorized in the high frequency/low amplitude range, most of the "loss" occurs among subtle shifts that are largely indiscernible by the human eye. This concentrates the bulk of the compressed file information on low frequency/high amplitude changes like edges and corners.

For example, Figure 2.19 has many shades of gray that are the high frequency/low amplitude changes. If the grays blended together, your eye probably wouldn't notice. The highest amplitude change is between the gray suit and the white shirt. If this was blended into a mottled gray, it would be extremely noticeable because the edge would be lost and two

Figure 2.19 JPEG breaks image into blocks of 8×8 pixels.

colors dramatically shifted. JPEG's quantization mechanism avoids this by focusing most of the loss where it won't be noticed.

After quantization, the values are further compressed through RLE using a special zigzag pattern designed to optimize the compression of like regions within the image.

At extremely high compression ratios, more high frequency/low amplitude changes are averaged, which can cause an entire pixel block to adopt the same color. This causes a blockiness that's characteristic of JPEG-compressed images.

JPEG's relatively simple mechanics make it extremely fast. It is also a symmetric algorithm, meaning that decompression is exactly the opposite process to compression and occurs just as fast. JPEG is used as the intra-frame technique for MPEG (Moving Pictures Experts Group).

Vector Quantization

Like JPEG, vector quantization, or VQ, also divides the images into 8×8 blocks, but the information quantized is completely different. VQ is a recursive, or multistep algorithm, with inherently self-correcting features. Here's how it works.

The first step is separating similar blocks into categories and building a "reference" block for each category. The original blocks are all discarded. During decompression, the single reference block will replace all of the original blocks in the category.

After selecting the first set of reference blocks, you decompress the image and compare it to the original. Typically there will be many differences, so you create an additional set of reference blocks that fill in the gaps created during the first estimation. This is the self-correcting aspect of the algorithm. Then you repeat the process to find a third set of reference blocks to fill in the remaining gaps—more self-correction. These reference blocks are all posted in a lookup table to be used during decompression. The final step is to use lossless techniques like RLE to further compress the remaining information.

VQ compression is obviously computationally intensive. However, decompression, which simply involves pulling values from the lookup table, is extremely simple and fast. VQ is a public domain algorithm used as the intraframe technique for Cinepak and early version of Indeo, but it was abandoned by Intel in favor of wavelets for their most recent release, Indeo video interactive.

Wavelets

Wavelets combine a completely different method of image analysis with the best features of JPEG and VQ. The first step is to filter the image with a high-pass and a low-pass filter, essentially creating multiple views of the image. This clearly identifies the location of low frequency/high amplitude information and high frequency/low amplitude information. A tree-based encoder works through the different views of the image, starting with low-frequency data.

After each encoding run, the codec checks the encoded information against the next image view. This is similar to the self-correcting aspects of VQ. If the higher frequency information doesn't accurately describe the next view, the difference data is encoded. Otherwise, no additional information is encoded and the codec begins searching the next level, checking for accuracy at each level.

This layered approach provides "scalability," a key feature leveraged by Intel in Indeo video interactive and by VDONet Corporation in their VDOLive Internet streaming technology. Briefly, when sufficient bandwidth or decompression horsepower exists, all layers are transmitted to the viewer and quality is optimized. However, rather than dropping frames when bandwidth gets tight or when the decompressor starts lagging, the codec can send fewer layers of information, which degrades picture quality but maintains motion.

Once the image is completely encoded, a simple quantization method similar to JPEG's is used to compress the data. Once again, the high frequency/low amplitude information is compressed more than the low frequency/high amplitude information. This preserves edges and targets the bulk of the compression toward areas not readily noticed by the human eye. The final step is lossless compression through Huffman encoding, an advanced variant of RLE.

Wavelets is a symmetric technology that compresses and decompresses very quickly. Indeo and VDONet are the two primary developers using wavelets.

Fractal Compression

Fractal compression results from a patented process invented by Dr. Michael Barnsley, Iterated Systems' cofounder and chief technical officer. Like JPEG and VQ, fractal compression starts by breaking the image into blocks. The next step, similar to that in VQ, is comparing blocks to other larger blocks to find similar blocks. However, rather than storing this information in a lookup table, the fractal process converts these self-similar regions into equations that can be used to recreate the image. In essence, the process converts the original pixel-related information into a mathematical model of the image.

This mathematical model is technically resolution independent, meaning that fractal images can be zoomed to any resolution, irrespective of the original size. This characteristic, also called scalability, is the primary advantage of fractal techniques.

Searching for self-similar regions is a lengthy process and fractal compression is extremely time consuming. However, the technology is asymmetric and decompression is extremely simple and fast. Fractal compression is the intraframe technology used by Iterated Systems for their fractal video codecs, including ClearVideo, their recently introduced streaming video codec.

SUMMARY

1. Video compression is a process whereby a collection of algorithms and techniques replaces the original pixel-related information with more compact mathematical descriptions. Decompression is the reverse process of decoding the mathematical descriptions back to pixels for ultimate display.

2. Video compression utilizes two basic compression techniques: interframe compression, or compression between frames, and intraframe compression, which occurs within individual frames.

3. Lossless compression techniques create compressed files that decompress into exactly the same file as the original, bit for bit. Lossy compression techniques create files that decompress into files that are similar to the original but different in digital makeup.

4. All relevant video codecs are lossy—it's the only way to achieve the required compression. This sets up the classic compression trade-off, video quality for file size. It's also the first reason why digital video doesn't look as good as analog video.

5. Decompression and display is a four-step process, down from five steps last time out. The remaining steps are:

   (a) Retrieval from storage and transfer to RAM
   (b) Decompression
   (c) Transfer to video card
   (d) Paint in video memory

   In contrast, your television simply receives the analog data, transfers it to the tube, and points scan lines down the screen. No conversions, decompressions, or restricted bus transfers. No wonder a $200 TV looks better than your Pentium when it comes to video.

6. Interframe compression uses a system of reference frames, called key frames in Video for Windows parlance and I and P frames in MPEG, and difference frames (delta/P and B frames) to eliminate

redundant information between frames. All interframe techniques derive their effectiveness from interframe redundancy, or the absence of motion. Videos with low motion content compress more effectively than high motion videos, which means better video quality at the same bandwidth.

7. Plan your video shoots to eliminate extraneous motion. Keep in mind that pans, zooms, and especially hand-held cameras degrade video quality. The best approach is to analyze which motion is critical to delivering the intended message of the video and then minimize all others. Minimize the hidden sources of noise, like complicated foregrounds and backgrounds and multiple video generations.

8. Intraframe compression is compression performed solely with reference to an individual frame. It's performed on pixels in differenced frames that remain after interframe compression and on key and I frames. While intraframe techniques are generally the most hyped, usually codec performance is related more to interframe techniques rather than intraframe.

Chapter

Windows Development Environment

IN THIS CHAPTER

When you develop video under Windows, you're on Microsoft's playground. Good thing, too, since before Microsoft took over with Video for Windows in 1992, the digital video playground was a confused place, populated by largely incompatible products used in highly specialized vertical markets. Not surprisingly, no consumer or even corporate mass market existed.

Video for Windows (VFW) stabilized the market, providing a file format that stimulated the development of VFW-compatible tools and well-defined APIs for integrating video into CD-ROM and other applications. In early 1996, Microsoft introduced ActiveMovie, a Windows 95 multimedia architecture that will serve as the basis for the next generation of video development tools.

Virtually every Windows tool used to develop video content is or will be affected by one of these two standards, and even if you're not familiar with these standards, you work with them every day. So let's get a bit familiar with Microsoft's digital video playground.

Overview

Before Video for Windows, the video market was composed of many separate and incompatible products. All codecs used proprietary programming interfaces that complicated video creation and integration. Most capture boards were codec specific and there were few mechanisms to convert to and from the different codecs. This scenario was fine for Intel and IBM but a problem for small codec vendors without the expertise or financing to build their own hardware.

Multimedia market growth on the Windows platform was retarded by the lack of standards that were in full bloom on the Macintosh platform with Apple's QuickTime standard. This was the problem Microsoft sought to address with Video for Windows, first introduced in November 1992 as a retail product priced at $199.

Video for Windows started as both an architecture and an application suite, with Microsoft later dropping its highly regarded applets as others performing the same functions became available. As an architecture, VFW provides both inbound and outbound interfaces.

The inbound architecture is built around a standard file format, called the audio/video interleaved (AVI) format, which ensures that various digital video creation technologies, including capture cards, video editors, and codecs, work together seamlessly. This allows the developers of each discrete tool to focus solely on their specialty area. For example, simply by supporting the AVI file format, VFW codec developers can access video captured by all VFW-compatible capture cards and work within the framework of VFW video editors.

Technically, while VFW provides the "harness," or architecture for video codecs, and ships with several codecs, it's not a codec itself. You can't "compress a file with Video for Windows," you compress using a VFW-compatible codec like Indeo or Cinepak from within a VFW-compatible application like Adobe Premiere.

Note also that only files with the AVI extension work with VFW, meaning that you can't access MPEG compression or playback through the VFW architecture. As we'll see, this limitation was one of the primary reasons that Microsoft later implemented ActiveMovie.

Outbound APIs

The Video for Windows playback APIs revolving around extensions to the Media Control Interface (MCI) introduced by Microsoft with the release of VFW. Briefly, MCI is an API for communicating with multimedia devices jointly released by Microsoft and IBM in 1991. In addition to VFW, the MCI interface controls the playback of analog video decks like laserdiscs and the playback of digital formats like animation and WAV audio.

By now, virtually all presentation and authoring programs directly support VFW files, making it extremely simple for even nonprogrammers to integrate video into their presentations. For example, Asymetrix Compel, a popular presentation program, directly supports most MCI-based multimedia formats, including digital video (see Figure 3.1).

Some business-oriented programs like word processors and spreadsheets still don't directly support AVI files. However, you can still trigger video playback from within these applications using Microsoft's Object Linking and Embedding (OLE) specification.

Media Player, an accessory shipped with all versions of Windows, is an MCI device that recognizes and plays MCI formats, including Video for Windows' AVI files. Media Player is also an OLE server which can link into and play back supported multimedia elements into OLE Client applications like Lotus 1,2,3 and Microsoft Word (Figure 3.2).

Developers using programming languages like C++ and Visual Basic can opt to write directly to the MCI command structure. Although more complicated from a programming standpoint, this affords much greater control and flexibility than either of the first two methods.

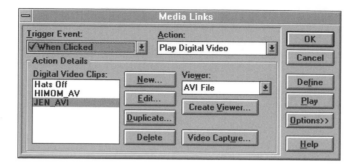

Figure 3.1   AVI files integrated into Compel presentation through direct
MCI suport.

Codec Architecture

On the inbound side, Video for Windows provides a standard interface for
multimedia tools and subsystems, including codecs. Microsoft has licensed
or developed four codecs to ship first with Video for Windows and then
with Windows 95. The famous four are Cinepak from Radius, Intel's Indeo,

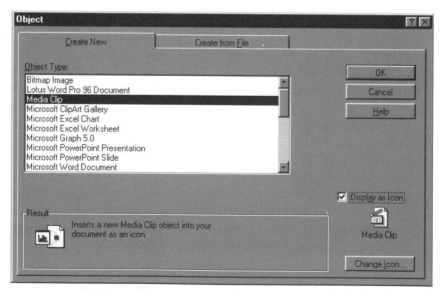

Figure 3.2   Embedding a video file into Microsoft Word through Media Player
and OLE.

Microsoft's RLE, and Video 1 (see Figure 3.3). This same interface houses other VFW codecs, offered by their developers under a variety of commercial arrangements.

Although all Video for Windows codecs produce files with the AVI extension, the internal structure of the files are different. To decompress a file created by Iterated Systems FVF Compressor, for example, you need that codec installed on your computer, which is typically why most CD-ROM title developers install a VFW "runtime" with all necessary codecs when installing their products.

Distribution of video files created with codecs bundled with Video for Windows is royalty free. This means that you can compress a video file with any codec and distribute the file internally or commercially without royalty. You can also distribute the dedicated playback module, or run time, royalty free, as we have with the bundled CD-ROM.

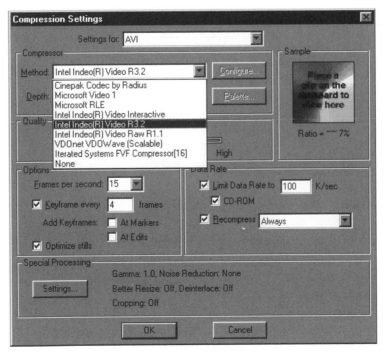

Figure 3.3 Premiere's codec selection screen showing the original four VFW codecs plus several others.

ACTIVEMOVIE

ActiveMovie, Microsoft's new Windows 95 multimedia architecture, was in beta form at the time of this writing. In general, ActiveMovie enables more precise synchronization of multimedia data, including the playback of MPEG files, which wasn't possible under the Video for Windows structure. ActiveMovie also works with MPEG audio, .WAV audio, and Apple QuickTime files.

As shown at the bottom of Figure 3.4, ActiveMovie uses a series of "filters" to separately operate the file retrieval, decompression, and display tasks performed by one code module today. For example, under the MCI architecture, one monolithic code segment is responsible for retrieving an MPEG file, decompressing both the audio and video segments, and sending both media types to the sound board and graphics card. This makes it difficult for developers to access lower level functions to merge different media types into one integrated display.

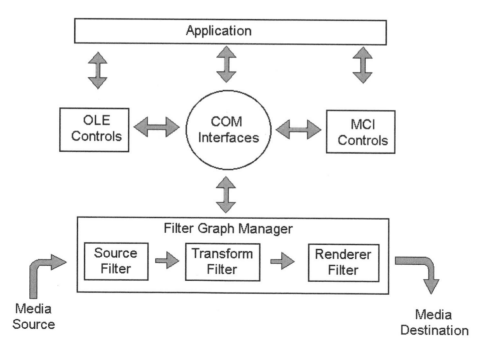

Figure 3.4   ActiveMovie flow diagram.

Under the ActiveMovie architecture, a "source" filter reads the data from disk, "transform" filters decompress respective streams, and "rendering" filters send the streams to the proper output device. All these services work under the control of a Filter Graph Manager. During the ActiveMovie press tour, this structure allowed Microsoft to demonstrate video playing back on three-dimensional objects rendered in real time.

In addition, ActiveMovie enables greater end user control and interactivity with video playback. During the same tour, Microsoft demonstrated controls enabling end user adjustment of video hue, color, brightness, and contrast, allowing each user to customize video playback for their graphics card and monitor.

This architecture opens up new dimensions in multimedia programming flexibility, but most won't be realized until 1997 and beyond. In the short term, ActiveMovie's most significant impact will relate to the MPEG video format, discussed in Chapters 16–18. By bundling a free software MPEG player with ActiveMovie, Microsoft will stabilize the MPEG playback API and make MPEG playback free to Windows 95 developers, much like the bundled Video for Windows codecs. Both of these should do much to advance MPEG's usage by developers.

ActiveMovie APIs

Controlling the Filter Graph Manager is a set of Component Object Models, the COM interfaces shown in the circle in the middle of Figure 3.4. As made clear in the figure, however, ActiveMovie will continue to support both the MCI and OLE interfaces, enabling backward compatibility with applications relying on these APIs.

Going forward, here are Microsoft's recommendations for adapting ActiveMovie.

ActiveMovie is the architecture to use for most new multimedia applications for Windows 95 or Windows NT®. With a few exceptions, it replaces multimedia playback services, APIs, and architectures provided by Microsoft in earlier versions of the Windows Software Development Kit (SDK). However, libraries will continue to be available and supported for applications that use the earlier Microsoft multimedia playback services, such as Microsoft Video for Windows. The first release of ActiveMovie does not provide a corresponding replacement for every solution found in the previous multimedia technology. For example, there is no video capture capability built into the runtime. In these cases, you may find an opportunity to use the ActiveMovie architecture to provide your own solutions with the help of the many samples provided in this SDK.

Choosing the Right Programming Model

ActiveMovie is accessible at many levels, and the approach you use depends on your requirements and the investment you plan to make in development. You might plan to rewrite an existing multimedia program, write a new multimedia program, or perhaps add multimedia capabilities to an existing program. Typically, existing applications that use the MCI command set are easily ported, whereas applications that access lower-level multimedia services will require more time to rewrite. For new applications, ActiveMovie playback services can be quickly added by using the ActiveMovie ActiveX control, or with a few direct functions, calling the COM interfaces. For C or C++ programmers, you can write filters that add specific processing capabilities to multimedia data already managed by existing filter graphs.

Rewriting Existing Applications

If you are adapting an application that currently plays AVI-encoded movies and sounds to use ActiveMovie, you have several choices. These choices depend on the services the application uses and your goal. If your application uses MCI commands, you can use the MCI subset provided by ActiveMovie. In the majority of cases, this will be a straightforward upgrade that maintains AVI playback and adds MPEG and QuickTime playback capabilities to your application. If your existing C-based application uses Video for Windows API, you can replace most of these with calls to the filter graph manager COM interfaces.

Writing New Applications

When writing a new application, you have some options. For example, if you only want to add MPEG playback to your application, you can incorporate the ActiveMovie ActiveX control in your application or directly access the COM interfaces on the filter graph manager. Both Microsoft Visual Basic® version 4.0 and Microsoft Visual C++® allow access to the ActiveX control or the COM interfaces. Filters within a filter graph are typically written in C++ using the ActiveMovie class library.

If your application must process the media stream in some way, you can incorporate both the filter graph manager and a custom filter into your application. The instantiated filter graph manager generates and manages the filter graph; the custom filter could be inserted into a preconfigured filter graph (created and saved using the Filter Graph Editor tool in the ActiveMovie SDK). Or the filter could be inserted at runtime into an existing filter graph.

This documentation makes it doubly clear that you won't be left out in the cold if you continue to support the Video for Windows MCI interfaces discussed above—at least in the short term. Also clear is that those desiring simple video playback gain little from the new architecture, whereas developers seeking the ultimate in features and flexibility have much to gain.

For Professional Video Developers

As with any new specification, much is left to learn, so we're turning to some industry experts to help supplement our knowledge. Montreal-based Matrox develops high-performance digital video capture and editing products and outstanding high-end graphics cards. An early ActiveMovie beta tester and Microsoft development partner, Matrox introduced one of the first digital video editing products based on the new specifications.

We've included Matrox's excellent White Paper entitled "The Impact of Microsoft's ActiveMovie Multimedia Architecture on the Professional Video Marketplace" for further reference. Those wishing to learn more about Matrox can reach the company at www.matrox.com.

SUMMARY

1. Video for Windows was introduced by Microsoft to spawn multimedia development on the Windows platform. Judged by that standard, it has been a remarkable success.
2. Video for Windows is primarily an architecture, although initially it shipped with an application suite that was later discontinued. The architecture centers around the AVI file format (Audio/Video Interleaved), which provides a common ground for capture card

manufacturers, codec developers, video editing developers, and other peripheral products.

3. Video for Windows is an Media Control Interface (MCI) device, accessible through direct AVI support in presentation or authoring programs, Object Linking and Embedding with Media Player, and by writing directly to MCI commands in programming languages.

4. Video for Windows ships with four codecs, RLE and Video 1 from Microsoft, Cinepak from SuperMac, and Indeo from Intel. Use of these codecs is royalty free. Other codecs fit into the same architecture but commercial terms vary, as discussed in Chapter 6.

5. New on the scene is ActiveMovie, solely for the Windows 95 architecture, which provides free software MPEG-1 decompression for digital video developers. Most developers seeking simple linear playback of AVI files can continue to use MCI calls, which are still supported in ActiveMovie. Those seeking to push the video features envelope may want to start working with Active-Movie.

The Impact of
Microsoft's ActiveMovie Multimedia Architecture
on the Professional Video Marketplace

By
Alain Legault, Director of Engineering
Janet Matey, Marketing Manager
Matrox Video Products Group
March 4, 1996

OVERVIEW

The desire to use economical PCs in professional video applications continues to grow. It started with nonlinear editing in the late 1980s but technology is rapidly advancing to make PCs usable in a wide variety of applications including:

- Digital Disk Recorders (DDR)
- Virtual VTRs
- Video-On-Demand Servers (VOD)
- Near Video-On-Demand Servers (NVOD)
- Interactive TV
- Live Video Switchers
- M-JPEG to MPEG Transcoders
- Commercial Insertion Systems
- Instant Replay Systems
- Time Delay Systems
- CATV Barker Channels
- 2D and 3D Animation Stations
- Animation Recorders
- Graphics/Paint Workstations
- Character Generators (CG)
- Closed Captioning and Teletext Systems
- Audio-Follows-Video Digital Audio Workstations (DAW)
- Visual Effects/Compositing Systems

Manufacturers of all of these types of systems have been held back by the lack of a robust software architecture standard that can meet the demanding requirements of handling multimedia data types in realtime.

Currently the PC standard is Microsoft's Video for Windows (VFW) multimedia architecture and the Mac standard is Apple's Quicktime. Both architectures lack important features that would make them usable by the professional video industry. For example, both schemes limit I/O throughput. Digital video file format structures and media synchronization methods are inadequate. VFW does not even support alpha channel keying. Developers have been forced to come up with proprietary software approaches to overcome these limitations of VFW and Quicktime which makes interoperability among vendors difficult, if not impossible. The need for proprietary code also limits the ability of developers to support multiple hardware platforms (video adapters, host processors) under multiple environments (Windows NT, Windows 95 and Mac-OS).

Effort is wasted porting the same software source code over and over, limiting the time available to respond to users' requests for new features. Also, the development of massive pieces of proprietary code leads to longer development and testing (SQA) cycles and less reliable applications. It is well known to programmers that software code reliability is directly related to the amount of testing it undergoes and the size of the user base. More reusable code with a larger user base would mean more reliable products with less down time—a real boon to professionals who cannot tolerate system crashes. And, who hasn't noticed that every editing system vendor takes much, much longer than promised to release the products they announce every year at NAB! This is an industry-wide problem due in large part to the software architecture limitations described above.

This paper focuses on Microsoft's new ActiveMovie multimedia architecture, that promises to overcome these limitations and deliver a standard, reliable software framework robust enough to meet the demands of the professional video industry.

First we review the limitations of Video for Windows, then we introduce the general theory of the Component Object Model (COM) programming structure upon which ActiveMovie is based. A discussion of the specific implementation of ActiveMovie as it applies to professional video applications follows, then we lay the ground work for future enhancements to the ActiveMovie model. Finally, we assess the impact that this new software architecture is expected to have on the video industry.

Throughout this discussion we use real-world examples of the benefits of the ActiveMovie architecture based on its implementation in Matrox's new DigiSuite family of hardware modules and software development tools.

Limitations of Video for Windows

The limitations of VFW have been clear to professional video application developers for some time. They include:

Inadequate Audio/Video File Format

In its original form, the AVI file format did not support the performance required by professional audio/video/film applications. The definition of enhancements to make the VFW AVI file format more useful for professional applications was the first project undertaken by the Open Digital Media (OpenDML) coalition. Established in late 1994, OpenDML is a group of software and hardware vendors dedicated to making Windows the platform of choice for professional video, audio, and film producers.

The enhanced AVI file format specification was released by OpenDML in November 1995 and has been incorporated by Microsoft into the ActiveMovie architecture. The enhanced AVI file format has the following features:

- backward compatibility with AVI

Applications with conventional AVI file format support can work on new codecs and applications that support the extended AVI file format can work on conventional codecs improving the performance of all VFW systems.

- interoperability among different hardware vendors' codecs

Up until this point, there have been as many motion-JPEG standards as there were motion-JPEG codecs on the market preventing interoperability of any sort. The extended AVI file format provides interoperability among different hardware and software vendors' motion-JPEG codecs using ISO 10918 motion-JPEG DIB (Device Independent Bitmap) as the standard.

- support for larger file sizes

The 1 GB practical limit on standard AVI files restricts D1-quality video playback to under two minutes at a 10 MB/s data rate. The OpenDML file format allows practically unlimited playback time subject only to the size of the storage media attached to the system.

- field indexing

AVI was originally designed to reference a frame index. The index, or reference list of video locations in the AVI file, provided access to frames as the smallest discrete element. Professional video applications, however, require the ability to sequence individual fields, not frames. The new field indexing scheme offers a number of important advantages including improved video effects support, film and video frame-rate support, disk seek-time minimization, support for incremental file growth, and references to source information.

Limited I/O Throughput

VFW transfers (copies) compressed video data, frame by frame, between different steps in the video processing operation using the conventional host CPU memory copying capability. Typically, these transfers need to occur between the storage device and the system memory, then from system memory to the video codec and finally from the video codec to the display device. The overall throughput of the system is thus limited by the performance of the CPU. In addition, VFW limits transfers to a maximum of 64 KBytes, which is very small relative to the enormous quantity of data needed to represent video. Even near-Betacam-quality compressed video requires at least a 4 MB/s bandwidth. System performance increases dramatically with larger data transfers.

The need for larger transfers introduces the concept of data streaming. A good analogy is to imagine transporting water to put out a fire. We could use water buckets (representing video frames) and a human chain (representing the CPU) from the source to the destination but that would be slow (buckets are small) and require a huge effort from the carriers (CPU). It is easy to see that using a hose (data stream) to accomplish this task would be much more efficient.

Inconsistent Driver Models

The number of data types supported by VFW is limited to audio, video, graphics, and MIDI. The driver models for these devices lack uniformity because VFW was designed to be backward compatible with legacy code for audio (WAV driver) and graphics (GDI driver). Inconsistency in the driver models greatly complicates the developer's job.

Limited Software/Hardware Interoperability

There are two major barriers to hardware/software interoperability inherent in VFW—software drivers are monolithic and the Installable Compression Module (ICM) interface is limiting.

Monolithic software drivers make it difficult to replace a specific function inside a software driver without major work. Multimedia device drivers provide services for a specific data type such as digital video playback, audio playback, graphics animation, and video effects. Conceptually, the drivers are made up of a large number of individual operations called primitives. In the case of a motion-JPEG video codec, for example, these primitives are memory/storage data management, color space conversion, raster block conversion, discrete cosine transform (DCT), quantization, Huffman decoding, and display.

Current software drivers associated with each media type are not broken down into these sub-elements of functionality. They are monolithic in nature. This all but prevents an individual function that was originally coded in software, say color-space conversion, to be enhanced by hardware control and acceleration.

The ICM interface of VFW allows some hardware/software interoperability but it is limited to the replacement of a software-only codec with a hardware codec. A much more generic approach to software/hardware interoperability, for all media types, is needed to achieve various price/performance products.

No System-Level Synchronization of Various Media Drivers

VFW ensures synchronization between audio and video playback by dropping or repeating video frames. This is a major shortcoming since professional video applications depend on timing accuracy down to the video field level. Synchronization for other media types is not supported.

Drivers Are Incompatible Between Windows 95 and Windows NT

Incompatibility between the Windows 95 and the Windows NT environments practically doubles the amount of work for vendors who want to support both operating systems. One example of the incompatibility is the 32-bit NT driver interface structure vs. the 16-bit Windows 95 software.

COMPONENT OBJECT MODEL (COM)

The Component Object Model (COM) architecture is the basic software foundation of ActiveMovie.

This extensible software architecture exploits object oriented programming techniques to offer interoperability between software and hardware and among different vendors' products. Perhaps the best known implementation of COM is Microsoft's OLE (Object Linking and Embedding) which provides a powerful means for applications to interact and interoperate. Microsoft's strategy is now to use COM in all new software architectures including ActiveMovie.

What is a component object ?

A component object is software code and associated data that perform a specific processing function in a system. In multimedia applications, we care about data processing. Data processing involves transformations. In electrical engineering terms, transformations are produced by filters, so one component object is called a "filter" in ActiveMovie terminology. For example, reading an AVI file from disk, decompressing a motion-JPEG stream and controlling the volume of audio playback are all functions that can be performed by a filter. Filters isolate the internal complexities of the code for each function from the outside world. One could think of each filter as a "black box" whose internal workings need to be understood only by the designer of the box. These "black boxes" or component objects are controlled through software via interfaces. An interface exhibits only the necessary information and a communication method to the other filters and the external world. To make use of a particular filter, one need only understand the interface, not the internal workings of the entire filter.

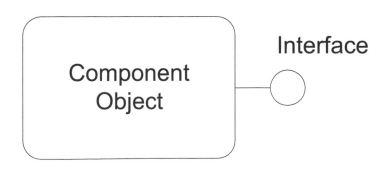

COM offers multiple advantages beyond the current VFW model:

- operating system and programming language independence

Conventional programming techniques result in incompatibility problems when interfacing software modules compiled with different software languages (C, Basic, Pascal). Similar incompatibilities occur between different CPUs (Alpha, Pentium, PowerPC, MIPS) and various operating systems (NT, 95, UNIX, Mac-OS).

COM defines a binary standard that eliminates this problem—binary descriptors are the lowest common denominator of all.

- versioning and Globally Unique Identifiers (GUID)

One basic problem hindering multi-vendor interoperability is: How can we ensure interoperability between different pieces of code that were designed at different times, in different parts of the world, by different software developers?

COM solves this problem by assigning a globally unique identifier (called GUID) to every interface and component object. This 128-bit integer code is guaranteed to be unique in the world across space and time. (There are 3.4×10^{38} different codes possible.) Because each component object is uniquely identified, there is no risk of confusion in trying to interface to the wrong component object.

- self-adapting system definition

COM provides the ability for an application to dynamically query the capability of a given filter and its interface. Thus, application software can adapt (without any code changes) to the availability of certain features in a particular system at a given time. For example, an editing application can query a particular video effects plug-in module, understand the specific effects that are provided in the module and allow the user to access these capabilities.

- distributed processing and multi-tasking are supported

COM allows interfaces to communicate between different hardware processors, different operating systems, different software processes in the same machine and even between multiple processors through networks.

- reusable code

COM technology provides the facility to use code over and over. In fact, existing component objects can be easily incorporated into new ones. The new component object inherits the features of the parent component. This speeds development and also ensures more reliable software. New code gains an immediate level of reliability by virtue of being built on an existing, thoroughly-tested, component object.

ACTIVEMOVIE

ActiveMovie is a specific implementation of COM for multimedia that overcomes all of the limitations of VFW. The improved audio/video file format described above that was originally proposed by OpenDML has been incorporated in ActiveMovie. High-performance I/O throughput is ensured by the new data streaming architecture. Driver models now have a consistent Application Program Interface (API). They support more data types and are modular leading to a high level of software/hardware interoperability. System-level, accurate synchronization for all media types is provided and ActiveMovie API is identical for Windows 95 and Windows NT minimizing the work required for software developers to support both operating systems.

ActiveMovie also benefits from all of the COM advantages defined above.

ActiveMovie Data Types

ActiveMovie allows the system designer to define a wider variety of data types than was possible under VFW. For example, in the Matrox DigiSuite implementation of ActiveMovie, the following multimedia data types are defined:

- Digital video data from various types of codecs—M-JPEG
- Digital audio data—PCM WAV
- Digital video F/X control attributes—2D or 3D DVE attributes
- Digital audio F/X control attributes—EQ, mixing and panning
- Graphics and still images—32-bit RGB-Alpha images

- Scroll and crawl of graphics overlays and titles—Inscriber scroll and crawl files
- VCR control—RS-422 Sony Betacam protocol control

The ActiveMovie data streaming architecture allows the optimal interchange of time-based data of all of these data types between various ActiveMovie filters. There are three major benefits to the data streaming approach. Data throughput is maximized by the ability to use large data buffers (more than 64 KBytes). CPU intensive memory copying operations are eliminated by the use of shared memory buffers. System-level synchronization is ensured through the use of time stamps on all data streams.

ActiveMovie Filters

A filter is a COM object that performs a single task in a multimedia system. For example, in a complex sub-system such as the Matrox DigiMix digital video mixer, individual filters perform such tasks as background and wipe generation, chroma keying, layer priority selection, proc amp adjustments, 2D DVE, etc.

More complex functions can be performed by interfacing multiple filters together to act on a specific data type. Filters are connected together by interfaces called "pins" in ActiveMovie terminology. It will typically take multiple filters grouped together to replace the functionality of the monolithic driver from VFW. Different types of ActiveMovie filters can either provide, transform, or consume data. These three functions are accomplished using:

- Source filters
- Transform filters
- Renderer filters

A source filter provides data such as digital audio, digital video, or graphics to other filters downstream. Alternatively, it can provide control information such as video and audio keyframes. For example, a data source filter would typically perform functions such as an AVI file reader, WAV audio file reader, and title animator. A source filter can get its control information from a file or from interaction with the user via a user interface device like a scroll bar or fader control. A source filter typically has only an output pin.

A transform filter accepts a data stream at its input pin, performs a transformation on the data and provides the processed data to its output pin. For example, in Matrox DigiSuite, the video codec, the 2D DVE processor, the audio equalizer and the Movie-2 bus interconnect are just a few of the many hardware assisted transform filters.

A renderer filter is responsible for consuming the processed data and relaying it to a presentation device such as a video display or a speaker. The renderer will ensure presentation of each media stream at the correct time, based on the system-level synchronization mechanism. In Matrox DigiSuite, for example, the "correct time" is defined as presentation of each media stream accurately synchronized at the video field-level. Typically, a renderer filter has only an input pin.

ActiveMovie Pins

Two types of pins are defined in ActiveMovie: shared memory buffers and implicit hardware connections. Shared memory buffer pins are used whenever a filter interfaces to another through the use of computer memory. For example, a source filter reading an AVI file from hard disk will provide the video data to the video codec through a shared memory buffer, given that the data read from disk is stored somewhere in system memory. ActiveMovie provides the ability to share these memory buffers from one filter to the next, without the need to perform the expensive CPU memory copying operations needed by VFW. In addition, the shared memory buffer can be used to transfer large blocks of memory (easily in the MByte range as opposed to VFW's 64K limit) at once, thus achieving significantly higher I/O throughput than the VFW approach.

Hardware connections are made when a filter employs hardware acceleration. For example, a connection made between two video adapters through the Matrox Movie-2 bus would occur through a hardware pin. Because pins are standardized for a given data type, a shared memory buffer pin can be easily replaced by a hardware connection without affecting the interface with the application software. This transparency between hardware and software allows the same application to easily migrate from software-only operation to higher performance using hardware accelerators.

ActiveMovie Filter Graph

A multimedia system requires the connection of multiple filters to accomplish system-level functions. A representation of the multimedia system is called a filter graph. Filter graphs are customized connections performed between many filters in order to accomplish a specific task.

In order to establish a connection between the input pin of one filter and the output pin of another filter, a negotiation of data type takes place. A connection can be established between two filters that share the same data type (i.e., motion-JPEG digital video) but cannot be successfully established between two inconsistent data types. This prevents feeding a digital video stream into an audio equalizer, for example. One output pin can feed many filter inputs using a tee filter.

System-Level Synchronization

The goal of system level synchronization is to present all streams of data to the presentation device in a timely manner. The multimedia system designer must decide what the timebase or reference clock will be for his application. For example, in Matrox DigiSuite the timebase is the video field (60/s NTSC, 50/s PAL) so the reference clock is derived from the hardware vertical synchronization signal provided by the DigiSuite video board. In the film industry, a system designer would likely choose a reference clock of 24 frames/s.

The rendering filters for all the data streams in the multimedia system must be controlled by this single reference clock. ActiveMovie accomplishes this by employing the concepts described below.

- samples

Each data stream is made up of samples. A sample is the smallest time element that the system designer decides that any particular data type can be divided into in his multimedia system. For example, Matrox has determined that, in DigiSuite, there will be 48,000 audio samples/s and that there will be 60 NTSC video fields/s.

- media position

Any media segment that is available to the multimedia system has a finite length. The media position interface in a renderer filter allows the application to seek to any position inside the media segment at any time.

- media control

At any given time a media segment is in a given state such as STOP, PAUSE, PLAY, FF, etc. The application can change the state of the media by sending information to the media control interface. The state of the media will determine the rate at which the renderer filter consumes the data. For example, media in STOP mode consume no data.

- quality management

Since there is a single, unchanging reference clock in an ActiveMovie-based multimedia system, one could envision a scenario where one renderer filter for some reason either receives information too quickly or too slowly. ActiveMovie provides a mechanism that resynchronizes the data stream if necessary by dropping or repeating samples. In a professional video system such as the Matrox DigiSuite, this phenomenon is avoided but in some multimedia systems this elegant system degradation is an important benefit of ActiveMovie.

For example, a media server designed to deliver digital video streams to multiple users over a network might encounter a situation where there are more simultaneous requests for data than the server can handle. Each user would experience a degradation in the quality of the MPEG stream he receives until the server catches up to the demand placed upon it.

The Next Step—Standardized ActiveMovie Media Types

The next project being undertaken by the OpenDML group is the definition of standard media types and device driver models. A Device Driver Workgroup made up of individuals from companies interested in this subject is currently being formed. The goal of this group is to define a standard Application Program Interface (API) for drivers to allow interchange of various vendors' hardware and software without the need to modify applications. The driver models will define interface characteristics and address various data types including:

- digital video data from various types of codecs
- digital audio data
- digital video F/X descriptors including 2D and 3D DVE attributes
- digital audio F/X descriptors for EQ, mixing and panning
- graphics still image loading of 32-bit RGB-Alpha images

- scroll and crawl of graphics overlays and titles
- VCR control protocol

WHAT WILL ACTIVEMOVIE DO FOR THE VIDEO PROFESSIONAL?

ActiveMovie is an important enabling technology for professional video systems. As vendors complete development using this model and start to introduce products based on ActiveMovie, users will realize many significant benefits. Individual products will be more reliable and offer higher performance than ever before. Development cycles will accelerate because ActiveMovie is such a modular, flexible architecture. Product upgrades will be easier for manufacturers to introduce so we may finally see NAB delivery promises met. A wider variety of price/performance solutions will be available and systems will be easily upgradeable. And perhaps the most significant benefit of all will be a high-level of multi-vendor, multi-platform interoperability.

Chapter

Streaming Multimedia

INTRODUCTION

Without question, the most significant new medium for transmitting information is the Internet. Very few digital products of any kind—in-house or commercial, reference or entertainment—are being developed without some vision for using the Net for marketing or for disseminating the same data over the Internet.

Unfortunately, the multimedia elements that enrich our titles are extremely bulky, resulting in an almost audible sigh of relief when double-spin (2X) CD-ROMs became standard. Although Internet hype is available in unlimited supply, Internet bandwidth isn't, making the Net quite inhospitable to multimedia data formats.

How inhospitable? Well, consider that the 150 kilo**bytes** per second capacity of the now obsolete single-spin CD-ROM drive is roughly 41 times faster than a 28.8 kilo**bits** per second modem. Even ISDN, the digital network that represents the next bandwidth increment for most businesses and consumers, is still nine times slower than a 1X drive.

But don't be daunted by mere statistics. Necessity is the mother of invention, and the Internet, as the next big computer marketplace, has created an urgent need for low-bandwidth multimedia. This has spawned some very innovative approaches toward delivering multimedia over these narrow pipes in more or less real time.

This chapter overviews technologies providing video, animation, and electronic documents over the Internet, with audio covered in much greater detail in Chapter 15. It's a fairly basic treatment suitable primarily for beginners, so if you're an experienced webmeister, you may want to skip

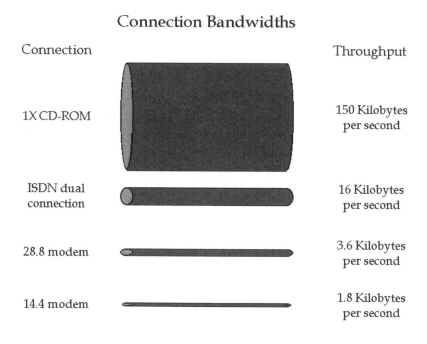

Connection Bandwidths

Connection		Throughput
1X CD-ROM		150 Kilobytes per second
ISDN dual connection		16 Kilobytes per second
28.8 modem		3.6 Kilobytes per second
14.4 modem		1.8 Kilobytes per second

Figure 4.1 You know you're in trouble when the bandwidth of a 1X CD-ROM drive looks huge compared to what you've got available to transfer data to your user.

to Chapter 15. We start by examining the new concepts and buzzwords common to all formats.

Technology Primer

Internet Architecture

Let's start with a scenario, then fill in the pieces. Assume we're surfing by the White House (www.whitehouse.gov), running Netscape Navigator. We click over to the President's area to hear a State of the Union message (www.whitehouse.gov/WH/NEW/Other/stateunion-top.html). If everything's configured correctly, a program that looks like Media Player automatically launches and you begin to hear President Clinton's address.

As you may know, when you arrived at www.whitehouse.gov, the White House Internet server downloaded information to your browser in HTML (Hypertext Markup Language) format. Even though it looked as if you were pressing buttons in the White House basement, all information displayed on your screen was present in your computer.

Servers, Players, and Tags

When you pressed the button "President's greeting," your browser called the RealAudio helper application, which sent a message to the White House server to begin sending you the audio file. After a few moments of buffering time, audio playback starts, sounding a touch warbled, but quite understandable.

All Internet multimedia delivery involves these common programs and processes. The multimedia data file is stored on the Internet server, or in some cases another server connected to the Internet server. The Web pages contain an HTML "tag" that references the data file and tells the server to start transmitting the data when activated. This tag structure is identical to how other data types are integrated into the Web page—if you know how to embed an icon, you can embed streaming video.

On the client side, the browser requires a helper application, generically called a player, compatible with the multimedia data format. The player must be installed and registered with the browser, or the browser will send an error message when receiving the data instructing the client to configure a player for that format or store the file to disk.

All first-generation players launched and ran separately from the browser, in effect presenting the user with two programs and two interfaces. In our example, the audio player that let you stop, start, and rewind President Clinton's voice ran separately from the browser, almost as if you had loaded Media Player and played the file from disk.

Netscape's Navigator 2.0 premiered an advanced level of integration called a "plug-in," which allows Web developers to integrate helper applications directly into the Web pages. Continuing with our example, this would let the White House webmeister integrate the audio controls directly into the page so that the user wouldn't know that a separate application was running.

To function as a Netscape 2.0 and above plug-in, the player must conform to a set of specifications available on Netscape's Web site (www.netscape.com). Eager to benefit from this advanced level of integration, most leading developers of Internet-delivered multimedia have elected to support the new specification.

Not to be left out, Microsoft has also proposed their own plug-in specification for their Internet Explorer browser, based upon the Object Linking and Embedding specifications, now called ActiveX. Since Internet Explorer is rapidly gaining in popularity, many developers have chosen to support ActiveX as well.

All multimedia data formats referenced in this chapter have at least two components, a program that creates the multimedia file, commonly called

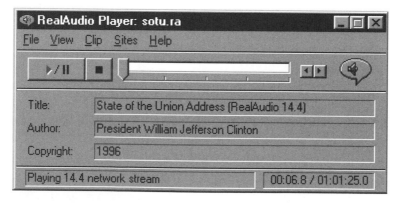

Figure 4.2   President's State of the Union message, courtesy of RealAudio.

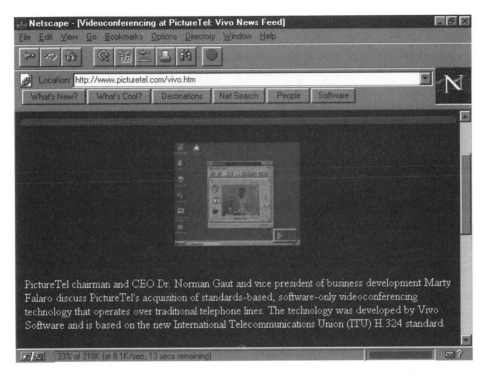

Figure 4.3   Video controls embedded in the Web page using Netscape's
plug-in specification and Vivo's video player.

an encoder, and the helper application or player. Several formats also have
"server" applications that reside on and work with the Web server software.
These servers provide advanced functionality during data delivery and
also to moderate data flow for greater overall server performance. We'll
address the server side of the equation in the individual sections.

Data Delivery Paradigms

Download and Play

The mode of data delivery is one of the critical implementation issues
affecting both initial and continued responsiveness. The status quo, tried

and true method of data delivery is called "download and play," where the entire file is downloaded before playback begins. All multimedia files can be downloaded over the Internet, stored on the client computer, and then played without special programming or software. The problem with this approach is responsiveness.

For example, a one-minute 11 kHz/mono/8-bit audio file would take three minutes to download at 28.8 kbps, stretching the patience of most casual Net surfers. A one-minute AVI file compressed to 150 KB/s would take 42 minutes to download, way past the attention span of your average Generation X-er.

"Streaming" Data Formats

The most common alternative for real-time technologies like audio and video is called "streaming," where playback starts after a short period for

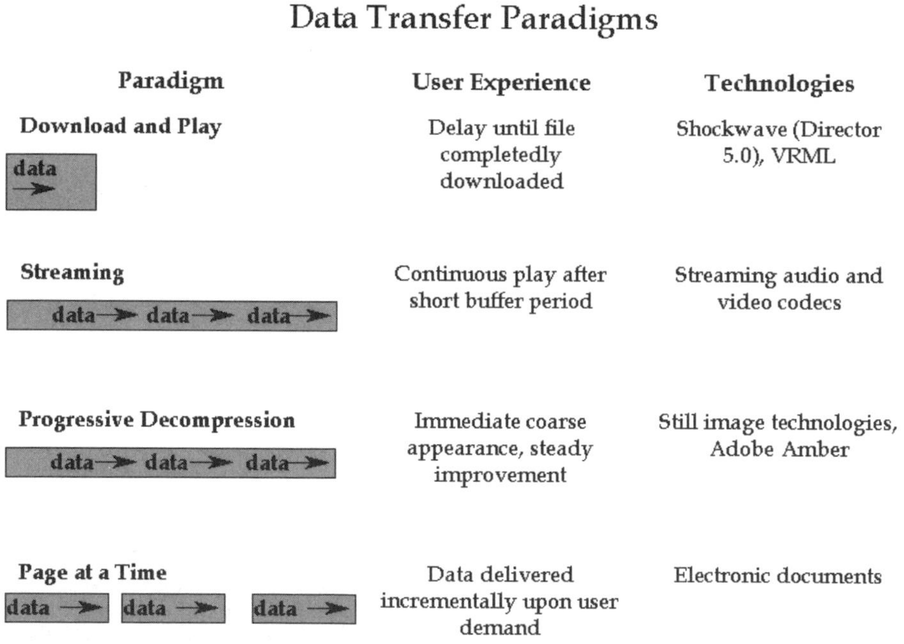

Data Transfer Paradigms

Paradigm	User Experience	Technologies
Download and Play	Delay until file completedly downloaded	Shockwave (Director 5.0), VRML
Streaming	Continuous play after short buffer period	Streaming audio and video codecs
Progressive Decompression	Immediate coarse appearance, steady improvement	Still image technologies, Adobe Amber
Page at a Time	Data delivered incrementally upon user demand	Electronic documents

Figure 4.4 The four methods used to send multimedia data from Internet servers to clients.

data buffering. During playback, data streams from Internet server to the user, providing essentially real-time playback.

Like the video compression technologies used for CD-ROM publishing, Internet streaming technologies are "codecs" that shrink bulky audio/video bit rates down to Internet bandwidths. Given the Internet's comparatively narrow bandwidth, however, compression rates are much greater than those used for CD-ROM publishing, or the data won't stream smoothly, causing noticeable breaks that interrupt audio or video playback.

Also like CD-ROM video codecs, streaming Internet codecs are all "lossy," meaning that the data thrown away during compression degrades quality. We'll discuss the impact of compression on video and audio quality in their respective sections.

Progressive Decompression

Progressive decompression is the technical term describing the now-familiar effect of an image or icon that initially appears blocky on your screen but gains detail as additional information is received. Initially used only for still images, progressive decompression is now used by other formats like Adobe's Acrobat to provide a rough but readable image very quickly and then improve fidelity over time.

Formats that progressively decompress are similar to streaming technologies in two aspects. First, they divide the information into sequential blocks of data for measured delivery to the user. For real-time technologies like audio and video, the logical division is time, and streaming encoders package and deliver the data from start to finish. Still image technologies

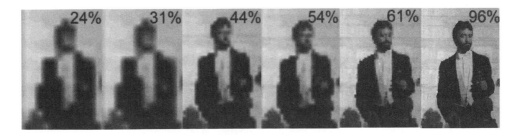

Figure 4.5   Scenes from LA, courtesy of Iterated Systems' fractal viewer. As more bytes get transferred, image quality progressively improves.

divide images into layers, each containing more detail, and send the layers sequentially.

The second common aspect is the player's ability to work with file segments rather than a complete file. Where most computer programs work only with complete files stored on disk, Internet players must store and display information as it's being downloaded. This is why programs like Media Player can't play streaming audio or video files as they're being downloaded, even if they can play the same files once downloaded and stored to disk.

Page-at-a-Time

Page-at-a-time technologies are a hybrid approach, used primarily for electronic documents like Adobe's Acrobat and Common Ground's Digital Paper. When both Adobe and Common Ground built their first Internet players, they couldn't handle incomplete data and essentially functioned like normal computer programs, displaying the electronic document after the file was downloaded and stored to disk. This forced the user to download an entire document before viewing the first page, a decidedly unresponsive approach.

The next logical step was page-at-a-time, where the encoder divides the document into pages, transmitting only the first page to the user when activated. When the user turns the page, or hyperlinks to another location, the browser sends a message to the server to transmit the appropriate target page. Overall, this provides users with much faster access to the first document page at the cost of repeated slight delays when turning pages inside the document.

Comparing the Contenders

With this background as prolog, let's take a look at the individual technologies. Our analysis will focus on high-level issues, like those to consider before incorporating one of these formats onto your Web page. Once you make the decision to go forward and start comparing alternatives, make sure you evaluate the following criteria for each reviewed technology:

Encoder: How does the encoder compare from a feature/function standpoint? For example, for audio delivery, does it allow batch compression of multiple files or real-time compression from a live source? Also, what environments does it run on, what types of inputs does it support, and how simple is the program to operate?

Player: Feature/function comparison, with emphasis on player environments, like Macintosh and UNIX support, since this defines the limits of your audience. Also integration issues like whether the player supports the Netscape 2.0 plug-in format or Microsoft's Active X.

Format quality: Comparing output side by side and analyzing which technology produces higher quality. For example, at similar audio bandwidths, which audio format sounds better?

Server: If there is a server, what environments does it support? A Windows NT server can't run on a Sun Web server. Also, a feature/function analysis, comparing performance and feature set.

Price: Finally, how does the technology compare pricewise with others in its class, considering prices for all of the above components?

We'll be looking at format quality for streaming audio and video technologies in the upcoming two chapters.

INTERNET MULTIMEDIA TECHNOLOGIES

Streaming Audio

At the risk of gushing (bad form for technology writers), streaming audio is here, it's now, it's today. Despite the 150:1 compression ratios required to squeeze audio down to below 14.4 kbps, quality is acceptable for many applications.

Note that speech is much less complex than music and compresses much more effectively, meaning less distortion. Still, if judged only by the quantity of music available on the Internet, audio quality is sufficient for the casual surfer, if not the dedicated audiophile.

At the time of this writing, five companies produced streaming audio technologies; DSP Group with TrueSpeech, RealAudio from Progressive Networks, Internet Wave from VocalTec, Toolvox for the Web by Voxware, and Streamworks from Xing Technologies.

Three of the technologies, TrueSpeech, Internet Wave, and Toolvox, were free, but business models change quickly on the Internet so be sure to check early in your decision-making process. Xing and Progressive Networks both charge for their server components, and Xing charges for their real-time encoder.

The first point on your streaming audio decision tree is the number of simultaneous streams you want your server to support. Xing and Progressive Networks have server programs that manage the outflow of data more efficiently than the Web server software itself, allowing more simultaneous streams. These servers also provide advanced features like random access to the audio stream, pause, and fast forward, all useful when playing long audio files.

What's the magic number beyond which you need server software? The DSP Group reports satisfying over 50 simultaneous streams without a problem, but the server was a Silicon Graphics workstation. On a Pentium box, with sufficient outgoing bandwidth, it's probably safe to assume that most technologies can support up to five or six simultaneous streams. Of course, you can always try the free technologies and upgrade to Real-Audio/Streamworks if performance is unacceptable.

The next consideration is playback feature set, where Progressive Networks dominates, not only by providing free real-time encoding but also with an advanced Application Programming Interface (API) that functions almost like an authoring system. For example, you can trigger page changes at specific points in the audio stream, letting you build a cost-effective kiosk on the Net.

Xing also scores high on advanced features, with proven, industrial strength real-time encoding and a stand-alone player that works almost like a car radio, letting you configure buttons to switch URLs at one touch.

Another key consideration is helper application. Support for Netscape's plug-in specification and Microsoft's ActiveX is obviously important, as are functionality and appearance.

Most players include status bar and volume control. As mentioned above, server-based technologies also offer random access to various points on the audio stream and pause and resume.

Helper appearance is key when you chose not to embed the player. Where DSP Group, Progressive Networks, and Voxware created simple, Media Player–like interfaces, VocalTec built an engaging, less buttoned-down player with a boom box toting character reflecting player status. The character plugs the box into the wall when you select a file, dances happily

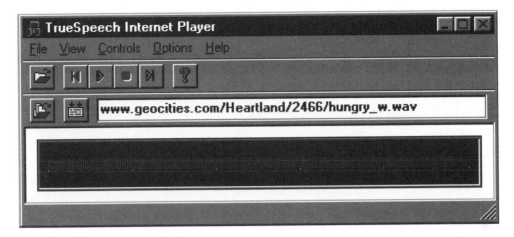

Figure 4.6 TrueSpeech offers great low-bandwidth audio fidelity and is free—really, really free.

when audio is playing, and jumps up and down on the box when playback is interrupted. This interface would be very desirable if distributing music to Generation X-ers.

Moving down the decision tree to audio quality, let's start with simple rules. First, dismiss Voxware if your page contains content other than simple speech, as Voxware handles speech incredibly well but mangles music beyond recognition. Contrary to its name, TrueSpeech works well with music at low bandwidths, but compresses to only one bandwidth —14.4 bps—so it can't scale quality for intranets with higher bandwidths.

Chapter 5 analyzes server, encoder, audio quality, and player for these five technologies in some detail.

Streaming Video

Streaming video is probably the most technically and artistically challenging multimedia format. Publishers currently working with video are familiar with the production, lighting, filming, and other issues related to analog video and the capture and compression issues relating to digitization. On the Internet, add the fact that your bandwidth suddenly shrinks from 150 KB/s to as low as 14.4, *including audio.*

As a result, even at 28.8 kbps, video quality is much, much lower than even the 160×120 video that graced many of our early CD-ROMs. On the other hand, at 128 kbps, double line ISDN, or simply a compact data stream for intranets, quality looks surprisingly good.

The Candidates

At the time of this writing, there are five streaming video technologies, VDOLive from VDONet Corporation, VivoActive from Vivo Software, ClearFusion from Iterated Systems, Streamworks from Xing, and Web Theatre from VXtreme, Inc. Unlike streaming audio technologies that are fairly homogenous, the two video technologies are striking in their key contrasts.

Streaming video technologies have all the same concerns as streaming audio, which we'll cover in more detail in Chapter 6. One unique consideration is the technology's "scalability," or ability to throttle video quality

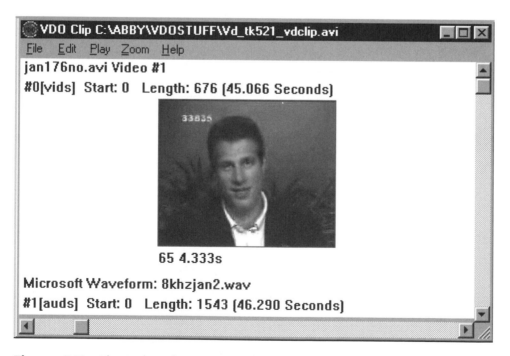

Figure 4.7   The author, the morning after handing in the last chapter. Actually, this is VDOLive compression at work, Jan at 28.8.

to maintain unbroken audio playback. Xing and VDOLive are both scalable and maintain audio playback even when bandwidth becomes limited.

In most instances, Xing, which uses MPEG-1–based technology, preserves audio by slowing or ceasing to deliver video frames, and at 28.8 kbps frames update as slow as one every five or six seconds. In contrast, using its scalable wavelet technology, VDO first drops the quality of the individual frames, then slows the frame rate, stopping video delivery, like Xing, if required to preserve the audio transmission. The obvious victim here is video quality, either as a result of dropped frame rate, à la Xing, or degraded frame quality, courtesy of VDO.

Vivo, which uses H.261 technology, and ClearFusion, based on Iterated's patented fractal algorithms, have no scalability mechanism, so when bandwidth drops, audio and video playback simply stops, restarting when bandwidth allows. This works well over high-bandwidth intranets, less well over the Internet if you prioritize audio over video quality. Those who favor video quality, however, like the fact that video quality never drops, per se, it just starts and stops a bit.

The one caution about streaming video is that of all the multimedia technologies, it is most adversely effected by the Net's challenging data delivery environment. This means that for the most part, the frame per second rating quoted by each manufacturer—e.g., 15 fps @ 160×120 @ 28.8 kbps—is optimistic at best and probably unattainable in anything other than a laboratory environment.

Electronic Documents

Although HTML has come a long way since its inception, viewed and printed output quality doesn't approach what you can achieve with a good word processor like Lotus Word Pro. This is obviously frustrating to those who spend hours (or thousands of dollars) beautifying their brochures and product specifications.

One alternative is electronic documents, like those produced by Adobe Acrobat or Common Ground Software's Digital Paper. These documents can contain both text and images, and once created, can be viewed and printed on a multitude of platforms, while looking virtually identical to their original form.

Electronic documents can also contain internal and even external hyperlinks and are searchable, both key advantages over HTML or native word processing documents. Long a favorite for CD-ROM publishers, neither format significantly penetrated the Internet because of two significant disadvantages.

First was the fact that both companies used the download and play metaphors, so the entire document had to be downloaded before viewing even the first page. A 10-page document could easily be 100–250 KB/s and take 30 to 90 seconds to download. This would be acceptable if you *knew* you wanted to view and print, but not if you're just window shopping.

The second objection to portable documents was integration, since before the Netscape 2.0 plug-in there was no way to integrate portable documents *into* a Web page. The forced the user to spawn a second full screen player which was slow and unwieldy. In addition, although hyperlinking *within* an electronic document was possible, linking to outside URLs was not. Unlike the eminently linkable and viewable HTML, electronic documents were like inert lumps of information, useful perhaps, but clearly foreign objects.

Both Adobe and Common Ground have dramatically improved Web functionality over the last 12 months. Both support the Netscape 2.0 and ActiveX plug-in specification, so the formats can be seamlessly integrated into a Web page. Both are also moving toward page-at-a-time paradigms to improve interactivity.

Common Ground has an early lead over Adobe in this regard, having shipped their "page-on-demand" technology in October 1995. Essentially, this breaks the document into multiple pages and transmits pages to the client as requested. For example, page 1 of the document downloads and displays immediately. If the user selects the next page, page 2 is downloaded. However, if the user selected a hyperlink to page 15, this page would be loaded, saving the interim load time of pages 2–14.

In December 1995, Adobe announced and shipped the initial components of their Web-enhanced Acrobat software, codenamed Amber, which ultimately shipped in the summer of 1996 as Acrobat 3.0. In addition to page-on-demand technology, Adobe implemented a progressive rendering, which sends text first, then graphics, then final font and sizing instructions.

Operation

By way of background, Adobe uses PDF (Page Description Format) files. Not surprisingly, the format is based on Adobe's crown jewel, the Postscript specification. Acrobat 3.0, which retails for $295, includes the three utilities necessary to create PDF files from word processors and similar applications

(Exchange), convert them from stand-alone EPS files (Distiller), or scan them from hard copy (Capture). To implement Adobe's page-on-demand technology, your Internet server must support "byte range serving," either directly or through a CGI (Common Gateway Interface) script (see http://www.adobe.com/acrobat/3beta/byteserve.html). You also need the Adobe 3.0 plug-in, which you can download from the Adobe Web site.

Common Ground uses the DP (Digital Paper) format, based upon their own proprietary format. Their Common Ground application ($185) creates .dp files, and a server program called the Common Ground Web Server Tools ($995) is required to implement their page-on-demand system.

For both technologies, creating electronic documents is as simple as printing. When you install Exchange or Common Ground, the programs add a printer driver that converts print output to their respective formats. This driver contains controls for image compression, embedding fonts, and other characteristics.

After finishing the document in your word processor or publishing program, you select the correct driver and print. The software prompts you for a file name and a few seconds later you have your file.

The next step is to load the file into the respective programs and create the inter- and intradocument links. At this stage, you can also add security features protecting your data from copying, editing, or even printing, if so desired.

Both companies take an extra step to prepare their files for the Web. Adobe Exchange "linearizes" the document, placing all assets like fonts and graphics in the most efficient order and compressing the result using a mix and match of lossless technologies like LZW, Group III and IV facsimile and RLE, and lossy JPEG for graphics. This process also catalogs all internal hyperlinks by byte range so that the player can request a specific page directly.

Common Ground's Web Server System is a bit more complicated, cataloging all documents and creating all HTML pages necessary to view the document. In both cases, programming is not required.

Once you're set up, Net surfers requesting a document prepared in either format from a Web page will receive one page, which Adobe will display progressively and Common Ground will display when fully received. Thereafter, touching any hyperlink in either format will launch the retrieval of the corresponding page. While waiting for each page to download may feel a touch unresponsive, it's tons better than waiting for a 500 MB document to download before you can even tell if you really want it.

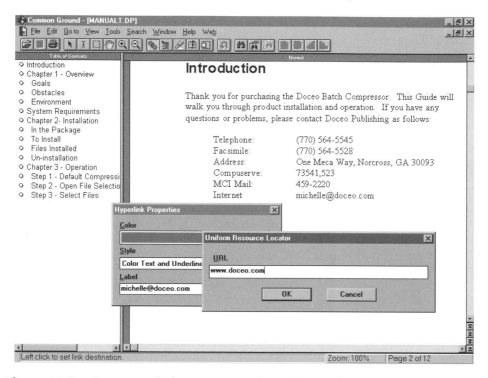

Figure 4.8   Creating a link to an external URL from within Common Ground.

Both Adobe and Common Ground freely distribute their players over the Internet, so your documents can be downloaded, viewed, and printed without charge to the user. Adobe has taken the lead on the plug-in side, as the Acrobat 3.0 player is fully embeddable under both Netscape 2.0 and Internet Explorer 3.0, in fact defaulting to embedded mode even when displaying pre–version 3.0 documents. Common Ground's player isn't embeddable and in fact doesn't even install itself as a helper application, a significant issue for those selling to nontechnical users.

A note to Acrobat users: If you've got PDF files up on your Web site, you'll need to download the new version of Exchange to linearize your files and register their byte order for page-at-a-time download. Otherwise, your viewers won't be able to move from page to page without downloading the entire file.

The Future

With the HTML 2.0 specifications recently finalized, the industry is moving toward 3.0 definitions, and two camps are emerging. On one side is Adobe, Netscape, and Apple, pushing the Postscript-based standard. On the other is Microsoft, once again hoping to break through Adobe's format monopoly with a TrueType-based standard.

Whatever the result, the advancement of HTML allows Web developers to improve the quality of their video both on screen and during printing. However, neither spec will be in place in the short term, and it's unclear whether either will deliver as much quality as Common Ground or Acrobat.

While the situation is in flux, Web architects should consider portable documents for two different purposes. First is for integrating more elabo-

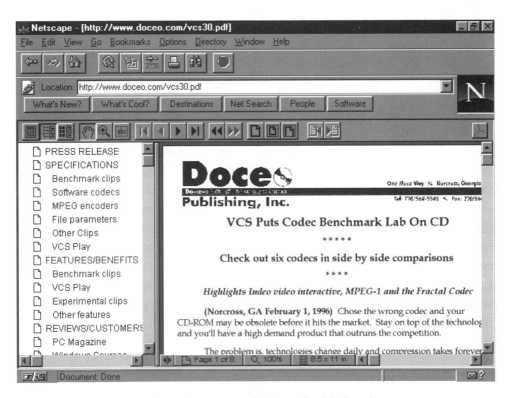

Figure 4.9 The Acrobat plug-in seamlessly embedded within Netscape Navigator 3.0. Note that middle layer of controls are from Acrobat.

rate text and formatting into their pages using the Netscape 2.0 plug-in specification.

Those who chose not to integrate should still consider distributing specifications, press releases, and other product literature from their Web site in Acrobat or Common Ground format. Remember that you're counting on this literature to sell your product or services, and while it's an unfair fact of life, sometimes the best-looking document wins.

Shockwave and VRML

Shockwave

One of the most visible multimedia on the Web developments has been Macromedia's Shockwave for Director. Director is an extremely flexible and capable hybrid used by many CD-ROM developers as both a stand-alone authoring program and to create animations embedded into other authoring programs. Shockwave is a player or helper application that lets Internet clients play Director files from within their browsers.

As it exists today, Shockwave is a download-and-play technology rather than a streaming technology. In most instances, this limits its use to small files in the "spinning logo" category, interesting appetizers but not a substantial main course.

This summer, Macromedia shipped Shockwave for Director 5.0, which supports streaming technologies like VDOLive and RealAudio but will not stream itself. Developers can now create a Director 5.0 front end for RealAudio playback, download the file to the client, and then initiate audio playback of the RealAudio stream.

By the end of 1996, Macromedia promises a postprocessing program called Afterburner that will arrange the bitmapped graphics, video, and audio assets in a Director file to enable streaming. It will be interesting to see exactly how the company manages the trade-offs necessary to accomplish full streaming.

At its essence, streaming technology implies the ability to maintain some measure of synchronization, usually with audio. Without sound, for example, you couldn't tell whether slow-motion television was an instant replay or some snafu at the station. Similarly, you couldn't tell if one frame per second animation was relaxation therapy or a bandwidth problem unless the audio was breaking up or clearly out of synch.

A streaming Director file means that the animated sequences will maintain synchronization with the audio. Note that the two key streaming technologies, audio and video, have established strategies for maintaining synchronization, all of which trade bandwidth for quality and degrade the overall experience to maintain synchronization. For example, audio and video codecs use lossy compression, which shrinks the stream but degrades quality. Video codecs also shrink the viewing resolution and drop frames to maintain synch.

Figure 4.10   Duckman, one of the more famous Shockwave creations.

In the "there ain't no such thing as a free lunch" Internet environment, Macromedia will have to employ some or all of these technologies. Let's assume a simple case, where a full-screen 24-bit bitmap (768 KB) changes every 4 seconds with accompanying audio commentary. This would be a piece of cake for a dual-speed CD-ROM but impossible over a 28.8 kbps connection unless you degrade image quality beyond recognition.

This raises two key issues. First, will there be some degradation trade-off to maintain synchronization? Second, with or without this trade-off, will there be development tools like bandwidth monitors to help developers create Director files that stream at bandwidths relevant to the developers?

One thing not in question is Macromedia's commitment to Shockwave and streaming. At press time, the company announced a Shockwave component for their popular Authorware product that will operate similarly to Shockwave for Director.

VRML

While not quite as loudly, the Internet has also been buzzing about VRML (Virtual Reality Modeling Language), a language that enables 3D graphics over the Web. Like Shockwave, VRML files are download-and-play technologies. Open a .VR file, and you'll see structured text instructions that list the audio and video files manipulated in the 3D sequence.

For example, one instruction might tell the computer to draw a triangle in the upper left-hand corner and texture it with a certain JPG bitmap. Another might start a certain audio file playing three seconds after animation starts.

This mode of operation means that all the required assets must be present on the client computer before a VRML file can start playing. Absent an initiative like Shockwave and Afterburner, VRML will remain a download-and-play technology.

SUMMARY

1. Multimedia on the Internet is just another phenomenon that looks easier than it is. At bandwidths up to 40 times *smaller* than that of even an obsolete CD-ROM, there will be trade-offs for every multimedia format.

2. Netscape's plug-in specification and Microsoft's ActiveX have enabled the seamless integration of HTML and multimedia formats like audio and video.

3. There are four data delivery paradigms: *download and play*, where you wait for the entire file to download before anything happens; *streaming*, where playback starts soon after calling for the file and continues (in theory) unbroken until the transfer is complete; *progressive decompression*, where a very rough image appears very quickly with additional detail filling in over time; and *page-at-a-time*, where the first page of a document is transferred immediately and subsequent pages are transferred upon demand.

4. All Internet multimedia formats have at least two if not all three of the following components: *Encoder*, which compresses the material into final format for placement on the server; *Player*, which resides at the client to decode the compressed stream; and *Server*, usually to dole out the compressed bandwidth or enable special features like fast forward or page at a time.

5. Audio is the most mature of the streaming technologies, with good alternatives at all price ranges, including free. Read all about them in Chapter 5.

6. Streaming video is still in its infancy. Over the bandwidth-limited Internet, it's suitable primarily for Generation X-ers and those seeking technology demonstrations. On intranets, however, the quality of a 128 kbps talking head video stream is remarkably high.

7. If your home page has brochures, spec sheets, pamphlets, and other marketing or sales materials, HTML probably can't duplicate the quality of your normal hard-copy output. Electronic documents, however, like Adobe Acrobat, can and also perform remarkably well in the Web environment.

8. Shockwave is currently a download-and-play technology best suited for very short movies of the spinning logo genre. If Afterburner succeeds in converting Shockwave to a streaming technology, however, hundreds of thousands of rabid Director authors will be set loose on our Internet, and things may never be the same.

Chapter

Streaming Audio Technologies

IN THIS CHAPTER

We had so much fun on our video Tour de Codec (Chapter 6) that we decided to do the same for streaming audio technologies. Here we look at five, RealAudio from Progressive Networks (www.realaudio.com), Voxware's ToolVox for the Web (www.voxware.com), Xing Technologies' StreamWorks (www.xingtech.com), VocalTec's Internet Wave (www.vocaltec.com), and DSP Group's TrueSpeech (www.dspg.com). We focused our testing and evaluation on three areas.

First and foremost is audio quality, where we compressed six clips to two different bandwidths with all five technologies and ran blind jury tests to pick a winner. Five of the six clips are included on the CD-ROM (chap_5 subdirectory) in both original and compressed forms. We couldn't get rights to include the symphony clip, and while I was up for including it anyway, well, you know how picky those publishing types are.

Then we evaluated encoder performance and usability, assessing factors like compression time, compatibility with existing tools, and ease of use. Finally, we looked at decoder performance and usability, focusing on features like volume control, ease of use, and whether the technologies leveraged the advanced integration capabilities offered by the relevant plug-in (Netscape) or DirectX (Microsoft) specifications.

Unfortunately, time didn't allow us to fully analyze the server side of these technologies. We also weren't able to study the "how-tos" of producing good quality streaming audio, or of HTML integration, which, hopefully, will be the subject of another book to be released in 1997.

Test Summary

Test clips: We compared six benchmark clips, three speech clips, including both male and female voices, and three music clips ranging from hard rock to symphony.

AUDIO QUALITY

Speech

Conference: This clip is the audio segment of video recorded on Panasonic M-2 format during a live conference and tests how the codec compresses audio from a slightly noisy source.

Alternating: This clip, recorded from a laser disc, alternates a male and female voice.

Female Speech: This clip was recorded in a sound booth, professionally dubbed to cassette and captured.

Music

Hard Rock: This clip is hard rock, with both live instruments and dubbed effects, captured from a cassette.

Soft Rock: This clip combines electric guitar with minor synthetic effects and was captured at high quality from a CD-ROM.

Symphony: This clip contains violins, reed instruments, minor percussion, and light horns and was recorded from a CD-ROM.

We compressed all clips to two bandwidths, 14.4 and 28.8, since none of the test compressors supported bandwidths in excess of 28.8. The encoders had varying input parameters, so we digitized each clip four times to optimize the input for each encoder and compressed output setting.

Jury Tests

Our jury comprised two individuals, with the test moderator casting the deciding vote when required. Tests were completely blind, with the jury sitting with their backs to the computer and comparisons always between technology A and B rather than Xing versus RealAudio.

Table 5.1 presents the rankings of the various technologies, and Table 5.2 analyzes low- and high-bandwidth performance and compressed quality for speech and music.

Table 5.1   Comparative ranking in jury tests, lower numbers better.

		DSPG	*Progressive*	*VocalTec*	*Voxware*	*Xing*
Conference	14.4	1	2	3	5	4
	28.8	2	1	4	5	3
Alternating	14.4	1	2	4	5	3
	28.8	3	4	2	5	1
Female voice	14.4	1	2	4	5	3
	28.8	3	2	4	5	1
Hard rock	14.4	1	2	3	5	4
	28.8	4	2	1	5	3
Soft rock	14.4	1	2	4	5	3
	28.8	3	2	4	5	1
Symphony	14.4	2	3	4	5	1
	28.8	3	1	4	5	2

Discussion

Overall, TrueSpeech was the low-bandwidth leader, winning five of six jury tests. In general, Progressive's RealAudio was second best in low bandwidth, beating Xing soundly in low-bandwidth speech and edging Xing in 14.4 music. Xing was the overall high-bandwidth champ, outperforming Progressive in speech but falling behind somewhat in music.

VocalTec was disappointing overall, winning one or two competitions but placing fourth in most. Voxware, a very specialized, speech only, low-bandwidth technology fared very poorly, failing to win even one competition.

TrueSpeech   TrueSpeech excelled in low-bandwidth tests, winning five of six juries. The codec held up well in high-bandwidth tests, especially voice, where it placed second in the noisy conference test and third in the two others. Note, however, that the difference between TrueSpeech and the category winners was relatively slight, even at twice the bandwidth. In high-bandwidth music tests, however, TrueSpeech fell to fourth overall, slightly behind VocalTec.

As you would expect from an algorithm tuned by real-world application, TrueSpeech degrades gracefully when stressed by noise or complicated music, becoming somewhat fuzzy and noisy but creating few artifacts and only minor distortion.

RealAudio   Overall, RealAudio provides good quality across a range of audio types, ranking first in two categories, third and fourth in one, and second in all others. In general, RealAudio quality degrades gracefully when compressing noisy speech or music, creating somewhat fuzzy audio, but generally without artifacts.

Table 5.2 Comparative ranking by categories, lower numbers better.

		DSPG	Progressive	VocalTec	Voxware	Xing
Total	14.4	7	13	22	30	18
Total	28.8	18	12	19	30	11
Speech	14.4	3	6	11	15	10
Speech	28.8	8	7	10	15	5
Music	14.4	4	7	11	15	8
Music	28.8	10	5	9	15	6

In general, Progressive consistently ranked behind TrueSpeech in low-bandwidth tests, and Xing in high-bandwidth tests, but outranked Xing in tests involving high-bandwidth music.

Xing   Overall, Xing was more effective at 28.8 than at 14.4 and slightly more effective at music than speech at the higher data rate. In general, Xing degraded differently than most other technologies, producing a hollow, warbling sound with some echoing, but little of the fuzziness or noise characteristic of other technologies.

While other technologies may have sounded "better" and closer to the original, Xing was almost always "clearer." Where most jury comparisons were generally fairly obvious, tests involving Xing were almost always controversial, especially when music was involved.

VocalTec   Much like TrueSpeech and RealAudio, IWave became fuzzy and distorted when stressed by noisy speech or music, but generally to a greater degree. In fact, few if any clips made it through the compression process without some obvious artifact.

IWave also became faint and somewhat distant during the higher quality speech recordings, a characteristic not shared by either TrueSpeech or RealAudio. Finally, among the scalable codecs, IWave seemed to benefit the least from the increase in bandwidth from 14.4 to 28.8, these factors combining to produce VocalTec's dismal benchmarks.

ToolVox   Overall, ToolVox performed poorly in all tests and exhibited extreme sensitivity to noise and very ungraceful degradation. When stressed by noisy audio, most other technologies become slightly more fuzzy or hollow. In contrast, ToolVox distorted beyond recognition when encountering even moderate noise. ToolVox is also totally unsuited for music, mangling even relatively simple music streams.

ENCODER PERFORMANCE

We judged encoders based on compression time, compatibility with existing tools, ease of use, and feature set (Tables 5.3, 5.4).

Time comparison proved Xing the fastest, but all encoders were clearly capable of real-time performance.

Table 5.3 Compression time, 38-second clip (in seconds).

DSPG	Progressive	VocalTec	Voxware	Xing
12	28	5	8	3

In terms of compatibility with existing tools, all encoders started with WAV files, eliminating compatibility hassles. Since TrueSpeech was licensed by Microsoft, users can access TrueSpeech compression via Media Recorder, Microsoft's Windows 95 capture/compression utility. All other technologies used proprietary encoders.

All encoders except for Xing were Windows-based application programs that were relatively straightforward to operate. For our tests, we used Xing's DOS command line program, but a Windows-based utility implementing the same technology became available just before our publication date.

DECODER PERFORMANCE AND USABILITY

We tested all decoders live on the Internet and, when possible, from files on disk. We tested the stand-alone performance and attempted to verify Netscape 2.0 plug-in capabilities when claimed.

Most important for all players was integration, meaning support for the Netscape 2.0 plug-in specification and Microsoft's OCX controls for Internet explorer. Next are features like volume control, fast forward, and random access. These are summarized in Table 5.5 and addressed in the individual reviews.

Table 5.4 Streaming audio encoder features.

Encoder	DSPG	Progressive	VocalTec	Voxware	Xing
Installation	N.A.	Self-extracting/installing EXE	Unzip and run EXE, no installation required	Self-extracting/installing EXE	Hardware encoder is turnkey, software is DOS command line
Encoder environments	Windows 95 and NT/Win 3.11	Windows NT/95, Macintosh, Linux, Solaris, Irix, SunOS, HP/UX, AIX, FreeBSD	Windows 3.11	Windows 95, Windows 3.11, Macintosh	DOS/real time via separate hardware
Encoder cost	free	free	free	free	$2500—audio (free software encoder)
Real-time encoding	no	yes	no	no	yes
Batch encoding	yes	yes—via DOS program	no	no	no
Inputs	8 kHz/16-bit WAV files	WAV, AIFF, AU	WAV/AU	WAV/AIFF	WAV/any recorded or live stream
Output	.WAV	.RA	VMF (media)/VMD (information stub)	VOX	.lbr (low bit rate)
Presets (e.g., bandwidth/content)	N.A.—all files 8500 bps	14.4/28.8	5.5, 8, 11, 16 kHz, music/speech	N.A.—all files 2400 bps	8–16 kbps
Recording capabilities	In sound recorder	yes	no	yes	

Help topics (on-line or read-me files):

Recording advice	yes	yes	yes	no	no

(continued)

Table 5.4 Encoders *(continued)*

Encoder	DSPG	Progressive	VocalTec	Voxware	Xing
Capture parameters	yes	yes	yes	Only Voxware program	no
Embedding audio into HTML	yes	yes	yes	yes	no
Audio placement on the server	yes	yes	yes	yes	no
Plug-in	yes	yes	no	yes	no
Special features	none	Play file during encoding, real-time encoding, input file description	Input file description	Recording/ fast forward/ compressed audio playback	Batch capabilities via command line
Uninstall	yes	yes	no (no real installation)	yes	no

Table 5.5 Streaming audio player features.

Player	DSPG	Progressive	VocalTec	Voxware	Xing
Playback environments	Windows 3.11, 95, NT/Mac	Windows 95/NT, Windows 3.11, Mac OS 7.X, OS/2, Linux 1.2.x, Solaris 2.4/2.5, SunOS 4.1.x, Irix 5.3	Windows 95/Windows 3.11/Windows NT	Windows 95, Windows 3.11, Macintosh	Windows 311/Macintosh, SGI, Sun, Linus
32-bit player for Win95 (y/n)	yes	yes	no	no	no
Browser integration	Plug-in/OCX	Plug-in/OCX	Helper plug-in pending	Plug-in helper application	Helper/stand-alone
Decoder cost	free	free/$29 (manual/ sample files)	free	free	free—$29 for support

Table 5.5   Players *(continued)*

Player	DSPG	Progressive	VocalTec	Voxware	Xing
Player features					
Installation	Self-extracting, separate installation	Self-extracting/self-installing EXE	Self-extracting/ self-installing EXE	Self-extracting/self-installing EXE	Self-extracting, self-installing
Status bar	yes	yes	yes	yes	yes
Timer	no	yes		yes	yes
Start at random points	no	no—but can move randomly once file starts	no	no	yes
Stop and resume	no	yes	yes	no	no
Volume control	no	yes	yes	no	Not in helper application but in stand-alone
Bookmark	yes	yes	no	no	no
Adjust memory buffer size	yes	yes	yes	no	yes
On-line help	no	yes	yes	no	limited
Optimize audio settings	yes	yes	yes	no	no
Server time out adjustment	yes	yes	no	no	yes
Uninstaller	yes	yes	no	yes	no

TECHNOLOGY REVIEWS

TrueSpeech (DSP Group, Inc.)

Overview   The DSP Group (DSPG) considers their streaming Internet product as inexpensive advertising for TrueSpeech compression technology, focusing on licensing deals with OEMs like Intel, Microsoft, and US Robotics rather than trying to profit directly from their streaming audio product. This is a shame, because with TrueSpeech's unparalleled low-bandwidth quality and DSPG's apparent deal-making abilities, the company could give Progressive Networks serious competition for leadership in this nascent market.

TrueSpeech is a family of compression algorithms marketed by DSPG for a diverse range of products and markets, including digital answering machines, telephones, and DSVD modems. DSPG offers both software and chip-based implementations and different algorithms that trade compression and playback complexity for compression ratios and audio quality. Significant OEMs include AT&T, US Robotics, Siemens, and TRW.

In 1994, DSPG licensed TrueSpeech 8.5 to Microsoft for inclusion in Windows 95. This version provides 15:1 compression, reducing an 8-MHz, 16-bit audio stream down to roughly 8.5 kbps, and plays back in real time on 486/33 computers and faster. In August 1995, DSPG announced TrueSpeech for the Internet, also built around TrueSpeech 8.5. More recently, the International Telecommunications Union selected TrueSpeech as the G.723 speech coder for the H.324 videoconferencing standard, a selection later endorsed by Microsoft, Intel, and companies like VDONet and NetSpeak.

As suggested by its name, TrueSpeech is optimized for speech, and the algorithm uses sophisticated modeling techniques to achieve relatively high compression and high-quality playback across a surprising range of clips. In our jury tests, TrueSpeech won five of six low-bandwidth tests, while falling no further than fourth in one 28.8 competition and twice placing second.

This quality is somewhat squandered by the relative lack of player amenities and absence of server-enabled features like stop and resume and random access to the audio stream. Overall, it seems that DSPG is content to license TrueSpeech to others who will butt heads with Progressive, winning the low-bandwidth compression battle but choosing not to compete seriously in the streaming audio war.

Audio Quality

Conference: TrueSpeech filtered out the background noise very effectively at the price of just a hint of slurring, winning the 14.4 competition and dropping only to second place against the higher bandwidth competition.

Alternating: TrueSpeech produced crisp results, with just an occasional hint of fuzziness.

Female Speech: Overall, TrueSpeech produced very good quality, with just a hint of a lisp on some of the "S" sounds.

Audio Quality—Music

Hard Rock: TrueSpeech tended to blend the instruments into a jumble, creating fuzzy audio with significant background noise. Still, TrueSpeech produced sufficient quality to win the 14.4 competition, while dropping to fourth at 28.8.

Soft Rock: TrueSpeech was again fuzzy and made the electric guitar twang like a cheap, toy guitar.

Symphony: TrueSpeech jumbled all instruments into a fuzzy, furry jumble, scoring its only second place finish in the 14.4 jury tests.

The Encoder

Installation: TrueSpeech is a standard component of Windows 95 and NT, so there's no encoder to download or install for these platforms. DSPG also provides a DOS batch encoder and Windows 3.11 compression program. DSPG has announced that they are developing a Mac encoder but hasn't set a release date.

Operation: On the tested Windows 95 platform, you encode with Microsoft's Sound Recorder, which also provides recording and simple cut-and-paste audio editing. You encode using the Save As command, changing the file type from PCM to TrueSpeech before saving. There are no bandwidth or audio type options, and all files are compressed to approximately

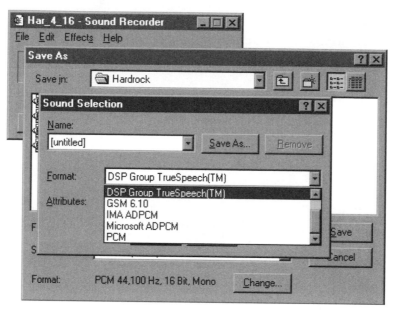

Figure 5.1 TrueSpeech encodes in Windows 95's Sound Recorder or virtually any 32-bit audio editing program.

8.5 kbps, roughly three times faster than real time, taking about 12 seconds to compress our 38-second test file on a Pentium 133.

Sound Recorder has no TrueSpeech specific help, a situation that DSPG seeks to remedy with read-me files shipped with the player. This documentation covers the basics of recording, converting, and embedding but provides little detail.

Player Features   TrueSpeech creates standard WAV files that will play from Media Player and other applications on the Windows 95/NT platforms without special drivers or player applications. However, playing *streaming* audio from the Internet requires a special player, even on these platforms. In addition to these platforms, DSPG provides players for the Mac, Power-Mac, and Windows 3.1 environments.

Installation: The Windows 95 player is a self-extracting EXE that produces a setup program that must be run separately by the user. The installation program creates a program group on the tool panel, loading

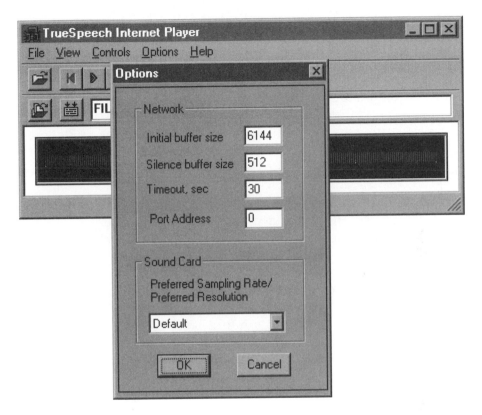

Figure 5.2 DSP Group's TrueSpeech player.

the player, uninstaller, and read-me file. After installation, the player automatically loads and plays a short greeting from DSPG.

Operation: The player is austere in function and appearance. As a serverless technology, TrueSpeech doesn't offer stop and resume or random access to the audio stream. Volume control is another important unsupported feature.

On the plus side, DSPG lets you adjust the initial download buffer size to decrease buffering related latency. You can also add bookmarks, useful when playing compressed audio files outside the browser environment. In terms of browser integration, DSPG supports the Netscape 2.0 plug-in specification but hasn't announced plans to support Microsoft's OCX program.

RealAudio (Progressive Networks)

Overview   Progressive Networks is a gilt-edged start-up founded by a former Microsoft VP with an executive team and board of directors that includes Lotus founder Mitch Kapor, a former U.S. congresswoman, and the obligatory scientist from Oxford. Their RealAudio streaming technology was first out of the gate, announced in April 1994. Strong PR, word-of-mouth, and some peachy customers that include NPR and ABC Radio have propelled Progressive Networks to the early lead in market share with close to 4,000,000 downloaded players.

Progressive Networks provides consistently high-quality audio and polished, full-featured encoder and player programs with excellent on-line help and additional documentation available on their well-traveled Web site. In fact, their Web site is so busy that it contains advertising from several companies, including Microsoft.

Progressive also excels at building a useful infrastructure for deploying streaming audio like synchronized HTML page turning in version 2.0, which converts static home pages into a Net-based kiosk. They're also masters of the art of promotion and strategic relationships. In short, Progressive is ahead of the field when it comes to making streaming audio a business, with Xing, the only competitor seeking profit from streaming audio, barely on the radar screen when it comes to commercialization.

Audio Quality

Conference: At 14.4, RealAudio exhibited good noise handling, producing good quality audio with just a hint of slurriness, placing second. At 28.8, audio quality improved significantly, with RealAudio taking first place.

Alternating: RealAudio performed well at 14.4, placing second, but didn't improve significantly at 28.8, dropping to fourth in this category.

Female Speech: RealAudio performed well with this crisp, clear segment, placing second in both categories, producing occasional artifacts at 14.4 and only the barest of slurs at 28.8.

Audio Quality—Music

Hard Rock: At 14.4, the singer's voice comes through clearly, but most of the instruments are indistinct, sounding withdrawn and jumbled together. At 28.8, the dynamic range increases but the music sounds faint, as if played back from within a tunnel or stairwell, and still noisy and fuzzy. Still, RealAudio placed second in both bandwidths.

Soft Rock: At 14.4, the guitar sounded metallic and playback was marred by background noise and fuzziness. Much of the fuzziness disappears at 28.8, but the metallic sound remains. Still, RealAudio again placed second in both competitions.

Symphony: At 14.4, all instruments jumbled into a big fuzzy audio mess that overwhelmed the melody, resulting in a third place ranking, Progressive's worst 14.4 placement. The individual instruments reappear at 28.8 with only a slight fuzziness and faint background noise during various solos, boosting Progressive to first place.

The Encoder   The encoder is available free on Progressive Network's Web site. Progressive Networks ships versions for Windows NT/Windows 95, Macintosh, Linux, Solaris, Irix, SunOS, HP/UX, AIX, and FreeBSD. The download size for the Windows 95 version is 487 KB.

Installation: The encoder is a self-installing EXE that creates a Windows 95 program group on the Taskbar and a hotlink to the encoder. The installation program also installs comprehensive help and an uninstaller.

Compression Controls: The RealAudio encoder is a simple, intuitive program with two windows, one for audio source, which can be a live stream or file, the other for destination, which can be a disk file or the RealAudio server for broadcasting applications. Both sides show a histogram of their respective audio files, which is useful for maintaining the proper volume during encoding.

The encoder can play a file during encoding, but playback is often marred by audio pops and other artifacts not actually present in the compressed file, limiting the utility of this feature for quality control purposes. You can't play a previously compressed RA file from the encoder—you have to use the player. Similarly, you can't play the input file from the encoder interface, forcing the user to load Media Player or a similar program.

RealAudio supports two bandwidths, 14.4 and 28.8, selectable via a simple control on the program face. There are no customization controls

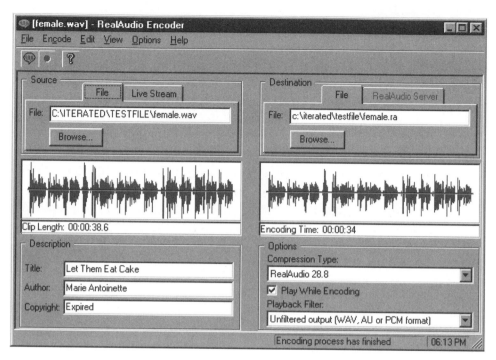

Figure 5.3   The RealAudio encoder program.

for audio type like speech or music, or any batch processes. RealAudio does offer a DOS batch processor.

Header information includes title, author, and copyright, which is input on the encoder screen and displayed by the player during audio playback. You can't change header information without recompressing the entire stream, which would have been a useful option.

On a Pentium 133, compression is approximately 30% faster than real time when audio playback is disabled, making RealAudio one of the slowest encoders. Compression is real time, of course, when audio playback is enabled or during live broadcasts.

Help files are extensive, describing program controls as well as input types and quality-related source issues. Progressive Network's Web site contains additional information about creating high-quality RealAudio streams.

Operation: The program worked as advertised, proving stable during all testing.

Player Features   Progressive Networks offers two player packages, a free downloadable player from their Web site and $29 player with priority e-mail support, manual, audio content, and the version 2.0 encoder.

Installation: The downloaded EXE is a self-extracting installation that runs the installation program and installs the player and bookmark to RealAudio home page. During installation, the program searches for browsers on the system and queries the user whether to install helper applications for all located browsers. The program also searches for and uninstalls previously installed RealAudio players, and creates a shortcut to the player on the Windows 95 desktop.

Features: The RealAudio player is extraordinarily feature rich. In addition to volume control, slider bar, elapsed time information, random access, and pause and resume, RealAudio offers the following features:

Options

- File: The player enables selection of location and/or file, like most players, but also remembers the URL/file name of the more recently visited sites, or bookmarks, useful for those who frequently visit one or more particular sites.
- View: The player is very configurable as to size and feature set. The default configuration presents the status bar, clip information, and volume control, or you opt to streamline the player down to just the slider bar and on/off control. This is in addition to being

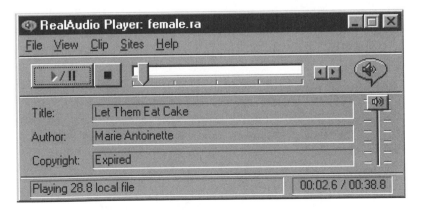

Figure 5.4   The near-ubiquitous RealAudio player.

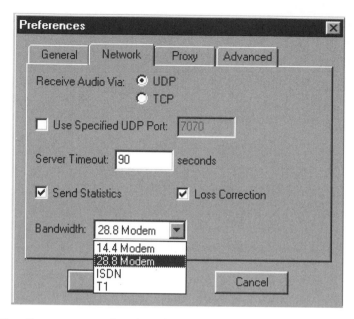

Figure 5.5   Options in RealAudio's feature-rich player.

able to embed the player under the Netscape 2.0 specification and ActiveX.

- Preferences: Controls allow the user to specify the number of recent clips maintained in the ini file; whether to optimize audio quality or CPU usage; whether to use UDP or TCP as the transmission protocol and to select the UDP Port and timeout period; to opt to send connection statistics back to the RealAudio server; to specify your connection speed to allow the server to automatically negotiate the optimal stream bandwidth; to enable/disable loss correction, which compensates for lost packets; to use a proxy server for security reasons; and to force your sound card to play 8 bit or 11 kHz only to compensate for older cards.
- Clip: Allows the user to page backward and forward between previously played clips.
- Sites: Automatic links to the RealAudio home page, guide, or help page.
- Help: Help is comprehensive and concise and augmented by additional help on Progressive Network's home page.

The player supports the Netscape 2.0 plug-in specification, and Progressive has several examples on their Web page.

Server 2.0   Server software is necessary for some of the advanced features found in version 2.0 of the RealAudio server, which include:

- Synchronized multimedia: This lets Web developers place hooks in the audio to change HTML pages at specified points in the audio stream, essentially converting the home page into a kiosk.
- Bandwidth negotiation: Lets the server query the client to determine the correct bandwidth to transmit, allowing the server to seamlessly deliver a higher quality stream to 28.8 connections while continuing to support 14.4 modems.
- The option to receive files using either UDP or TCP.

Servers are the primary source of revenue for Progressive. The company bases *Internet* pricing on the number of simultaneous streams supported by the server, while *intranet* pricing is based on streams and the number of licensed players. Intranet pricing is somewhat cheaper, with unlimited streams and 100 licensed players available for $3995 while 100 streams for an Internet application cost $8495.

Progressive strongly encourages support sales, which cost as much as 60% on small servers, shrinking to around 35% for large servers. Faculty, staff, and students of accredited colleges, universities, and K–12 schools are eligible for a 25% discount on server and support pricing.

Progressive ships server software for Netscape, O'Reilly, Mac HTTPD, NCSA HTTPD, Emwac HTTPD, CERN HTTPD, and Webstar for Macintosh. Progressive supports both the UDP and TCP protocols but recommends UDP for most applications. This has caused problems with listeners behind corporate firewalls.

To address these problems, Progressive has aggressively pursued direct support for the RealAudio format from firewall vendors. Progressive has also provided proxy support in the player and provides source code to companies willing to write their own proxy.

The Personal Server   The Personal Server is a new server with functionality similar to that of Server 2.0 except that it runs solely on Windows 95/NT and Mac OS 7.5x platforms and supports only two simultaneous external streams. The product costs $99.

Internet Wave (VocalTec)

Overview   In February 1995, VocalTec made fame and some fortune with the Internet Phone, a product that enables long-distance phone calls over the Internet. An early Internet technology darling, VocalTec successfully OEM'd the Internet Phone to several prominent modem vendors, including Motorola, Boca Research, and Zoom Telephonics. In September 1995, VocalTec followed with Internet Wave, a free technology apparently intended to stimulate demand for the Internet Phone.

Internet Wave (IWave) has three components, an encoder, a player, and a limited server that enables random access to the audio stream on a small set of server types. Audio quality was surprisingly poor given VocalTec's compression experience. While IWave experienced a few high points, like winning the high-bandwidth hard rock jury test, the technology rated a distant fourth overall and was fourth in every average category, whether 14.4/28.8, voice, music, or combined. Absent the highly specialized Voxware, VocalTec would have been the bottom of the barrel.

VocalTec doesn't appear to have updated any IWave components since shipping in late 1995, which could also indicate their lack of seriousness about a product with no revenue potential. Overall, IWave is not a serious competitor in the streaming audio market and may not be intended to be.

Audio Quality

Conference: IWave was usable at 14.4 but was noisy and fuzzy and the speech was somewhat slurry, placing third. Conversion to 28.8 did not significantly improve the results, dropping IWave to fourth.

Alternating: VocalTec's clips sounded faint, as if recorded in a tunnel, and IWave placed fourth. Clip quality improved in the 28.8 competition, boosting IWave to second.

Female Speech: At 14.4, IWave again sounded hollow and fuzzy and ranked fourth, and the increase in bandwidth produced only a slight improvement, stranding IWave in fourth position at 28.8.

Audio Quality—Mus.

Hard Rock: At 14.4, IWave tended to blend the instruments together and produce extraneous noise and some echoing, but it ranked third overall. At 28.8, IWave's artifacts sounded like additional percussion, blending in and even enhancing the music, accounting for IWave's sole winning jury score. Still, this was one of the closest races, and IWave could easily have dropped to third behind both Xing and Progressive.

Soft Rock: IWave placed fourth in both bandwidths, blurring the distinct guitar sound into a fuzzy mess at 14.4 and improving only slightly at 28.8.

Symphony: IWave again produced fuzzy, noisy audio, which didn't improve at higher bandwidths, and placed fourth in both categories.

The Encoder

Installation: The Internet Wave Encoder comes in a zipped file that, once unzipped, needs no further installation; you simply double click on the encoder EXE from Windows Explorer or set up a shortcut. The downloaded file includes a short read-me file, a lengthy and useful white paper, and on-line help.

Operation: While the encoder looks somewhat dated, the program works well, has several nice features, and is well documented. Like RealAudio, IWave includes slots to describe audio source and content and also includes information about the base URL address, which is required for server integration.

During compression, the encoder creates two files, one containing the compressed audio, the other a stub file to use during HTML preparation. Compression is extremely fast, taking less than six seconds for our 38-second test file. On the negative side, we could never successfully play a compressed file using the Encoder's play feature.

The encoder can compress to four different data rates suitable for 9600, 14,400 and two levels for 28,800 bps modems and provides presets for speech and music. The encoder warns the developer before adjusting the sampling rate of an audio file, which is significant because subsampling can degrade audio quality.

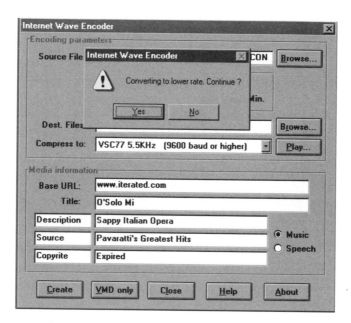

Figure 5.6 VocalTec's Internet Wave Encoder.

Between the help and read-me files, VocalTec covers most of the critical recording and encoder bases, including extensive help on recording from different sources like microphones and internal CD-ROM players and providing HTML and server integration details. Overall, from a program and documentation standpoint the encoder's only disappointing feature was that it produced subpar quality audio.

Player Features

Installation: The IWave player comes bundled with a demo version of the Internet Phone, comprising a hefty 1.3 MB file. The file is a self-extracting, self-installing zip file that creates a VocalTec program group and installs the Internet Phone, Internet Wave, and associated help and read-me files.

Operation: The IWave player is very graphical, using an animated figure with a boom box to illustrate playback status of music files and a figure turning pages of a book to illustrate playback of a speech file. The player is also reasonably well featured, with volume control, status bar, a digital readout of playback time to completion, and stop and resume.

Display of audio file details like author, content, and source is a user-selectable option. Advanced controls include the ability to adjust download cache size to modify preplay buffering time and to adjust the amount of downloaded audio stored to disk.

Server Features VocalTec provides a small server component for enabling fast forwarding through a file on the client end. The utility must be compiled on the server and has been tested only on the Solaris 2.4 and SunOS 4.x servers.

Figure 5.7 VocalTec's engaging player.

ToolVox for the Web (Voxware, Inc.)

Overview   In theory, an extremely low-bandwidth, voice-specific audio codec would seem ideal for the Web environment, especially given the increasing focus on Internet telephones, live conferences, and other voice-centric activities. Unfortunately, while ToolVox meets the low-bandwidth requirement, producing even adequate quality compressed audio with ToolVox is elusive. ToolVox placed last in *all* tests, failing to win even one comparison.

Founded in 1993, Voxware's entire product line centers around its Meta-Voice technology, which analyzes digitized audio to create a mathematical model of the individual's speech characteristics. This produces outstanding compression ratios and enables manipulation of playback speed for fast forwarding without distortion or changes in tone.

Voxware introduced ToolVox for Multimedia, a Software Development Kit (SDK) targeted at the CD-ROM title community, in June 1995. The technology gained a measure of technical credibility in November 1995, when it was licensed by Microsoft for use with the Microsoft Bookshelf reference CD-ROM. Voxware launched ToolVox for the Web in December 1995 and gained additional credibility when Netscape licensed the technology and then made an equity investment in Voxware.

ToolVox has two components, a simple, somewhat fussy encoder and a very basic player, both free. Voxware does not plan to introduce server technology, selling its technology on bandwidth rather than features like random access and pause and resume that server components enable. Voxware has hinted that they will release a "Pro" encoder that costs $100 and produces higher quality audio at the same data rate, but has made no firm announcement.

As noted on Voxware's Web page, however, the company subsidizes their free Internet technology with license fees paid by other software companies for their general-purpose compression technology. This tends to indicate their status as a "technology company," shipping remarkable but largely unusable technology for others to refine and productize. On the other hand, Netscape's equity investment, viewed in the light of their announced intention to include Internet Phone-like capabilities in Navigator 3.0, may mean that usable technology is closer than it appears.

Audio Quality

Conference: Voxware clearly struggled with the noise, moving in and out of usable quality with very obvious flubbing and some echoing.

Alternating: This clip, recorded from a laser disc, alternates a male and a female voice. Even though the voices were relatively clear, quality was frequently marred by short segments of distorted audio.

Female Speech: This clip was recorded in a sound booth, professionally dubbed to cassette and captured. Voxware produced the best results with this clip, which was similar to that used in the *PC Magazine* testing. Still, because the clip was extremely simple and clear, all codecs performed well, and Voxware again placed last even in 14.4 tests.

The Encoder

Installation: The encoder is a self-installing EXE that creates a Windows 95 program group on the Taskbar and a hotlink to the encoder. The installation program also installs a help file, read-me, and uninstaller.

Operation: The encoder is bilateral in layout, with source file on the left and compressed file on the right, both capable of being played from the encoder program, a useful feature. The program also converts compressed VOX files back to WAV format.

Voxware designed in capture capabilities, automatically producing the 8-Hz, 16-bit mono audio stream required by the encoder. While strong in concept, this feature's benefit is diminished because of the lack of even simple cut-and-paste capabilities, since it's almost impossible to capture the precise audio stream without heads or tails that need to be clipped. Note that unlike RealAudio, these capture facilities do not enable real-time compression to VOX format, simply capturing the stream to disk for subsequent compression. Voxware does not provides batch capabilities, but compression is extremely fast, taking roughly eight seconds to compress a 38-second file on a Pentium 133.

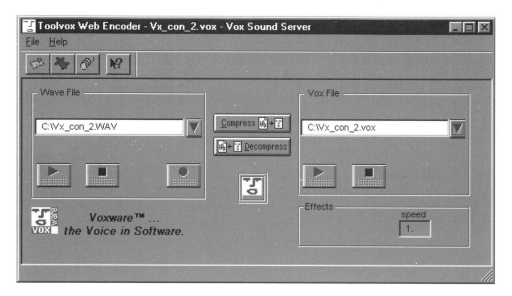

Figure 5.8 The Voxware encoder program.

The Voxware encoder has no compression-related options or features, always producing the same 2400 bps bitrate stream, roughly one third of the lowest data rate of the other codecs. While simple in operation, the program frequently shows its first-generation roots, including failure to warn before overwriting a previously compressed file and somewhat erratic operation. For example, the program was unable to save a compressed file to a directory other than the source file, a hassle during production.

Voxware includes both help and read-me files which cover basic HTML and server integration issues. Voxware doesn't address how to digitize audio for maximum quality, discussing only how to record from a microphone using the encoder's recording functionality. Voxware also doesn't highlight that the encoder requires 8-Hz audio, automatically subsampling higher values down during encoding, which can cause distortion. This is surprising given ToolVox's sensitivity to noise.

Voxware touts their ability to accelerate and slow down the playback of their files without obvious distortion as a key component of their technology. While these functions worked largely as advertised, their appeal was not obvious, at least within the realm of business-oriented applications.

Player Features

Installation: The ToolVox WebPlayer also ships as a self-installing EXE file that automatically configures the player as a helper application for Netscape Navigator, Internet Explorer, and NCSA Mosaic. The program ships with an uninstaller and a short read-me document, and after installation is complete, the player loads and plays a short greeting audio.

Operation: The Voxware player is extraordinarily simple, containing status bar, elapsed time indicator, and little else. Notably absent is volume control, a key. Since Voxware doesn't offer a server, the player can't pause and resume or seek random locations. This is a significant disadvantage for Web sites containing long audio content, although it is somewhat lessened by the ability to fast-forward through a file using ToolVox's native acceleration capabilities.

The player supports the Netscape 2.0 plug-in specification, and Voxware has several examples on their Web page. Voxware's Web page indicates that they also plan to support Microsoft's OCX plug-in strategy.

StreamWorks (Xing Technologies, Inc.)

Overview   Xing is unique in that they also offer streaming video technology in addition to their low-bit-rate audio. Xing is also the only company other than Progressive attempting to profit directly from their streaming audio technology. Unlike Progressive, however, which has invested significantly in marketing and productization, Xing is just now starting to polish and sell StreamWorks, using the proceeds from a private offering and devoting internal resources previously dedicated to their XingCD product line.

Figure 5.9   The extraordinarily simple Voxware player.

StreamWorks 2.0 was designed to alleviate many of the earlier documentation and ease-of-use issues that plagued StreamWorks 1.0, supporting, for example, the Netscape plug-in and Microsoft OCX specifications, which illustrates Xing's decision to move away from the stand-alone browser paradigm of version 1.0. Xing also made several server enhancements discussed below.

From a pure technology perspective, Xing's codec is extremely interesting, producing clear, high-bandwidth audio often indistinguishable from the original. Even its lower bandwidth audio is remarkably clear, if somewhat distorted. Xing is the only truly scalable codec, able to increase audio bandwidths to ISDN rates, and the only proven extensible codec, via its propagation servers. Xing also has the most experience with real-time encoding.

This adds up to a product line that's ideal for broadcast customers like TV and radio stations and networks, which make up most of Xing's customers, and large intranets. While Xing can't match Progressive feature for feature, StreamWorks' proven brute-force muscle is clearly more important in Xing's critical target markets.

The StreamWorks line has three components: encoders, including the free software encoder that we tested and a turnkey hardware audio encoding station, including computer, that costs $2500; servers, which are priced according to connection bandwidth, starting at $3500 for a 1.5 Mbps system; and decoders, which can be downloaded for free but cost $29 for support. All pricing is for version 1.0, since Xing hasn't announced prices for the new version.

Audio Quality

Conference: At 14.4, the clip sounded hollow with consistent ringing and flurriness. At 28.8 the ringing went away, boosting Xing from fourth to third.

Alternating: The 14.4 clip sounded hollow with slight echoing, which improved to near-original quality at 28.8, where Xing rated first among all competitors.

Female Speech: Xing performed well at 14.4, producing a clear, crisp sound that sounded faintly hollow. The 28.8 clip was virtually identical to the original, with Xing again winning this category.

Audio Quality—Music

Hard Rock: At 14.4, Xing performed poorly, producing background ringing and blending the guitar and audio tracks. This improved dramatically at 28.8, where Xing lost split decisions to both Progressive and VocalTec, falling from first to third by the slightest of margins.

Soft Rock: At 14.4, Xing produced slight warbles that sounded as if the audio were being played under water. At 28.8, the audio was virtually indistinguishable from the original, and Xing again claimed first place.

Symphony: In the low-bandwidth tests, Xing produced the most engaging audio artifact of all tests, a rhythmic ringing that sounded like a baroque organ in the background—only when comparing the clip to the original did the artifact become obvious. At 28.8, quality improved dramatically, and Xing lost another split decision to drop to second behind Progressive.

The Encoder   Xing offers two encoders, a real-time hardware-based encoder and a software-only encoder that we used that is operated via a command line argument. The encoder's only compression parameter was bit rate, which ranged in size from 8 to 16 kbps. While clearly not elegant, the program worked well and was fast, compressing our 36-second benchmark clip in under three seconds.

Player Features

Installation: Xing's player ships as a 437 KB/s EXE file that self-extracts and automatically segues into the StreamWorks installation program. The installation program searches for Netscape Navigator 16-bit and 32-bit programs, CompuServe's Spry, and Microsoft's Internet Explorer, enabling each installed browser application. After creating a Program Group on the Taskbar, the installation deletes all setup files, a nice feature.

Operation: One of the most irritating features of the StreamWorks player is that it doesn't play files from disk. Xing was kind enough to provide us with an internal utility that plays files from disk for our testing, but we can't distribute it. Accordingly, you can't play the files on the CD-ROM from the CD-ROM, and in fact can't play them at all unless you find a StreamWorks server on which you can load them.

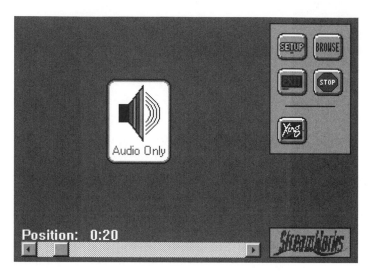

Figure 5.10 The StreamWorks stand-alone player, push-button radio to the Net.

A server-based system, Xing matches many Progressive features like random access to the clip and fast forward. Originally, StreamWorks shipped primarily as a stand-alone player that functioned more as push-button radio station than an embeddable player. With version 2.0, however, Xing also started shipping a sleeker player that was visually similar to the RealAudio and TrueSpeech players and eminently more embeddable than their stand-alone player.

With both players, the user can elect to play audio in both mono or stereo quality, and, in the case of streams containing both audio and video, elect to optimize audio quality or video quality or let the StreamWorks player balance the resource allocation issues.

Both players also provide a great deal of data about the server and streaming file, including server name (either domain name or IP address of the StreamWorks server), stream name, stream length, total data rate, video data rate, video resolution, audio data rate, sample rate, channels, and compressed audio format.

The characteristics of the audio data generated by the StreamWorks player can affect your computer's overall playback performance; for example, stereo audio contains twice as much data as monaural audio. Depending on the nature of your computer's sound system, the overhead processing associated with transferring this additional data to your computer's sound board may adversely affect overall playback performance.

Figure 5.11   StreamWorks' more compact player.

Xing's recent announcement hopefully signals their intention toward greater integration, and their decision to support the Netscape 2.0 plug-in specification and Microsoft's OCX is a step in the right direction. We should probably expect that Xing will retain much of the flexibility of their initial player (in stand-alone operation) while beefing up documentation.

Server Operation   Like Progressive Networks, Xing uses UDP as opposed to TCP/IP, opting for broadcast efficiency over the risk of quality degradation. Xing's approach to firewall incompatibilities is to provide a patch to system administrators to route StreamWorks packets around the firewall, which maintains firewall integrity.

One of Xing's key advantages is extensibility, or the ability to use multiple servers to deliver one live feed to more clients than one server could support. Xing enhanced these capabilities in version 2.0 and announced "on-the-fly bit rate scaling and stream thinning" which reportedly will allow a content provider to use one stream to satisfy multiple audio requests of different bandwidths.

SUMMARY

1. There is a great deal of quality difference between the various technologies. Among the free technologies, TrueSpeech is by far your best bet over VocalTec and Voxware. Of the two companies attempting to make a profit from streaming audio, Progressive Networks is generally stronger in low-bit-rate tests, while Xing excels at higher bandwidths.

2. The server versus nonserver decision relates primarily to two technology items: number of simultaneous streams and playback feature set. Server-based technologies are generally more efficient and can handle more simultaneous streams because they meter

out the high-bandwidth files rather than blasting them out as fast as possible. On the other hand, free is good and you can always try TrueSpeech until it clearly "breaks."

The feature side is a bit tougher. If your page has longer files (over a minute), the ability to fast-forward, stop, and resume become much more important. For generally shorter files, however, this isn't such a big deal.

3. Beware the UDP versus TCP/IP protocols. UDP is a blasting protocol that works well for broadcast applications but may cause firewall issues, although both Xing and Progressive are aggressively working to minimize these issues. If significant groups of target customers are behind firewalls, this may be an issue.

Chapter

Tour de Codec

INTRODUCTION

Welcome to the Tour de Codec, where we compare compression technologies for applications ranging from streaming Internet delivery to CD-ROM publishing. The first section takes an admittedly one-dimensional look at streaming video, focusing only on pure video quality and ignoring the server component offered by two of the four technologies. This gives us a sneak peek at the potential of these innovative products while allowing us to focus most of our energies on CD-ROM–related technologies. And, hey, it even leaves fertile grist for another book.

Then we'll move into the big-bandwidth codecs, from which you'll likely choose when publishing the video fruits of your capture and editing labors. In analyzing these products, we look at ease of use, quality, performance, and special features. Reflecting the expanded usage of video codecs, we encoded both quarter-screen and full-screen animations, plus the usual talking head and high-motion videos. We also look at game-oriented features offered by Indeo video interactive and other codecs.

For pure compression freaks, this is your chapter. For the rest, the principles and conclusions reached here will affect the codec choices made in Chapter 12 and many of the capture decisions studied in Chapter 10.

STREAMING INTERNET CODECS

In 1992, in the dawn of multimedia, video codec developers released grainy, distorted 160×120 resolution video that barely played at 15 frames per second (fps) from single-spin CD-ROM drives. Heralded by some but discounted by most, these codecs spawned the term "postage stamp" video and a stigma that digital video has only recently overcome.

In 1995, or perhaps Year 1 AI (after Internet), video codec developers released grainy, highly distorted 160×120 resolution video that barely played at 1 or 2 fps on a 28.8 connection. Video over the Net immediately became the next *big thing*, codec developers got frantic calls from venture capitalists, and the TV industry started dreaming of "narrowcasting" to upper middle class yuppies with demographics to die for.

What a difference a medium makes.

In truth, things have gotten better. Like most first-generation technologies, the initial streaming Internet products fell into the realm of "Gee, isn't it lovely that we can send video over the Internet?" Well, at display rates often less than one frame every two or three seconds, it wasn't really video, and with the distorted video received at low data rates, it certainly wasn't lovely.

Then codec developers discovered the intranet, with bandwidths as high as 100 mbps and network administrators paying 150 KB/s for Moving Pictures Experts Group 1 (MPEG-1) video, complaining all the while about the drag on network resources. The second streaming generation delivered relatively artifact-free video at a mere 15 KB/s, or 120 kbps, under dual-line ISDN rates. Sure, the window is small (176×144), but it zooms easily to quarter-screen resolution using video scaling features standard on graphics cards for the past two years.

These data rates truly enable applications like ISDN-based distance learning, intranet video delivery, and headache-free video over the corporate local area network (LAN). Imagine putting 10 hours of video on a standard CD-ROM or almost 15 minutes on a floppy.

Here we look at the quality produced by four streaming video codecs, ClearVideo from Iterated Systems, VDOLive from VDONet, VXtreme from Web Theater, and VivoActive from Vivo Software. Unfortunately, we couldn't get our hands on Xing Technologies StreamWorks 2.0 because of scheduling difficulties.

While most of the hype, of course, relates to the Internet, applications for these technologies may be much broader. We start by looking at performance at Internet-type bandwidths and then examine high-bandwidth quality to gauge suitability for more mainstream corporate uses.

Technology Review

Perchance to Stream Let's briefly review what we covered in detail in Chapter 4. The Internet is a bandwidth-limited delivery mechanism, a *very* narrow data pipe. Digital video is a data hog, requiring 27 MB/s of data throughput to play freely. A 28.8 kbps modem provides exactly 1/7500 of this requirement, and an ISDN connection, at 128 kbps, does little better at 1/1500.

To be really effective, video must "stream," or become available after only a short buffering period and play through to the end without interruption. Two techniques help squeeze the combined data rate down to Internet bandwidths.

First and most important is scaling, in resolution and frame rate for video and in sampling size, channels, and frequency for audio. The native resolution of analog video is 640×480. Scale this down to 176×144 size and you've cut your data transfer requirements from 27 MB/s to roughly 2.2 MB/s. Scale from 30 fps to 15 fps, and you're down to an infinitely more manageable 1.1 MB/s.

CD-ROM quality audio is 44-kHz, 16-bit stereo, adding up to a healthy 176 KB/s. Most technologies scale down to 8-kHz, 8-bit monaural audio, reducing the data rate to approximately 8 KB/s.

After scaling comes compression, which replaces the original data with more compact mathematical models. Most streaming video products are audio and video "codecs," which *co*mpress at the front end and *de*compress during playback. In addition, they're all "lossy" codecs, which means that as compression rates increase, quality suffers. For the two media that make up video, pictures and audio, loss means visual blockiness, blurring, and artifacts, as well as cracks, pops, and other audio distortion.

The fundamental measure of lossy technologies is quality at a given bit rate, or for video, which codec looks and sounds best when the same video source is compressed to the same bandwidth. Ergo, our tests: compress a bunch of files to similar bandwidths and compare the results.

Although three of the four products offer audio compression as an integral component of their streaming technology, Iterated Systems doesn't bundle audio compression with ClearVideo. The practical limitations imposed by this decision are significant, since without audio compression you can't *stream* ClearVideo content, you can only download it quickly and then play it.

However significant, this restriction is probably short lived. By the time you read this chapter, Iterated should have announced an agreement with a prominent streaming audio vendor that effectively adds audio compression capabilities to their product offering. In the meantime, our tests of ClearVideo focus solely on video.

Deliverability   In addition to quality, the Web's harsh environment adds another key factor—deliverability—measuring how effectively a technology can maintain smooth playback through the inevitable bandwidth shortages experienced on the Web. Due to the constraints of this analysis, we'll describe the approaches taken by each technology but won't test the results.

Fortunately, our product offerings represent the extremes in each category, with Vivo and Iterated offering good low-bandwidth quality and VDO and VXtreme providing the ultimate in deliverability. Before analyzing each system as a whole, let's examine the basic components of all streaming video technologies.

Technology Components

The process of creating streaming video is identical to that of creating other forms of digital video. First you film, then capture, then compress. Instead of integrating video into a multimedia presentation, however, you integrate streaming video into your Web page and server.

Like CD-ROM–oriented video codecs, streaming video codecs have both encoder and decoder components. VDO and VXtreme also have server components that reside on the Internet server, but Iterated and Vivo do not. These server components determine the theoretical architecture of the streaming video product, which dictates the product's deliverability. We'll start our analysis here.

Architecture   There are two kinds of streaming architectures: scalable systems and nonscalable systems. Scalable systems always have a server component that monitors the flow of audio/video data between the client and server and can adjust that flow to ensure a continuous video stream. If effective throughput drops, for example, the server can send fewer frames or even less information per frame to ensure the continued delivery of data. When bandwidth is really restricted, the server may send only audio.

Nonscalable systems have no dedicated server component, using the server software found on the Web server just like any other HyperText Transfer Protocol (HTTP) format. Since there is no dedicated video server, there is no server/client regulatory mechanism, and if bandwidths drop, video playback stops until more data arrives.

Server-Based, Scalable Systems   Scalable systems have several advantages in addition to maintaining continuous video streams. First is that they can *regulate* the flow of streaming video to the various Internet clients. In contrast, nonserver systems transmit the entire video file as quickly as bandwidth allows, which can interrupt the operation of the Internet server, especially when blasting long video files out to multiple clients. Since most Net surfers don't watch every video through to completion, most video data is sent for no reason, wasting server and Internet bandwidth.

The second key advantage relates to the first: since the video flow is regulated, server-based systems can generally service more clients than nonserver systems. In other words, a server-based system can easily service 10 simultaneous streams of low-bandwidth video, even if the videos are fairly long. In contrast, serverless systems service requests serially, one after the other, delaying the delivery of video to all subsequent clients until previous requests are completely filled.

Finally, the server component enables advanced features like fast forward and random access to the points in the video file. This is because the logic in the server program can view the video file as a streaming file with a beginning and end and many temporal points in between. In contrast, serverless systems view the video file as an inert lump of data and have no mechanism to understand that the viewer wants to jump 15 seconds forward in the video file. That makes features like random access impossible until the video file is completely downloaded to the client.

To accomplish these basic tasks, server-based systems typically use the Universal Datagram Protocol (UDP) instead of TCP/IP, the Internet's lingua franca protocol. UDP is a bandwidth-oriented streaming protocol without error correction, efficient for broadcasting multiple streams of information, but lost packets can and do occur. This means potential drops in quality in addition to the loss imposed by the compression technology itself.

In addition to lost packets, UDP can cause problems with internal firewalls, which automatically pass through TCP/IP data but can choke on UDP information and refuse to pass the data through. This means that many potential corporate viewers may have difficulty playing back streaming video files using this protocol. Although there are workarounds, they all require action on the part of the network administrator, who may be reluctant to open the firewall simply to enable casual viewing of Internet videos.

Nonscalable Systems   Nonscalable systems have no mechanism for scaling back quality, so full bandwidth, high-quality video is delivered to each client, every session. This is a mixed blessing, of course, since the cost of full-quality video may be video stoppages. That is, when bandwidth drops, the video simply stops until the necessary data gets to the client. Because there is no server, nonscalable systems use TCP/IP rather than UDP, ensuring in-order packet delivery and total firewall compatibility. Mindful of the benefits of TCP/IP, most server-based vendors are moving toward offering dual-protocol servers that can transmit files using either UDP or TCP/IP.

In summary, scalable systems can and often do transmit scaled-back video that looks degraded at the client site and can run into compatibility problems with corporate firewalls. However, the video tends to be more robust in terms of continuous playback.

Nonscalable systems send only top-quality video, but the files frequently stop and start during low-bandwidth playback. By using TCP/IP, however, these systems typically have no firewall problems.

Of our four products, Iterated's ClearVideo and Vivo's VivoActive are nonscalable technologies without server components. Both VDO and VXtreme have server components that enable scalable operation using UDP, which VXtreme leverages to offer features like fast forward and pause and resume.

VDO and VXtreme are working hard to minimize the downsides of their server-based offerings. For example, VDO's most recent release can encode a "lite" version of their file format that is nonscalable and targeted for HTTP servers using the TCP/IP protocol. With a view toward avoiding firewall issues altogether, VXtreme lets the client decide whether to use the UDP or TCP/IP protocol to stream the video from the server.

Table 6.1 summarizes the architectural features of the four products.

The Encoder   Streaming video encoders have two aspects: technology and implementation. The technology side measures pure output quality and factors that add to the "deliverability" capabilities offered by scalable systems. Implementation issues look at both output flexibility and ease of use. We'll start with the technology side.

Encoding Technologies: Interframe compression algorithms are at once the most hyped component of most video technologies and the least important when it comes to video quality. That's because interframe compression plays a much greater role in the ultrahigh compression ratios necessary to achieve streaming bandwidths. Nonetheless, I'd lose my union card to the video writer association for not mentioning the algorithms used by the various technologies, so here goes.

Iterated's fractal codec is the most recent iteration of the fractal transform technology percolating around that company since long before I was there from 1991 to 1993. Interestingly, although fractal technology is inherently scalable, this feature is not implemented in the current ClearVideo release. As mentioned, Iterated bucked tradition by not offering an audio codec, a situation hoped to be remedied in early 1997.

Table 6.1 Architectural issues and server-related features.

	ClearVideo	VDOLive	Vivo	VXtreme
Architecture	Nonscalable	Scalable/ nonscalable	Nonscalable	Scalable
Server	no	Optional	no	yes
Protocol	TCP/IP	UDP	TCP/IP	UDP/TCP/IP
Features				
Pause/resume	yes	no	yes	yes
Rewind	Once file downloaded	no	no	yes
Fast forward	Once file downloaded	no	no	yes

VDOLive's wavelet algorithm is an integral component of its scalable delivery system. In addition to providing high-quality, low-bandwidth performance, wavelet-based algorithms are inherently scalable, which improves streaming performance.

During compression, VDO divides each frame into multiple layers, each providing additional detail and image quality. When sufficient transfer bandwidth exists, all layers are sent for optimum quality. When bandwidth constricts, however, fewer layers are transmitted, degrading video quality and slowing playback frame rate but minimizing audio breaks. On the audio front, VDO uses a TrueSpeech variant, licensed from the DSP Group.

Vivo takes a more standardized approach, using compression technologies standardized in the H.324 plain old telephone system (POTS) videophone standard. The video codec, H.263, is a transform-based, motion-compensated technology similar to MPEG but optimized for low-bit-rate video. The audio codec, G.723, is a speech-oriented codec also licensed from DSP Group.

VXtreme is hush mouthed about its algorithm, but the Gibbs effect and mosquitoes evident in our sample videos are very reminiscent of MPEG-1 artifacts.

Image Quality   We used three test videos, two talking heads and one high-motion clip, captured at 176×144×15 (talking head/high motion) and 320×240×15 (talking head) and compressed them to 28.8, 64, 128, and 256 kbps. Since Vivo doesn't support 320×240 resolutions, they weren't considered in two of the five comparisons. As always, we attempted to compress files within each class to similar bandwidths, but at times they varied more than we would have liked.

To compensate for Iterated's lack of audio support, we compressed the ClearVideo clips to bandwidths of approximately 8–10 kbps under the test data rate to simulate the inclusion of 8 kbps of audio. We compressed all VDO clips using the "lite" option, discussed below.

We played back the files in both 16-bit and 24-bit modes and captured screen shots in 24-bit color. We evaluated both still-frame and full-motion performance, looking at the quality of the foreground and background and the number of dropped frames per video. For Vivo and VXtreme this last metric was an approximation, since we had no mechanism to step through the files.

Files are included on the CD-ROM for your viewing pleasure. To view them, you'll need to download and install the player module from each company's Web site.

After downloading the players, you can use VCS to play VDO and ClearVideo files, since both are audio/video interleaved (AVI) format. The simplest way to play the Vivo files is to double-click on the file from Windows Explorer, which will launch your browser program. Use the same technique to play the VXtreme files, except double-click on the hypertext markup (HTM) files in the respective subdirectories rather than the VLO. I apologize if the VXtreme files don't play—time was short and their authoring program somewhat difficult to assimilate in real time.

Naming conventions are as follows: The first two letters relate to technology. CV is ClearVideo, VD is VDO, VV is Vivo, and VX is VXtreme. The second two letters stand for the clip. TK is the 320×240 talking head file, JA is the 176×144 clip of me, and AC is the similarly sized action clip. Finally, the last two numbers are bandwidth, with 28 translating to 28.8 kbps, 64 to 64 kbps, 12 referring to 128 kbps, and 25 describing the 256-kbps files.

Now on to the results.

28.8 kbps, 176×144×15 Talking Head: Figure 6.1 shows a simple clip of me taken in a studio setting, an easy to compress, low-motion file representing a low degree of difficulty, albeit at a murderous data rate.

> **ClearVideo: Third Place** One ClearVideo trademark is blockiness at the start of the video and at subsequent key frames. Iterated apparently opted for extremely small key frames, a bandwidth-pleasing and fast-response approach that nonetheless causes extreme blockiness for the first few frames. The blockiness largely clears up after a few frames, fading into almost a lizard-like pattern of not quite square blocks in the background that undulates as the video plays. Once the foreground clears up, it remains fairly stable with good image quality until the next key frame, which starts the process over. Iterated recommends not using frequent key frames,

Figure 6.1   Compressed to 28.8 kbps, even a simple 176×144×15 fps talking head video is challenging for these technologies.

which looks like good advice. Unlike several other technologies, Iterated did not drop frames during compression to meet the data rate target.

VDOLive: Fourth Place   VDO dropped every other frame during compression and still suffered from foreground fuzziness and background banding throughout the clip. Unlike most other technologies, the situation didn't improve over time, contributing to VDO's fourth place finish.

VivoActive: First Place   Vivo retains good image fidelity throughout, with the clearest, most consistent foreground image and just the barest hint of blockiness in the background. Vivo appeared to drop occasional frames throughout the video, however, and showed both Gibbs effect and color bleeding.

VXtreme: Second Place   Background blockiness was apparent throughout the video, as were banding and facial distortion. The blockiness and Gibbs effect convinced us that while VXtreme might not be a full-blooded derivative, MPEG-1 is certainly in its genes.

64 kbps, 176×144×15 Talking Head: Same video, higher bandwidth. Getting into a zone where some of the codecs can even look good (Figure 6.2).

ClearVideo: Second Place   Slight blockiness and banding in background; foreground blockiness is minimal except for the trademark first frame.

VDOLive: Third Place   Some background banding, but a slight fuzziness throughout mars facial quality and movement generates ghosting and additional blurriness.

Figure 6.2   At 64 kbps, several of the products start to shine.

VivoActive: First Place Some ghosting during motion, but not even a hint of blockiness. The background is extremely stable, and there were few if any facial artifacts. Problems with color bleeding kept Vivo from sheer perfection.

VXtreme: Fourth Place Blockiness and color banding never quite go away, and foreground image still suffers from frequent artifacts. Mosquitoes, another MPEG-1 artifact, follow the head as it moves throughout the video.

64 kbps, 176×144×15 Action Sequence: Motion is the enemy of inter-frame compression, the most potent fuel for all the streaming technologies. All technologies dropped tons of frames, and blockiness and other artifacts ran rampant (Figure 6.3).

High-motion sequences at this bandwidth are strictly for Generation X-ers and other surfers with too much time on their hands. Few if any business folks could find a use for this level of quality in business-to-business applications.

ClearVideo: Fourth Place ClearVideo reduced color drastically and became extremely blocky at high-motion sequences, with large blocks of pixels creating a checkerboard pattern.

VDOLive: Second Place VDO produced the smoothest motion, fewest artifacts, and least apparent blockiness but merged many video regions into indistinct cloudlike masses.

VivoActive: First Place Severe color bleeding and tons of dropped frames, but blockiness and other artifacts were limited.

VXtreme: Third Place Blocky and distorted with severe dropped frames.

 Figure 6.3 High motion and low bandwidth don't belong in the same sentence.

128 kbps, 320×240×15 Talking Head Sequence: A very challenging con-figuration, four times the area of the smaller talking head, although roughly five times the bandwidth (Figure 6.4). Again, Vivo is not rated because their maximum resolution is 176×144.

> **ClearVideo: First Place** After its usual blocky first frames, some-thing "clicked" with fractals, creating a crisp file that (gulp!) actually compared well to MPEG-1 files at close to 10 times the data rate.
>
> **VDOLive: Second Place** Quality was generally fair, but the video stayed slightly fuzzy throughout.
>
> **VXtreme: Third Place** Choppy and fuzzy throughout, clearly not presentable.

256 kbps, 320×240×15 Talking Head Sequence: An interesting configu-ration for intranet delivery, or even ultralow-bandwidth CD-ROM. 256 kbps is 32 KB/s, roughly 20% the bandwidth of MPEG-1 (Figure 6.5).

> **ClearVideo: First Place** Iterated took full advantage of the extra bandwidth, creating a file almost twice the size of the 128-kbps file. Since the original file looked so good, however, visual improvement was marginal, so you might consider compressing high-resolution ClearVideo files to 128 kbps rather than 256 kbps.
>
> **VDOLive: Second Place** Compressing at 256 kbps as compared to 128 kbps increased the actual bandwidth by less than 1%. Accordingly, image quality was virtually identical to that with the smaller bandwidth file. Still not bad, but not quite as crisp as ClearVideo.

 Figure 6.4 What's up with fractals? I've seen MPEG-1 clips that looked worse than this, even at 10 times the bandwidth.

Figure 6.5 Fractals everywhere, our big picture star.

VXtreme: Third Place Like VDO, VXtreme didn't double the data rate of the 128-kbps file when compressing to 256 kbps, increasing video bandwidth by about 23%. Although this improved quality somewhat, VXtreme was still way behind the other two technologies.

To test whether VXtreme simply was "allergic" to our 320×240 test image, we compressed another similarly sized image to 256 kbps. The result, shown in Figure 6.6 and on the CD-ROM in the \vxtreme\lisa subdirectory, tends to indicate that VXtreme has difficulty with high-resolution images at 256 kbps and lower. We also hunted for 320×240 videos on VXtreme's Web page to disprove this theory but all exhibited similar choppiness. Table 6.2 summarizes our results.

Creation Tools In terms of implementation, all four encoders support Video for Windows (AVI) files, so you can use most Windows-based capture cards for input. Both ClearVideo and VDOLive are Video for Windows codecs, so you can compress files to these formats with video editing packages like Adobe Premiere or Ulead MediaStudio. VDO ships its own capture and editing tools, but they're finicky and limited in function, so plan on using your Video for Windows editor for all but the simplest jobs.

In contrast, Vivo's proprietary VIV format forces you to use their encoder, which is fast, simple, and reasonably comprehensive (see Figure 6.7). VXtreme takes this one step further, with capture, compression, and HyperText Markup Language (HTML) authoring tools all tailored for their proprietary file formats, VLO for video, and SPH for audio (see Figure 6.8). Although the initial learning curve is steep, the tools work well at their

Table 6.2 Technology and quality.

Technology	ClearVideo	VDOLive	Vivo	VXtreme
Video compression algorithm	Fractal	Wavelet	H.263	Proprietary (MPEG derivative)
Audio compression algorithm	none	TrueSpeech (licensed from DSP Group)	6.723	Proprietary
Quality rankings				
Talking head, 176×144×15, 28.8kbps	3	4	1	2
Talking head, 176×144×15, 64 kbps	2	3	1	4
Action, 176×144×15, 64 kbps	4	2	1	3
Talking head, 320×240×15, 128 kbps	1	2	n.a.	3

Figure 6.6 Lisa told me I could use her video as much as necessary, but only if I never make her look bad. Hope she doesn't see this one.

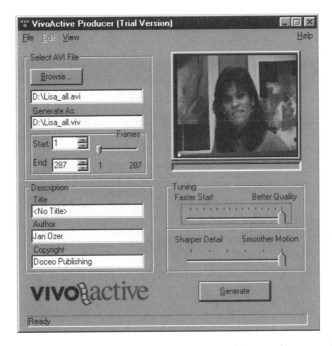

Figure 6.7 Vivo's proprietary encoder is simple, fast, and comprehensive.

assigned functions. Given the work that went into both companies' tools and how well they work, their proprietary nature is not a significant disadvantage.

Output Flexibility Output flexibility describes your ability to output video at the desired data rates and video resolutions. Vivo is the most restrictive, offering a maximum of 176×144 resolution at a maximum bandwidth of 115 kbps. On the other hand, within its proprietary interface, Vivo lets you adjust the frame rate from 2.5 up to 30 fps, a nice convenience.

VXtreme is next lowest on the flexibility curve, not because of technology limitations but because of design decisions made by the company during development. For example, although at larger resolutions VXtreme supports up to 512 kbps, the maximum data rate allowed at 160×120 resolution is 56 kbps. This prevents the developer from using higher data rates at the lower resolution to create pristine, artifact-free video. In addition,

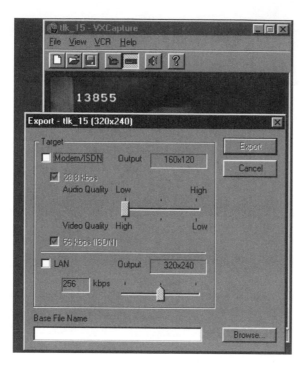

Figure 6.8   VXtreme creates a complete development environment, including capture, encoding (shown), and HTML creation tools.

VXtreme's encoder doesn't enable frame rate changes, reducing compression time flexibility.

When VXtreme encodes a file, it creates multiple bit streams to enable scaling. For example, when compressing a 28.8-kbps file, the encoder also creates an 18-kbps file for use when bandwidth is limited and another much smaller file to support fast-forward functions. The multiple files contained in the single VLO file push the total file size well above that produced by other products, so don't compare files and expect them to be similar in size.

Iterated Systems supports any video resolution as long as both the height and width are divisible by four, at any data rate up to the maximum 256 kbps. If your video resolution isn't divisible by four, ClearVideo won't crop the video; it simply won't appear as a compression option.

With ClearVideo, you can select a video data rate ranging from 14.4 to 256 kbps, but this number is *video only*. Since you have to choose one of the Iterated presets, compressing files with audio becomes somewhat confusing. For example, if your target is 56 kbps, you can't use this preset because the audio data rate will push you over the required bandwidth. The next smaller bandwidth is 28.8 kbps, which might work depending on the audio compression technology that you choose (Figure 6.9).

Other ClearVideo compression controls let you elect to maintain a constant bit rate, auto-detect key frames, and smooth individual frames. Using a slider bar, you can chose higher quality video, which increases compression time, or faster compression to the possible detriment of video quality.

VDO offers the most flexibility, supporting resolutions from 64×64 pixels to 352×288 and bandwidths up to 256. VDO also supports five output modes: Movie (up to 15 fps), Flipbook (up to 2 fps), Storybook (one frame and accompanying audio), audio only, and the aforementioned "lite" version of their file format (see Figure 6.10).

In Movie mode, the encoder packs redundant video data into the file to support the format's scalability, making it impossible to compare VDO's file sizes to those of other technologies. For this reason, we compressed in "lite" mode, which provided close to equivalent file sizes, albeit, as VDO's release notes state, at some potential loss of quality.

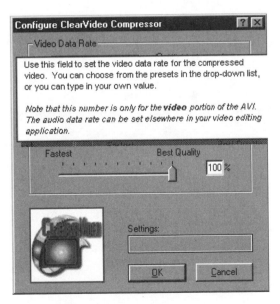

Figure 6.9   Iterated's encoder seems to forget that audio is integral to video, a situation that should be resolved when they announce their partnership with a streaming audio vendor.

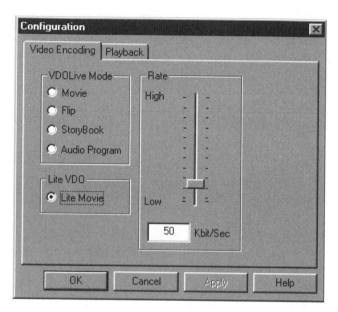

Figure 6.10   VDO's flexible encoder showing its "lite" version. Wonder if Miller's attorneys will come calling.

While on the subject of encoders, we'll deal with compression time. In this regard, ClearVideo is the slowpoke of the bunch, although clearly worth it at big picture videos. We timed all encoders on a Pentium 133, compressing the smaller talking head clip to 64 kbps. Table 6.3 includes both raw time scores and how long it would take to compress one minute of video.

Note that Iterated's scores don't include audio compression, but all others do. That makes their compression times even a touch longer.

The Players   Once again, the player is the decoder, or helper application on the client site enabling video playback. Although most players were originally stand-alone applications that launched and played separately from the browser, the overwhelming trend is toward embedded players that integrate directly into the Web page. All products supported embedding under both Netscape 2.0 and Microsoft's Internet Explorer under the platforms shown in Table 6.4.

Other relevant features include buffer control, which controls how quickly the video starts to play on the client; volume control, a slider bar that lets you gauge progress through the clip; and the ability to zoom the

Table 6.3 Architectural issues and server-related features.

	ClearVideo	VDOLive	Vivo	VXtreme
Format	AVI/MOV	AVI	VIV	VLO (video)/SPH
Tool set	Any AVI/MOV	Any AVI/MOV	Proprietary	Proprietary
Resolutions	Any divisible by 4	64×64 pixels to 352×288	176×144 maximum	160×120 to 640×480
Bandwidths	Up to 256 kbps	Up to 256 kbps	Up to 115 kbps	Up to 512 kbps
Compression time for 45 seconds of video	109 minutes	64 seconds	66 seconds	5 minutes, 41 seconds
Time to compress 1 minute of video	145 minutes	84 seconds	88 seconds	7 minutes, 27 seconds

clip by a factor of 2 for larger sized viewing. Both VDO and Vivo offer austere players, with VXtreme offering the most functionality (Figure 6.11) with Iterated close behind.

On the player front we also measured responsiveness by timing how long it took for a video to start playing after requesting playback from the respective company's home page or a big site designated on the page. This duration includes how long it takes to load the player and start downloading the file.

In its current form, ClearVideo can't stream, so we couldn't include it in this test. Of the remaining three, VXtreme was by far the slowest, even when playing back from disk, which probably reflects the company's decision to use Java applets for its control panel. This problem was compounded by frequent crashes in this, their initial product release. All other technologies proved extremely stable during all testing.

Pricing

Pricing information is capsulated in Table 6.5. Both Vivo and Iterated charge only for the encoder, $495 and $995, respectively, and give away the player. Both server-based technologies charge by the number of streams that the

Table 6.4 Player-related features.

	ClearVideo	VDOLive	Vivo	VXtreme
Player name	ClearFusion	VDOLive Video Player	VivoActive Player	Web Theater Client
Platforms	Windows 95/NT and PowerMac	Windows 3.X/95/NT and PowerMac	Windows 3.X/95/NT and PowerMac	Windows 95/NT, PowerMac, UNIX
Netscape plug-in	yes	yes	yes	yes
ActiveX control	yes	yes	yes	yes
Buffer control	no	Stand-alone player only	no	yes
Volume control	yes	Stand-alone player only	no	no
Slider bar	no	no	no	yes
Zoom	yes	yes	no	no
Responsiveness (seconds)	n.a.	6 seconds	4 seconds	34 seconds
Stability	Stable	Stable	Stable	Some crashes

server can support. VDO gets $1195 for a five-stream server, which includes one encoder. Annual support is $360.

For $1995, VXtreme will ship you an encoder, five-stream server, and 25 full-featured Web clients. VXtreme's free decoder, available on their Web site, is a limited-use version that can't play back streams compressed to over 64 kbps.

Summary

ClearVideo   Not technically a streaming product until Iterated deals with audio, but effective at quick download and play applications. High-resolution quality was extraordinary, but our test video has extremely low motion.

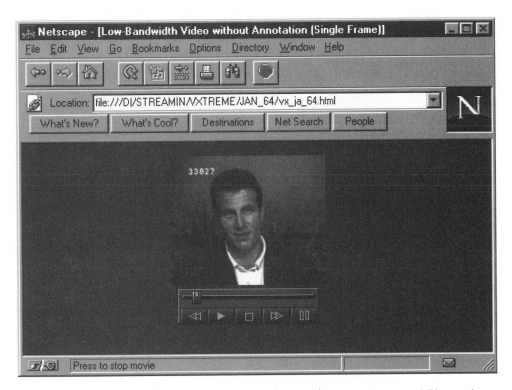

Figure 6.11 Your author, coming at you live and in Netscape via VXtreme's feature-rich player.

Table 6.5 Product costs.

	ClearVideo	VDOLive	Vivo	VXtreme
Encoder	995	Included with server	495	One encoder included
Server	n.a.	(Five-stream server)	n.a.	Stream server included
Player	Free	Free	Free	25 clients included
Limited bandwidth player	n.a.	n.a.	n.a.	Free

Don't expect the same results on videos with even moderate motion. Pricing structure seems reasonable.

VDOLive   Consider VDO when deliverability is key. The only third-generation product we reviewed, VDO has clearly gone out of its way to meet its customers' needs, nice to find in a bleeding-edge technology vendor. Quality results were mixed, but you may get better results with regular movie files in the full UDP environment. Don't be too stressed out by firewall issues; VDO and other UDP vendors like Progressive Networks are well on their way to minimizing or eliminating them completely.

VivoActive   My fave. Cheap, good looking, none of those messy firewall issues. If you've got to implement in the short term, I'd be tempted to use VivoActive unless and until too many customers complain about stopped videos.

VXtreme   An extremely ambitious product that takes all video development—not just streaming video—a few steps in the right direction. The most significant downside is responsiveness: 24 seconds to play a file from disk just doesn't cut it. Video quality was a bit disappointing given the hype, but deliverability looked very solid. Big resolution performance was a puzzle.

CD-ROM PUBLISHING

Probably the most significant paradigm shift facing video developers is a shift away from a "one size fits all" codec to application-specific codecs. There are low-bandwidth codecs, covered in the last section, codecs for high-bandwidth power platforms, codecs for 486/66 computers still running in 8-bit graphics mode, animation codecs, and game codecs. This dynamic forces developers to scrutinize their target markets and content to pick the right codec for the job.

This section analyzes the codec choices available to developers, matching their strengths and weaknesses against a range of target platforms and video requirements. We'll start by looking at the linear playback market, which incorporates MPEG-1, and then analyze the advanced capabilities provided by several codecs, including Intel's new Indeo video interactive.

Linear Playback

Introduction to Category   This category focuses on pure linear playback, no tricks, no treats. There are two gross measurements: quality at a given file bandwidth and playback rate on the target platform. The codec that looks the best and plays back most smoothly wins.

In terms of the first measurement, quality at a given bandwidth, MPEG-1 is still the clear leader, even after the introduction of Intel's Indeo video interactive. This is because MPEG-1, designed originally for hardware-assisted decompression, uses more sophisticated interframe compression algorithms than codecs like Indeo and Cinepak.

In 1995, MPEG-1 shed its hardware-only clay feet, as three companies commercialized software-only players that produced 25-plus frames per second on a Pentium 133. By the end of 1995, most first-tier graphics card manufacturers like ATI, Diamond, Matrox, and Number 9 shipped software MPEG-1 decoders with their newer products, and IBM and other manufacturers bundled software MPEG-1 with their computers. In the second half of 1996, Microsoft started shipping ActiveMovie, which contained a software MPEG-1 player licensed from MediaMatics. Since ActiveMovie is free and works fairly well, this completes the transition of MPEG-1 from an expensive, ungainly hardware codec to a cheap, freely distributable codec like Cinepak or Indeo.

Clearly, whereas hardware-based MPEG-1 never really got off the ground, software MPEG-1 playback is becoming pervasive (see Chapter 13). At the same time, MPEG-1 compression options are cheaper and more technically accessible than ever before (see Chapter 14).

MPEG-1's quality makes it the odds-on favorite in the linear play competition. The only question is, can it play back smoothly on your target platform?

Other Codecs: In part, the overwhelming interest in MPEG-1 relates back to the early Video for Windows days, when windows were small, quality was poor, and performance was even worse. Despite the hype over MPEG-1, video compression remains the ultimate embedded technology—end users don't want MPEG-1, Indeo, or MPEG-2 for that matter, they want high-quality video.

The codec shot heard 'round the world in 1995 was Indeo video interactive (IVI), Intel's new wavelet-based codec. At one level, IVI deserves the hype, creating a new feature-oriented codec paradigm while setting records for quality as well. On the other hand, as we'll see in a moment, the codec's power profile is very similar to that of software MPEG-1, which might limit its appeal in strict linear play applications.

Horizons Technology made some noise of their own with Power!Video Pro, an intraframe-only algorithm based upon technology licensed from Duck Corporation. Under Horizons' tutelage, quality and performance improved, and the product became much more polished and accessible. While not for everyone, Power!Video Pro fills several important niches in the stratified codec market.

In 1996, the Duck Corporation incorporated interframe compression with TrueMotionS and started licensing the codec to PC developers. With cross-platform capabilities including the SEGA, Sony, and 3DO game platforms, TrueMotionS is now very popular among games developers worldwide. We look for the first time at this rejuvenated codec.

RAD Game Tool's Smacker is a versatile codec that performs well in both linear play segment and animation conversion. Unlike the other codecs in this roundup, Smacker isn't a Video for Windows (VFW) codec, which means that files can't be produced, edited, or played back with any VFW-compatible tools. However, RAD has taken some serious steps to make the technology more accessible to authoring programs like Director and Authorware, which should significantly broaden Smacker's appeal to a wide audience of developers.

Long-time favorite Cinepak, now owned by Radius, has been static for the past two years but still leads the field in low-platform performance. A major revision promised for early 1996 died on the vine, leaving the codec we test here remarkably similar to what we tested in 1994.

Indeo video interactive certainly didn't obsolete Indeo 3.2, which should continue to play a significant role in CD-ROM publishing well into 1997. We tested version 3.24, released in 1995, which delivered minor quality improvements over previous versions. We also tested another codec old-timer, Video 1, specifically for low-motion and animation performance.

Criteria

Compression Controls: Job number one for all codecs is to *achieve* and *maintain* the data rate target over the duration of the clip. These are two very separate tasks, since *averaging* below target data rate doesn't prevent data spikes from interrupting smooth CD-ROM playback, a significant issue for CD-ROM title developers.

There are two basic compression control paradigms (see Table 6.6). The first and best is the *data rate* paradigm, which lets the developer set a target data rate which the codec achieves and maintains by adjusting video quality according to video content. The other paradigm is *control oriented*, in which the developer sets certain compression controls that maintain uniform quality over the duration of the video by adjusting the data rate upward and downward according to scene complexity.

Figure 6.12 uses VCS's frame profile to illustrate the two approaches. On the left is Cinepak, a staunch and exacting data rate codec with a penchant for maintaining precise key and delta frame sizes. Note that the wavy line hovers uniformly just above the 150 KB/s line. On the right is Power!Video

Table 6.6 Compression details by codec.

Compres-sion	Cinepak	IVI	Indeo 3.2	Power!-Video Pro	True MotionS	Video 1	Smacker
Compres-sion paradigm	Data rate	Data rate	Data rate	Control	Data rate (with drop frames)	Data rate	Data rate or control
Quality setting	Ignored	Ignored	Ignored	Grayed out	Grayed out	Compre-hended	n.a. proprietary interface
Other controls	None	Quick, bi-directional, scalability target platform	None	Compress (high/ low), color resolution, detail slider, others	Intraframe, interframe options, with temporal quality and filtering	None	Key frame trigger
Time to compress 1 minute of video (15 fps) on Pentium 133 (hr:min)	:25	Bidirectional 1:32; no bidirectional 1:24; quick :04	:13	0:14	:26	:15	:37

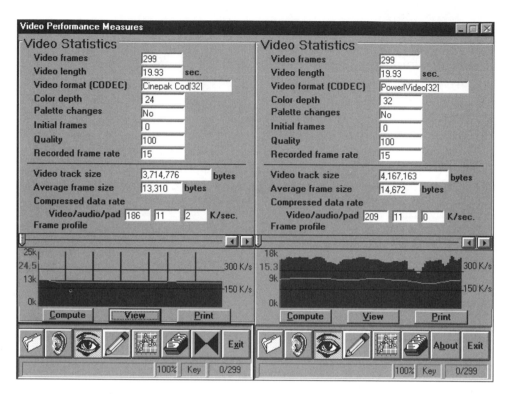

Figure 6.12   Data rate–oriented codecs like Cinepak meet and maintain the
data rate target, while control-oriented codecs like Power!Video
Pro adjust frame size upward and downward to deliver
consistent quality over a range of video scenes.

Pro, a control-oriented codec. Note how frame size varies over the clip with
the resultant increases and decreases in streaming data rate.

For the most part, CD-ROM developers prefer *data rate*–oriented codecs
because they ensure that the video will stream successfully from your target
CD-ROM drive. At the end of the day, uniform quality does you no good
if your customer can't play the video smoothly from CD-ROM. On the other
hand, developers working on kiosks and similar hard-drive–oriented projects may prefer control-oriented codecs that deliver uniform quality irrespective of scene complexity.

Note that data rate–oriented codecs often have an apparent conflict
between the data rate and quality setting (see Figure 6.13). After all, you
can't meet 100% quality at any data rate, so something has to give. All

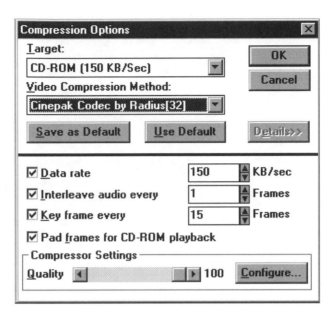

Figure 6.13   When both quality and data rate settings are engaged, which
does the compressor ignore? Cinepak unabashedly ignores the
quality setting and meets the data rate. We like that in a codec!

codecs handle this differently, as described in Table 6.6, some ignoring
quality, some comprehending it, and some simply graying out the control.

Indeo 3.2 and Cinepak both use the data rate method and usually hit and
maintain the target within 5%. Both also ignore the quality slider during
compression, though I usually set it to 100 just in case a customer finds this
setting in the file header and wonders why I thought 85% quality was
sufficient for their incredibly valuable videos. Video 1 adopts a similar
approach but monitors adjustments to the compression slider, taking longer
to compress and producing higher quality video when you select higher
values.

Indeo video interactive is a staunch data rate codec with some unique
compression controls that trade quality for display rate (Figure 6.14).
Bidirectional interpolation is very similar to MPEG's "B" frame structure,
adding computational complexity to both encoding and decoding to
squeeze out maximum quality. We test with bidirectional interpolation
enabled and disabled to gain a sense of this feature's benefits and costs.

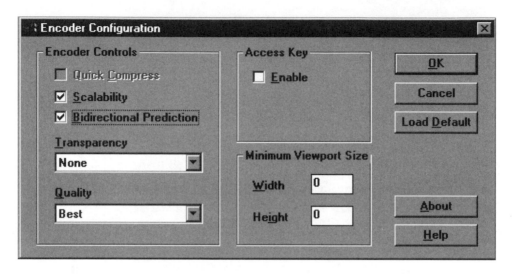

Figure 6.14   Indeo video interactive offers some innovative controls to optimize quality for your target platform.

IVI also enables scalability, like VDO's above, which allows partial decompression of files to maintain display rate. We enabled this feature for all compressions. IVI also has a "quick" compression mode that operates roughly 25 times faster than the normal mode at the cost of some quality. Once again, we tested quick mode compression output to learn if the quality differential outweighs the faster compression.

Finally, IVI lets you target good, better, and best quality levels, with the higher quality files requiring more CPU horsepower to decode. To assess the feature/benefit trade-off of these options, we compressed at both good and best quality and compared video quality and display rate.

Smacker is a switch-hitter that allows the developer to compress to either constant quality or constant data rates. The data rate control is new in version 3.0, as is a video analyzer that, like VCS's frame profile feature, helps verify that the data rate target has been met.

TrueMotionS is a data rate–oriented codec with a very coarse mechanism for maintaining the data rate—it simply drops frames when stressed to the max. There are filtering and quality sliders you can use to attempt to minimize dropped frames, but at the end of the day, if the scenes get too complex, frames drop (Figure 6.15). This means that it will meet your target,

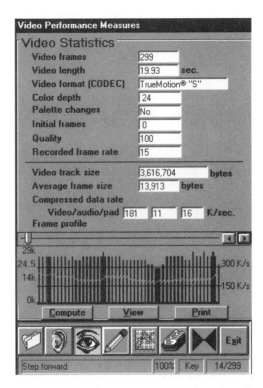

Figure 6.15 TrueMotionS is a data rate–oriented codec that drops frames to meet the target data rate when really stressed. The tall blue lines are compressed frames, while the valleys between the peaks are dropped frames.

but the frames dropped during compression will make the video appear jerky upon playback.

Power!Video Pro is the only pure control-oriented codec in our review. Note that the compression interface does not provide direct data rate control and doesn't maintain a constant data rate over the duration of a file. Instead, users set the controls shown in Figure 6.16 and the codec compresses away, with data rate rising and falling according to the complexity of each individual frame. This delivers consistent quality but makes it tough to achieve and maintain target data rates.

Compression Time: CD-ROM publishing is a "compress once, decompress many times" medium for which compression time wouldn't seem critical. That is until you start thinking about prototypes, beta testing, and

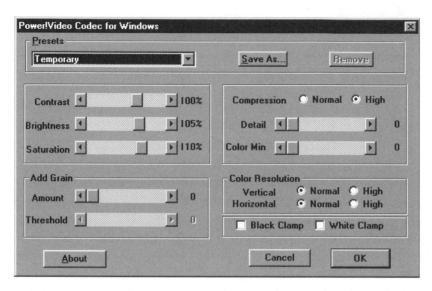

Figure 6.16   Power!Video Pro is our sole control-oriented codec, which uses these controls to compress to consistent quality but highly variable data rates.

all other compressions that occur before final. Then compression time becomes mission critical.

Indeo video interactive is by far the slowest encoder, taking 92 minutes to encode one minute of video with bidirectional encoding enabled, 84 minutes without. IVI is also the fastest encoder, taking four minutes to encode a minute of video in Quick mode. This feature alone makes it a remarkable tool for prototyping and fast-turn applications. All other encoders fell into the not-too-fast, not-too-slow range of three to 27 minutes per minute of video. All tests were run on a Pentium 133.

Performance   Now that we've achieved our target data rate, it's time to see how well the codec performs on our target computers. Display rate, or the number of frames displayed per second, is the most important factor in your codec decision, since irrespective of still frame quality, if the video doesn't play back at close to its nominal display rate it's a slide show, not video.

Target computer is a bit of a slippery concept, referring to the installed base of computers that will ultimately play the videos you compress. I say slippery because this can frequently be a shifting target, and as we'll see in a moment, the stakes are fairly high.

For example, the quality offered by Indeo video interactive is very appealing, but it plays at only five frames per second on a 486/66. Pentium owners who consume your video will be pleased, but what if many of your ultimate end users have 486 boxes? Use Cinepak to satisfy your low-power users and the Pentium owners will be underwhelmed by the video quality.

Complicating your decision is the fast-moving market. Perhaps software MPEG-1 is a stretch today, but in six months your average customer may very well own a Pentium 133. You may have the ability to rerelease your product then or ship two versions as many publishers do, one using Indeo or Cinepak, the other MPEG-1.

Be aware that most commercial publishers are extremely conservative when it comes to codec decisions. For Christmas 1996, publishers like Byron Preiss Multimedia and Imagination Pilots still targeted 486/66 computers. Unofficial word from Disney Interactive is that for Christmas 1996, 486/33s were still in the mix, though Disney relies more on animation than video. Christmas 1996 came and went with few if any unbundled MPEG-1 titles on retail shelves and only a sprinkling of Indeo video interactive CD-ROMs.

Given the broad range of target markets and the unique nature of most applications, the only universal advice I can offer is this: Before choosing a codec, study the performance charts that follow and *understand* how your codec decision affects those in your target market. Consider that low-power users might see single-digit frame rates or high-power users suboptimal quality. At least make this very important decision consciously, and be ready to respond to potentially unhappy users.

A reasonable goal is a display rate of 15 fps at the midrange of your target market, with no fewer than 10 frames per second at the low end. Let's see which codecs deliver this performance.

Display Rate: We ran two playback tests, the first with a 30-fps, 250 KB/s file to test pure decompression speed and the second with a 15-fps, 200 KB/s file to determine the lowest available platform that could play 15 fps for each codec.

All machines were running the latest version of ActiveMovie and the most up-to-date version of all codecs we could find. We used VCS to compute the display rate for all files except for Smacker, which we ran in free run mode and timed to calculate the frame rate.

Briefly, our 486/66 computer was a clone with an ATI Mach 32 graphics card, the Pentium 60 a Gateway 2000 with a Matrox Millennium graphics card, the Pentium 90 an NEC VERSA 4050H with an embedded graphics controller from Chips and Technologies, the Pentium 133 another Gateway 2000 box with a Diamond Stealth 3D 2000, and the Pentium 166 a clone with an S3 Trio64V+ chip embedded on the motherboard.

All computers were running Windows 95, the 486/66 with 8 MB of RAM, the others with 16 MB. All computers were configured in 16-bit graphics mode except the VERSA, which supports only 8-bit graphics. We tested from the CD-ROM drive on all computers but the Pentium 60, which we tested from the hard drive since it had difficulty reading the gold "one-off" disk.

We didn't test 30 fps Power!Video Pro or TrueMotionS files because they strained to meet our 15-fps, 200 KB/s cutoffs. We also ignored 30 fps tests for IVI's good compressor and Quick compressor, since neither compression mode is suitable for 30 fps encoding.

Whew! The results are presented in Table 6.7.

Clearly, developers targeting the 468 and low-end Pentium market should stick to Cinepak, Video 1, and Indeo 3.2 and perhaps consider Smacker or Power!Video Pro. TrueMotionS is an option with Pentium 60 computers and above.

In terms of Indeo video interactive's relative flavors, the range in display rate was nominal. Even without bidirectional interpolation, and compressed at the lowest quality setting, IVI was clearly inappropriate for 486/66 computers and very marginal on Pentium 60s, even from a hard drive. We'll reserve final judgment until reviewing the quality results, but IVI's advanced encoding options seem to do very little to expand its relevant target market.

Finally, Software MPEG-1, at least via ActiveMovie, shouldn't be considered unless your target computer is a Pentium 133 or higher.

Certain other observations are also worth mentioning. The first relates to Indeo video interactive's problems with start-up latency. When first released, files often took eight to 10 seconds to load, especially on 8-MB computers, primarily because of IVI's huge memory footprint. In addition, the codec suffered from playback latency, which caused most files to stutter for the first three or four seconds before starting smooth playback.

A new IVI version released in June 1996 reduced but didn't eliminate these problems. In our testing, we found that the first IVI file loaded on nearly all test computers stuttered somewhat before playing smoothly.

Table 6.7 Display rate by computer and codec.

Display rate	486/66		P60		P90		P160		P166	
Quality by codec	15 fps	30 fps	15 fps	30 fps	15 fps	30 fps	15 fps	30 fps	15 fps	30 fps
Cinepak	15	30	15	29	15	29	15	29	15	30
IVI, bidirectional	5	4	9	4	15	24	15	28	15	30
IVI, no bidirectional	7.5	5	10	4	15	26	14	29	15	30
IVI, no bidirectional, good compression	5	n.a.	11	n.a.	15	n.a.	15	n.a.	15	n.a.
IVI, quick compressor	9	n.a.	10	n.a.	15	n.a.	14	n.a.	15	n.a.
Indeo 3.2	15	6	15	26	15	27	15	29	15	30
Power!Video Pro	14	n.a.	15	n.a.	15	n.a.	15	n.a.	15	n.a.
TrueMotionS	9	n.a.	14	n.a.	15	n.a.	15	n.a.	15	n.a.
Smacker	15	30	15	24	15	25	15	30	15	30
MPEG-1	n.a.	3.7	n.a.	9	n.a.	19	n.a.	23	n.a.	28
Video 1	15	n.a.	15	n.a.	15	n.a.	15	n.a.	15	n.a.

Subsequent files, however, generally played smoothly from the start, probably because all the necessary drivers were loaded and operational.

There are several ways to work with these limitations. When loading your program, you could run a short, unobtrusive video file, possibly of your company or product logo, to get the drivers set. If the same video plays first every time, you can include two or three seconds of no activity in the front of the video, either a long, slow fade in from black or simply two or three seconds of static video, so that the latency isn't obvious. The latency is worse with higher bandwidth files, so you can also try compressing down to lower data rates like 150 KB/s.

Also worthy of note was the relative slowness of MPEG-1, both to load and to move interactively through the file. If your CD-ROM depends on lots of fast jumps within a file, test the responsiveness of your MPEG-1 driver early to get a feel for overall performance.

Quality   Now that you know which video plays best on your target platform, it's time to measure video quality, which we broke into four categories, still frame detail, moving quality, color fidelity, and 8-bit appearance. We ranked all codecs on a range of one to five, with five being the highest grade.

Still frame tests compare a single compressed frame to the uncompressed original, noting the differences in color or detail. Motion tests play the video back at full frame rate, looking for background noise and artifacts that appear only in real time.

For all tests, we compressed two video sequences at 15 fps to 200 KB/s, a reasonable target used by many CD-ROM developers. The only exception was MPEG-1, which we compressed with Xing's Software MPEG-1 encoder at 30 fps, 150 KB/s. We compared the results in moving and still frame tests using VCS' dual display window.

A quick glossary will help you work through our thumbnail descriptions:

- *aliasing:* Aliasing refers to jagged lines in straight objects like railings or posts, usually when placed at an angle in the video. During compression, aliasing is caused by the codec subsampling down into four or eight pixel blocks and then not having the resolution to display a smooth line.
- *banding:* Banding occurs where smooth regions in the video are marred by bands of pixels grouped together. When compressing, many codecs reduce the number of colors saved in the compressed file, making it impossible to display subtle changes like gradations in a face or wall. The codec has to group regions of similar-colored pixels into a band, describing it with one color. Banding also occurs when 24-bit codecs reduce colors for displaying in 8-bit graphics mode.
- *blockiness:* Blocky regions typically relate to how a codec breaks an image into pixel blocks during compression. Generally a sure sign of MPEG-1.
- *color shifting:* A motion artifact characterized by colors shifting bizarrely during playback.
- *jaggies:* A nontechnical name for aliasing.

- *mosquitoes:* Another typically MPEG-1 artifact where small lines and other artifacts hover around an object displayed on screen and look like flying mosquitoes.
- *pulsing:* Another motion artifact where key frame appearance is so different from that of delta frames that the video appears to pulse whenever a key frame is displayed.

With these descriptions on file, let's compare some videos.

Low-Motion Videos: Low-motion results are presented in Table 6.8. Overall, all IVI flavors were quite impressive, with bidirectional encoding apparently worth the wait, but only barely for these easy-to-compress, low-motion videos. Without careful scrutiny, however, the differences between the Quick compressor and full bidirectional encoding were fairly small, and you should feel comfortable using the codec for all but the final, final compression. Even at double the frame rate, MPEG-1 was also impressive, particularly in moving quality.

Table 6.8 Still frame and moving quality for low-motion videos.

Low-Motion Video: Quality by Codec	Still Frame Quality: Score, Description	Moving Quality: Score, Description	Total
Cinepak (Figure 6.17)	2; noticeable blockiness; virtually all detail is obscured, but no jaggies or ragged edges.	3; soft crinkling in background and face; no blockiness or distortion.	5
IVI, bidirectional (Figure 6.18)	5; first few frames mottled, almost perfect thereafter, image very clean and stable.	5; quiet, soft movement in background very much like real analog footage.	10
IVI, no bidirectional (Figure 6.19)	4.5; same first frame problems; colors seemed a little bit off.	5; all movement very slight, no bands, no blockiness, no color shifting.	9.5
IVI, no bidirectional, good compression (Figure 6.20)	5; a touch "brighter" than the bidirectional, no noticeable difference from best setting.	5; no noticeable difference upon playback from best setting.	10

(continued)

Table 6.8 *(continued)*

Low-Motion Video: Quality by Codec	Still Frame Quality: Score, Description	Moving Quality: Score, Description	Total
IVI, Quick (Figure 6.21)	4; slightly less "crisp" and a touch more grainy than other IVI videos, but we had to struggle to find it; very slight color bleeding; no first ugly frames.	4; slightly more pulsing than the other IVI videos, but difference very slight, noticeable only on zoomed viewing.	8
Indeo 3.2 (Figure 6.22)	3; colors and brightness are uneven through image; some banding in background, face appears filtered, obscuring facial details.	2; shifting forehead and obvious artifact patterns in the background.	5
Power!Video Pro (Figure 6.23)	1; color bleeding throughout with a washed-out look; most edges slightly ragged, the face blurry, background choppy with small blocks, banding, and discoloration.	1; interframe-only algorithm shows significant change between frames; noisy and blocky; snowy effect all over.	2
Duck TrueMotionS (Figure 6.24)	2.5; a touch blotchy in both the foreground and background, which ruined uniformity; not as sharp or crisp as some of the higher scores.	3; pulsing effect at key frames, blockiness and banding in smooth surfaces; face a touch fuzzy, looks like a 16-bit codec.	5.5
Smacker (Figure 6.25)	3; slight noise in the background, face slightly blotchy, with some banding in the jacket; edges clear.	3; colors uniform throughout, but slight blockiness in forehead and on background.	6
MPEG-1 (Figure 6.26)	4; face slightly softened as if filtered; colors a bit deeper and richer, changing some colors from dark gray to black.	5; very high quality in the motion, perhaps the slightest hint of distortion in the face, but perhaps not.	9
Video 1 (Figure 6.27)	2; noticeable distortion, a bit ragged around the edges, some blockiness in the background.	2; a lot of background movement, and jaggies in collar that don't go away or get clearer through the video.	4

Figure 6.17

Figure 6.18

Figure 6.19

Figure 6.20

Figure 6.21

Figure 6.22

Figure 6.23

Figure 6.24

Figure 6.25

Figure 6.26

Figure 6.27

If your target systems can't play videos compressed with these codecs back at close to full frame rate, you'll have to consider second-tier codecs. TrueMotionS won in this tier by half a point, but royalties apply. Cinepak and Indeo 3.2 were next, followed by Video 1. As we've seen in all of our tests, Power!Video really wasn't meant to play at these data rates and performs poorly at 200 KB/s.

High-Motion Videos: Table 6.9 contains our observations regarding the respective quality of the tested codecs. Here's a summary.

Action: Indeo video interactive clearly carries the day with high-motion videos. Unlike the case of the talking head video, where we saw very little difference between videos compressed with the various options enabled and/or disabled, here bidirectional encoding and compressing using the "best" setting created significant differences. If your target platform can play back full-bore IVI, these options will pay real quality dividends.

Developers courting the installed base of 486/66 computers will have to settle for artifact-ridden videos, since neither Cinepak nor Indeo 3.2 can handle high-motion files without visibly dropping quality. TrueMotionS does a great job with still frame quality, but the dropped frames used to maintain the target data rate kill playback smoothness. Power!Video Pro is

Table 6.9 Still frame and moving quality for high-motion videos.

High-Motion Video: Quality by Codec	Still Frame Quality: Score, Description	Moving Quality: Score, Description	Total
Cinepak (Figure 6.28)	2; noticeable blockiness; virtually all detail is obscured, but no jaggies or ragged edges.	3; very smooth playback, but some background noise, especially around difficult scenes. Cinepak also places key frames where needed, a great feature IVI still didn't have.	5
IVI, bidirectional (Figure 6.29)	5; best looking by far; just the slightest hint of mosquitoes.	5; Indeo looked like it dropped frames early, but background was clear throughout.	10
IVI, no bidirectional (Figure 6.30)	4; non-bidirectional showed mosquitoes around face and head, some aliasing on vertical lines.	3; aliasing apparent in some sequences, as are mosquitoes around subjects' heads.	7
IVI, no bidirectional, good compression (Figure 6.31)	3; significant blockiness and faces almost totally obscured; aliasing also present.	3; noisier throughout, but only slightly.	6
IVI, Quick (Figure 6.32)	3; noticeably blocky, with faces somewhat distorted.	3; noisier throughout.	6
Indeo 3.2 (Figure 6.33)	2; jagged edges indicate subsampling, background mostly obscured, faces mostly obscured.	2; noisy, tons of edges, bad, bad sky blockiness and discoloration; frequent aliasing visible throughout—most sharp edges look jaggy.	4
Power!Video Pro (Figure 6.34)	2; ragged around all edges, background blurred.	2; sky sequences look snowy and other sequences show static, resembling TV with a bad cable connection.	4
Duck TrueMotionS (Figure 6.35)	4; very good quality.	2; noisy with some streakiness and banding; dropped frames mar playback smoothness.	6

(continued)

Table 6.9 *(continued)*

High-Motion Video: Quality by Codec	Still Frame Quality: Score, Description	Moving Quality: Score, Description	Total
Smacker (Figure 6.36)	1; most definition lost, main characters look like putty figures.	1; constant blockiness and block shifting in the sky and other sequences; appeared to drop frames to meet the data rate; banding very evident in more demanding scenes.	2
MPEG-1 (Figure 6.37)	4; slight blocks and lines mar appearance; most facial detail obscured.	5; very smooth, picture is very clear, colors very deep and rich; minimal blockiness in most sequences.	9

Figure 6.28

Figure 6.29

Figure 6.30

Figure 6.31

Figure 6.32

Figure 6.33

Figure 6.34

Figure 6.35

Figure 6.36

Figure 6.37

also outmatched by the high-motion sequence, with low scores in both still frame and real-time playback tests.

Finally, even MPEG-1 had difficulty maintaining still frame quality in this sequence, with slight blockiness marring our test frame. Moving quality was still outstanding, however.

The Skinny on IVI: What's our advice on IVI? Well, all in all, the options designed to increase the display rate on low-power machines had only a marginal effect. At the same time, the quality-related options had a significant effect on video quality, albeit only for higher motion videos.

You're probably best advised to stay away from IVI altogether if a significant portion of your target market falls in the Pentium 60 range and below. If you choose IVI, however, go full bore, and compress using bidirectional interpolation, scalability, and the best quality setting. Dropping to lower power parameters will make your video look noticeably worse and probably won't make it play significantly faster.

Quality Honorable Mentions: *Low bandwidth:* Smacker deserves recognition for extremely high quality low-motion videos. In 320×240×15 fps tests, Smacker produced an excellent quality talking head video at around 82 KB/s (video only). At this data rate, you could pack close to two hours of high-quality talking head videos on one CD-ROM.

High bandwidth: Comparing Power!Video Pro to other codecs at 200 KB/s is like comparing a sumo wrestler to a gymnast in a tumbling competition—you see all of the negative and few of the positives. Where Power!Video Pro really excels is at high-data-rate, quality-oriented presentations. It is one of the few codecs that keep adding quality as data rates increase, approaching MPEG-1 levels at 350 KB/s and above, which is increasingly accessible in this age of the 4X CD-ROM drive. In instances in which only top quality will do and bandwidth or disk real estate isn't an issue, Power!Video Pro is worth considering.

8-Bit Appearance: Most Windows-based video graphics cards display in 8-bit, 16-bit, or 24-bit color depth with 8-bit systems predominating. When a computer is in 8-bit graphics mode, display is limited to 256 colors. This collection of 256 colors is called the palette, since all screen elements must be painted with colors contained in the palette. The 256-color combination is not fixed—palettes can and do frequently change. But at any one point, only 256 colors can be used to describe all the objects on the screen.

When displaying in 8-bit mode, all codecs are limited to 256 colors. For 8-bit codecs (Smacker, Video 1) this isn't a problem; their video is already described in 256 colors or less. This means that 8-bit codecs look as good in 8-bit mode as they do in the higher color depths. Conversely, this means that the appearance of videos compressed with 8-bit codecs doesn't improve in higher color depths.

All other codecs are native 24-bit codecs that use over 16 million colors to describe their compressed video. When displaying in 8-bit mode, they must drop from 16 million to 256 colors. To conserve file size and preserve display rate, all codecs decompress to the same fixed palette for all videos. To minimize distortion, all high-color codecs "dither" or draw minute geometric pixel patterns of various sizes to simulate colors not contained in the palette.

We judged the 24-bit codecs on two criteria. First, how well did the colors in each codec's unique palette match the requirements of our two test videos? Second, how noticeable or distracting was the dither pattern? The results are presented in Table 6.10. Note that we only tested one flavor of IVI, since color handling is identical across all encoder settings.

Microsoft's ActiveMovie MPEG-1 player is the star of this competition, producing video without a hint of color reducing or dithering. Of course, if you're planning on MPEG-1 you probably assume that most Pentium 133 owners don't configure in 8-bit mode anyway, so this functionality is somewhat wasted.

Among the rest, Indeo video interactive appeared the most natural in both the high- and low-motion videos, followed by Indeo 3.2 and Cinepak. Both Power!Video Pro and TrueMotionS appeared to use less than 256 colors, causing distracting banding.

Table 6.10 Still frame and moving quality for high-motion videos.

8-Bit Performance: Quality by Codec	Color Matching: Score, Description	Dither Pattern: Score, Description	Total
Cinepak	2; Cinepak doesn't allocate sufficient colors to facial tones, resulting in banding and a general brown appearance.	4; dither pattern very slight with little distortion upon playback.	6
IVI	4; most natural palette, with little banding evident anywhere in the video.	4; dither pattern very slight.	8
Indeo 3.2	3; face is reasonably natural, although some colors in the face are almost fluorescent.	4; very slight dither pattern; color shifting during playback mars appearance.	7
Power!Video Pro	1; 8-bit display is highly faded and cloudy.	1; dither pattern is very obvious and distracting, shifting continuously during playback.	2
TrueMotionS	2; face converted into two disparate colors with banding throughout background.	2; some background shifting but could have been worse.	4
MPEG-1	5+; it appears that MPEG-1 is displayed in 24-bit mode the quality is so good.	5+; no obvious dither pattern whatsoever.	10

IVI's dither pattern was also the most subtle, followed closely by Cinepak and Indeo 3.2. TrueMotionS' dither pattern was slightly more noticeable but wasn't distracting. Power!Video Pro really fell down in this category, with gross dither patterns that looked almost like space invaders crawling down the screen.

As 8-bit codecs, both Video 1 and Smacker look better than 24-bit codecs in 8-bit mode because they don't have to color reduce and because developers can assign a custom palette to the video rather than using a standard palette. When compressing low-motion video content for display in the 8-bit environment, both are excellent options.

However, neither codec performs well with high-motion videos, making them incomplete solutions at best. In most instances, developers will be forced to work with a 24-bit codec, at least for certain higher motion clips. We discuss the palette management issues surrounding how to work with 24-bit codecs in products bound for the 8-bit environment in Chapter 12.

Color Fidelity: Here we observed how compression affected the color and shading of the original video, more for informational purposes than to keep score. We didn't rate Smacker because it can accept any assigned palette. Here are our observations.

> *Cinepak:* Low-motion color fidelity was quite good. In high motion sequences, colors became washed out and the video appeared greenish in tint. When capturing high motion video sequences, experiment with bumping up color saturation values to counteract this effect.

> *Indeo video Interactive/Indeo 3.2:* In both high- and low-motion sequences, IVI does an outstanding job matching the color of the original video.

> *TrueMotionS:* Appears to bump the colors up slightly during compression to good effect.

> *Power!Video Pro:* At high data rates, Power!Video Pro is very accurate, but colors tend to fade at higher compression ratios. Horizons includes brightness and saturation controls in their compression interface to adjust this during compression.

> *Software MPEG-1 (Xing encoder):* Most MPEG-1 solutions tend to darken video slightly, so bump up the brightness during capture.

Note that these aren't hard-and-fast rules. You'll get the best results by understanding that compression can subtly change the color composition and brightness of your videos and experimenting to minimize these effects.

Special Features

Converting Animations   Converting Autodesk FLC files to video files is one of the most popular uses of Video for Windows in game CDs. Until very recently, the FLC format wasn't interleaved, so there was no other way to synchronize audio and FLC playback, especially from CD-ROM.

Note that 8-bit codecs have a distinct advantage over 24-bit codecs when compressing 8-bit animations. The 24-bit codecs, like Indeo, IVI and Cinepak, must first convert the compact 8-bit FLC format to 24 bits, tripling the amount of data compressed. Power!Video and TrueMotionS can't even compress 8-bit files, forcing you to convert to 24-bit color depth before making the encoder available.

In contrast, RAD Software's Smacker is an 8-bit codec that was designed for animation conversion. Video 1, another 8-bit codec, also performs well in this role and is royalty free. As discussed earlier, these 8-bit codecs also can compress to an assigned palette, so they can deliver a more accurate representation of the original FLC than the 24-bit codecs.

We tested quality, display rate, and compressed file size. The results are presented in Table 6.11.

Quality: As expected, the 8-bit codecs, Smacker and Video 1, delivered compressed video virtually identical to the original FLC file. TrueMotionS delivered bipolar performance, showing some aliasing on the smaller animation but delivering nearly flawless quality for the full-screen animation. Cinepak performed surprisingly well on both animations, preserving edges and detail, but IVI and Indeo 3.2 ruined sharp edges with pixelation and blockiness and blurred background detail. Power!Video Pro didn't meet data rate requirements for either test.

Smacker was the clear winner in motion quality, producing video that looked identical to the original FLC file. Video 1 fell down on the major transitions, where remnants from the initial sequence often took 15 frames to disappear completely. This problem can be avoided by compressing the animation in parts and then piecing together the whole, but this takes extra time and effort.

Table 6.11 Moving and still image quality for quarter-screen animation compressed to under 150 KB/s and full-screen animation compress to under 250 KB/s. Display rate tests on a Pentium 133 from CD-ROM.

Animation Quality by Codec	Cinepak	IVI (all flavors)	Indeo 3.2	True-MotionS	Power! Video Pro	Smacker	Video 1
Still Image Quality							
Quarter-screen	4	1	1	3	n.a.	5	5
Full screen	3	1	1	4	n.a.	5	4
Moving Quality							
Quarter-screen	4	2	2	4	n.a.	5	5
Full screen	2	1	1	5	n.a.	5	3
Display Rates—P133							
Quarter-screen	14	14	14	14	n.a.	15	14
Full screen	2	2	2	14	n.a.	15	12
File Size							
Quarter-screen	936	1.7 MB	895 KB	745 KB	3 MB	372 MB	1 MB
Full screen	2.23 MB	3.97 MB	3.05 MB	1.8 MB	n.a.	449 KB	2.6 MB

 All compressed animation files are located in the \chap6\animation\ bigani and \smallani subdirectories under their respective names.

Playback Rate: All codecs produced 14 fps for quarter-screen playback, but the 24-bit codecs all performed very poorly at full screen. TrueMotionS performed well at 14 frames per second, while Video 1 produced 12 fps.

Smacker really shined in full-screen playback tests. Not only did it achieve the full 15 fps, it speeded up to 95 fps for the full-screen file in free run mode, indicating that it would perform well on slower computers. For the record, RAD works with animated files much faster than real-world videos, compressing the full-screen, 285-frame animation in under one minute.

File Size: Most codecs priced themselves out of the park with compressed bandwidth. Smacker was the efficiency leader, followed by TrueMotionS. Video 1, your only realistic free compression option, was five times larger than Smacker on the full-screen animation, three times larger on the quarter-screen.

Summary: Smacker is clearly your best option when it comes to converting animations. If you're working with these types of files, you owe it to yourself to download their free sample codec (www.radgametools.com) and try it on for size. TrueMotionS is next but currently doesn't offer as convenient a test package as RAD—you have to contact Duck directly and ask them to encode some files.

Video 1 is your best free option, but results will vary widely by animation footage type. You should also be prepared to invest significant time disassembling and reassembling files to achieve the highest possible quality. We cover these techniques in Chapter 12.

Game-Oriented Features

Indeo video interactive To understand the real significance of Indeo video interactive, you must first recognize one essential truth. That is, at least in the linear play arena, mama Intel doesn't really care if Indeo beats software MPEG-1 or not. Software MPEG-1 requires lots of megainstructions per second (MIPS), which sells Pentiums and keeps the lights on in Santa Clara and Hillsboro, where IVI was developed.

For this reason, Intel isn't targeting IVI against MPEG. Rather, it's an enabling technology in Intel's march against dedicated game platforms like the SEGA Saturn and Sony PlayStation, which steal Pentium sales from Intel.

Game developers would love to switch to the Intel platform, if only to avoid royalties paid to the SEGAs and Nintendos of the world. Until very recently, however, a $3000 computer couldn't compete with a $300 dedicated game machine when it came to pure game performance.

With Windows 95 true 32-bit performance and a host of "DirectX" technologies in place, this situation is set to reverse. One key element still lacking, however, was a video technology enabling the effects possible on the dedicated game machine. This is the true focus of Indeo video interactive. Here's a summary of the new key elements:

Transparency support: Enabling video sprites and other video overlays that can be interactively controlled during playback with a mouse or keyboard.

Local window decode: Allowing the developer to decode regions within the compressed video rather than the entire video during run time. This sets up the ability to include multiple views in a video stream for real-time switching. For example, in an airplane simulation, users could press F4 and look out the right wing, press F5 and look out the left wing.

Random key frame access: Letting the developer insert key frames randomly into the video to maximize quality and interactivity.

Saturation/contrast/brightness controls: Letting users customize video characteristics for their graphics card/monitor combination.

Password protection: Protecting the intellectual property interests of the developer from editing and alteration.

Transparency: We've included an Intel demo application and some sample files to help illustrate these features. Load IndeoApp.exe by double-clicking on the file in the \chap6\indeovi subdirectory. First we'll experiment with transparency.

In essence, transparency is like chroma keying, explained in Chapter 11. Your goal is to overlay a segment of a video over a background bitmap. To do this, you film the video in front of a blue screen, such as the one TV stations use to film weatherpersons for overlaying over weather maps.

Editing programs like Premiere can eliminate the blue regions and "composite" the remaining video over the bitmap. However, this must be done in production, creating a finished video file that isn't interactive. IVI lets you do this in real time, on the user's computer, and, as we'll see in a moment, interact with the video.

What we'll be doing is loading a background bitmap and then playing the video over the bitmap with the background blue screen keyed out (see Chapter 11). First let's load the video by using IndeoApp's file/open command. Load \chap6\indeo\trans\surfera1.avi. Play the video using the arrow commands on the program's taskbar and you'll see a faux surfer on a blue background.

Next we'll load the bitmap. Using the same file/open command, load strt3.bmp. Notice how the program loads the bitmap and then places the surfer over the bitmap, with the blue background present.

If you play the video now, the bitmap will disappear and the blue screen will stay behind the surfer. If you press the two colored buttons on the taskbar, or select transparency and backgrounds from the video options screen, you'll see the surfer overlaid over the video as shown in Figure 6.38. As the video plays, you can grab it by touching it with your mouse and holding down the left mouse key and drag it around the screen. Pretty cool, huh?

Local Window Decode: Local window decode lets you create a composite video file composed of multiple "views" of a scene and then toggle instantaneously between views. In a flying simulation game, for example, you could switch between front and back, and left and right views at the touch of the keyboard.

Figure 6.38   Surf's up, dude, with IVI's transparency feature. Load IndeoApp and you can play too!

Development has two stages. First you film the various views, capture them separately, and combine them in one file. If you double-click on RAC_smnb.avi in the \chap6\indeo\local subdirectory, you'll see the file depicted in Figure 6.39, showing four views of a car racing at Portland International Raceway. These are the files we'll test and the views we'll be switching among.

The next stage is the script, where you tell the program which video sections to play at which commands. This is the 320×240.edl file in the same subdirectory.

Close IndeoApp and then reopen the program. Load the AVI file *first*, then the EDL file. Your screen should resemble Figure 6.40, with a small "output" file. Play the file, and then press 1, 2, 3, and 4 to switch views of the video. You can also pan the video in real time by holding down the keyboard arrow keys.

We've included Intel's documentation (appread.doc) in the chap6\indeo subdirectory, which includes more detail on both functions. To create applications utilizing these features, check Intel's Web site (www.intel.com) for more documentation.

Figure 6.39   Four views of a racecar driving down the track. See what great demos you can do when you're Intel?

Figure 6.40 IVI's local decode feature lets you switch rapidly between views in a video.

Other Interactive Efforts: To be fair, Intel was not the first to market all these features. For example, Duck Corporation debuted its "comprending" technology, similar to IVI's transparency feature, several months before IVI's launch. Horizons, developer of Power!Video Pro, offers a special Power!Video that allows you to zoom, pan, and reverse video playback, making your video much more interactive.

What's important with IVI, however, is not pure innovation but a critical change in focus. Intel conceded a war that they didn't need to win in the linear play arena to focus on markets affecting their bottom line. This will inevitably cause other codec developers to follow in this pursuit, which can only help their ultimate cause.

Programming Interface   All codecs except for Smacker are Video for Windows codecs compatible with all capture, editing, compression, authoring, and presentation tools that support Microsoft's AVI format. Most also support Apple's QuickTime format on the Macintosh and QuickTime for Windows.

Smacker offers two programming interfaces. First and most comprehensive is a proprietary programming interface primarily available to hardcore programmers working in C++ and similar languages. RAD recently released an MCI interface accessible from most authoring programs, which should open up their market substantially.

As we mentioned, while Indeo video interactive is an AVI codec, the game oriented are accessed through a new proprietary Indeo API that isn't currently supported by most authoring and presentation programs. Nonprogrammers can still access normal playback functions via the Video for Windows interface, but not the new features.

Economics   Table 6.12 shows commercial costs for compression and decompression.

Horizons' Power!Video Pro costs $495, but an EZ version, without data rate controls, costs only $99. Decoders are free.

RAD Game Tools offers three different products. Smacker utilities provides basic encoding and decoding, but each time you play a file the Smacker copyright notice displays. This option is free and available via download from www.radgametools.com. The second option is Smacker

Table 6.12   SDK and royalty costs per codec.

Costs Per Codec	Cinepak, Indeo 3.2, Indeo VI, Video 1	PowerVideo! Pro	TrueMotionS	Smacker
Compression	Free	Pro, $495 EZ, $99	Custom	Free
Decompression	Free	Free	Custom	$995–$3000 per title depending on use.
Contact	n.a.	www.horizons.com	212-941-2400	www.radgame-tools.com

HL, which includes an encoder Xtra for Macromedia Director and distributable versions of an MCI-compatible player with no copyright notice. This product is targeted toward the business user authoring in IconAuthor or ToolBook and costs $995 for unlimited decoders.

Their top-level product, Smacker SDK, is designed for CD-ROM title developers seeking to integrate Smacker playback into the core of their games. The SDK costs $3000 per title.

To date, Duck Corporation has cut very custom deals with a number of different game developers and computer manufacturers. Contact them directly for more information.

Chapter 1

Analog/Digital Overview

IN THIS CHAPTER

There's a revolution going on in the low-end camera business, a fundamental shift from analog to digital storage formats. Over the next several years, this will dramatically change how we film and capture video and significantly improve video quality.

What's so cool about digital? Well, for one thing, you can edit without creating another generation, the video equivalent of photocopying as many times as you want without degrading quality. It's just like copying a bitmapped image, which you can do hundreds of times without fading, discoloration, or any other artifacts created when overdubbing an analog tape.

Second, when you "capture" digital video on a computer, you're actually "converting" the signal, not capturing. This is more like converting a TGA file to a BMP file, which, theoretically at least, shouldn't degrade quality at all. In contrast, traditional capture introduces a host of artifacts into the digitized video, not only from the capture process but also from the compression that accompanies capture.

Today, however, most digital video starts life as an analog signal on film, and a working knowledge of analog standards and formats is essential to successfully navigating the analog-to-digital conversion. This section starts with an overview of analog storage formats like SVHS, BetaSP, and Hi-8 and then moves on to review broadcast, signal, and other analog standards.

Then we'll move to the Great Analog Source test, where we examine how these analog characteristics affect ultimate compressed video quality. The answers will affect both how you film and how you capture video.

We finish with a sneak peek at Sony's new low-end digital format and a look at "Firewire," a specification for a really, really fast serial port. When I say your next capture card will be a serial port, I mean a Firewire card.

> *Note to readers:* Many of the analog tests shown in this chapter were performed for the first edition using the capture cards of the day. Since the analog standards haven't changed since the first edition, our findings and conclusions remain valid. We apologize for not updating but note that using the first-edition tests gave us time to compare the Sony Digital camera and capture card.

ANALOG STANDARDS

Let's jump right in and attack the maze of analog standards using Figure 7.1 as a guide.

Capture/Storage Formats

Whenever you film or edit, you store the video in a particular analog video format, represented in the upper left-hand corner of Figure 7.1. At a

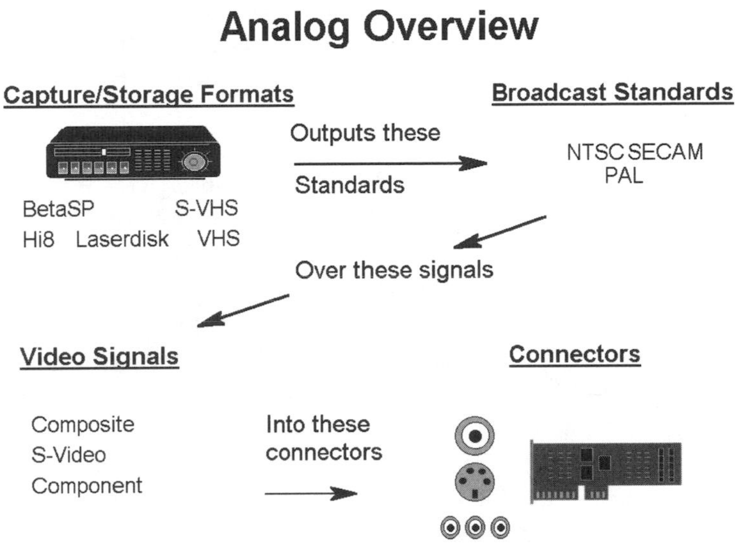

Analog Overview

Capture/Storage Formats

Outputs these
Standards
→

BetaSP   S-VHS
Hi8 Laserdisk VHS

Broadcast Standards

NTSC SECAM
PAL

Over these signals

Video Signals

Composite
S-Video
Component

Into these
connectors
→

Connectors

Figure 7.1   Analog tape, broadcast, and signal standards.

minimum, you're probably familiar with VHS, SVHS, and Hi-8. As we'll see in a few moments, differences between the formats relate to issues like lines of resolution, signal bandwidth, and how color information is stored.

The highest quality format shown in Figure 7.1 is BetaSP. While there are higher quality analog formats like one inch, equipment costs for components handling these formats are sky high. In contrast, although BetaSP cameras and decks are out of the purchase price range for many developers (Doceo included), these components are widely available for rental at reasonable rates. For this reason, we included them in our survey and testing.

Broadcast Standards

Broadcast standards, in the upper right-hand corner of Figure 7.1, define how the signal is represented when transmitted to a receiving device like a television. NTSC, which stands for National Television Standards Committee, is the reigning standard in North America, Central America, and

Japan. We'll look at the background and color composition of NTSC in a moment. For now, remember that NTSC signals define the screen with 525 lines per frame and update the screen at just under 30 frames per second or, more accurately, at 60 fields per second.

PAL, for phase alternation line, dominates in Europe and is also found in the Middle East, Africa, and South America. SECAM, for Systeme Électronique pour Couleur avec Memoire, is a PAL variant used in France, Russia, and other pockets in Africa. Both PAL and SECAM use 625 lines of resolution and 25 frames per second.

For the most part, VCRs, decks, and other analog players handle only one format. Fortunately, if you're working in the United States, you'll rarely run into PAL or SECAM materials, and I assume the inverse is true in other geographic areas. If you get handed a PAL or SECAM tape, check your Yellow Pages under Video Production Services and start making phone calls. I'm sure someone local can either convert the tape to NTSC or recommend a regional resource that can do the work.

Video Signal Standards

Video signal standards, in the lower left-hand corner of Figure 7.1, relate to how color and other video information are stored and transmitted. The transmission method also affects the type of connector used on the video capture card, shown in the bottom right-hand side of Figure 7.1. A composite signal, which carries all information in one channel, uses a one-hole jack called the RCA Phono connector. The S-Video signal, composed of two channels, uses a four-pin connector called the mini-DIN connector. A true component signal, made up of three separate video signals, hooks into three separate connectors.

The key concept to remember is that all U.S. video decks record and play, and all U.S. capture boards receive, an NTSC signal. The signal may be stored on a laserdisc or BetaSP deck and may be transmitted as composite, S-Video, or component video. However, all these formats are under the umbrella of NTSC video.

While we'll cover this in detail later in the chapter, note that formats like D-1, D-2, and Digital BetaCAM, although digital, still adhere to these same rules. They output one of the three broadcast standards, store the video as either composite or component format, and can usually output analog video to one of the connector formats as well as at least one digital format.

THE EVOLUTION OF ANALOG SIGNALS

It all started with television—but you probably already guessed that. Back in 1953, the NTSC committee had a problem. Black-and-white televisions were pervasive, but color was coming. They had to design a standard that would work with both.

Black-and-white televisions receive one video signal, called luminance, which is often referred to as the "Y" signal. Each screen pixel is defined as some range of intensity between white (total intensity) and black (no intensity). To maintain compatibility with older black-and-white sets, the NSTC had to set a color standard that kept the luminance signal separate and also provided the color information required for newer color television sets.

In the digital world, we're comfortable with colors described with red, green, and blue, or RGB values. Your first color monitor probably said RGB right on the case. The analog world has also embraced the RGB standard, at least on the acquisition side, where most cameras also break the analog signal into RGB components.

However, the NTSC couldn't use RGB as the color television standard because the old black-and-white television sets couldn't decode an RGB signal. They had to send a luminance signal for the black-and-white sets and fill in the color information with other signals, called hue and saturation, or U and V. For this reason, where the digital world works around RGB, the analog world, especially around television broadcasting, works in YUV.

Component, S-Video, and Composite

Figure 7.2 traces the evolution of the analog signal from RGB to composite. On the extreme left-hand side of the chart is RGB capture. Here, storage channels are maintained for each of the primary colors.

However, RGB is an inefficient analog video storage format for two reasons. First, to use RGB, all three color signals must have equal bandwidth in the system, which is often inefficient from a design perspective. Second, because each pixel is the sum of red, green, and blue values, modifying the pixel forces you to adjust all three values. In contrast, when images are stored as luminance and color formats, as in the YUV format, you can modify a pixel by changing only one of the values. For this reason, the Y, R-Y, and B-Y shown in the middle of the chart were adopted by CCIR601 as the international component video standard.

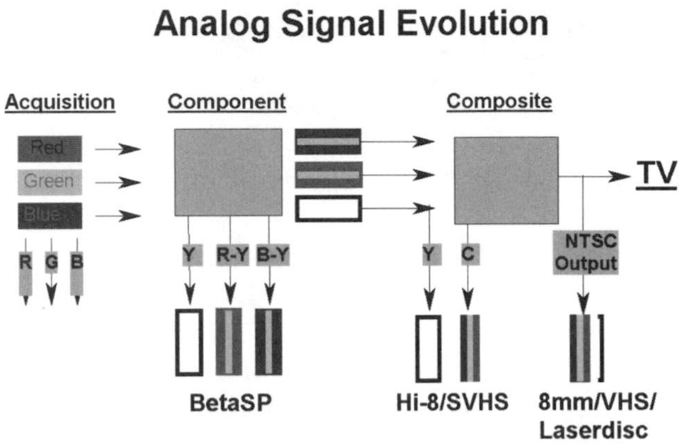

Analog Signal Evolution

Figure 7.2   The evolution of an analog signal from RGB to NTSC.

Component video means that separate channels are maintained for each color value, both in the recording device and on the storage medium. This minimizes noise that occurs when two signals are combined in one channel.

After NTSC encoding, the hue and saturation channels (U and V) are combined into one chrominance channel, also called the C channel. A video signal called S-Video carries separate channels for the luminance (Y) and chrominance (C) signals. This is also called Y/C video.

To play on our old black-and-white televisions, we know that all color and other information must be ultimately combined into one video signal, called a composite signal. This is represented on the extreme right-hand side of the screen. Technically, a composite signal is any signal that contains all the information necessary to play the video. In contrast, any one individual channel of component or Y/C video would not be sufficient to play the video.

Capture and Storage Formats: The Contenders

As you can see from Figure 7.2, the first major difference between the capture formats is how the color information is stored. BetaSP stores the color information as component video with three separate channels. Hi-8 and SVHS use the two-channel Y/C video, while lowly VHS, 8 mm, and laserdiscs store all color information in one channel.

Which signal produces better video quality? The composite signal combines all signals into one channel, which inevitably introduces noise into the signal. Noise is manifested, in the terms of one extremely technical manual on the subject, as "any random fleck that shows up in the display." I couldn't have said it better myself. So obviously the composite signal is the noisiest.

The S-Video signal (also Y/C or separate video) produces less noise, because the two signals are isolated in separate channels, not merged together. This minimizes flicker and color blur, not to mention flecks, random or otherwise. Finally, the component signals provide the highest quality signal because all components are maintained in separate channels.

To preserve this color fidelity, you should transmit the video to the capture card in as separate a video signal as possible. This relates back to the video signals and connectors shown in Figure 7.1. For example, virtually all BetaSP decks have composite out signals, which combine the three component signals into one channel. This obviously negates some of the benefits of using BetaSP, and component or S-Video signals are preferred.

Unfortunately, the inverse is also true. For example, SVHS decks usually play VHS tapes as well. Broadcasting a VHS signal through the S-Video cable doesn't reverse noise that may be present in the original signal. You may get a slight improvement in quality if the deck performs a cleaner color separation than the capture board, but you won't get SVHS quality.

The tape formats also differ in other characteristics, as shown in Table 7.1.

Table 7.1 Analog capture and storage standards.

	BetaSP	SVHS/Hi-8	Laserdisc	VHS/8 mm
Color	Component	Y/C	Composite	Composite
Lines of resolution	360	400	240	240
Signal bandwidth	7.5 MHz	4.5 Hz	4.5	2.5 MHz

Lines of resolution are a characteristic related to how each format stores the analog data, specifically with respect to the number of vertical lines used to describe each video frame. For example, SVHS cameras store 400 vertical lines of information for each frame. When outputting the signal, which has approximately 480 vertical lines, the deck must perform some minor interpolation to boost the 400 lines to 480.

Contrast this with VHS, which stores only 240 vertical lines and has to double each line to compose the 480 required by the NTSC standard. This forces a pretty dramatic interpolation that degrades the video quality. For example, imagine stretching a bitmapped image to over twice its original size. While the deck filters and interpolates the pixel-replication artifacts, fundamentally the information isn't there and picture quality and sharpness both suffer.

Bandwidth describes the amount of data within the signal. As you'd expect, the more information the better. Probably the best analogy is to dots per inch for still-image graphics. An image stored at 200 dpi looks grainy compared to an image stored at 600 dpi. Similarly, the video quality of VHS's 2.5 MHz bandwidth can't match up to higher bandwidths of other storage formats.

Signal to noise relates to the amount of noise in the signal, with higher numbers being better. Note that when differentiating between the formats the comparison isn't linear—each drop of 3 dB means an *additional 50% of noise in the signal*. When dropping from BetaSP's 53 to VHS's 43, this isn't a noise increase of 20%, it's an increase of over 150%.

All other things being equal, you're probably guessing that BetaSP is the preferred format, and you would be right. But if your name isn't Rockefeller, and you've checked the prices of BetaSP equipment lately, you're probably asking yourself, just how much does it help?

The answer is, it helps a lot, in certain places under certain circumstances. To see exactly where, let's trace the flow of analog video from the original filming to digitization.

FROM ANALOG TO AVI

Filming

This is the part where you buy makeup and klieg lights, invite all your friends, and shout things like "quiet on the set," "cut," and my personal favorite, "print it." It's the fun part, before all the serious work begins.

Anyway, when you film, you have a range of options, from your personal Hi-8 camera to the local BetaSP deck that rents without operator for about

$500 per day. Does choice of format matter here? Yeah, it does. Here's how we tested.

The Lens Test

We shot the same video with three cameras: a Sony 3CCD BetaSP camera that cost around $25,000, a Canon A1 digital that cost around $3000, and a Sony TR101 Hi-8 camera that cost around $1100. We filmed at the GTE Visnet studios in Atlanta.

Through GTE, we hired a professional camera operator for the BetaSP camera. He was also familiar with the Canon A1 and configured the camera to match the BetaSP as closely as possible. The Sony TR101 was configured with care by an associate who is a practiced video enthusiast out to prove that his TR101 could match the Canon costing three times more. He was motivated.

Rather than shoot from exactly the same camera angle in sequence, which would yield similar lighting but cuts that would be difficult to compare, we positioned the two Hi-8 cameras as closely as possible to the BetaSP camera and shot once. While we got as close in angle, height, position, and focus as we could, I'll be the first to admit that the videos created were slightly different in many respects. Overall, however, I think the results were instructive.

As was our practice, we edited the "keeper" takes from the original BetaSP film onto a one-inch master. One-inch tape is a component format with a higher signal bandwidth than BetaSP. This one-inch tape was therefore "second generation."

While preparing the tests presented in this chapter, we transferred the clip from the one-inch master back to BetaSP (third generation), which was ultimately transferred to Hi-8 tape for capture and comparison to the other two cameras (fourth generation).

To explain, we transferred to Hi-8 format to isolate the impact of lens quality on ultimate video quality. Had we captured from the original BetaSP film or one-inch master, we couldn't be certain how much of the quality differential, if any, related to media and how much related to the cameras.

We captured all three Hi-8 tapes using a Sony CVD-100 deck and VideoLogic's Captivator board. We captured at 15 frames per second, 320×240 resolution in RGB format in step. We captured using step frame mode—which we'll cover in the next section, and compressed the video to about 150 KB/s with Indeo 3.1. The results are presented in Figures 7.3, 7.4, and 7.5.

Subjectively, the gap between the high-end BetaSP camera and the two Hi-8 cameras is much more dramatic than the difference between the two lower end cameras. When you consider that the BetaSP footage was ultimately captured from a fourth-generation source, you get the strong feeling that it pays to invest in quality equipment during the original analog capture.

 The videos are contained in the Chapter 7 subdirectory on the CD-ROM under Fig7_3.avi, Fig7_4.avi, and Fig7_5.avi, and I urge you to play them. Here are our observations.

BetaSP   The most striking image from a warmth and depth standpoint. The high-end camera handled the lighting most smoothly, without the white foreheads and nose present in both other videos—even taking into account that this camera was directly in front and the others were off to the side. The gray back wall was the smoothest and least mottled of those depicted with the three cameras. However, we were surprised to find some patches of green in the black coat, indicating some color slippage.

You may notice that this camera was focused on the subject, which left the back wall softly out of focus. This seems to be a fairly useful filming technique, since flat surfaces are the bane of most codecs. By filming the back wall out of focus and somewhat fuzzy, you limit the flat, static detail that the codec can turn into a boiling mass of motion. This promotes the perceived quality of the back wall.

Canon   Showed better color fidelity than the Sony TR101, producing a smooth back wall and crisp black coat texture without swatches of green. Note, however, the relative lack of contrast in the facial colors, especially compared to the high-end camera. By contrast, we mean the number of colors used to describe the face. Where the Sony 3CCD camera shows a wide variety of colors, including rich tans and browns, the Canon video appears faded, with only a few colors describing the face.

As you play the video, you'll notice that the frames seem to jump around a bit; however, this tape jitter could have been caused by the Sony capture deck, as we noticed it on several other step captures.

The Canon video was the most impressive from a clear compression perspective. At 126 KB/s, the image was clear and virtually artifact free.

Figure 7.3 Video filmed with a high-end Sony 3CCD camera and dubbed to
a Hi-8 tape for capture. Colors are rich, deep, and smooth,
although the author would like to point out that the camera added
at least 10 imaginary pounds. On the negative side, whether the
result of the lens or simply the three generations that passed
between filming and capture, this image showed some artifacting
upon zooming that wasn't present in the Canon video at 20 KB/s
less.

While editing your many takes into one reel of final footage saves a lot of
time, you may get the best results capturing from the original footage.
Notwithstanding the higher color quality and bandwidth of the BetaSP
format, the first-generation capture from the Canon produced the clearest,
most artifact-free video of the bunch.

Sony Same deal with the relative lack of contrast, only slightly worse. The
TR101 also didn't like the gray back wall, which becomes more apparent

Figure 7.4　Video filmed with the Canon A1 camera. Color contrast in the face is noticeably absent, resulting in an image with much less warmth than the Sony 3CCD. On the other hand, the Canon image compressed down to a virtually artifact-free 126 KB/s, and the back wall is the smoothest of the three. Like vegetables from the garden, the best captures may come directly from the original film.

at higher magnifications. It also produced the most green patches in the black coat. However, the camera performed exceptionally well for an $1100 device, producing facial colors that were subjectively superior to those obtained with the Canon.

Obviously, high-end cameras exist in Hi-8 and SVHS format as well as in BetaSP. In fact, many high-end cameras don't come with bundled recorders, they simply have analog feeds out to your storage format of choice. So although we referred to the camera as the BetaSP source, equal or greater lens quality could almost certainly be found in other formats.

 Figure 7.5 Video captured with the Sony TR101. The Sony produced very credible video that trailed the Canon in pure compressed quality and both other cameras in contrast. Note, however, that the camera angle is at least partially responsible for some of these problems. The camera showed some muddling in the back wall and mottled green patches on the coat.

However, this experiment proves two things. First is that even after slicing and dicing the video during scaling, capture, and compression, higher quality equipment can make a difference. Cameras like the Sony and Canon are absolutely essential to the overall production process, especially for rehearsals and proofs of concept. However, you'll produce a higher quality result for final production with a higher end device.

The second point is that BetaSP's 7.5-MHz bandwidth allows the signal to hold up over multiple generations. If you plan exotic transitions or special effects that require multiple generations, BetaSP may be absolutely required to retain quality. On the other hand, we also noticed some degradation in video signal when comparing the first-generation Canon Hi-8 video with third-generation footage from the higher end camera. Although it may be a real pain in the rear, you may want to eschew an edited master and capture directly from the original tapes.

Finally, what this test didn't establish is whether BetaSP produces superior results when used as the analog format for capture. Here we learned that filming with a higher end camera produces better compressed video and that BetaSP holds up remarkably well through multiple generations. Still to come is whether sending a BetaSP stream to the capture board produces appreciably better video than Hi-8, SVHS, or even VHS and laserdisc.

In Search of the Perfect Wave

OK, I admit it. There is a CPA in my background, those early years of the 1980s when I was fresh out of grad school and still running on that preprogrammed "you have to be a professional" course set in high school and college. I bailed out of public accounting one step before the cold auditor debited me out, leaving surprisingly little residue save a couple of old club ties and a nagging feeling that there is order in the world, if one could only quantify it.

Naturally, when I started compressing video, I felt there was a *right way* to capture video. I left Iterated Systems secure in my knowledge that step frame capture from a laserdisc was *the* best way.

Then I learned that laserdiscs use a composite signal, the analog equivalent of being a smoker amidst nonsmokers. I polled my publishing brethren and saw platinum titles captured from VHS with $300 Video Spigots. I learned of mythical analog formats like BetaSP and million-dollar capture stations that churned out perfect files in near real time.

So, although somewhat less romantic than the *Endless Summer's* search for the perfect wave, but only somewhat, I began my quest for the perfect capture system. Or maybe Diogenes is a better analog.

I took my lamp, my surfboard, and my trusty Gateway 2000 computer figuratively around the world, testing analog decks from Japan, capture boards from Europe and the United States, and a good old, made in the US of A, eight cylinder with overhead CAM supercomputer that converts analog to digital without ever touching a capture card.

And while I never saw the sun set over the Australian barrier reefs or smelled the salty morning tide off Honolulu, I have seen perfect raw footage that takes your breath away and learned the truth of how to video capture. These bring their own form of spiritual harmony and peace.

Hmmm. I have been working too hard on this book.

Anyway, I'll start with a story that's also an excuse. I began my high-tech career in fax boards. Seemed like a great place to be back in 1987.

In developing our little product, called the JT Fax, we tested with a relatively small sample of fax machines, primarily our office fax—a Sharp unit—and a small sprinkling of other units located in friends' offices. You see, group III facsimile is standard, and we figured if we worked with these machines, we'd be in great shape. In truth, we tested real hard, sent multipage faxes at all hours of the day and night, testing during storm and sunspot, and released our product with full knowledge that it would be the most compatible fax board ever introduced.

I hear you chuckling. Yup, didn't work with fully half the fax machines out there, including those made by market leader Ricoh. Well it took a while, but we got things squared away, as much, I later learned, as any fax device vendor gets things squared away. Sometimes I'm amazed fax machines work at all.

Segue to seven years later. I design what I believe is the perfect test for analog formats and capture boards, have my tapes dubbed by one of the best facilities in Atlanta and my laserdisc mastered at a world-renowned facility. I play them all from professional quality equipment, and guess what?

The analog world is no better than the digital one. All the clips look different. Oh, just in color and shade and brightness and darkness, but different nonetheless.

We captured with seven or eight of the best capture boards in the world, took great pains to make the input signals look as similar as possible, and guess what? They all look different. Well, in truth, given time we could tweak and adjust and get the final products looking a little bit more similar. But it's really a diminishing returns kind of thing, and my editor is telling me it's time to shoot the author and ship the book.

So. When you look at the clips, try to ignore the facts that (1) they're all of me and (2) sometimes I look like a Martian. Try to judge the formats not on absolute color, because that can be adjusted, but on color fidelity, as in why are there green spots on his black jacket? Also focus on resolution—which formats look like they delivered the most detailed information to the capture card.

When you look at capture cards, compare quality and color fidelity. All were captured from the same BetaSP tape, so artifacts and muddled colors relate strictly to the board.

Usable Quality: Capture Technologies

By now it's relatively clear that BetaSP is the highest quality format that's reasonably accessible from a budget standpoint. Does that automatically make it the best capture format? Again, sometimes yes and sometimes no. It all depends on your ability to access the quality.

Real Time versus Step Frame Capture

As we'll see, real-time capture cards almost always compress video during capture to shrink the video to data rates that can be successfully transferred to the hard drive without dropping frames. As we know, this compression is "lossy," which means that it degrades video quality in process.

The alternative to real-time capture is called "step frame" capture. In this mode, the capture software controls both the analog source and computer and feeds frames only when the capture board, bus, and storage subsystem are ready for them, usually around a frame per second. Step frame enables compression-free capture without dropping frames.

To step frame capture, the deck must have two characteristics. First, it must be frame accurate, which means that it can pause on a single whole frame and hold synchronization. Second, it must be controllable through a communication standard supported by your capture software.

If you've ever "paused" your home VCR, you've probably seen that it isn't frame accurate. Neither are any of the low-end BetaSP decks that I've experimented with. Which means that you can't practically step frame in BetaSP format.

The only low-end devices (read, affordable) that met both criteria are laserdiscs, including the Pioneer CLD-V2600 we use at Doceo and the Sony CVD-1000, a Hi-8 deck. Looking back at Figure 7.2, we see that both Hi-8 and laserdisc formats are inferior to BetaSP. However, since both formats can step frame, they can deliver the video without compression. BetaSP can't. So the real issue becomes—do step framed Hi-8 and/or laserdisc formats deliver better quality than BetaSP compressed during capture?

Step Frame versus Real Time: Experiment

Our test involves both BetaSP and laserdisc footage. Let's review the generations of the respective footage, which is all derived from the same video sequence filmed on BetaSP (Table 7.2).

Table 7.2 Generations of test formats.

	1st Generation	2nd Generation	3rd Generation	4th Generation
BetaSP	Filmed on BetaSP	Dubbed to 1 inch	Dubbed to BetaSP	Dubbed to BetaSP
Hi-8	Filmed on BetaSP	Dubbed to 1 inch	Dubbed to BetaSP	Dubbed to Hi-8
Laserdisc	Filmed on BetaSP	Dubbed to 1 inch	Pressed laserdisc	

As you can see, the laserdisc was one generation newer than the other two. However, since all previous generations were high-bandwidth analog formats, I believe that one extra generation had no impact on the ultimate test results.

We captured all footage with the venerable Intel Smart Video Recorder Pro, one of the few boards with a raw capture format. All video was captured at 15 frames per second at 320×240 resolution and compressed to 150 KB/s using Indeo 3.1.

As you would expect, both the BetaSP and the Hi-8 decks offered S-Video signals out. While the laserdisc stores the color information in composite format, the Pioneer CLD-V2600 also offers S-Video out. Although this can't convert the composite color signal back to pristine S-Video, it allows the $1000 deck to separate the colors rather than the $500 capture board. Accordingly, we used the Smart Video Recorder Pro's S-Video connector for all three sources.

The laserdisc puts out its own frame indicator, which is the number shown in the upper left-hand corner of the screen. Since we burned the frame numbers into the BetaSP tape after mastering the laserdisc, the time code found in the other footage isn't there.

All files were captured at 320×240 at 15 frames per second. Capture formats were YUV-9 for the step captures and Indeo 3.2 for the real time. All videos were compressed to around 150 KB/s with Indeo 3.2.

Here's what we focused on in comparing the results:

> *Color fidelity:* We focused on two areas, the black coat and smooth gray back wall. For the coat, we looked for patches of green and other color errors. We judged the back wall based on the smoothness of the color and presence of streaks or other artifacts.
>
> If you chose to follow along, we extracted frame 12:16 or 12:17 on the tape formats and frame 13244 for the laserdisc. This is obvious in the first few frames but not later.
>
> *Compression artifacts:* The cleaner the signal, the fewer the artifacts. Zooming in on the face, we observed the smoothness of the facial features, especially around the eyes and mouth.

The Envelope Please

Not surprisingly, the real-time BetaSP capture (Figure 7.6) showed minor artifacting below the eyes and in other smooth regions in the face. This is the double compression at work.

Overall, the laserdisc step frame was the champ (Figure 7.7). The face shows good detail and smoothness, and the back wall is smooth with good color fidelity. The laserdisc showed little of the color instability I had feared would result from the composite signal. Conversely, the higher color quality of the BetaSP signal didn't translate into significantly higher quality video. Perhaps this related to the S-Video signal in, perhaps the double compression.

Both formats showed some color smearing, evidenced by pockets of green in the black coat. However, the detail on both videos was extremely crisp and sharp, even after compressing to 150 KB/s.

Third in overall quality was the Hi-8 step frame capture (Figure 7.8). While the single frame picture quality was outstanding, we experienced several analog problems, like "jitter," where the tape bounces up and down,

 Figure 7.6   BetaSP captured in real time and compressed during capture.

 and "dropout," where spurious white lines randomly streak across the
bottom of the picture. Both of these will be clearly evident in Fig7_8.avi.

During compression, jitter looks like motion to the codec which retards
compression. In fact, the Hi-8 step frame capture ended up looking worse
than real-time Hi-8 capture because the real-time capture had no jitter and
compressed more smoothly.

These problems may be the delicate Hi-8 tape's not-so-polite way of
telling us that it's not quite up to the rigors of step framing, even if the deck
is frame accurate and computer controlled, thank you very much. On the
other hand, I used this test as a learning experience and ran through it 15
or 20 times, which may be beyond the half-life of Hi-8 tape. The jitter and
dropout seemed to turn up late in the game and maybe wouldn't have
appeared had I gotten it right the first time...or even the fifth time.

Figure 7.7   Step capture from a laserdisc.

In addition, the test footage appeared on the first two minutes of the tape. We later learned that analog video experts advise not using the first five minutes of the Hi-8 tape for precisely these reasons. During other testing, we captured footage located further along the tape with the CVD-1000 in step frame mode. Jitter was totally gone and dropout very infrequent, and the quality of the footage was close to but not quite equal to that of the laserdisc. To a degree, these subsequent results have convinced me to discount the test results presented here.

Overall, there's no doubt that laserdisc provides a physically stronger medium that holds up better over multiple captures. On the other hand, read on, and you'll see that laserdiscs have their warts as well.

We'll discuss the mechanics of the step frame capture in Chapter 8.

 Figure 7.8 Hi-8 step frame capture.

Format Hassles

You can shoot in Hi-8 format yourself, or shoot in BetaSP and dub to Hi-8 for capture. Dubbing the BetaSP tape to Hi-8 can be done in house by most studios or postproduction houses and should cost under $50. In contrast, creating a one-write laserdisc can be a real pain in the rear and costs between $250 and $500. You have to create a master tape that meets certain specified requirements. Most analog production facilities don't have a one-write laserdisc, so you have to send the master off to another city. The finished one-write disk only holds 30 minutes of video.

If you buy a *plastic* master ($250–$300), the first three to four minutes of video on the disk can be distorted. Color hue and saturation tend to change as you move through the laserdisc. *Glass* masters cost about $500 but offer better color fidelity. How much better? Probably about $200. What's that mean? I don't know!

Notwithstanding these problems, many CD-ROM developers swear by laserdiscs and claim to have fewer problems than I've had. If you decide to go this route, here's a list of steps to take before cutting the master.

1. Advise the one-write facility in writing that you're using the disk for step frame capture. There are two types of laserdiscs, CAV, for constant angular velocity, and CLV, for constant linear velocity. Most laserdisc players can step frame only from a CAV disk, which has a capacity of 30 minutes. You need to be certain that you're getting a CAV disk.

2. Get a written list of specifications for the master tape that you will provide to the one-write facility. This should include length of time required for tones and bars, which allow the one-write system to synch up the color signal, and length of time of pure black video. Keep this information on file and follow it to the letter.

3. Get a written description of the warranty for both the plastic and the glass masters. Determine the benefits of the glass over the plastic and see what faults aren't warranted in the cheaper disk. The first few minutes of color on the first disk I cut were unstable. Later, when I complained, I was told that I had been advised of this up front. If you have less than 30 minutes of video to master, ask if you can place the video starting five or six minutes into the disk.

4. Don't purchase your master until all your footage is completed. Multiple laserdiscs are not only expensive, they also usually look at least a little different from a color standpoint.

If you're working on a budget and doing your work in Hi-8 or SVHS, probably the best advice is to work in that format until all your video is finished and prototypes completed. Then, if you'd like to try and boost video quality, master the laserdisc and go from there.

To find the nearest facility, look up Video Tape Duplication and Transfer services in the Yellow Pages and call the company with the biggest advertisement. Normally, if they don't have a facility they will tell you who does. If you can't find a facility in town, try Crawford Post Production Services in Atlanta at (404) 876-7149.

THE GREAT ANALOG SOURCE TEST

Well, you have our advice—now let's see what it costs you NOT to follow it. If you're a real-time kind of guy or gal, can't wait in this step frame stuff, don't want to cut a laserdisc, you'll probably want to know how the other formats stack up.

Working in IBM's analog multimedia facilities here in Atlanta, we created equal generation copies of BetaSP, SVHS, VHS, and Hi-8 tapes (see Table 7.3). The laserdisc was one generation younger than the other formats. Once again, all generations previous to the test tapes were high-bandwidth analog formats and I believe the multiple generations had no impact on the final results.

Table 7.3 Generations of test formats.

Tested Format	1st Generation	2nd Generation	3rd Generation	4th Generation
BetaSP	Filmed on BetaSP	Dubbed to 1 inch	Dubbed to BetaSP	Dubbed to BetaSP
Hi-8	Filmed on BetaSP	Dubbed to 1 inch	Dubbed to BetaSP	Dubbed to Hi-8
Laserdisc	Filmed on BetaSP	Dubbed to 1 inch	Pressed laserdisc	
SVHS	Filmed on BetaSP	Dubbed to 1 inch	Dubbed to BetaSP	Dubbed to SVHS
VHS	Filmed on BetaSP	Dubbed to 1 inch	Dubbed to BetaSP	Dubbed to VHS

We tested with three different capture boards to normalize our results. These were the Videologic DVA4000, the miroVIDEO DC1 tv, and Intel's Smart Video Recorder Pro. Here are our observations.

Videologic DVA4000

Figure 7.10 shows clipped video segments zoomed to 200% in the respective formats. Overall, the clearest, smoothest image was produced by the laserdisc, even though we couldn't step frame capture with the DVA4000

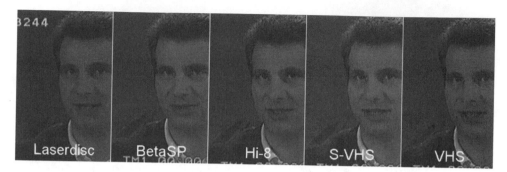

Figure 7.9   Videologic DVA4000 working with the respective formats.

because its capture application didn't provide step frame control. The best of the rest was clearly BetaSP, which showed fewer artifacts and less streaking than any other format.

Streaks on the back wall become evident with the Hi-8 video, which appears to be of slightly higher quality than the SVHS in this instance. In the original videos, SVHS showed fewer artifacts than Hi-8. However, the SVHS showed less blurring around the chin and looks better in the picture printed earlier. Overall, VHS was clearly the worst-looking image, with blotches of green in the black coat, a totally mottled back wall, and fairly apparent facial artifacts.

The respective videos are included in the Chapter 7 subdirectory of the CD-ROM as

>   DVABETA.AVI, DVAHI_8.AVI, DVASVHS.AVI, DVALASR.AVI, and DVAVHS.AVI.

miroVIDEO DC1 tv

The miro board held up surprisingly well through the first three formats with only minor differences between BetaSP, Hi-8, and SVHS. Quality for the VHS format is definitely a step below that of the other three.

In the great battle between the medians, I pick Hi-8 over SVHS both in Figure 7.11 and in the original videos. Probably wouldn't throw away my SVHS deck and buy a new Hi-8 player, however, because the quality difference is minimal.

Figure 7.10 Analog formats captured with miroVIDEO DC1 tv.

The respective videos are included in the Chapter 7 subdirectory of the CD-ROM as MIROBETA.AVI, MIROHI_8.AVI, MIROSVHS.AVI, and MIROVHS.AVI.

The Intel Smart Video Recorder Pro

No surprises here. The laserdisc again produced the cleanest back wall and most artifact-free finish. The black jacket was black through and through. The BetaSP also showed excellent color fidelity in the jacket and wall.

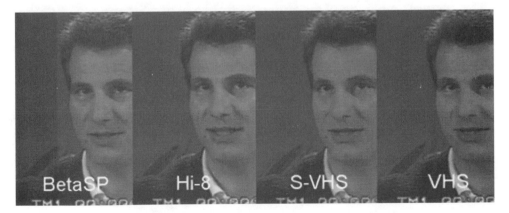

Figure 7.11 The Intel Smart Video Recorder Pro runs the analog format gauntlet.

SVHS shows less artifacts than Hi-8 but greater irregularity in the back wall. SVHS bled more green into the black coat than Hi-8. VHS clearly lags all the formats, showing gross breakup and artifacting in the face and streaking in the back wall.

Just to Prove We're Not Total Slackers

We did the same experiment with the FAST/AV Master, looking at frames converted to MPEG format Xing Technologies' software MPEG encoder, with the results shown in Figure 7.12. While the difference between the two images may not be visible in the image on the page, if you look at the source video you'll notice three things.

First, the back wall on the Hi-8 video exhibits significantly more chroma crawl, or color noise in the back wall. Second, you'll see the "Gibb's effect," a well-known JPEG artifact, around the SMPTE time codes on the bottom of the image. What's Gibb's effect? Just take a look, you'll know it when you see it. Finally, notice the mosquito artifacts around the edges on the Hi-8 side that aren't present on the BetaSP image.

Summary

What have we learned? Well, I recall a politically incorrect, not funny then, not funny now, but very appropriate kind of joke. It goes like this.

What's a six, then a seven, then an eight, then a nine, and finally a ten? The answer? A person of the opposite sex in a bar on Saturday night at 9:00 PM, 10:00 PM, 11:00 PM, 12:00 AM, and finally at 2:00 AM.

In the digital video world, it's the same question, but the answer is— your video on VHS, SVHS, Hi-8, BetaSP, and laserdisc. Clearly, your results will suffer if you capture from VHS, especially if you film in that format as well.

If you work in BetaSP, SVHS, and Hi-8, you can improve your video by transferring the video to a laserdisc and step capturing. Note, however, you can only achieve this benefit if your capture card captures raw, not compressed.

Now onto the digital side of the world.

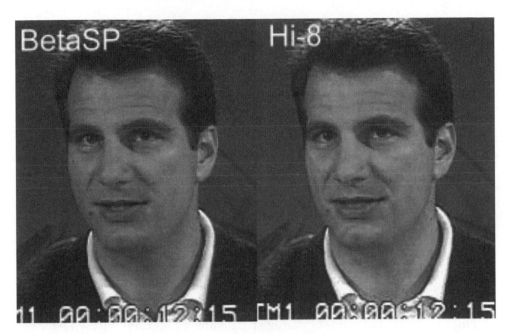

 Figure 7.12   Comparing BetaSP and Hi-8 video using the FAST AV/Master
and a software MPEG encoder.

THE DIGITAL REVOLUTION

The Digital Advantage

Digital formats store video information on tape in digital format, zeros and
ones, just like computers. This means that they *digitize* the video during
filming, converting from analog to digital between acquisition from the lens
and storage to tape. On lower end decks, this often involves compression,
usually some form of JPEG derivative. For example, Digital BetaCAM
cameras use JPEG to compress the video by approximately 2:1.

JPEG is a "lossy" compression algorithm, meaning that conversion to
JPEG format theoretically degrades video quality. Digital BetaCAM's 2:1

ratio, however, isn't noticeable in most applications. This is especially true given the unique advantages of digital formats in traditional analog activities, such as video editing, where they avoid the generation loss associated with A:B roll transitions, titling, and special effects.

Digital formats also bring unique benefits to the video compression world. As we'll see when we look at MPEG encoding systems, most MPEG service bureaus and high-end real-time capture cards convert serial digital input (SDI) from these devices digitally, like converting an AmiPro file into Word for Windows format. This makes video capture a "lossless" file conversion.

In contrast, traditional capture cards digitize by isolating each pixel in a video frame and assigning a YUV value to that pixel. This is less accurate than a direct digital conversion, creating noise that degrades compressed quality. In addition, all capture cards compress during capture, usually much more than the 4:1 compression implemented in digital cameras. This is always a lossy compression that further degrades video quality.

The problem for the average multimedia developer has always been cost. A Digital BetaCAM camera can cost upward of $60,000 and a D-1 deck $150,000 or more. Thus, while we *knew* about the benefits of digital analog formats, they were financially inaccessible.

All that changed in early 1996 when Sony introduced two low-end digital cameras, the DCR VX-1000 and DCR VX-700 digital cameras. The 3CCD VX-1000 costs around $4000, while the 1CCD VX-700 costs about $1000 less, available in discount camera stores for under $3000. Both cameras record video in digital "DV format" on DV cassettes that fit where the Hi-8 cartridges used to go. Here's what Sony says about the DV Format (all information from http://www.sel.sony.com/SEL/consumer/camcorder):

> With the new Digital Video format, your images will have more precise detail and accurate color than you ever thought possible with an analog camcorder. Because the highly advanced digital technology delivers:
>
> - 500 lines of horizontal resolution achieved by a 13.5 MHz sampling frequency (Luminance)—for a resolution higher than the NTSC TV broadcast standard.
> - Digital Component Video Recording that divides the Chrominance (color) signal into separate R-Y and B-Y signals and uses a bandwidth that carries three times as much data as analog

NTSC video. The result is a virtual elimination of color blurring.

- An innovative data compression system—Discrete Cosine Transform system (DCT)—makes it possible to record vast amounts of digital video on a small cassette.
- Time Base Correction for stable picture and minimal jitter.
- Powerful Error Correction system that compensates for tape dropout or other errors.

How's it compare to Digital BetaCAM? Check it out in Table 7.4.

Table 7.4 DV format compared to Digital BetaCAM.

	DV Format	Digital BetaCAM
Video recording system	Digital component	Digital component
Sampling frequency: luminance	13.5 MHz	13.5 MHz
Chrominance (R-Y signal)	3.375 MHz	6.75 MHz
Chrominance (B-Y signal)	3.375 MHz	6.75 MHz
Key compression type/ratio	Discrete cosine transform/approx. 5:1	Discrete cosine transform/approx. 2:1
Horizontal resolution	About 500 lines	About 500 lines
Chroma bandwidth	1.5 MHz	3 MHz
Interface	S-Video, composite, DV interface	Composite, component, SDI interface
Time code	Drop frame time code	SMPTE time code

Like Digital BetaCAM, the DV Format is *component*, which means all the nice color separation we liked in the BetaSP format. The format uses the discrete cosine transform, or DCT, the compression algorithm used in JPEG, to compress images before storing them to tape. The compression ratio is 5:1, barely beyond the 4:1 threshold that purists claim equals "no compression" at all. Overall, Sony's digital camcorders provide near Digital Beta-CAM quality specs at about 5% of the cost.

Course, it don't mean a thing if it ain't got that swing, which means that it's all useless if you can't transfer the DV formatted frames to your computer and convert them to a usable format. Being big in the music business, Sony knew this, and was also first with a capture card and software that lets you grab frames totally digitally, performing the same conversion that the higher end systems do, though for only a frame at a time.

Sony's DVBK-1000 is an ISA card with a DV connector for video transport and a Control L (LANC) protocol connector for controlling the camera during capture. Sony supplies all required cables and two software programs, Capturer and DV Viewer, that manage the conversion process.

Designed for graphics artists and Web developers, the product snaps only one frame at a time and is incapable of real-time video capture. But it serves as a taste for what is to come in early 1997, when companies like miro and Truevision launch PCI cards based on a fast new serial port specification called Firewire that can haul in 30 frames per second in real time. When someone says that your next capture card will be a serial port, this is what they mean.

We got hold of a DVBK-1000 just before deadline and decided to benchmark the digital conversion against that produced by a traditional capture card, FAST's AV/Master, reviewed next chapter. We filmed a bunch of low- and high-motion footage with the DCR VX-700 and selected two clips, a talking head clip (for those of you *already* sick of me, or at least videos of me, check out Figure 7.13) and a high-motion clip of traffic outside our offices (Figure 7.14).

Once again, the DVBK-1000 couldn't capture video, so we advanced the camera a frame at a time, captured the frame, and then moved on to the next frame. And so on, for about 900 frames over two clips. We captured audio separately and then pasted the two files together in VidEdit. Then we captured the same sequences with the AV/Master and compressed all footage to MPEG format using Xing's MPEG encoder.

Here's what we found. First and foremost is that the DCR VX-700 produced outstanding quality, with seemingly much higher contrast than the Canon A1 reviewed previously. We scanned a number of converted frames looking for JPEG artifacts, finding just a touch of blockiness on one or two frames but nothing major. Overall, color quality was extremely impressive, as was the camera's ability to maintain detail. While we can't

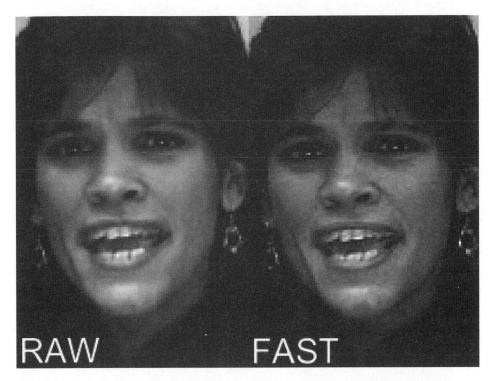

Figure 7.13   Low-motion sequence captured digitally with the DVBK-1000 and FAST AV/Master.

say that that the picture quality was up to BetaSP levels, it certainly looks very close.

In the low-motion sequence, the difference in still frame quality between the two videos is very modest, but the DVBK-1000 wins out. The difference is most noticeable in the two pictures hanging behind Lisa, especially in the grid detail in the picture on the right. When you play the video back in real time, the FAST video also looks slightly more noisy. In the high-motion sequence, the still frame quality differential is much more apparent, as is the difference between full motion quality.

So, what have we learned? Clearly, if you have a Sony Digital camera, hold off on any capture card purchases until a real-time, Firewire converter is available, which, once again, should be early 1997. These will produce the absolute best quality video.

What didn't we learn? Well, Jan's law of exponential testing (or testing gone out of control) is that once you run one test, you automatically think

Figure 7.14 High-motion sequence captured digitally with the DVBK-1000 and FAST AV/Master.

of six others that would magically illuminate six points that are much more important than those you've previously established. This rule is obviously antithetical to the publisher's law that a book in galleys is worth two in the ozone, so stop testing Jan and ship the book.

We would have liked to test the difference between the DV format, captured digitally, and first-generation BetaSP, captured through the FAST card. This would identify whether the 5:1 JPEG compression used in the DV format is more damaging than the approximation and compression incident to capturing with the AV/Master. Another test, potentially more relevant, would be capturing third- or fourth-generation BetaSP footage, since editing in analog form typically adds at least this number of generations. Oh well, maybe next edition.

You don't need any additional testing whatsoever to see that the quality of the DCR VX-7000/DVBK-1000 videos is vastly superior to that produced by the Sony TR101 and Canon A1 in Figures 7.4 and 7.5. While we can't say the quality of the compressed video is as good as that of BetaSP, the video looks really good, especially since it was shot in a convenient conference room using overhead fluorescent lighting plus one, strategically placed lamp. And you certainly have to like the new subject a heck of a lot better than the old.

SUMMARY

1. VHS, BetaSP, Hi-8, SVHS, and laserdiscs are analog filming and storage formats with different characteristics related to color information storage, lines of resolution, and signal strength. These characteristics translate directly to capture and compression performance.

2. There are three types of video signals. Component video signals maintain three separate channels for color information, which reduces video noise. The only reasonably accessible component filming format is BetaSP. S-Video signals maintain two channels, a chroma or color channel and a luminance channel for black-and-white information. This format, available on SVHS and Hi-8 formats, is cleaner than composite, which maintains one channel for

all video information. Composite formats include VHS, 8 mm, and laserdisc.

3. Signal bandwidth quantifies the strength behind the signal. If you anticipate multiple video generations, you should film with a stronger format like BetaSP or transfer lower formats to BetaSP before editing.

4. The quality of your camera and lens translates to ultimate compressed video quality. Prototype with inexpensive cameras, but shoot your final footage with as high quality a camera as possible.

5. Step frame capture avoids compression during capture. To step frame from an analog source, it must be frame accurate and computer controlled through a protocol supported by your capture software. The two most accessible step frame devices are most laserdiscs and the Sony CVD-1000 Hi-8 deck.

   Our tests revealed that step framing from a laserdisc produced superior results to real-time capture from BetaSP, proving that signal strength and color fidelity don't outweigh the negatives of double compression. If you decide to go the laserdisc route, take the following steps:

   (a) Get a CAV disk.
   (b) Request written specifications for the master analog tape from which the laserdisc will be cut. Follow them to the letter. Request a written explanation as to the advantages and disadvantages of glass versus plastic disks.
   (c) Understand your warranty.
   (d) Don't purchase a master until you're sure that filming is complete.

6. Results from the CVD-1000 showed jitter and dropout. However, single-frame video quality was excellent, and subsequent tests revealed that the analog faults could have been related to over-stressing the tape or capturing too close to the start of the tape.

   Other multimedia producers have also reported good success with this technique. Hi-8 format is much more accessible than laserdisc and you should at least experiment with this technique. Make sure you start all filming at least five minutes into the Hi-8 tape.

7. In step frame tests, a Targa 64 frame grabber produced better color fidelity but more artifacts than the Smart Video Recorder Pro.

Purchasing the more expensive card for step frame capture will not produce overall higher quality video.

8. In real-time tests performed with three different capture boards, the BetaSP format was always superior to the other three tape-based formats. Hi-8 seemed to have a slight edge over SVHS in most tests, and VHS always produced the worst results.

9. Digital formats store video information on tape in digital format, zeros and ones, just like computers. This eliminates generational loss during traditional editing activities and allows lossless capture to disk for computer-based editing or compression.

10. Sony brought digital to the masses when they introduced the 3CCD VXR-1000 ($4000) and the 1CCD VXR-700 ($3000). Both use Sony's DV format, which provides near Digital BetaCAM quality specs. Sony's DVBK-1000 ($799) capture card can grab frames in digital format from the camera and store them to disk, but captures still frames only. Real-time capture cards should be available for the Sony cameras by early 1997.

Chapter

Capture Karma

IN THIS CHAPTER

This is the capture chapter. We start by analyzing features to look for in your capture board, covering both the hardware and the software side. Then we'll review the current crop of PCI-based capture cards to see how they compare.

Along the way, we'll see that "less is often more" and that "bigger isn't always better." We'll find (with relief) that plug and play has, in fact, replaced plug and pray as the most efficient installation mantra, unless, of course, your computer mistakes a WakeBoard for an MPEGator, but that SCSI card + sound card + capture card + graphics card = no network card.

ANATOMY OF THE PERFECT CAPTURE CARD

Capture cards are multifunction tools, and a card proficient at one task won't necessarily perform as well as others. Our goal here is to identify the functions that capture cards perform and test each card's performance.

We'll be working with four cards: Digital Video Arts' WakeBoard ($995), FAST's AV/Master ($1195), miro's DC30 ($995), and Truevision's Bravado 1000 ($795). All boards are PCI based, all run under Windows 95, and, as you can see, all cost around $1000.

The following are the basic functions we'll test for.

Nonlinear Video Editing

Install any of these cards on your computer, and you can be the next Steven Spielberg, capturing video from your camcorder, editing in Premiere or MediaStudio, and sending the resultant video back out to tape to the amazement of your spouse and friends. Well, sorta, anyway. Windows 95 and the limitations of these capture cards may inject some ugly realities on your feature length movie.

First and foremost is that Windows 95's file size limitation restricts your final movie to one gigabyte (GB) in size. All of these cards capture at least 3 MB per second, or 180 MB/minute, so your finished movie can't be longer than about five minutes, surely long enough to reveal your brilliance but not long enough to really worry Mr. Spielberg.

So you'll build your movie in five-minute chunks and merge 30 chunks into your 90-minute flick? Well, not without some additional software or the visual equivalent of the eight-track tape "THUNK" between movie segments. None of these programs offer machine control, so you can't control your target deck accurately enough to place the last frame of chunk one next to the first frame of chunk two.

So what can we do with these boards? Well, within the context of a professional video editing suite you can do some pretty amazing things. The video you send back out to tape can be frames accurately edited into a cohesive whole, if you have about $15,000 in decks and deck controllers. In this situation, the $1000 capture card can perform titling, transitions, and special effects that replace a $10,000 or higher analog video editor.

In the home, you can edit your hours of vacation footage down to an exciting five minutes, and heck, that's probably all you could expect someone to watch anyway.

Performance Criteria

First and foremost is getting the frames to disk at full NTSC resolution (640×480×60 fields) at as high a quality as possible and then turning the video around and sending it back out to the deck again. Note the balancing interests here.

First, unlike capture for compression, where we capture as high a data rate as possible, compress, and distribute a much smaller digital file, here we capture a fat video file and then send it back through the capture card and out to tape. Two high-bandwidth transactions, one coming, the other going. Thus we tested both ways, determining the maximum data rate the board could sustain on our capture system to and from the hard drive.

Capture for Compression

Here we shift from full-screen, 60 fields to 30, 15, or even 10 fps at resolutions ranging from 320×240 for MPEG and AVI files to 160×120 for low-bit-rate video streamed over the Internet. Quality is king here, as well, and there are two unique capture card features that help preserve capture quality.

First is the presence of a raw capture mode. As we know, Motion JPEG is a lossy compression format that degrades video quality. When capturing full-screen, 60-field files for video editing, compression is an absolute necessity. But it's not when capturing 160×120×15 fps files for low-bit-rate conversion or perhaps even when capturing 320×240×15 fps files bound for AVI compression.

Second key is the ability to capture directly to the smaller resolutions like 160×120 in raw mode, which none of our main test boards could do. In general, when scaling from 640×480 to postage stamp size, say for Internet delivery, onboard chips using complex scaling and antialiasing algorithms produce better results than editing programs that shrink by throwing away every other pixel.

One noteworthy exception is Adobe Premiere, which in version 4.2 added the scaling algorithms from their After Effects program to come close to hardware-like performance. These capabilities notwithstanding, our ideal capture card would capture directly to all relevant capture resolutions.

Now we move toward more general capture card features.

HARDWARE FEATURES

To Get in the Game

Don't even consider a new board if it's not a PCI, plug and play, bus master board with onboard audio. Plug and play made installing all these cards bearable (don't tell my publisher) and reduces tech support calls as well. I know I'm preaching to the choir on this one, so 'nuff said.

Bus mastering takes most of the file transfer burden from the host CPU, which is how boards like the AV/Master and DC30 push 4.5 MB/s or more over the PCI bus. Since data rate usually (but not always) translates directly to video quality, more is better and bus mastering delivers more.

Onboard audio also helps push data rates up, since the CPU doesn't have to deal with all those pesky interrupts required to move digitized audio data over the antiquated ISA bus and doesn't have to interleave the streams in main memory. Speaking of interleaving, onboard audio lets you assign a random DSP or two to audio/video synching, providing more precise sound synchronization.

Another consideration is that BetaSP and similar decks output high-gain audio that can really fry cheap sound cards. Since capture cards with audio are built with these applications in mind, overall sound levels and quality will probably be better.

Jan's rule of I/O conservation is the final and a most compelling reason, at least to me. Simply stated, you can't ever be too skinny, too rich, or have too many free interrupts—you heard it here first. Both the FAST and miro boards, with onboard audio, were dreams to install, requiring only one interrupt and one memory address. In contrast, your average consumer sound cards are black holes of I/O, requiring at least two interrupts, two DMA channels, and several I/O ports, primarily because they also provide wave table and MIDI support and a joystick port. Cards like these are almost impossible to squeeze in with a capture card, SCSI card, and CD-ROM drive, and heaven forbid you should want a network card or a modem.

Input/Output

All of the reviewed boards have both S-Video and composite inputs. On future models, S-Video should be considered a minimum and component a bonus. If you're interested in video editing, you'll need a board with

VGA-to-NTSC capabilities and video out ports. Once again, all reviewed boards support both NTSC and composite outputs.

Other Hardware Features

Overlay Capabilities   Video overlay lets the capture card display video on your computer monitor in real time, useful for both capture and editing. Without video overlay, you absolutely need an NTSC monitor, adding between $300 and $800 to your setup cost. From a usability standpoint, an NTSC monitor is acceptable for capture, but not really for editing, since you're forced to look at two screens at one time, your computer monitor for moving the mouse and the NTSC monitor to watch the video. Although this is not as bad as it sounds, focusing on one screen via video overlay is vastly more preferable.

Video overlay used to be a bad word (OK, a bad phrase, but it doesn't have the same ring) because it meant a cable connector from capture card to graphics card that generally limited the color depth of the graphics card to 8-bit color or less. One card we reviewed long ago at *PC Magazine* had video overlay that limited the usable color depth on our graphics card to 16 colors, pretty nasty in itself, but ludicrous when you consider that the editing software shipped with the board—Premiere 1.0—needed 256 colors or higher. It should have been called the video Catch-22 board, because you could capture but not edit.

Today, you don't need a cable for overlay, you just need to support DirectX, which lets you send the video directly to the graphics card over the PCI bus. No muss, no fuss, and if your board is a bus master, no drain on the CPU.

There are different levels of overlay support. The Bravado doesn't support overlay at all, and anytime you look at an original video file, you're looking at the NTSC monitor. Note, however, that once you lay the video on the time line, you can see the individual frames, which Bravado and Windows have converted to bitmaps.

The only board with DirectX support is miro, which can overlay in real time, even during capture, albeit at reduced quality. Video update during editing is at full quality and virtually instantaneous. Both the WakeBoard and AV/Master support overlay through Windows Graphics Device Interface, or GDI. During capture, the video windows stop, but they do update the computer screen during editing, although rather slowly. All three boards send a signal out of their video ports during video editing, so you can use an external monitor if desired.

Data Translation's Broadway was one card that shipped with filtering that couldn't be disabled. The board got dinged in several reviews and by some of their more sophisticated users, and they put a disable feature into their first software revision.

Filtering Controls   Several boards, like the AV/Master and WakeBoard, claim to filter the incoming video, which can improve video quality in two ways. First, decimation or antialiasing filters remove the ill effects from scaling down from 720×480 to MPEG-1's 352×240 resolution, commonly seen as the jaggies in diagonal lines.

Filtering can also decrease noise in the raw video, which helps in both compression and nonlinear editing applications. Noise filters come in several flavors. Interframe or temporal noise filters analyze the differences between frames, setting thresholds to distinguish between real motion and noise. Median filters remove small, discrete data spikes in adjacent regions in a frame, like those resulting from analog dropout or other artifacts. Softening or low-pass filters average pixel values in adjacent regions.

As we'll see, filtering is often a double-edged sword, helpful for high-motion sequences but somewhat damaging in low-motion sequences like talking heads, where it blurs edges and creates a vague, gauzy-type look. In general, if filtering is strong enough to help the high-motion sequences, it's also strong enough to cause these bad effects. For this reason, when filtering is a provided, the manufacturer should also describe which filter types are used and at least the ability to enable or disable it depending on footage type.

Real Time to Usable Format/Compression Acceleration   Now we're getting along to some specialized requirements. Many publishers seek a board for prototyping or fast turn productions that captures video that can be instantly plugged into an application or presentation. In real time, the Wake-Board outputs Indeo files of surprisingly good quality at reasonable data rates, which almost in itself makes it valuable to have around.

One caveat is that Intel, with the release of Indeo video-*interactive* 4.2, enabled a "Quick" mode producing similar quality to the WakeBoard at about 6:1 compression times. This means six minutes to compress a minute of video, vastly preferable to the normal IVI compression time, roughly forever, but still quite a bit slower than real time.

One feature you should expect in the near term is compression coprocessing, or the ability to accelerate MPEG or IVI to closer to real time. This is one of the more attractive features of Data Translation's Broadway product, which, of course, can't serve as a video editor since it doesn't have video out capabilities. C-Cube, which makes Broadway's enabling chipset, also produces Motion JPEG encoders, and it wouldn't be shocking to see a more general-purpose board for nonlinear editing and MPEG encoding from one of their OEMs.

Software Features

Incoming Video Input Controls

Of all the software features we'll discuss, this is the one you shouldn't possibly do without. Probably 90% of video quality, if not more, comes from a precise adjustment of incoming brightness, contrast, and color. This fact comes to fore each capture card roundup when we capture from the same source and, despite our best efforts, end up with video clips that look vastly different.

All cards in our roundup provided incoming video adjustments, usually via a slider bar *and* precise digital values (see Figure 8.1). This second feature is incredibly important since it's almost impossible to duplicate a position on a slider bar but a digital value is simple to replicate. This will help when you're recapturing video for the fourth time in the hope of eliminating that Martian glow from your boss' face.

Note that these features, while implemented from within the capture program, actually belong to the capture card. For example, while Figure 8.1 shows the DC30's incoming controls inside VidCap 32, a screen shot taken in MediaStudio or Premiere would bring up the identical box. The same holds true with capture formats and capture resolutions, which belong to the capture card, not the editing program.

Input Resolutions

We briefly discussed the benefits of capturing directly to the intended compression resolution. Here's a list of them.

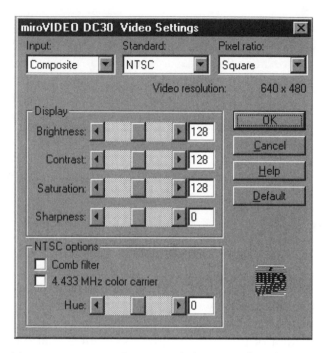

Figure 8.1   Miro's incoming video controls let you adjust brightness, contrast, saturation, and sharpness with digital readouts that help you duplicate previous efforts.

640×480: Full-screen NTSC resolution for most nonlinear video editing.

352×240: MPEG-1 standard image format (SIF), useful when encoding MPEG for display on NTSC monitors.

320×240: The standard capture format for Video for Windows AVI files, and also the "square pixel mode" for MPEG compression bound for display on computer screens.

240×180: The last bastion of CD-ROM–based video bound for low, low, low end computers, like 486/66s and lower.

176×144: The quarter common intermediate format (QCIF), the standard resolution for H.263 low-bandwidth video files produced by technologies like Vivo Interactive.

160×120: The official postage stamp–sized video that ruined digital video's good name for at least four years, now relevant for low-bandwidth video like VDO's and Iterated Systems.

Raw Capture Formats

Most capture cards implement some form of lossy compression to squeeze the incoming video down to bandwidths than can be stored to disk in real time. As we've seen, however, the flip side of lossy compression is degraded image quality.

As we'll see in the next chapter, some analog devices can deliver a discrete frame of video to the capture card in nonreal time, allowing the system time to store the frame before asking for another. In these instances, quality is maximized if the capture card can capture in uncompressed format. In addition, at certain video configurations like 160×120×15 fps, most PCI buses can support uncompressed capture data rates. If you plan to work with these types of analog formats or capture low-bandwidth video for streaming Internet delivery, raw capture formats are a big plus.

External Device Control

On a related note, higher end products offer external device control to supplement the VISCA and laserdisc controls included with Windows 95. External device control is helpful not only for step capture but also for more precise starts and stops during capture and batch capture of multiple clips.

Video Offset Controls

If you look closely at some of the videos in this chapter, you'll see several lines of black pixels along the bottoms or the sides of the video window. This happens when the analog source doesn't precisely synch up with the capture board. On the MPEG side of the house, several cards provide video offset controls that let you adjust the position of the video in the window. This would be a great feature not currently offered by any of the boards in this review.

Editing and Capture Software

We cover editing programs in detail in Chapter 11. Although most editing programs also include capture capabilities, several capture cards also include a 32-bit version of VidCap, Microsoft's venerable capture program from the original Video for Windows application suite. Not only does VidCap load faster, it's also much more straightforward, and I use it for most capture tasks.

CAPTURE CARD REVIEWS

As promised, here are our thoughts on four capture cards: FAST's AV/Master, Truevision's Bravado, miro's DC30, and Digital Video Arts' WakeBoard. A few words about our results and how we tested before getting started.

Nonlinear Editing

We tested nonlinear editing with a three-minute BetaSP video segment composed of six separate clips, each starting and stopping with a sharp cut and separated by three seconds of black. We captured at 60 fields per second for all boards, at 640×480 for the AV/Master and Bravado. The DC30 offers a clipping mode that eliminates television overscan, reducing the capture resolution from 640×480 to 608×456. We captured in 320×480 resolution with the WakeBoard, the only resolution capable of 60 fields per second capture.

We started capture at each board's rated bandwidth capacity, dropping the data rate by 100 KB/s until the board dropped 10 frames or less over the life of the clip. We found 10 frames acceptable because most boards dropped the initial frame of each new sequence regardless of actual capture rate.

After capturing successfully, we attempted to write the video segment back out to Hi-8 format. If the board dropped significant frames when writing to tape, we started the process over, dropping the data rate by 100 KB/s until the board stopped dropping frames. Capture and playback results are shown in Table 8.1.

We compared the technologies by playing the Hi-8 tape back out to a ProScan 20-inch color television set. We also compared seven frames captured from each video stream in side-by-side comparisons on the computer. The results are presented in Table 8.2.

We tested sound synchronization by capturing a 10-minute talking head segment with each board, writing the resultant file back out to tape and playing the tape. None of the boards showed any tendency to lose synchronization.

You should note that for the top three boards—FAST, miro, and Truevision—the difference in these tests was very, very minor, and the difference between first and third is very much smaller than the raw scores would indicate. In general, Bravado won because its video was slightly less noisy than the AV/Master and colors slightly brighter and more vivid than the DC30.

As we'll see, however, video quality often relates more to equalizing the incoming video by adjusting color and brightness controls than actual board quality. While we tried to reflect this in our scoring, it's awfully difficult to do. Between these three boards, it's entirely possible that if we had spent numerous additional hours fiddling, the results may have been different.

On the other hand, the WakeBoard was a distant fourth, clearly outmatched by the task. While all of the top three boards were clearly capable of professional quality editing, if not broadcast quality, WakeBoard wasn't and probably should be avoided if nonlinear editing is a major job requirement.

Capture for Compression

We tested capture for compression with three separate clips, one talking head shot from a Hi-8 deck, the same talking head from a BetaSP deck, and

Table 8.1 Maximum capture rates.

	AV/Master	Bravado 1000	DC30	WakeBoard
Resolution	640×480	640×480	608×456	352×480
Maximum capture	4.3 MB	2.8	5.1	1700
Maximum output	4.3 MB	2.8	4.8	1000

Table 8.2 Nonlinear editing comparisons.

	AV/Master	Bravado 1000	DC30	WakeBoard
Still frame quality	2	1	3	4
Real-time playback	2	1	3	4

a 30-second action sequence. We compressed each clip with Xing Technologies Software MPEG Encoder and Radius' Cinepak codec.

In round-robin testing, we compared each clip to every other, focusing on both still frame quality, where we evaluated five frames from each clip, and real-time playback quality, essentially evaluating the extent of background noise and interframe distortion. The results are presented in Table 8.3.

In the capture for compression tests, all boards were very close, including the WakeBoard. In general, miro won because its files had less visible background noise, although it lost points on the talking head sequence because of filtering that blurred the face.

Once again, FAST got dinged by a little extra noise in the video but clearly performed well overall. Bravado also produced excellent compressed quality, either tying for first or placing second in all four tests. Bravado's Cinepak clips tended to be a bit grainy at times, although color fidelity was excellent. WakeBoard was exceptionally sharp in detail, but the color was marred by subtle green shading that feels typical of Indeo-driven capture

Table 8.3 Capture for compression evaluations.

	AV/Master	Bravado 1000	DC30	WakeBoard
Cinepak				
Still	2	3	1	4
Motion	2	3	1	4
MPEG				
Still	3	2	1	4
Motion	1 (tie)	1 (tie)	1 (tie)	4

devices. Given time, we may have been able to clear these out, but we couldn't within the time constraints of the book.

These clips are included on the CD-ROM and many of you may have different thoughts on the rankings. Oh, well, that's why we included them. You should know going in that any of these boards should perform very well in capture for compression tasks, which makes the usability rankings all that more important.

FAST AV/MASTER

FAST Electronics, Inc.

FAST's $1099 AV/Master is a big bandwidth board that produced high-quality video, placing second in our nonlinear editing tests and tying for first in MPEG compression quality. Easy to install and operate, the AV/Master should be a strong candidate for all video capture applications.

The AV/Master is a plug and play, bus master card with support for both audio and video. The full-length board features a cutaway design that eases installation in slots bordered by heat sinks. FAST designed in the Zoran 36050 chipset, with a maximum throughput of around 5 MB/s, with stereo quality audio provided by Analog Device's SoundComm 9605. A separate ASIC provides hardware audio/video locking for rock-solid AV synch. In terms of I/O, given the onboard audio, it was a welcome surprise that the AV/Master required only one interrupt and one memory address.

The AV/Master supports NTSC, PAL, and SECAM standards and includes connectors for S-Video and composite video input/output and stereo audio I/O. The board ships with Ulead's competent MediaStudio 2.5 video editing software, Crystal Graphics Flying Fonts LE, and a 32-bit version of Microsoft's venerable VidCap capture program, still the favorite of many video developers. FAST also provides MediaCache, a proprietary program that smoothes AVI playback jitters when writing video back out to tape. S-Video and composite cables and stereo minicables round out the product bundle.

Installation was simple, with Windows 95 recognizing the board and requesting the required drivers. Two diskettes contain all basic programs with MediaStudio provided on a separate CD-ROM.

Capture Controls

During capture, data rate is controlled by a single horizontal slider bar with digital readouts of frame size, per second, and per minute data rate at the various capture locations. The slider is overlaid over a bar with green, orange, and red zones representing capture rates that are safe, aggressive, and probably too high for the capture drive. The color keys were supposed to change according to the capacity of the capture drives, but we noticed no change when toggling between drives despite fairly dramatic capacity difference. Capture rates range from 6.9 MB/s, way in the red zone, to a skimpy 0.3 MB/s (Figure 8.2). Screen updates change according to the quality setting, so you can preview quality before capture.

There are only two resolution settings, "capture both fields," which automatically defaults to full screen, and "capture for MPEG or AVI conversion," which switches to 320×240 resolution. Slider bars with digital values adjust the hue, brightness, contrast, and saturation of the incoming video, with changes reflected in real time. Audio capture rate is controlled by the familiar Media Recorder dialog box that lets you select either 8, 11, 22, or 44 Hz, all in 16-bit stereo.

Before capture, the AV/Master updates the screen every tenth frame. This slows dramatically during capture. Preview in the capture window before actually starting capture was acceptable, but during capture you get much better results when you turn off the preview, so you'll need an external NTSC monitor for precise start and stop times.

Capture/Editing Performance

Several times during various test captures, the board sputtered, simply stopping to capture frames while continuing to capture audio. The program didn't crash but spread the actual captured frames ratably over the captured audio sequence, creating a file with a frame rate well below the target. This usually happened early in the capture; once you got past the first 800 frames you were safe.

FAST technical support hadn't heard of the problem before and guessed that this related to edit points in our clip that somehow diverged from the NTSC specification. We couldn't verify or disprove this claim, but no other board exhibited the same tendencies.

The AV/Master tended to drop frames after quick cuts, when the quantization compression table changes dramatically, which was expected. At

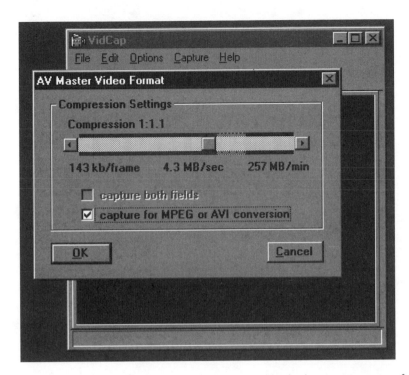

Figure 8.2   The color-coded slider bar tells you which data rates are safe
(green), which are touchy (orange), and which are probably too
high for the board and drive (red).

higher data rates, the board also seemed to hiccup occasionally, dropping
two or three frames at a time, creating noticeable gaps and breaks during
playback. After dropping 15 frames at 4.5 MB/s, the AV/Master settled
down to an acceptable eight dropped frames at 4.3 MB/s, which was our
test bandwidth for nonlinear editing.

Moving the clip in Premiere's clip window was a bit jerky, making it
difficult to find the initial frame of the sequence. Heavy users will benefit
from running a monitor from the card's composite output port, since the
screen updates are so much faster from the card than through Windows to
the graphics card.

To output to tape, you simply load the file in Media Player or similar
application and start playing the file. During this process, the video is
transferred directly from the AV/Master to the target deck, and the com-

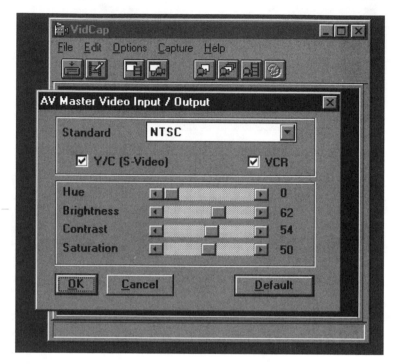

Figure 8.3   FAST's incoming color control screen.

puter screen is not updated. This makes an external NTSC monitor extremely useful, if not essential.

Capture Quality

The only visible degradation in FAST's nonlinear output was a touch more noise both in the background and on foreground dark surfaces. Detail was extremely well maintained. We also noticed some problems with color, with chroma crawl throughout the video with touches of pink frequently showing through. Black sequences between clips were very noisy as well, making us wish that we had lowered brightness during capture.

The AV/Master captured 2.2 MB/s in our 30 fps, 320×240 capture for compression tests, the highest of any card. FAST rated third in our Cinepak compression tests, with slightly grainy video marred by random pink and red tinges in the backgrounds of sequences. FAST improved to tie for first in our MPEG compression tests, producing artifact-free video with clear backgrounds and crisp details.

I had the benefit of working with the AV/Master for the better part of three months, using it to capture all the clips for the software MPEG tests and many other uses. In all instances, the card was extremely stable and integrated well into our production workstation, which included both network and SCSI cards, and played a big part in convincing me that onboard audio is essential, if only for ease of integration. The card also produced top-quality video in all applications, and I recommend the card without reservation.

 Tour the AV/Master interface by clicking on Fst_tour.avi. Sample files are Fst_cp.avi and Fst_mpg.avi.

TRUEVISION BRAVADO 1000

Truevision, Inc.

Let's be honest—we prefer capture cards with onboard audio because they're easier to install, push higher data rates, and help ensure audio/video synchronization. That said, Truevision's Bravado 1000's David-like data rates produced better looking video in our nonlinear tests than the Goliath numbers produced by FAST and miro, and at $799 Bravado was our cheapest board by $200. Bravado also performed well on capture for compression tests and showed no signs of audio drift in our 10-minute A/V synch tests.

The Bravado 1000 is a plug and play, bus master card with video capture provided by Zoran's 36050 chip but no audio capabilities. The full-length card doesn't have a cutaway design like the AV/Master, which forced us to swap the PCI boards in our test system because the only open slot was limited by the processor and heat sink. We also didn't like the absence of the always helpful input/output labels on the back bracket.

Installing Bravado was very simple, but only after installing a separate sound card, which proved much more complex. After trying three cards, the Ensonic plug and play board that shipped with our test bed computer, a Turtle Beach Tahiti, and an old Microsoft Sound System card, we settled on a Creative Labs SoundBlaster PnP, which—shades of reviews past—still forced us to remove our network adapter and required us to manually change the interrupt settings in our Windows 95 Device Manager. In contrast, both the miro and FAST boards installed without incident and without removing any other peripherals.

Capture Controls

The Bravado 1000 supports NTSC, PAL, and SECAM and is configured with one S-Video and two composite inputs and an S-Video and composite output. Truevision ships drivers for Windows 3.11/NT/95 and should have Mac support by the end of 1996. The software offering is rather austere, consisting solely of Adobe Premiere 4.2, but no VidCap 32, disk bench marking software, or other analog device control software. Truevision also supplies no audio or video cables, so be sure to pick some up when you purchase the board.

Bravado captures in four resolutions, 320×240, 320×480, 640×240 and 640×480. You have four options to set the data rate from the obscure bits per pixel and compressed field size to the familiar data rate or compression ratio. Expressed in terms of KB/s, the incoming data rate must range between 75 and 3600 KB/s, pushing the theoretical limit of the Zoran chip. Since Truevision provides no benchmarking utilities to check hard disk capacity, capture was a trial-and-error process.

Bravado lets you adjust incoming brightness, contrast, saturation, and hue, providing digital values to help reproduce our results. Software also controls incoming video source, allowing you to switch easily between any of three analog sources.

During preroll, the video previews slowly in the capture window, working through GDI. Preview stops at capture, however, forcing you to use an external NTSC monitor. Once captured to disk, Bravado displays only on an external NTSC monitor, a big disadvantage against cards like the DC30 that display via Direct Draw, eliminating the need for an external monitor.

Capture Performance

Like the FAST AV/Master, the Bravado tended to drop one or two frames when hitting a fast cut from black into a new scene during major scene changes, which stress the Zoran Motion JPEG compression chipset. This may tend to make drop frames less noticeable than frames dropped during a high-motion sequence or even talking head. Even at 2 MB/s, the board dropped an occasional frame, so we used the first setting that dropped less than 10 frames over the three-minute clip, which was 2.8 MB/s.

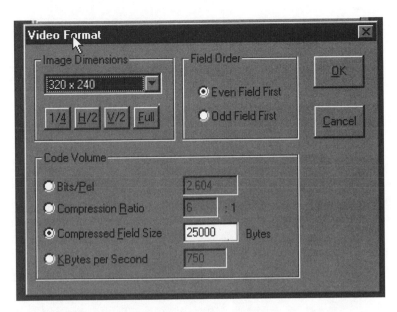

Figure 8.4   Bravado provides four data rate options, two rather obscure, the other two useful.

Working in Premiere felt a touch more responsive than FAST AV/Master, but not significantly more, and any efficiencies could relate more to warming to the task than Bravado's acceleration. As with the AV/Master, you output to tape by playing the clip in Media Player and pressing "record" in your target deck. Unlike some other boards, it felt as if the video was leaping off the disk onto the awaiting tape, with the tapes playing smoothly with no evidence of dropped frames.

Capture Quality

Working with codecs like Cinepak, I've seen where higher compressed data rates actually created additional noise that detracted from playback quality. In this review, the Bravado, at roughly 66% the data rate of other competitors, seemed to work the same way, exhibiting less noise than the other boards while maintaining good detail and striking colors that seemed to jump off the screen of our ProScan television. Remarkably, Bravado won both still image and real-time nonlinear editing competitions, although, once again, margins were extremely small.

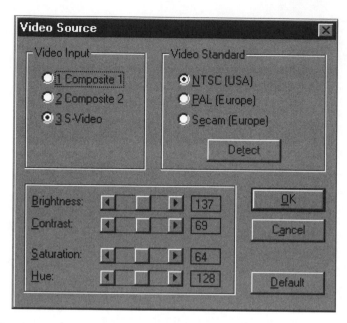

Figure 8.5 Bravado's incoming video adjustments.

Bravado also produced excellent compressed quality, especially with Xing's MPEG, where it tied for first in moving quality and placed second in still frame. When compressed with Cinepak, Bravado's video tended to be a bit grainy at times, although color fidelity was excellent and background noise minimal. Bravado also had more trouble working with the lower quality Hi-8 format, producing noisier video than either the FAST or miro boards. On the other hand, despite the lack of onboard audio, Truevision had no problem with audio/video synchronization, with synch remaining rock solid at the end of our 10-minute test clip.

Overall, Bravado performed very well, and at $799 it was our cheapest board by $200. You're absolutely going to need an NTSC monitor, however, making up this difference and more. In addition, like the old "three on a match" warning in World War I—one to sight, two to aim, and three to fire—it seems like your fourth plug and play peripheral, especially if it's an ISA-based sound card, always causes problems, forcing you to either pull other cards or manually adjust your system configuration. Call it a bias, call it unreasonable, call it subjective, but I like capture cards with audio because they're easier to install and maintain in a fully loaded system.

Tour the Bravado capture controls by clicking on bra_tour.avi. Sample files are bra_cp.avi and bra_mpg.avi.

MIROVIDEO DC30

miro Computer Products, Inc.

Miro computer products has a well-deserved reputation for producing affordable, top-quality video capture cards, and their latest product offering, the $999 miroVIDEO DC30, will enhance this status. The DC30 pushed the highest data rate of all cards and was the overall winner in our capture for compression tests. Although miro's product faired less well in our nonlinear editing comparisons, the board is the easiest to install, fast and responsive during editing, and an excellent choice for virtually all video capture tasks.

The DC30 is a three-quarter length, plug and play bus master card with video capture provided by the Zoran 36050 chip, and 48-kHz, 16-bit stereo audio capture via the Analog Devices SoundComm 9605 chip. Onboard DSPs also accelerate the display of video thumbnails, preview, and final rendering.

The card supports NTSC, PAL, and SECAM and contains S-Video and composite in and out jacks and a custom audio connector leading to four labeled stereo in and out jacks. Miro includes Adobe Premiere 4.2 deluxe edition with custom presets, VidCap32, and Asymetrix 3D/FX, but no additional software for analog deck control. Miro doesn't supply *any* audio or video cables, so run a quick inventory and pick up any additional cables when you buy the board. Remember you'll need inbound and outbound audio and video cables for nonlinear editing and transfer back to tape.

The CD-ROM–based installation was simple and slick. Windows 95 recognized the board, installed the drivers, and, after rebooting, installed the miro programs and Premiere presets. Then the miroVIDEO DC30 configuration program automatically loads to test all board functions, the PCI video overlay system, and hard drive capacity.

Overall, a very impressive installation.

System resources are nominal, with the board requiring only one interrupt and one memory address. An interesting comparison is the miroVIDEO

DC1, an ISA capture board we reviewed in the first book. Without audio, the DC1 required an I/O address, video memory range, interrupt, and DMA channel and miro provided no diagnostics to help you along the way. Maybe there's something to this plug and play stuff, after all.

Capture Controls

Miro's resolution configuration screen is visually complex but full featured, providing a range of capture inputs from a high of 640×480×60 fields to 288×216×30 frames. The board supports 320×240 capture, useful for AVI and square pixel MPEG, and 352×240 resolution, normal SIF resolution for MPEG files played on NTSC monitors.

The board supports cropping, which you can use to remove overscan areas that aren't usually seen anyway from the top, bottom, and sides, preserving data rate for the on-screen segments. We performed all of our tests cropping out the television overscan, reducing the normally 640×480 screen down to 608×456.

Miro provides slider bars for adjusting incoming brightness, contrast, saturation, and sharpness with digital values. If you use composite video, miro provides a Comb filter, which helps clean up signal quality.

Miro includes a disk analysis utility called the miroVIDEO EXPERT that determines the maximum input/output capacity of your various hard drives and suggests a maximum capture data rate. Our fastest drive rated at 6219 write and 6085 read, which translated to a reachable video data rate of 4851 KB/s. Miro stores this information and sends a message when your target capture rates exceed drive capacity. Working within the "green" zone, or within the rates computed by miro, minimized capture and writing to tape errors.

Miro includes a control program that toggles output between your graphics card, via Direct Draw, for use during preroll and your video out port for writing the finished video to tape. There is also an "overlay" mode for use during capture that displays a pixelated version of the video sufficient in quality to eliminate the need for an external NTSC monitor.

Capture and Editing Performance

The full potential of the board was somewhat limited by the fact that data rates varied by content. On our 5 MB/s clip, most of which played back without a problem, there was a low-motion segment that inexplicably

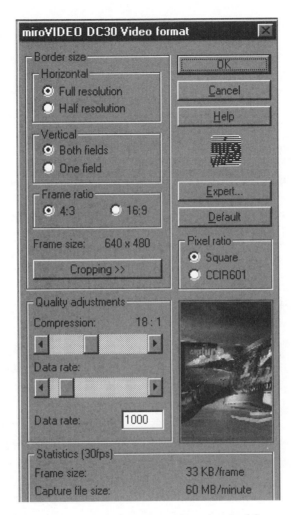

Figure 8.6   The DC30's capture screen packs a load of functionality in a slightly busy interface.

bounced the data rate up to around 5300 KB/s, too high for playing back. This forced us to either recompress the entire movie to 5 MB/s, and risk the degrading effect of double compression, or capture at a lower rate, which is what we did, finally settling in at 4.8 MB/s.

We also experienced some minor anomalies with the DC30's onboard audio control, which seemed stuck at one of two levels—too low and too high. This made it difficult to work with analog sources without volume control.

On the other hand, editing in Premiere was pure joy, as the board was very responsive with virtually no hesitation between mouse click and action. This is a welcome change from other boards and, if you spend a lot of time editing video, a very relevant differentiator.

Capture Quality

The DC30's quality performance was puzzling, once again along the lines of the "less is more" concept. In nonlinear editing, where its data rate was by far the highest, miro placed third behind both the Bravado and AV/Master. Once again, the differences were minor, but bigger certainly wasn't better.

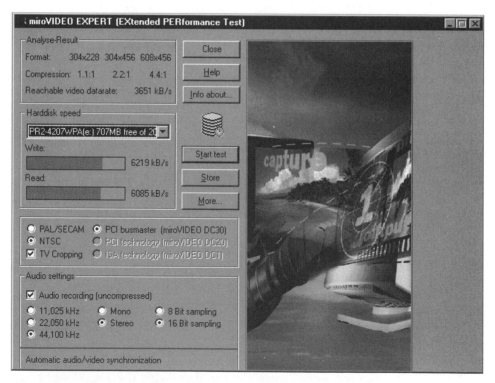

Figure 8.7   Miro's excellent hard disk benchmarking utility saves time by isolating the maximum data rates for capture.

At our 320×240, 30 fps capture configuration, capture bandwidth was limited to 1500 KB/s, in contrast to the 2.2 MB/s produced by the AV/Master. Nonetheless, the DC30 was our top performer in both the MPEG and Cinepak compression tests, placing first in all moving video and still image comparisons.

If you work with a lot of talking head sequences, you're going to wish that miro provided the opportunity to turn off some of the filtering that appears to happen during capture, which caused some blurring. On the whole, however, miro's clips resisted noise and random discoloration much better than the other codecs.

Working with the DC30 is not for the meek or unwary. You'll need 32 MB for RAM to optimize DC30 performance—with only 16 MB installed, we couldn't write even 3.5 MB/s files to tape without noticeable jerks. You'll also have to disable the write behind cache and disable write ahead optimization, both fairly simple to do, but more than what's required from the other boards, which pretty much work out of the box.

On the other hand, Ferrari owners typically don't complain about maintenance issues or small operational quirks, they just kind of smile and talk about performance. The DC30 is clearly the exotic car of the bunch and definitely worth the extra effort.

 Tour the DC30 interface by clicking on DC30_tour.avi. Sample files are DC30_cp.avi and DC30_mpg.avi.

WAKEBOARD

Digital Video Arts

Digital Video Arts' WakeBoard is unique in its ability to capture directly to an Indeo video-interactive file that can be used instantly for prototyping and publishing. In more traditional capture activities, WakeBoard performed reasonably well in capture for compression tests, though ranking behind all other boards, but was totally outmatched by our nonlinear editing tests.

WakeBoard supports both NTSC and PAL and comes configured with unlabeled S-Video and composite inputs and outputs. For about $995 you get the board plus Premiere LE. The more expensive model, estimated street prices of $1495, comes with the deluxe version of Premiere, Crystal Graphics Flying Fonts Pro 3.0, and Caligari trueSpace 2.

WakeBoard is a plug and play, bus master half-card powered by the 8×8 MEP chip. Unlike most other capture boards, the WakeBoard is powered by Wavelets, rather than Motion JPEG, and offers both compressed and uncompressed modes.

WakeBoard doesn't have audio, and we ran into the same kind of sound card problems we experienced with the Bravado—e.g., rollup sleeves, remove network card, manually set configuration options like interrupts.

We also ran into a totally unexpected case of mistaken identity when our computer recognized the WakeBoard as the MPEGator and kept installing the wrong drivers. We briefly pondered the cosmic significance and irony of a real-time Indeo capture card being confused with a real-time MPEG card and then installed updated drivers in the system properties dialog box.

Capture Controls

WakeBoard is the only board that can capture real time in Indeo video-interactive format, although supporting only key and delta frames (I, P frames) but not IVI's bidirectional interpolated frames (B frames). Configurations supported in this capture mode are 320×240 at a maximum frame rate of 24 fps and 160×120 up to 30 fps. Advanced controls during IVI capture include key frame interval and compression ratio, from a low of 1.3:1 to a high of 9.3:1.

WakeBoard also supports Intel's YVU9 mode, an uncompressed mode capable of 320×240 at 15 fps, ideal for MPEG encoding, and higher resolutions to 640×480 at slower frame rates. YVU9 isn't a lossy compression format, so there are no data rate options with this format; the capture program simply encodes all incoming video in this format, dropping frames if data rates get too high. Unfortunately, the minimum resolution for YVU9 capture was 320×240, which was too large for direct capture in a low-bit-rate format at 30 frames per second.

Wake Video is a proprietary hardware codec tied to the 8×8 chip used for big frame, high frame rate capture for applications like nonlinear editing. WakeBoard's maximum capture rate for fields, however, is 320×480×60 fields, or half-width NTSC, with horizontal pixels being duplicated when writing to tape. Capture rates range from 250 KB/s to 3 MB/s.

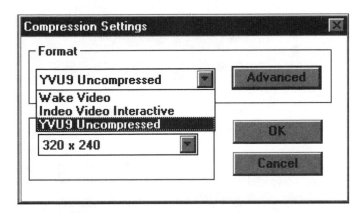

Figure 8.8   WakeBoard is the only product that captures
in uncompressed format, producing exceptionally
clear video.

Of the three capture formats, Wake Video is the only one that requires the
board installed for further editing.

Incoming video input controls include saturation, brightness, contrast,
gain, and hue, controlled by slider bars with digital readouts, and buttons
for switching between composite and S-Video capture and NTSC and PAL.
Program controls don't make it clear when you're capturing frames versus
fields. Apparently, you capture fields in only one mode—Wake Video at
320×480, but this appears to be stated only in the manual.

Capture Performance

As with the other boards, we started capturing for nonlinear editing at
WakeBoard's theoretical maximum of 3 MB/s, dropping down by 100 KB/s
at each failure. We got nervous until we reached 1700, when the board
captured smoothly but couldn't output to tape without significant dropped
frames.

A quick call to technical support produced their recommendation to try
1200 KB/s, which still exhibited some shudders, as did the 10-minute clip,
captured at 1050 KB/s. Given the degraded quality experienced even at
these levels, it's tough to recommend this board for NLE.

In addition, editing Wake Video felt sluggish, with the board taking a
couple of extra seconds to set up for all operations, including capture and
editing. This forced you to work slowly and deliberately, which became

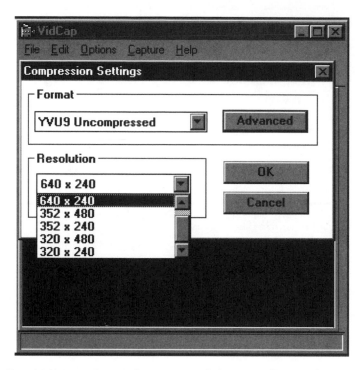

Figure 8.9 WakeBoard's resolution control doesn't tell you when you're capturing frames versus fields.

frustrating at times. Operation also was a touch unstable, and we had to reboot the computer several times after capturing. At one point, we lost use of the keyboard from within Premiere, which prevented us from saving a project or creating a title. Premiere crashed repeatedly when attempting to create a title to send out to tape.

Although the last-place finish was the same, WakeBoard's performance in the capture for compression tests was much closer to that of the top three boards. While WakeBoard's images were typically sharper than those of the other boards, especially in the talking head shots, frames were marred by subtle green tinges that we couldn't eliminate via the incoming color controls.

Cinepak footage was also a bit noisier than with the other boards, especially when capturing Hi-8 footage, which manifested as chroma crawl in the backgrounds and slight artifacts in the face. MPEG footage was strikingly crisp but again rated downward because of noticeable green traces throughout the video, especially in Hi-8 footage.

Real-time capture to Indeo video interactive format was much more promising. At 320×240 resolution and at 15–24 frames per second, we captured video from 180 to 220 KB/s, with very good results. Video quality was impressive, with minimal background noise or artifacts. Unlike Intel's venerable Smart Video Recorder Pro, which captured only key frames, WakeBoard also captures P frames, making the video instantly usable for publishing or prototyping.

WakeBoard's YVU format was also very crisp, although not capable on our system of 30 fps at 320×240 mode. We compressed a 15-fps file to Cinepak format, and it compared very well against the leaders in sharpness, once again getting dunned for the slight green tinges.

The capture card market is a tough battleground, and miro, FAST, and Truevision are experienced competitors. Standing alone, the WakeBoard is an impressive first product, with a unique capture to final format capability that may in itself justify the purchase for short-run jobs and prototyping. Compared to the other products, however, the WakeBoard is clearly outmatched in nonlinear editing and probably one software driver update from competing in capture for compression.

Happily, Digital Video Arts issued a software update as we finished our testing, targeted at the stability issues described above. With careful tweaking of the incoming video adjustments, you may now have the ability to produce exceptionally crisp video unmarred by the green flecks that we experienced.

 Tour the WakeBoard feature set by clicking on Wake_tour.avi. Sample files are Wake_cp.avi and Wake_mpg.avi.

The Future

We touched on this briefly in the last chapter, but in two or three years most low-end cameras will be completely digital like the Sony Digital Handy-Cam (DCR-VX700), and capture cards will be firewire-based cards that convert from Sony's or Panasonic's format to AVI files. By early 1997, miro and Truevision will have shipped Firewire cards for Sony and Panasonic, respectively, that cost about the same as their current cards but deliver much more flawless quality.

Of course, we need tools to produce video today and tomorrow, as well as in three years, and it's definitely time to trade in your Smart Video Recorder. Just remember that a whole new breed of inexpensive tools is on the horizon, and that you'll probably be switching over to them before the new millennium.

SUMMARY

Company	Miro	TrueVision	Digital Video Arts	FAST
Product	DC30	Bravado 1000	WakeBoard	AV/Master
Price	$999	$799	$995 est'd street	$1,099
Operating systems	Windows 95	Win 3.1/95/ NT/Mac (10/96)	Windows 95	Windows 95
Video standards	NTSC/PAL/ SECAM	NTSC/PAL/ SECAM	NTSC/PAL	NTC/PAL/ SECAM
Bundled software	Adobe Premiere 4.2 deluxe edition, Asymetrix 3D/FX	Adobe Premiere 4.2 deluxe edition	Adobe Premiere Deluxe, Crystal Graphics Flying Fonts Pro, Caligari TrueSpace II	MediaStudio 2.5 VE, Crystal Graphics Flying Fonts 3.01 LE, VidCap 32
Hardware				
Plug and play	yes	yes	yes	yes
Bus master	yes	yes	yes	yes
Burst DMA		yes	yes	yes
Compression chipset	Zoran 36050	Zoran 36055	8×8 MEP	Zoran 36050
Audio/video/ both	Both	Video only	Video only	Both
VGA > NTSC	yes	yes	yes	yes

Company	Miro	TrueVision	Digital Video Arts	FAST
Video I/O	S-Video/ composite in/out	Two composite and S-Video in/composite out	S-Video/ composite in/out	S-Video/or composite in/S-Video and composite out
Audio I/O	Stereo in/out	no	n.a.	Stereo in/out
Hardware A/V sync	yes	no	no	yes
Accelerated transitions	yes	no	no	yes
Preview mechanism	Direct Draw	All NTSC—external monitor only	Direct Draw/NTSC	Inlay—signal to VGA card (GDI)
Accelerated compression	no	no	no	no

Software

Capture resolutions	640×480×60 fields to 288×216×30 frames	320×240, 320×480, 640×240, and 640×480	Format dependent, from 160×120 to 640×480	640×480/ 320×240
Deck control	In Premiere	In Premiere	In Premiere	MediaStudio
Incoming video adjustments	Brightness/ contrast/ saturation/ sharpness	Brightness/ contrast/ hue/saturation		Hue/brightness/ contrast/ saturation
Deck control	In Premiere	In Premiere	In Premiere	MediaStudio
Disk benchmarking	yes	no	no	yes
Uninstall	yes	Manual	no	yes

Capture formats

Compressed	Motion JPEG	Motion JPEG	WakeVideo (proprietary), IVI Key/Delta, no B)	Motion JPEG
Raw	no	no	YUV 9 raw	none

Chapter 9

Surviving Your Capture Board Installation

INTRODUCTION

Installing a capture card in a Windows 3.1x system involved a familiar, but very inefficient technique called plug and pray. Windows 95, along with Intel and a bunch of happily compliant vendors, brought about a new paradigm, plug and play. Never in the history of computing has one consonant made such a difference.

As I mentioned in a recent *PC Magazine* article (have to name drop a little bit, plus it probably got cut!), plug and play (PnP) has taken the whole "don't try this at home" feel from the video capture arena. So much so that we almost left this chapter out. But then I started thinking about some of the wonderful surprises and experiences that I've had with Windows 95 and decided to write the chapter, even if only to tell the stories. What can I say—book's been short on new stories (so far).

Like the time that I installed the Digital Video Arts WakeBoard and Windows 95 thought it was the MPEGator. Kept installing and uninstalling both boards, to no avail. Or the first time I got a message that Windows 95 couldn't automatically configure all of the plug and play devices installed on the system. "What do you mean you can't configure all the PnP devices?" I thundered silently to myself. "Your ads never mentioned this one." Or the time I caught my first computer virus.

They say that anything that doesn't kill you makes you stronger. Learning to work with a new OS—no matter how well designed and executed—well, I'm just surprised we don't all look like Arnold Schwarzenegger.

Since you've read this far into the introduction (thank you very much), I'll pass along Jan's amazing fact number one about Windows 95. You can actually still run File Manager, the old Windows 3.1x file system, under Windows 95. Just push Start\Run, then type "winfile" in the open line and press OK. Should come right up.

When I first met Windows 95 Explorer, I spent four hours trying to figure out how to open up multiple windows. Can't do it. Then I spent a couple of hours trying to make the computer show me file extensions, like AVI, BAT, or TIF. Figured that out. Then I spent a couple of hours trying to figure out how to show file sizes down to the byte level, instead of being rounded to the nearest 1 K. Couldn't do that.

I don't mean to sound parochial or small minded, but multiple windows and these file details were crucial to how I work, so I was about to remove Windows 95. Throw it out, along with my entire collection of Rolling Stones CD-ROMs. Then Steve the Video Genius told me about File Manager. "Heck," he said, "you can even run Program Manager, they're both 16-bit programs." I left Windows 95 on the computer, and the rest, as they say, is history.

PLUG AND PLAY

The goal of PnP is to automatically assign each peripheral the required input/output resources and resolve any conflicts between cards. Let's have a quick look at what these resource requirements are.

Interrupts, I/O Ports, and DMA Channels (Oh My!)

Interrupts are signal lines used by peripherals to notify the CPU that it needs attention. You've heard the term "interrupt driven"? For the most part, the host CPU goes merrily along on its way, doing what processors do, until some function in the computer "interrupts" and says "hey, I need something." This need could be video capture, a mouse movement, a modem transfer, or whatever.

Computers have 16 interrupts, which sounds like plenty until you realize that totally mundane devices like modems, keyboards, mice, floppy drives, and similar peripherals all need one. As do infinitely cooler devices like network cards, SCSI cards, sound boards, and CD-ROM drives. Then 16 starts to sound like way too few, which about describes it for most video capture stations.

DMA stands for Direct Memory Access line. DMA channels are the data paths to and from system memory. Most computers have eight DMA channels, which is usually more than sufficient.

I/O ports or addresses are areas of memory used by the CPU to communicate with and identify the various peripherals. Your computer has plenty of I/O ports and typically won't run out—problems will arise only if two devices are placed at the same address.

Virtually all computer peripherals require these resources, and some, like sound cards, get pretty greedy. Complicating matters are peripherals with limited configuration options, like those, for example, that can be installed only in interrupt 5 or 7.

So, how to manage all this? Under DOS and Windows 3.1x, there were no mechanisms for efficiently distributing available I/O over a range of devices, forcing you to manually track used and available I/O. This was often close to impossible, even for technically sophisticated users, because there were no hardware or software tools that listed the I/O used by each peripheral. The resultant installation problems caused CD-ROM and multimedia upgrade kit return rates of 40 to 50%, which ultimately sank multimedia vendors like Media Vision and several others.

This is the problem that plug and play was designed to solve. Though imperfect, the new specification really has made it much easier to work with a range of computer peripherals, including capture cards.

PnP Overview

Here's a quick PnP overview. For PnP to work at all, you need a PnP motherboard and PnP peripherals. All PCI cards are supposed to be PnP, and ISA cards *can* be but don't have to be. Each PnP peripheral has a unique identifier stored in on-board ROM (read-only memory) that tells Windows 95 what type of board it is and describes its I/O requirements and any restrictions (e.g., interrupts 5 and 7 only). This is how Windows 95 knows that new card you just installed is the miro DC30.

Each time you boot your computer, Windows 95 polls all PnP devices regarding their I/O requirements and then attempts to distribute I/O like a mother bird doling out worm bits to her chicks. Most of the time it works fine, but PnP sometimes can't service all requirements, primarily because the resource allocation algorithm isn't exhaustive and the process isn't iterative. Rather, Windows 95 hands out I/O linearly, starting at the first device and ending at the last, and if there's no worm left over, this little peripheral has none.

When this happens, once again, you're in charge of making manual adjustments to allocate I/O to the respective devices. You're also in charge of finding and allocating I/O for non-PnP devices like older ISA cards. Fortunately, Windows 95 makes it a lot easier to both identify these problems and resolve them. But, as with Windows 3.1x, you have to roll up your sleeves.

SYSTEM PROPERTIES PROGRAM

Let's say you've just installed the DC30, and Windows 95 boots and tells you in rude, text lettering that it can't install all plug and play cards. Here's where you go look.

Hidden way down on the bottom of your Control Panel (Start/Settings/Control Panel, or My Computer/Control Panel) is a little program called System (see Figure 9.1). This is where you can identify both the conflicts and available resources and, in general, is the font of all sorts of good information about what's going on inside your computer.

If you double-click on the computer icon, you launch the Computer Properties screen (Figure 9.2), which conveniently shows you all used interrupts, DMA channels, I/O ports, and memory segments. This makes it very easy to tell if you have the open I/O to install additional peripherals.

When there are question marks or crosses in a peripheral, like those shown in Figure 9.8, it means you have some sort of configuration problem.

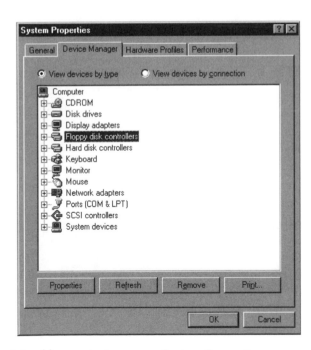

Figure 9.1   A healthy, post–virus scan System Properties screen. Contrast with Figure 9.8.

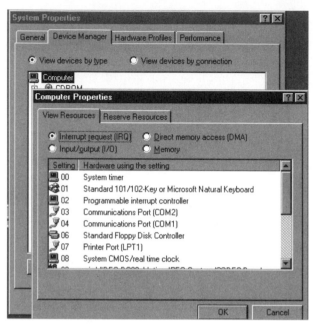

Figure 9.2   Computer Properties screen shows all used I/O. Double-click on
Fig9_2.avi for a never previously released video of the author's
Computer Properties screen.

Fortunately, this doesn't automatically mean the peripheral won't work,
since the hard drives the system's complaining about in Figure 9.8 worked
fine. Most of the time, however, when a peripheral isn't working, you can
find it here first. We'll talk about how to resolve these issues in a moment.

Double-clicking on a device launches a Properties screen, shown in
Figure 9.3, that provides general information about the peripheral and
identifies the drivers loaded and system resources. When a peripheral is
incorrectly installed, as in Figure 9.3, perusing the Properties screen will
typically help resolve the problem.

INSTALLATION: HOW IT SHOULD WORK

Under PnP, installation should be fairly painless, but products install in
different ways. Some ask you to install the software first, then the hardware.
Others tell you to opt out of the Windows 95 automatic routine and launch

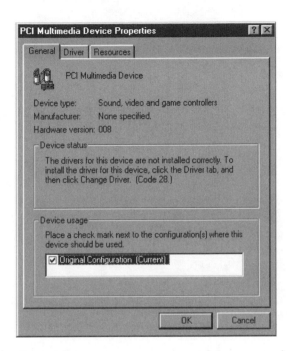

 Figure 9.3   The Device Properties screen. A quick tour around a "sick" PCI
multimedia Device Properties screen, and the resolution to the
problem is shown in Fig9_5.avi.

a setup utility. Others ask you to use Windows Explorer to find and
double-click the .INF file that accompanies the product to launch Windows
95 setup. It sounds trite, but following the instructions that accompany the
product gives you your best chance of an easy installation.

In all instances, the INF file that ships with the product tells Windows
95 which resources it requires, which files are needed and where to place
them, and, if you're lucky, how to uninstall the product as well. The typical
setup goes something like this.

Step 1: Turn off computer, install the board.

Step 2: Turn on your computer. In most instances, Windows 95 will
recognize the new board and request the diskette containing the
INF file. Plug in the diskette and you're on your way. If this doesn't
happen, check your installation guide to see if you're supposed to
run a separate setup program. If not, go back to Control Panel and
double-click on Add New Hardware (Figure 9.4). *If you have the*

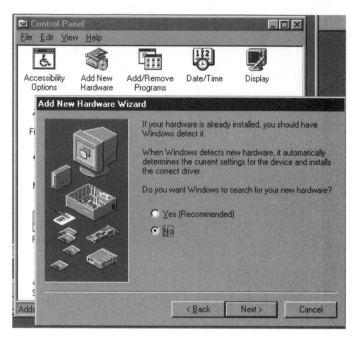

Figure 9.4 How to add new hardware when all else fails under Windows 95. Double-click on Fig9_3.avi for a prescreening of "Installing the miro VIDEO DC30" by Doceo Publishing.

disk with the INF file, don't let Windows search for your new hardware. In a couple of screens you'll have the opportunity to tell Windows 95 where to find the driver, which is the fastest way to get the job done.

WHEN THINGS GO WRONG

Note we said "when" things go wrong, rather than if. Not naturally pessimistic, just recognizing that the more stuff you add to your capture station, the more that can go wrong.

Let's say from the start that there is no definitive "right" way here—this is an operating system we're dealing with, not a crossword puzzle. So we'll simply list things that have gone wrong and what we've done to fix them.

PnP Finds Wrong Device

This happens only after you've installed a product, removed it, and then installed another that thinks it's the first. This happened after I tested the MPEGator (Chapter 14), removed it, and then installed the Wake-Board, which thought it was the MPEGator. Windows installed what it thought was all the right drivers, but, not surprisingly, the board didn't work.

The simple solution is to go into System Properties and double-click on the device to launch the Device Properties screen. Go to the Drivers screen

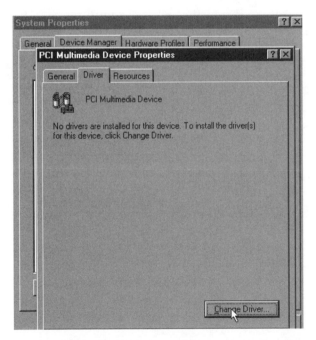

 Figure 9.5 Changing drivers is the easiest way to make Windows 95 recognize a new device—especially if it has confused it with another one. Check out Fig9_5.avi for a heartwarming video about a peripheral and operating system finding each other after a bad installation.

and press the Change Driver button (Figure 9.5). Point Windows 95 to the new installation disk, and the MPEGator magically becomes the Wake-Board.

You can use the same technique when a driver is incorrectly loaded for some reason—simply point Windows 95 at the right driver and wonderful things can happen.

PnP Can't Automatically Configure

As we mentioned previously, when PnP can't automatically configure all your peripherals, it's your job to get the boards installed. Usually it's a bad sign when you see the screen shown in Figure 9.6, your draft board notice that Windows 95 Wants *you* to fix the problem.

 Fortunately, Microsoft does provide a Hardware Conflict Trouble-shooter, shown in Fig9_6.avi, to help resolve the issue. Essentially, here's the drill. The Device Properties screen identifies the hardware you're conflicting with and the conflicting I/O. Figure 9.7 shows our Windows

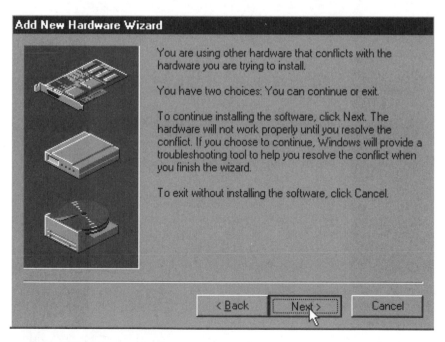

Figure 9.6   This is your draft notice—Windows 95 wants *you* to fix this installation problem.

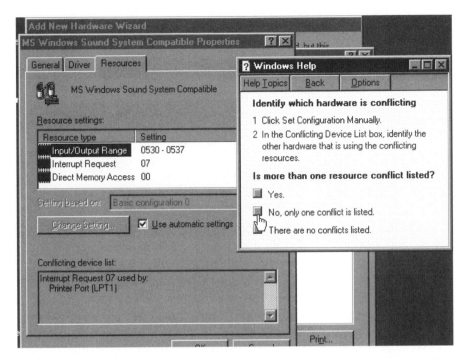

Figure 9.7   Conflict in the workplace—our Windows Sound System card conflicts with our parallel port. Just how important is printing to you, anyway?

Sound System conflicting with the printer port. You have four choices.

1. Change the settings of the new peripheral to a location that doesn't conflict. In this case, there were none.
2. Change the settings of the old device to allow the new one to install. You can do this only if the old peripheral enables manual adjustment of I/O parameters *and, of course,* if there is available I/O. As shown in the video, we couldn't adjust the parallel port, which probably wouldn't have helped anyway since there was no open I/O.
3. Give up on the new device, which we couldn't do cause we needed to capture audio, or
4. Remove the old device, which is what we did. Heck, we don't print much from our capture station anyway!

It's not elegant, but it works most of the time, and in all honesty both scenarios are worst case in terms of my experience. Usually, even in crowded computers, PnP peripherals install easily, unless, of course, you've been hanging out with the wrong types of software.

CAN WE TALK?

C'mon over here and sit down next to me. Don't be embarrassed. It's time we talked about something, well, personal. You're on the Net all the time, downloading drivers from hither and yon.com. You've got more bookmarks than B. Dalton's. You get even more files on CompuServe or AOL. You load demo disks from trade shows, install shareware screen savers from your users group and CD-ROM compilations of freeware games. Let's face it . . . your hard disk gets around. And if you get around in the computer game, it means a virus.

Remember this lesson, remember it well. Somehow, last year, our office got invaded by the Stealth_C virus, not the worst in the world, but a pain in its own right. First it hit my desktop computer, a clone, not the test station we rebuild every month, but the computer where I write, correspond, and do financial stuff. You know, the computer you never back up.

It started out as a boot problem, as in the computer didn't want to. I don't know about you, but I find reloading Windows 95 periodically somewhat rejuvenating, like fasting for a couple of days and losing 20 MB of wasted DLL's in your windows/system subdirectory. But I wasn't really up for the guaranteed day and a half it takes to get your machine right so I tried everything to avoid it, going so far as to (gulp) call the manufacturer. No help, no surprise.

About four hours into it I concluded that my hard drive was dead, so I called an old buddy to ask about those services that somehow retrieve your data from dead drives. This was Tom M., a guy I worked with in '86 – '90 and then again in '91–'93. Tom grew up with computers, supporting DOS, Windows, and even Novell Netware. Tom could build a computer from scratch, knew the difference between DOS 4.0 and 5.0, and could actually write batch files with Edlin—I saw it with my own eyes. I mean, he knew everything.

So when Tom said "sounds like a virus," I started sweating and thought about paging my wife, the doctor. But Tom reminded me that she was a sturgeon (we were all Kip Odata fans) and that a scalpel wouldn't help. Instead, he recommended that I surf over to www.mcafee.com and download their virus protection software. I did, and about 20 minutes later my computer was restored, good as new, with no loss of data, hallelujah.

The lesson? Get an antivirus utility before you run into problems. I've only worked with McAfee, and it has never failed me. You can even buy it over the Net (Mastercard and Visa only). Anytime your machine starts acting funny, whether it's a complete shutdown or just certain peripherals stop working, think virus. Think virus, think virus, think virus. Hate to repeat myself, but we frequently forget the lesson as well.

We never found the source of Stealth_C, and like a bad apple it keeps turning up again and again on our various computers, morphing each time, it seems, into a different form. It recently hit our venerable capture station, manifesting as a number of peripherals that refused to stay installed (see Figure 9.8). Since I had just tested a non-PnP ISA board, I naturally attrib-

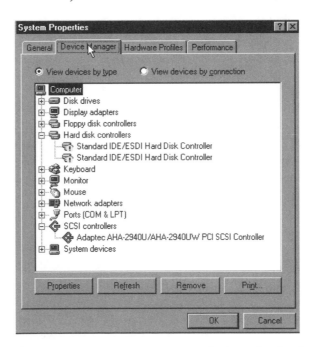

Figure 9.8 When your computer system starts looking this bad, start thinking virus.

uted the problem to that card, cursing the manufacturer liberally and spending the next three hours trying to figure out why my computer was acting sick. I admit it—I was in goober heaven, though a bit rushed.

Then, after crashing so badly that the computer ended up in safe mode, Windows 95 deigned to mention that perhaps there was a virus on my computer. My right hand smacked into my forehead like the Talking Heads lead singer, David Byrne, in "Stop Making Sense," but instead of "Same as it ever was" a loud *"duh"* escaped my lips.

One quick trip to www.mcafee.com and my computer was restored. We actually upgraded to the Windows 95 version, which checks for viruses on start-up and should help avoid most future problems. Not quite in time to meet this chapter's deadline, I'm afraid, but soon enough to avoid a Windows 95 reload. That's my story, anyway, Ms. Editor, and I'm sticking to it.

Uninstalling

Here's one area where most application developers could do better. In the INF files, developers are supposed to specify how to uninstall the program, available through the Add/Remove Programs utility located in the Control Panel and shown in Figure 9.9. They don't always.provide this information, which means you can't remove it using this utility. Other times, they provide incorrect data, which essentially prevents the uninstaller from working.

Either way, give it a shot before yanking out any hardware or deleting a software program—it's the only way to get your machine back to where it was before you installed.

Typically, it's not important to remove PnP hardware devices from the System Properties screen when you take them out of the computer. Since Windows 95 checks the hardware configuration each time it boots (one of the reasons it takes so long to boot), it will recognize that the peripheral is gone automatically. Once you configure in a non-PnP peripheral, it's good practice to make sure that it's removed, cause sometimes Windows 95 can't tell whether it's there or not and may reserve the I/O.

I should say for the sake of completeness that installing a program using the Add/Remove utility will *not* make it uninstallable if the developer

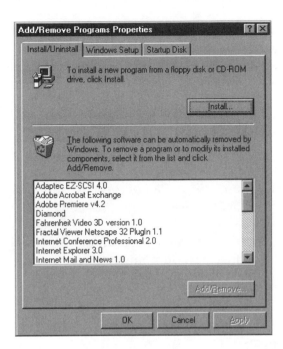

Figure 9.9 Windows 95 Add/Remove Programs utility doesn't always work, but always give it a try when removing a hardware or software product. Check out Fig9_9.avi for a quick video showing how this utility works.

doesn't provide the required information in the INF file. For this reason, it really doesn't (seem to) matter if you install using this program or the old-fashioned way via Start/Run/Setup.

PRECAPTURE CHECKLIST

Defragment Your Hard Drive

When you format your hard disk and start adding programs, all files are stored in continuous sectors on your hard drive. As you delete and add files, the system starts breaking files up and storing them in noncontinuous disk sectors. For example, if you delete a 1 megabyte file and then add a 2 megabyte file, the system might place one half of the new file in the space opened up by the deleted file and one half in other sectors. Over time, many of the files on your disk are fragmented, and most of the available storage space on your disk is located in noncontiguous sectors.

When you capture video, you achieve the best results by dumping all of the captured data into contiguous sectors. That way, the disk can write continuously, rather than writing, moving to a new sector, writing again, and so on.

Think of a cement truck trying to unload. If it dumps the cement in one large load, like the foundation of a building, it empties very quickly. If it has to unload into 40 or 50 wheelbarrows, it will take a lot longer.

When you capture video, if the disk has to seek new locations to store the newly captured video, you may drop frames. Overall operation will be most efficient if it can just start dumping into continuous sections. For this reason, it's best to start every capture session by defragmenting your hard drive.

Windows 95 ships with a Disk Defragmenter licensed from Symantec Corporation, which you can find by running Start/Accessories/System Tools (Figure 9.10, Fig9_10.avi). It's free and simple to operate, and always checks the drives for errors before starting, a useful early warning system.

Interestingly, defragmenting also helps video playback. When compressing a file, the system places video file chunks in available slots all over the disk. During playback, if the file is fragmented, the disk has to work a lot harder to retrieve the file, which can cost you a couple of frames per second. If you're compressing on one station and transferring to another for playback, you should defragment the playback station before or after loading the video files.

It's also not bad practice to scan your system disk frequently with ScanDisk, another Symantec utility included with Windows 95. It's in the start-up folder of most of our systems, checking for and repairing file allocation errors and lost chains, checking the file allocation tables, and maintaining a mirror image of disk information in case your drive is accidentally formatted.

With all of the devices and drivers you end up loading on your computer, the inevitable conflicts, and the memory-intensive tasks that continuously page information back and forth to disk, inevitably you end up with all kinds of errors on your hard drive. When I installed ScanDisk's predecessor, Norton Disk Doctor, on my home computer, I found 40 megabytes of lost

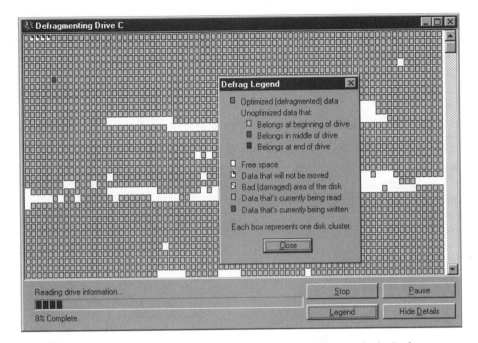

Figure 9.10 Windows 95's Disk Defragmenter. Brush regularly before capture.

chains. I locked the barn door and bought Norton after losing my first 1.4-gig drive. I've had some scares but no problems since.

Set File Nomenclature

In the course of capturing, editing, and possibly filtering a file for compression, you end up with four or five versions of the same file. Add two to three potential compressions to get it just right, and you've got a bunch of files on disk, all described with eight characters and the surname .AVI. That's just for one final file.

You do get more characters with Windows 95, but I switch back and forth between 16-bit programs like VidEdit and my 32-bit apps so often that I still typically use only eight letters. It's better to name a file in code than to have Windows 95 truncate the name into unrecognizable form.

For this reason, it's always a good idea to develop a naming convention for all generations of video files. We started doing this with the Video Compression Sampler, since it would have been impossible to manage the thousands of captured, intermediate, and final files without one. It's impossible to develop one naming convention that works for everyone, but here's the idea.

- *First two letters:* name/number of the video itself. S1 might be scene one, or V1 might be video one.

- *Third and fourth letters:* describe level or generation of the file.

  First generation: Use CA (capture) or RA (raw).

  Second generation: After preprocessing use ED (edited) or FI (filtered).

  Third generation: When compressing use the name of the codec, like IN (Indeo) or CP (Cinepak).

- *Fifth and sixth letters:* If you're experimenting to produce the perfect video file, use these letters to describe the parameters. For example, if you're playing with key frames to see which interval gives you the highest quality, you might use these two letters to record key frame interval.

Sometimes the file names are easier to read if you include an underline between the letters. Thus S1_IN_15.AVI would be the first scene, compressed with Indeo at a key frame setting of 15.

When you have a keeper, or the file you intend to finally use, you might name it something easier to read. For example, you could change S1_IN_15.avi to Scene1.avi.

About file management. I've gotten real conservative about deleting intermediate files and usually don't start deleting until absolutely necessary. Pretty much every time I delete a filtered or raw file, it seems like I need it again. We obviously do a bit more experimenting than most readers, but you may find the same thing.

Plan Your Directory Structure

Even the best file naming convention doesn't help when you've got 5000 files in one subdirectory. Think about logical ways to segment the capture information and then use separate subdirectories where you can.

Keep a Log

I'm the world's worst record keeper and resisted keeping a log for about eight months. But between the time you capture a file and the time you compress the final version, you'll deal with the following parameters:

- Color/brightness settings on the capture card
- Time codes or frame numbers on the analog source
- Color/brightness settings in Adobe Premiere or other editor
- Filter settings
- Compression settings

It's bad enough when you have to start over because the boss thinks the video makes her look like a Martian. It's really demoralizing when you have to start from scratch without a record of what worked before and what didn't.

Get Comfortable with Your Video Input Controls

In terms of pure video quality, the most valuable time you'll spend with your capture board is with analog video input controls. As you recall, these adjust the color and brightness of the incoming video. While some of the capture boards come close, default settings don't work 100% of the time, and adjustments are necessary to maximize video quality.

In the heat of the capture, you focus on getting the video to disk and your internal quality controls become more lax. Later, during preprocessing and compression, you get more critical and start thinking, gosh, this would look so much better if only it was brighter, or darker, or less green, or more green. Then you might talk yourself into starting over or trying to adjust the color in Premiere.

The key to one-step video quality lies with the analog input controls. Get to know them early.

Don't Delete More Than You Can Chew

This is kind of a silly one, but whenever I get ready to capture, I start deleting files left and right to clear the space. It's all backed up, mind you, but it's a pain to restore and I never end up capturing anywhere near as much as I thought I would.

SUMMARY

1. Plug and play should make your life a lot easier when installing capture cards and similar devices. Just remember to read the manual before you start installing, because most devices do it just a little differently.

2. The System Properties program is key to installing recalcitrant peripherals, or those who haven't read point one. It's one of Windows 95's high points; get to know it early.

3. Use the Add/Remove utility to uninstall programs—it's your best chance of restoring your computer.

4. Get an antivirus program on all of your computers, and use ScanDisk every day. Remember that a hard drive crash can ruin your entire day, so take these steps to protect against it.

5. Defragmenting your hard drive is key to real-time capture performance. Defragment before every major capture session.

6. Create a standard file nomenclature before you start capturing. Make up unique identifiers for the various clips you'll be capturing, as well as all stages from capture to compression. When you have 6000 similarly named AVI files on your disk, it's too late.

7. Keep a log of all your work. Track capture settings, start and stop points, filter and compression settings. This will help you recreate any video files, which inevitably you will have to do.

8. Get comfortable with your capture board's input color controls. Proper use of these controls guarantees maximum image quality. Improper use guarantees you'll have to redo the videos.

Chapter  10

Video Capture

IN THIS CHAPTER

In this chapter we start by counting down to capture, reviewing the various controls that implement our capture decisions and discussing critical capture parameters such as frame rate and video resolution. All supported by sample videos and abundant statistics, of course.

We'll be discussing four video applications throughout, since all have different capture requirements. These markets are capture for nonlinear editing, capture for software Moving Pictures Experts Group 1 (MPEG-1) encoding, capture for streaming Internet delivery and capture for encoding with a traditional software-only codec like Indeo video interactive (IVI) or Cinepak. *Con su permiso*, we will discuss these markets in different order as the mood strikes us but will include a table with each capture parameter for easy reference. Then we move to the capture itself, reviewing topics such as how to configure computer-controlled analog sources, how to work with the Media Control Interface (MCI) controls, and how to step capture.

This section is very hands on, best used when actually doing the work. So clear some space for me on your desk, right there near the keyboard, and let's get down to work. It's time to capture some video.

CAPTURE CHECKLIST

1. Set Capture File and Allocate File Space

Job number one during video capture is to avoid the dreaded "dropped frames," which occur when the computer can't store the video fast enough to disk. Job number two is capturing at the highest possible data rate, which maximizes the quality of the captured video. Both jobs rely on good disk performance.

If you read the last chapter, you're fresh and ruddy faced from defragmenting your disk drive. Always a pleasurable experience. To optimize capture performance, we now want to preserve that defragmented state throughout the capture session.

Video professionals approach video capture in a number of different ways, as do capture programs. It's important to select a procedure and understand how your capture program works to capture high-quality files most efficiently.

All video programs use the concept of a capture file that lets you reserve contiguous disk sectors on the drive. Set up a 200-MB capture file in VidCap32, as shown in Figure 10.1, and you end up with a 200-MB file called capture.avi on your E drive. Since your file system views this file like any other, even if it's empty, you can't save any data to this area, maintaining 200 MB of contiguous, unfragmented disk real estate ideal for video capture.

When capturing video, you have to choose between two basic techniques. When I started capturing video, I named each file separately, allocated the file 60 MB of disk space, and captured away. I quickly ran out of disk space, however, because even if the actual captured file took only 20 MB of space, the file size on the drive was the allocated 60 MB.

Figure 10.1 Allocating capture file space in VidCap32.

Then I turned to option number two, which was to set one capture file and then save each captured sequence after capture. In our example, you would set e:\capture.avi as your single capture file and then save each video sequence off to another name and disk location after capture, perhaps naming them scene1.avi, scene2.avi, etc.

This approach has one major problem, at least with VidCap, VidCap 32, and DVP: If you capture again without saving the first file, it's lost. Many developers, including yours truly, have lost more than one carefully captured file in this manner. If you're working with these programs, you need to remember to save the file between captures, or at least save the keepers. Both Premiere and MediaStudio let you set up a scratch file for capturing multiple files, but each warns you before overwriting.

How much space to allocate? If you've just defragmented and you're about to capture a few clips, it really doesn't matter; even if you allocate a small amount, any overrun will be stored to contiguous defragmented sectors anyway.

But if you plan on capturing, editing, and compressing without defragmenting again, and then perhaps capturing some more video, you should allocate enough space for the largest file you plan to capture. If your capture rate is 2 MB/s and your longest clip is 2 minutes, this adds up to 120 MB.

Note that the whole allocation/defragmentation issue becomes much less important when capturing for streaming Internet delivery or encoding to MPEG-1 or traditional software codecs, since the actual capture data rates of about 2 MB/s are very much under the 3–5 MB ceiling supported by even average SCSI drives. In these applications, I tend not to worry about frequent defragmenting unless or until frames start to drop during capture, or when reviewing products for comparison purposes, of course.

On the other hand, when capturing for nonlinear editing, managing your drives becomes an obsession, since capture rates typically directly reflect capture quality and rank a board among its peers. Not to mention a testosterone point between reviewers. Fortunately, the video capture card community is small and close knit, and I can call Jeff Sauer at *NewMedia Magazine* or Rich Popko at *DV* and say, "Hey man, wha'd you get with that new BrandX PCI card? I only got 3.3 MB/s."

If they say 5 MB/s, I get back to work; if they say 2.5, I tell *them* to get back to work. All this is a long way of saying that you have to worry about your drives and capture rate a whole lot more when capturing for nonlinear editing than for most other applications.

2. Audio Format

Choosing the Right Audio Parameters   You set audio capture parameters in a dialog box typically labeled Audio Format or Sound Selection (see Figure 10.2). All capture programs let you control incoming audio levels, though most simply allow you to choose between stereo and mono; 8-bit and 16-bit; and 11, 22, and 44 kHz audio. Other programs such as VidCap32, shown in Figure 10.2, and MediaStudio let you access Microsoft's Audio Compression Manager and capture in a much broader range of audio formats. As we'll see, this functionality becomes helpful when working with streaming video codecs for Internet delivery.

Traditional Software Codecs   If you're capturing for compression with Indeo video interactive or Cinepak, you want to capture at the parameters

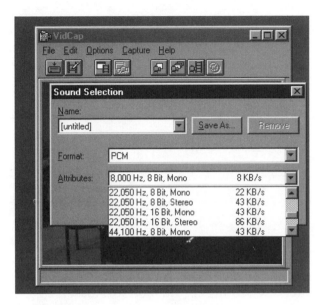

Figure 10.2 VidCap32's Sound Selection dialog box, for choosing audio capture parameters. All editing programs let you select audio parameters prior to capture.

that will ultimately be included with your video. Obviously, audio adds to the bandwidth of your captured video, meaning that higher quality settings add load that may cause you to drop frames during capture. For this reason, you should capture at the audio setting you intend to use, never higher. Table 10.1 illustrates the data rates associated with sampling frequency, channels, and sampling size.

Here's what these parameters mean. You're probably familiar with the difference between mono and stereo—stereo carries two channels and is twice as large. Sample size relates to the amount of storage used per unit of analog audio. As you would expect, 16-bit requires roughly twice the data rate of 8-bit.

Finally, frequency relates to the rate of sampling performed on the audio. The higher the sampling rate, the higher the fidelity of the captured audio. By way of reference, 44.1 kHz is used for audio CDs, 22.05 kHz sounds about the same as AM radio, and 11.025 kHz is about the same quality as a telephone line.

Table 10.1 Audio data rates at specified audio parameters.

	11.025 kHz	22.05 kHz	44.1 kHz
Mono Audio			
8-bit	11 KB/s	22 KB/s	44 KB/s
16-bit	22 KB/s	44 KB/s	88 KB/s
Stereo Audio			
8-bit	22 KB/s	44 KB/s	88 KB/s
16-bit	44 KB/s	88 KB/s	176 KB/s

As you can see, at the higher quality sound settings, the results are somewhat alarming, especially if you're working with CD-ROM products. Choosing the right combination relates primarily to the sound system on the target computer. Obviously, if you can't hear the difference, the additional quality isn't worth the bandwidth.

Whatever combination you choose, make sure you test on a computer with a very low-end sound board, which often yields some interesting results. For example, I've experienced a fuzzy sound ("white noise") when playing 16-bit audio on an 8-bit sound system. Other developers have reported audio distortion when high-quality audio is played on lower quality sound systems.

For these reasons, and to save bandwidth, most CD-ROM publishers seem to use either 22- or 11-kHz, 8-bit mono audio. All of the videos on the CD-ROM use 8-bit, 11-kHz mono audio.

MPEG-1 Compression   If you're capturing for conversion to MPEG-1 format, capture 16-bit stereo audio at 44 kHz, also known as CD-ROM–quality audio. This is the level called for in the MPEG-1 audio specification, so all MPEG-1 encoders are designed to work with this quality level.

Streaming Internet Formats   If you're capturing for conversion to VDO, Vivo, or similar formats, peruse the codec's documentation before capturing, since many encoders require very specific parameters. For example, VDO requires 8-kHz audio for their proprietary encoder.

Don't be shocked, however, if your capture card and software don't support all the exotic formats out there. Of the three programs we review in Chapter 11, only one, MediaStudio, could capture at 8 kHz. Since VDO is an AVI codec that works in Premiere, this wasn't so much of an issue: The VDO audio codec could convert to 8 kHz behind the scenes. When working with other technologies, however, be sure you're capturing at the right parameters, which will optimize audio quality.

Table 10.2 capsules our recommendations for the various formats.

Nonlinear Editing   When capturing for nonlinear editing your ultimate goal is to send the video back out to tape in as close to its original condition as possible. This means capturing at the highest possible quality setting, which is CD-ROM quality—16-bit/44 kHz/stereo.

That said, high audio capture rates can often drag performance on the video side, causing dropped video frames that force you to drop video capture bandwidth and video quality. This is especially true when working with capture cards *without* onboard audio, since the system has to stream the audio in from a separate, interrupt-driven ISA sound card that requires significant resources from the host CPU.

Many times, if you drop the capture rate to 22 kHz, the difference in perceived audio quality is minor, but you've cut the audio capture rate in half, to 88 KB/s. If you're working with fast-moving music videos this may not fly, but it may be a great strategy for talking heads and other primarily talking videos that don't have the dynamic range of music and don't need CD-ROM–quality audio.

All this is a long way of saying that there are no hard-and-fast rules with nonlinear editing. You're working to put the highest quality audio/video

Table 10.2 Summary of recommended audio capture parameters.

Capturing for:	*Recommendation*
Compression with traditional software codec	Capture at planned publishing parameters, generally not to exceed 22 KB/s, whether 16-bit/11 kHz/mono or 8-bit/22 kHz/mono
Software MPEG-1 compression	16-bit/44 kHz/stereo
Streaming Internet delivery	Check codec's documentation
Nonlinear editing	16-bit/44 kHz/stereo

combination to disk possible, which may mean trade-offs in audio or video quality.

Audio Format Controls   For several reasons, capturing audio is often more challenging than it would seem. I've learned the hard way that just because you hear audio coming out of your speakers doesn't mean that you're capturing audio. The only way to be certain that you've actually captured audio is to play back the file after capture and listen.

The problem starts with the fact that your capture program doesn't control audio input as it does video input. Instead, audio control is usually handled by the software that comes with your sound card. On Windows 95 computers, you access this control panel by double-clicking on the yellow speaker on the bottom right-hand side of the task bar, bringing up the screen shown in Figure 10.3.

For some reason, various Windows programs often have a tendency to manipulate these controls in some unforeseen fashion. You'll notice that in Figure 10.3, the wave balance is set to the bottom, not by design but by some strange, unseen software hand. If you were about to capture video, this could drive you crazy. Not only won't you hear any audio during capture, making you start scurrying around, madly checking your cable connections, you also won't hear it when you play the video back, even if you've successfully captured it, because your speaker volume is turned off.

To complicate matters, the Volume Control screen has two screens, one for recording and the other for playback. You flip-flop between the two via

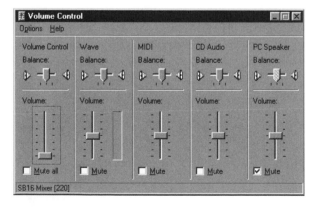

Figure 10.3   Windows 95 Volume Control screen, found by double-clicking the yellow speaker on the bottom right-hand side of the task bar.

the Options, Properties menu to get to the Recording Control screen found in Figure 10.4. This screen controls the incoming volume from your microphone and line-in, the latter of which you'll likely use to input the audio from your analog source.

With most sound cards, when you play video from your analog source, you should hear the audio coming from the speakers in real time, whether you're capturing or not. When you don't, it's a bad sign. Here's a list of things to try.

1. First, try to play a WAV file already on your hard drive. If you don't have any handy, you can always try the soothing Windows 95 theme song, typically located in Windows/media. You can either load Media Player (Start/Programs/Accessories/Multimedia/Media Player) or just double-click on the file from either File Manager or Windows Explorer. If you hear the lovely Windows 95 theme, you know that you're not getting the audio from the analog source into your system. Here's a list of things to try:

   a. Check the volume control, if any, on your analog source. Most higher end decks have gauges that reveal audio levels; make sure those levels are jumping. Most analog sources also have headphone output jacks; if you have a compatible headphone, make sure you hear audio.

   b. Check the cables from the analog source to the sound card. Probably the most common mistake is to plug the incoming line into the microphone input rather than line-in, complicated by the fact that some sound cards don't label their jacks (not that you could see them anyway, way back in the dark dusty area behind your computer). I can't tell you how many times I've had to look through a sound card manual to identify the right input jack. Usually, I end up photocopying that page of the manual and taping it to the wall over my capture station.

   c. Check the incoming volume control (Figure 10.4). Double-click on the old yellow speaker on the task bar, get to the recording control, and make sure your line-in volume is turned up.

2. If you don't hear a thing, you could have any number of problems. If you get an error message similar to that shown in Figure 10.5, your sound drivers aren't loaded properly. If you don't get the

Figure 10.4   Windows 95 Recording Control screen, found via the Options, Properties menu, controls audio coming into the computer.

message, the drivers are loaded properly but the sound isn't getting to the speakers. Try these:

a. Check the cables from sound card to speaker, and…heh, heh…make sure your speakers are turned on. Both of these have burned me more than once.

b. Check your software output controls and make sure they're not turned off. If the control looks like the screen shown Figure 10.3, you've found your problem.

Figure 10.5   Ruh, Roh, Scooby Doo. Your audio won't play 'cause your drivers aren't loaded.

3. If none of these work, swap your cables from your analog source to your sound card. Cables typically go bad before a sound card.

Ninety-nine percent of the time, one of these steps will fix your problem. The other 1% of the time you're in the realm of busted hardware or blown speakers and a trip to the old computer superstore.

Even when your system is working perfectly, it's good to check each file after capture to make sure sound is present. If you hear audio during capture but there's none during playback, you may have installed the analog input into the microphone jack. Check this and your recording controls to make sure you're properly set up.

Another problem I've encountered with professional quality BetaSP decks is that the sound card can't handle the high levels of audio output by the deck. The audio sounds fine coming from the speakers, but when you play the file back the audio is very loud and scratchy, clearly distorted. This happens most often with inexpensive sound cards.

You can cut the incoming levels from the deck or drop the levels on your Recording Control, but typically the audio will remain scratchy, even at lower levels. Your safest bet, if you haven't just purchased a new capture card, is to get one, like the miro DC30 or FAST AV/Master, that has audio input on board and expects the higher levels from an analog source. Or you can try a new sound card, but go name brand and buy from a store you can return it to if you experience the same problem.

Sound Synchronization A few words about sound synchronization. It's important. Really important. Video for Windows and your capture cards are supposed to handle all that, and pretty much do, but here are a couple of things to watch out for.

My experience with both the miro DC30 and FAST AV/Master is that when I play back videos captured with these boards *on the capture station with the board still installed,* the audio synch is consistently off by about one second. I have no idea why.

However, *when I swap a stand-alone sound card for either capture card,* synchronization is perfect. In addition, when I render video out to tape and play it on television, synchronization is also perfect.

Two lessons here. First is that something funky is going on with these boards, and if you attempt to synchronize audio with the video manually in an editing program, it will sound great on your capture station but not on other computers. Don't do it.

A more universal lesson is this: There's a terrible tendency to assume that your capture station represents the real world in all its exactitude. Unfortunately, it seldom does. If you confine your testing for sound synch, video color and brightness, and playback capabilities to your capture and compression station, you will have accomplished one thing—creating video that plays back perfectly on *your capture/compression station.* Assuming you want to distribute your video beyond this comfortable but admittedly restricted range, you could be in trouble.

I've said it before and will say it again, probably even in this chapter (boosts the word count, you know): Whenever you capture and/or compress your video, test early and often on computers other than your capture and compression station. Test other lab machines, computers with 8-bit graphics and ancient sound cards, and a reasonable range of machines in your target market. Otherwise, the fruits of your efforts could be video that looks and sounds great on one machine but few, if any, others.

3. Video Resolution

You choose video resolution from a screen that looks suspiciously like that shown in Figure 10.6, irrespective of the capture program. Figure 10.6 shows the options available for the Intel Smart Video Recorder III (ISVR3), a flexible board in both resolution and capture format. For example, in addition to four set resolution options, including 160×120, the ISVR3 lets you select custom resolutions. In contrast, the FAST AV/Master is unusually constraining, with only two resolutions, 320×240 and 640×480.

I'm telling you all this not to dis the FAST AV/Master but to let you know that these are *hardware options controlled by the capture card.* If you're frustrated by the lack of capture options in MediaStudio or VidCap32, both of which ship with the board, switching to Premiere won't help. Any Video for Windows capture program will pick up these options and these options only.

Choosing your video resolution also relates to how you're going to use the video, and we'll make some specific suggestions in a moment. In all instances, however, you should capture at the resolution at which you intend to distribute the video, so that the capture card, not the editing program, performs the scaling.

Capture cards use sophisticated interpolation and filtering to minimize scaling artifacts. Most editing programs simply subsample, or throw away pixels during scaling, which can produce noticeable pixelation and other

Figure 10.6 All capture cards have this or a similar screen, usually found under the Video Format label. This is the Intel Smart Video Recorder III from inside DVP's capture program.

artifacts, though Premiere claims some advanced resizing options that appear to work with good results (Figure 10.7). We also tested MediaStudio, which produced equally clear video, but DVP looked very much like VidEdit's video.

Either way, it's always best to capture at your target resolution when the capture board supports it. Otherwise, capture at the next highest resolution and scale down, but be certain that your editing program offers advanced resizing options or your quality will suffer.

Let's review the four market areas, dealing with the simplest first.

MPEG-1 When capturing for MPEG-1 conversion, capture at 320×240 unless the video will be played back on a National Television Standards

Figure 10.7   Video captured at 240×180 (center) compared to video
captured at 320×240 and scaled by VidEdit (right) and Premiere
(left) to 240×180. Although the Premiere image is vastly superior
to VidEdit's, it's still not as crisp as that produced by capturing
directly to the intended resolution.

Committee (NTSC) monitor via VideoCD or CD-I. If you are compressing
for playback on computer monitors, use 320×240, even though MPEG-1's
official resolution is 352×240. We explain this in detail in Chapter 14, but
the following is a brief explanation.

When developing the MPEG standard, the MPEG committee members
chose 352×240 as the standard image format (SIF) resolution, meaning that
the entire NTSC video image is subsampled down to that resolution for
compression. When played back on an NTSC monitor, the image looks
normal. However, when the 352×240 image is played on a VGA monitor, it

Table 10.3   Recommended video resolution parameters.

Capturing for:	Recommendation
Compression with traditional software codec	320×240 unless targeted toward extremely low power computers
Software MPEG-1 compression	320×240 unless for VideoCD or CD-I
Streaming Internet delivery	Check codec's documentation and formulate big picture versus fast motion strategy
Nonlinear editing	640×480 unless the board supports overscan cropping

looks stretched by about 10%—because it is stretched by about 10% (see Figure 10.8).

For this reason, the MPEG committee defined a "square pixel" mode for squeezing the video during playback to achieve the proper aspect ratio, leaving a slot in the MPEG file header to tell the decoder. The problem is that squeezing video in real time can dramatically affect the display rate of software-only decoders.

All software encoders can compress 320×240 resolution video to 320×240 resolution MPEG-1 video that looks like square pixel. This is what you want, so capture at 320×240.

Streaming Internet Delivery Here your resolution depends on your intended delivery strategy. All streaming video codecs except for Vivo allow

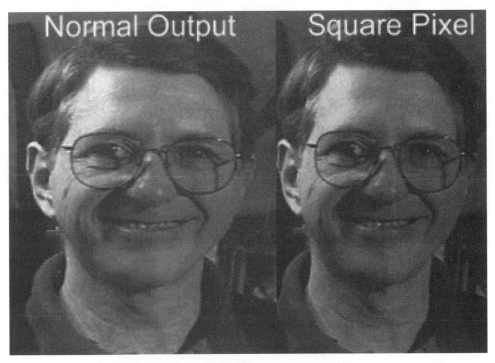

 Figure 10.8 Ken looks happier on the left, but the wider smile is strictly courtesy of the stretching effect of mapping NTSC video to VGA screens. Using square pixel mode, on the right, corrects the aspect ratio.

you to compress at resolutions ranging from about 64×64 up to 320×240. This gives you two options, even at low bandwidths.

You big-picture folks might use 320×240 resolution, scaling down the frame rate to one or two frames per second. This produces a fairly high quality, low frame-rate image. Others may opt for faster motion, which means capturing at 160×120 or 176×144 at 15 frames per second.

Either way, the important rule remains the same. Figure out what your ultimate delivery resolution will be, and capture at that resolution.

Traditional Software Codecs   For codecs like Indeo and Cinepak, the resolution issue has gotten very simple. Unless you're targeting extremely low end computers, like 486/33 computers and slower, you'll want to capture at 320×240 unless interface design calls for a smaller window. I have gotten a couple of inquiries about larger capture resolutions, like 400×300, but I try to talk the caller into 320×240 for a couple of reasons.

First, at higher resolutions, decompression rates slow and the data rates required for reasonable quality increase. For example, 400×300 is 56% larger than 320×240, which means the video data rate must be 56% higher to achieve the same quality.

If you're serving a high-power audience, chances are their graphics cards have scaling mechanisms that can boost video resolution to full screen without slowing down video playback. In most instances, this works better than bigger resolution video.

For most in-house training, sales support, customer testimonial, kiosk, and day-to-day, meat-and-potato applications, you'll want to capture at 320×240. Once the video is digitized and stored to disk, you can choose a codec that will play it back on your target platform at 15 fps.

Nonlinear Editing   When capturing for nonlinear editing, full screen is your mantra and 640×480 is your capture resolution. One exception is for boards like the miro DC30, which support cropping to remove television overscan. These edges on all four sides typically aren't seen anyway, and cropping lets you focus the data rate for the on-screen segments.

We performed all of our tests with the DC30 by cropping out the television overscan, reducing the normally 640×480 screen down to 608×456. During playback to television, the DC30 videos looked normal from a resolution perspective.

Digital Video Arts' WakeBoard didn't support 640×480 capture at 60 fields per second, required for nonlinear editing, so we had to use 320×480, with a bad result. Older cards like miro's ISA-based DC1 recommended capture at 320×240 and scaled the video to full screen when writing to tape. Neither of these situations is optimal, however, and if you're serious about nonlinear editing you'll need a card that supports full-screen capture.

4. Frame Rate

A quick NTSC review. Although we typically describe NTSC video as 30 frames per second, it's really composed of 60 separate fields that alternately scan down your analog monitor 60 times a second. First the odd lines scan down, then the even lines, to promote visual smoothness. In contrast, Video for Windows codecs and MPEG-1 are *frame based*, with a frame being the combination of the respective two fields.

When capturing for nonlinear editing, you have to capture at 60 fields per second to remain compliant when writing the video back out to tape. When capturing for AVI or MPEG-1 conversion, however, you have to capture frames. For this reason, most high-end boards like the FAST AV/Master support field-based capture as well as frame based (Figure 10.9).

In addition to choosing between frames and fields, you can set the number of frames per second captured to disk, or frame rate. VidCap32's Capture Video Sequence dialog box is presented in Figure 10.10.

Once again, specific recommendations relate to the intended use of your video, so let's look at your respective categories.

Traditional Software Codecs   As with video resolution, your frame rate goal is to capture just the number of frames per second destined for inclusion in the finished video. In English, this means that if you're going to publish 15 fps, capture 15 fps.

Why? Because capture is a demanding process that often requires compression to get the frames to disk. Often, the more frames per second captured, the more compression, which as we all know by now degrades video quality. If your goal is 15 fps video, capturing at 30 fps could force you to increase compression and damage your final output quality.

Few if any commercial titles have ever shipped with video compressed at more than 15 fps. This is related to a number of factors:

- At consistent data rates, more frames per second means degraded quality, since the encoder must spread the available bandwidth

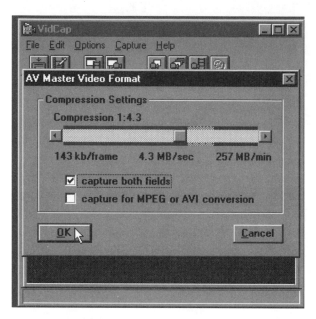

Figure 10.9 FAST AV/Master captures fields for nonlinear editing and frames for conversion to AVI or MPEG-1 formats. Note the capture data rate slider, which we'll discuss in the next section.

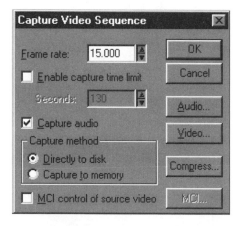

Figure 10.10 VidCap32's Capture Video Sequence dialog box, set to the frame rate value appropriate for most video to be compressed with traditional software-only codecs.

over more frames. While the video may play faster, the per-frame quality won't be as high.

If you bounce up the data rate to improve quality, you further increase the load on the host CPU to retrieve the data from the CD-ROM and display the extra frames. This bodes poorly for performance on even powerful computers.

- Many computers in their customer base couldn't play back faster than 15 fps video anyway, making the exercise a waste and perhaps decreasing overall display rate on some slower computers. In Table 10.4, you'll notice that the 30 fps IVI video played at 4 fps on the Pentium 60 compared to 9 fps for video compressed at 15 fps. This translates to fewer frames of worse-looking video, which generally sounds like a bad idea to me.

- High-motion videos compressed at 20 and 24 fps may look jumpy to some viewers. NTSC video is composed of 30 discrete frames per second. During capture, you digitize these discrete analog frames—you don't sample from a continuous analog steam. For example, when capturing at 24 fps, you drop every sixth frame—you don't capture 24 evenly spaced frames from the one second of video. At 20 and 24 fps, frames are being dropped irregularly from the video, one from every three frames at 20 fps, one from every six at 24 fps. This can cause the 20 and 24 fps video to look more jumpy than 15 fps.

  We've included four files in the chap_10 subdirectory, called AC_15.avi, AC_20.avi, AC_24.avi, and AC_30.avi. As you may have guessed, these are the same file compressed to 15, 20, 24, and 30 frames per second. I know that 30 fps looks really smooth and that 15 fps looks choppy. I can't tell whether the 20 and 24 fps files look better or worse since I'm biased (can't you just use 15 fps and let me go on!), but perhaps you can test an unsuspecting officemate and get his or her observations.

- With low-motion videos, higher frame rates don't look that much different from 15 fps, since the limited change between the frames doesn't need 30 fps to show smoothly. We've included four files in the chap_10 subdirectory, called TK_15.avi, TK_20.avi, TK_24.avi, and TK_30.avi, the same file compressed to the different frame rates. Once again, grab an officemate and see what an unbiased person thinks.

Table 10.4 Display rate by computer and codec.

Display Rate, Quality by Codec	486/66		P60		P190		P133		P166	
	15 fps	30 fps	15 fps	30 fps	15 fps	30 fps	15 fps	30 fps	15 fps	30 fps
Cinepak	15	30	15	29	15	29	15	29	15	30
IVI, bidirectional	5	4	9	4	15	24	15	28	15	30
IVI, no bidirectional	7.5	5	10	4	15	26	14	29	15	30
IVI, no bidirectional, good compression	5	n.a.	11	n.a.	15	n.a.	15	n.a.	15	n.a.
Quick compressor	9	n.a.	10	n.a.	15	n.a.	14	n.a.	15	n.a.
Indeo 3.2	15	6	15	26	15	27	15	29	15	30
Power!Video Pro	14	n.a.	15	n.a.	15	n.a.	15	n.a.	15	n.a.
TrueMotionS	9	n.a.	14	n.a.	15	n.a.	15	n.a.	15	n.a.
Smacker	15	30	15	24	15	25	15	30	15	30
MPEG-1	n.a.	3.7	n.a.	9	n.a.	19	n.a.	23	n.a.	28
Video 1	15	n.a.	15	n.a.	15	n.a.	15	n.a.	15	n.a.

- You're probably better off using a higher quality, slower playback codec like IVI at 15 fps than a lower quality, faster playback codec like Cinepak at 30 fps. That's because the overall *perceived* quality of the IVI video might be a bit higher. The only exception *might* be with high-motion files. Compare AC_30.avi, a Cinepak 30 fps file, with AC_15IVI.avi, an IVI file compressed at 15 fps. Which looks better to you (or your unbiased officemate)?

Note that your sound card captures a continuous audio stream irrespective of how many video frames per second your capture card is storing to disk. During compression, the encoder divides the audio stream into equal chunks and interleaves each chunk with (hopefully) the appropriate video frame. For example, if you encode at 15 frames per second, the audio is divided into 15 equal chunks, interleaved with their respective video frames.

Frame Rate Options Consider 10 fps if you want high-quality video on low-powered machines and the video has only moderate motion with no hard audio/video synchronization points. At 10 fps, talking head videos don't look synchronized and most action sequences appear choppy.

Consider 30 fps when you're trying to show off to the boss, but only at high bandwidths and from that screaming SCSI drive hooked to your capture station. Tell her you could deliver that quality video on CD-ROM at 200 KB/s if you could only buy more products from Jan Ozer's company, Doceo Publishing.

…Errr…Actually, tell her she can show it to potential investors but not to expect the video to look "quite" that good in the finished product (thank goodness Proposition 211 failed in California—all those computer marketing folks who would have been out of jobs just before Christmas, just too tragic to think about).

Seriously, if you go 30 fps, check Table 10.4 and make sure your compressed video will play back at this rate on your target computer. Remember that these test files were all compressed to 250 KB/s and that if you bump the data rate for quality, you probably will drop the display rate on marginal computers. Do yourself a favor and compress at 15 fps as well, and compare the two videos just to make sure that 30 fps does, in fact, look better.

Finally, remember that for linear play video at least, if your playback station is powerful enough for 30 frames per second, you probably should be looking at MPEG-1 anyway.

MPEG-1 Most MPEG-1 encoders accept video captured at 30 fps or 29.97 fps, the precise frame rate of NTSC video. I've always worked with 30 fps.

Many MPEG-1 encoders also work at 24 fps, but this option should be used only with material that originated as film. Even then you need some pretty sophisticated software to get rid of the extra six frames injected when the film was converted to videotape.

Streaming Internet Delivery Once again, frame rate is the other side of the resolution/frame rate equation. When working with limited bandwidths, you can choose either big-resolution (320×240) videos that play at 1 or 2 fps or smaller videos (160×120) that play at 10–15 frames per second. Either way, the important rule stands: Capture at your ultimate delivery frame rate.

Nonlinear Editing   Once again, the stated rate of NTSC video is 60 fields per second, and this is your goal, your Holy Grail, the only acceptable capture rate. At 60 fields, 640×480 capture, you're starting to strain the limits of your capture system, and most of the time you'll end up dropping your capture data rate to reduce frames dropped during capture.

In most instances, however, you'll never totally eliminate dropped frames. Even in the most highly tuned system, your disk might hiccup, or your capture card might hit an area so difficult to capture that a drop of one or two frames is inevitable. This happens often when cutting into a scene from black, because the amount of change overwhelms the capture card.

When testing capture cards for the book, over a 9000-frame test tape, several cards dropped three or four frames no matter how low the data rate. For this reason, we pretty much accepted any test in which the board dropped less than one frame per 1000.

Keep in mind that when a board drops a frame, it doesn't create a gap in the video stream. Rather, the board simply tells the file to repeat the frame immediately before the dropped frame. This means that 15 dropped frames over the course of a 15-minute segment don't create a half-second loss of synchronization; it's just that there are 15 times when the video stutters for 1/30 of a second. It's embarrassing to drop frames, of course, so don't admit it to your friends, but in most instances it's imperceptible to the human eye.

Table 10.5 summarizes our thoughts regarding capture rates.

5. Video Format/Frame Rate

When capturing video, your first goal is to get the frames to disk. If your target is 30 fps at 320×240 for MPEG-1 conversion, make sure you capture

Table 10.5   Recommended frame per second capture rates.

Capturing for:	Recommendation
Compression with traditional software codec	15 fps unless you're targeting only extremely powerful computers
Software MPEG-1 compression	30 fps
Streaming Internet delivery	Check codec's documentation and formulate big picture versus fast motion strategy
Nonlinear editing	60 fields

30 fps. Your second goal is to get the frames to disk at the best possible quality.

Let's review some simple rules.

Rule number one: All capture compression is lossy, which degrades quality, so it's best to avoid compression when we can. When capturing for nonlinear editing, however, you have to compress, since no hard disk that we can afford can store 30 MB/s of data to disk without compression.

Rule number two: All capture compression is lossy, so compress as little as possible while still getting the frames to disk. This means capture at the highest possible data rate.

All capture cards with compressed capture formats include controls for increasing or decreasing compression, usually in the form of data rate sliders (see FAST's in Figure 10.9). When capturing using these compressed formats, always capture at the highest possible data rate you can achieve without dropping frames.

Rule number three: Raw YUV (luminance, hue, saturation) formats typically produce better results than compressed formats. YUV formats typically throw away color information but don't compress the video. YUV formats, for example, allow Intel's Smart Video Recorder III to capture 30 fps at a data rate of 2.55 MB/s rather than the 6.9 MB/s data rate of raw RGB (red, green, blue) video. Since most capture subsystems can't store 6.9 MB/s in real time, the YUV format lets you capture without compression.

One caveat: depending on the board, some YUV formats can be off in color, usually on the greenish side. In these instances, compressed video that looks normal is superior to YUV formats that make your boss look like a Martian. Trust me on this one.

OK, one more caveat: note that YUV capture formats don't have data rate sliders, because they're not implementing a lossy compression, they're discarding some color information that hopefully won't affect quality. This means that if you're dropping frames and can't fix the situation by trying the steps listed here, you may have to use a compressed format. Remember that goal number one is getting the frames to disk.

How much difference does this make? Figure 10.11 shows two VDO videos, one captured in YUV mode with ISVR3 and the other captured in compressed mode with FAST AV/Master. Both videos are on the CD-ROM (fg10_11l.avi and fg10_11r.avi), though you'll have to surf over to www.VDOLive.com to get the drivers to play them.

To be honest, the FAST video was also captured at 320×240 and scaled to 176×144 in Premiere, which can create another set of problems (see earlier). However, the ISVR3 clip is slightly clearer than the FAST AV/ Master, with fewer visible artifacts. Whether it is attributable to the scaling or compression during capture is, of course, irrelevant, since you *must* capture with compression and scale with the FAST AV/Master, whereas you *can* capture directly to 176×144 resolution without compression with the ISVR3. Decisions, decisions.

How about on the MPEG-1 side? Figure 10.12 shows two clips compressed with Xing's MPEG-1 encoder, one captured with the FAST AV/Master, the other with the ISVR3. Note the aliasing on the counter ledge just above the label in the FAST clip, as well as the slightly increased distortion around the face and neck. Once again, both files are on the CD-ROM (fg10_12l.avi and fg10_12r.avi), so you can check them out for yourself.

In the old plug-and-play days, I'd hesitate to tell anyone to purchase *two* capture cards to use for different types of projects, since it could take weeks to get your machine right after swapping cards. On a good plug-and-play machine, however, you can swap cards fairly easily, which makes application-specific capture cards a reality.

You can't do nonlinear editing with the ISVR3, since it has no analog out ports, so if nonlinear editing is on the agenda, it can't be your only capture

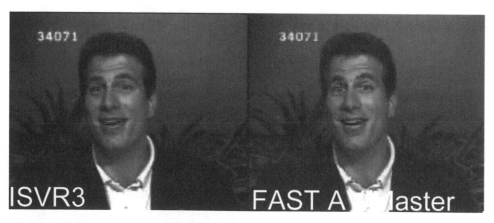

Figure 10.11   FAST AV/Master versus ISVR3 in 176×144 competition. Which do you think is clearer?

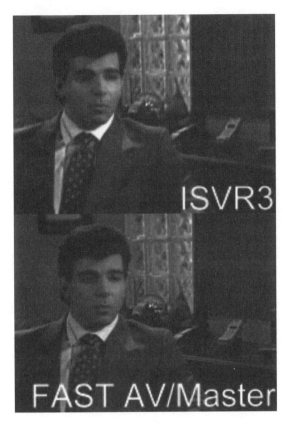

Figure 10.12   FAST AV/Master versus ISVR3 in MPEG-1 competition. Note
the aliasing on the ledge above the FAST label and the slightly
increased distortion in the face.

card. For $199, however, it's a damn good investment strictly for the various
flavors of capture for compression, be it Internet, MPEG-1, or good old
software-only codecs.

Rule number four: Although raw RGB formats should produce
superior results to YUV formats, we didn't find that to be the case
in any of the tests performed here. Go with RGB only if it's your
only raw format or if YUV is off-color.

Rule number five: Not all boards support all of these capture formats, which means that you won't always have all the options
presented here. Like video resolution, the format options relate to

Table 10.6 Recommended capture format.

Capturing for:	Recommendation
Traditional software codec	Uncompressed format (usually YUV) if possible; otherwise, compressed at the highest possible quality setting
Software MPEG-1 compression	Ditto
Streaming Internet delivery	Ditto
Nonlinear editing	Compressed format at highest possible quality setting

the board, not the capture software, so changing from VidCap32 to Premiere won't buy you any more capture formats.

All But Nonlinear Editing   When capturing for any purpose *other than* nonlinear editing, capture in uncompressed mode wherever possible. For MPEG-1 capture (e.g., 30 fps, 320×240), note that if the board supports only RGB, the only way to get the frames to disk will likely be via step capture, unless you've got a totally monster SCSI system. Essentially, this means that you may be forced into using a compressed format to get the frames to disk. On the other hand, if the board has a YUV format, you can probably capture in YUV without dropping frames.

For software codecs at 15 fps or streaming Internet delivery, you might try RGB before giving up and using a compressed format. The uncompressed data rate for 160×120×15 fps RGB video is about 1.75 MB/s, well within the capabilities of most SCSI systems.

Many boards don't support uncompressed formats, which is a crying shame, but there it is. If you have to capture in compressed format, *always capture at the highest possible data rate the board supports.* Don't try to capture down to your target data rate in one pass. When capturing for *any kind of compression*, the rule is *capture high, compress low.*

Nonlinear Editing   When capturing for nonlinear editing, you're going to have to capture in compressed format. When working with a capture card for the first time, you'll probably have a breaking in period in which you get to know the card's capabilities, which can be eased if the capture card has a utility, like miro's shown in Figure 10.13, that measures the capacity of your target drive and recommends a safe data rate.

When I test a board for capture capacity, I usually ignore the board's recommendations, which are generally conservative, and start capturing at the board's control capacity. If it goes up to 7 MB/s, that's where I start. Then I start capturing, stopping the capture once dropped frames get excessive, usually beyond one dropped frame for every 1000 frames. Then I lower the data rate by 100 KB/s and start again. Usually, the first few captures end quickly as the board immediately drops tons of frames. Then the tests lengthen gradually until the board passes.

When experimenting, keep two things in mind. First, you've not only got to get the frames to disk, you've got to get them smoothly *back out* to your analog source when writing to tape. This means that you've got to test writing capacity as well as reading before selecting a target. When working with the miro DC30, we could capture at up to 5.5 MB/s, but couldn't write

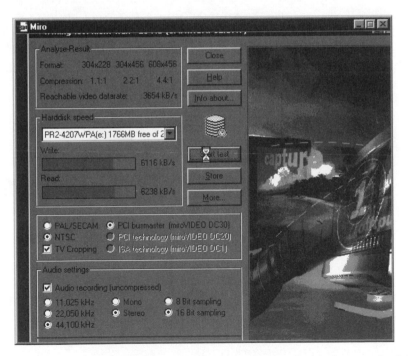

Figure 10.13   Miro's outstanding data rate capacity tool helps you find the optimal data rate.

successfully back out to tape at rates higher than 4.8. For this very obvious reason, we selected 4.8 as our capture rate.

Next, be aware that sometimes video doesn't write as smoothly after being edited and rendered. During editing, your editor has to decompress frames being edited, add the transition, effect, titling, or whatever, and then recompress the fields back to the motion JPEG capture format. When testing several cards, we noticed that a rendered file dropped frames when writing back out to tape, even when the originally captured file didn't.

Nonlinear video editing isn't for the meek or unwary. But if you follow one simple rule, you'll minimize the risk of being caught unawares toward the end of a project. As with capture for compression applications, always test your work procedures out to finished copy, be it analog or digital, before starting to work through the various project phases in parallel.

In other words, capture scene 1, edit it, and render it out to final format before starting on scene 2. Then, if your results were good, you can capture clips 2–10, edit clips 2–10, and then render them. You can end up with 10 useless clips if you *assume* your procedures are correct and jump right in and capture scenes 1–10, edit scenes 1–10, and then finally render them and test.

With any type of video development, the more you test at the start, the less you'll be hustling to try and clean up at the end.

Dropped Frames during Capture   If dropped frames become excessive, take these steps before dropping the quality levels dramatically.

1. Don't use the "preview" option during capture, since it takes CPU cycles to update your video card. Shutting off preview makes an NTSC monitor a virtual necessity, but job one is, after all, getting the frames to disk.
2. Check out Chapter 11, where we rate editing programs on capture efficiency. VidCap32 is generally more efficient than all other editors, so if you can get your hands on VidCap32, use it.
3. Change to 8-bit (256-color) video mode. This reduces the computer's overall workload, allowing more CPU cycles for capture, transfer, and storage.
4. Unload all extraneous memory-resident programs.
5. Uninstall your network card.
6. Defragment your hard drive (again).

6. Video Source

Selecting Your Analog Source   All capture cards let you select between composite and S-Video input. Note that some cards autodetect which signal is coming in, saving you a step, while others force you to manually select. Figure 10.14 shows the screen for the FAST AV/Master. It goes without saying that you should use S-Video whenever available, since this will deliver better quality video.

Note the VCR selection box, which customizes the program for capturing from a VTR (videotape recorder) or VCR (videocassette recorder) as opposed to directly from a camera or other source. VCRs can produce an irregular synchronization signal that is manifest in rolling, hooking, or jittery displays. In theory, when you check the VCR or VTR box, you enable compensation called time-based correction, which cleans up the signal.

In operation, check the box on and off and see how it affects your incoming video signal from whatever source. If it cleans it up, great. If not, click it off and don't worry about it.

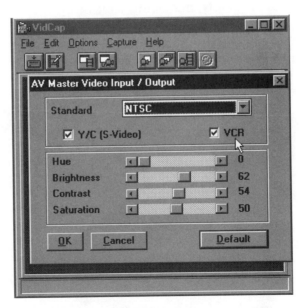

Figure 10.14   Video source selection from the FAST AV/Master. Note the VCR selection box and the controls for adjusting the incoming video.

Adjusting Color and Brightness   Note the controls for adjusting incoming hue, brightness, contrast, and saturation in Figure 10.15. Virtually all capture cards have such controls, and most of the time the default settings simply won't work—you'll probably have to customize the settings for each class of videos that you capture. Accept it, get used to it, don't fight it, or you'll end up redoing a bunch of video files.

The same clip from two versions of Richard Irwin's *Multimedia MBA* helps illustrate the importance of getting used to working with these controls. The video engineer, Chris Ewald, an outstanding compressionist now with Triad Interactive in Washington, DC, used the same capture card, the Intel Smart Video Recorder Pro, to capture both clips.

This is a challenging clip, with lots of cuts, some motion, some talking heads, and plenty of vivid colors. The first time out, on the left, the clip was slightly washed out in appearance, with minimal contrast between foreground and background settings.

When capturing the second time, however, Chris had enough time to perfect the incoming color and brightness settings. If you play the clip, you'll note more realistic colors throughout, as well as a generally richer feel to the entire clip. Clearly, managing your incoming video makes a big difference.

Unfortunately, selecting the optimal settings is a real pain. It's subjective, it's time consuming, and the controls are obscure. I mean, can anybody meaningfully explain what hue and saturation are?

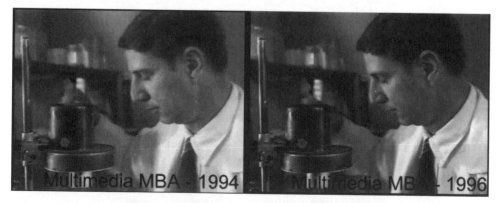

Figure 10.15   Same clip, same capture card, but the clip on the right, from a later version of Richard Irwin's *Multimedia MBA*, looks better because the incoming color and brightness settings were totally optimized.

If your analog source is frame accurate, like a laserdisc, it's somewhat easier to adjust because you can freeze the frame on screen and adjust the controls until you get it right. With other decks, you've just got to roll the video and experiment in real time. Here are some color control "gotchas" to consider:

- Don't expect the captured video to look like the video you modified on screen—the color always seems slightly different. This is especially so when capturing with an overlay card. Analyze small chunks of the actual captured video to make sure it's acceptable.
- Remember that compression may also change the color and especially brightness parameters of the video. This means that you should capture *and compress* your test clips to the target data rate with your chosen codec early in the design process to assess your capture performance. In Chapter 6 we summarize the effects that some codecs have on color and brightness; you might refer back to that chapter for a quick refresher.
- Once again, test early and often on computers other than your capture station. Note that while you see the world through the graphics card and monitor on your capture station, the rest of the world sees it through *their* graphics card and monitor. This means that you should test your compressed test videos on other computers before assuming you have a keeper.

  For example, if the graphics card and monitor are set too dark on the capture station, or your monitor is simply fading out, you may boost brightness to lighten up the video. If your controls aren't representative, your videos will look washed out to the rest of the world.

  If you're doing custom work for a limited set of computers, be it kiosk or sales laptop, test your videos early and often on these platforms.
- Don't expect your settings to work with all video segments on the tape, even if you don't change scenes. Sometimes color and/or brightness changes over the life of the tape, or maybe it was the lighting adjustment that you did halfway through the shoot. Either way, you may have to change the settings to keep your video looking consistent.
- If you've got disparate footage on the same tape, like outdoor and indoor shots, you should also check your parameters when adjust-

ing to the new footage. The "indoor" settings just may not work for the great outdoors.

- You should also calibrate when changing tapes. For example, if your video shoot took three BetaSP tapes, check your settings between them. You can calibrate the new video against the old by loading a file in VidEdit and keeping it on screen as a guide.

Once again, all this work can be a real pain. However, when the colors aren't just right, your video won't look good. While you can modify colors and brightness in Premiere, it's better to get it right the first time.

Preview Video/Overlay Video   Figure 10.16 shows the Preview toggle, which is usually available from both menu and icon. Preview makes the video show up live in the application during capture, which is convenient but can degrade capture performance significantly. If you start dropping massive numbers of frames, turning off Preview is a good first step toward improving performance.

Preview also tends to slow mouse responsiveness to a crawl as the CPU struggles to keep up with 30 frames per second of incoming video. When this occurs, it's usually easier and faster to work with the keyboard rather than the mouse.

Troubleshooting the Incoming Signal   At this stage you should have a clean video signal displayed on your monitor in either overlay or preview mode. Here are some problems that may occur and some possible solutions.

1. No video, period! This can be caused by everything from an improperly installed capture card to a loose cable. This is the most frustrating experience of all, since you really don't know where to start. Having an NTSC monitor really helps, because then you can tell if your analog source is working. Here are some things to try:

   a. Verify software setup. Typically, if you try to load your capture program and the proper drivers aren't loaded, you'll get an error message to that effect. We look at capture card installation fairly exhaustively in Chapter 9, so if you're not properly installed, check your installation manual and check out Chapter 9. If you're properly installed, try to 1.) Toggle the preview button to make sure preview is running. 2.) Make sure that you've selected the right input source (S-Video/Composite) and broad-

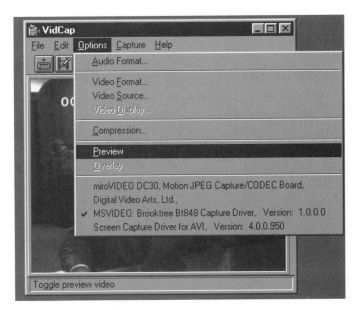

Figure 10.16 The preview toggle, which displays or hides video in your capture program's main screen during capture. While useful, Preview can cause dropped frames during capture, so disable it if you're having this problem.

cast standard (PAL/SECAM/NTSC). 3.) Toggle the VTR/VCR button to see if that makes a difference.

b. Verify hardware setup. If you have an NTSC monitor that's receiving the video signal, switch connectors and see if that brings the board to life. If it does, you'll know that your board is properly installed and that you may have a faulty S-Video cable.

If you don't have an NTSC monitor, try the composite signal (assuming you've been using S-Video) and see what happens.

Shut off the computer and make sure that the analog connectors are properly seated in the capture board. With my first capture card, properly seating the video cable required a lot of pressure, which got me in the habit of screwing in the board.

If all else fails, change cables.

2. Video jittery or otherwise distorted. This almost always seems to be attributable to an incorrect software setup. Check to make sure that you've properly selected the right input source and toggle the VCR/VTR button.

3. Video mottled or gray scale. This almost always seems to relate to a software setting as well. Some YUV formats can look pretty funky on screen, with greenish Martian types of effects the most frequent.

   Also check to make sure you've selected the proper input source. Sometimes when Composite input is checked but the input source is S-Video, the video appears in gray scale.

On occasion, I've lost all color information and captured black-and-white videos when an S-Video connector isn't seated sufficiently. Generally, this means it's time to throw away the cable, since these problems almost always relate to the cable, not the capture card or analog source.

7. Miscellaneous Options

Now we're getting close to the actual capture. The Capture Video Sequence dialog box shown in Figure 10.17 is where you implement your frame rate selection and take final passes at audio and video capture parameters. But first, the enable capture time limit option.

Enable Capture Time Limit   By selecting this option in the dialog box, you can set a time limit for the capture and have the software stop the capture automatically. I use this for timed test clips, and it may be useful for capturing long clips when you want to leave and get a cup of coffee or something. Check that, let's call it a cup of Java (publisher said I *had to* mention Java in the book).

Otherwise, remember this control is here if you find your video captures mysteriously stopping in midstream. Generally, it means you've somehow engaged this control at some duration shorter than the clip you're actually trying to capture. Check it off to disengage and you'll be in business.

The other buttons on this screen give you second looks at items that we've already discussed. The Audio button brings you to the dialog boxes shown in Figure 10.2. The Video button brings you to the dialog box shown

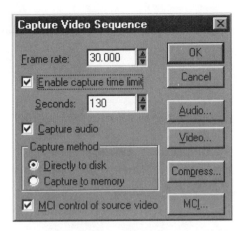

Figure 10.17 Capture Video Sequence dialog box contains several final capture controls.

in Figure 10.6. It's always helpful to review all these options just one more time before starting the capture.

The Compress button brings up the dialog box shown in Figure 10.18. This is some strangely vestigial control that, like your tonsils and appendix, seemed to have had some use in the past, but not one I can recollect. You can typically ignore this box during normal operation.

8. Capture

Manual Capture At this point, if your analog source isn't controlled through an MCI or VISCA controller, you're ready to go. Press MCI in Figure 10.17 to trigger the dialog box shown in Figure 10.19.

Now it's up to you to press OK at the right time. The video should be showing in the window underneath the dialog box in Figure 10.19. It's obviously easier to watch the video if you move the box away. When the target sequence begins, click OK.

Although the system looks ready to capture, in reality the board isn't quite ready and will need between two and five seconds to start the capture after you click OK. This means that you really have to press OK between two and five seconds before your target video appears, which takes some getting used to. However, you can easily crop extra frames after capture,

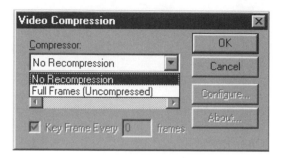

Figure 10.18 The vestigial Video Compression dialog box. Like our tonsils and appendix, we know it's there, but we're not sure why!

so it's usually faster to press OK early and capture too much than to try to time it right and miss the first couple of frames.

Once you press OK, a message appears in VidCap32's status bar advising you to press Escape to end the capture. During capture, you can keep the

Figure 10.19 Launching a non-MCI-controlled capture.

video running in VidCap32 by selecting preview, though it can detract from capture performance (e.g., cause dropped frames). Preview or no preview, VidCap32 presents running frame count and capture time, updated after each 100-frame interval, in the status bar below the capture window (Figure 10.20).

This lack of visual feedback makes an external NTSC monitor very helpful. Alternatively, you can time the clip or count the number of frames and use the capture information presented by VidCap32 to stop when appropriate.

After you've completed the capture, VidCap32 presents capture results, including duration, number of video frames, frames dropped, and audio bytes captured, in the status bar. Right after capture is a good time to either change the name of the capture file so that you don't write over it during the next capture or use the Save As command to save it to a new name.

Figure 10.20   Capture results presented in VidCap32's status bar.

Computer-Controlled Capture   Computer-controlled captures are useful in two instances. First, during real-time capture, computer control lets you start and stop your capture exactly where you want to, avoiding the trimming process. More important, if you record time code or frame settings, you'll be in great shape if you have to capture the same footage again—especially if your capture program does batch capture.

Computer control also comes in handy for "step" capture, which you can use to capture in raw mode and avoid compression, assuming your capture card has a raw mode, of course. Step capture requires an analog source that's both frame accurate and capable of being controlled by your computer. However, if your deck is computer controllable and not frame accurate, you can still use it to drive real-time captures.

Note that frame accuracy in the analog world differs from the concept of frame accuracy as it relates to video capture. Frame-accurate devices in the capture concept are those that can pause on a frame while providing perfect synchronization. If you've ever paused your home VHS deck on a single frame, you probably know what frame accuracy isn't.

Computerizing Your Deck   Let's look at how to "computerize" two devices that are both frame accurate and computer controlled, the Pioneer CLD-V2600 laserdisc and the VISCA-controlled Sony CVD-1000 Hi-8 deck. The procedure is roughly the same for all computer-controlled decks, whether frame accurate or not, so this should help those looking to perform real-time capture as well as step frame.

To computerize your analog deck, you need the required drivers and a cable connecting the computer to the device. This is in addition to the cables required for audio and video capture and transmission back to the deck after editing.

Drivers   Windows 95 simplified working with VISCA decks and laserdiscs by including the drivers in every installation. Wanna see? Let's explore.

Go to your Windows 95 Start (me up) button, touch Settings, and Control Panel. Somewhere in the midst of all those icons you'll see one with a video strip and some audio notes titled "Multimedia." Double-click on this icon and tab over to the advanced settings screen shown in Figure 10.21. Touch Media Control Devices and you're there.

We touched briefly on the Media Control Interface (MCI) back in Chapter 3. Briefly, MCI is an application programming interface for communicating with multimedia devices jointly released by Microsoft and IBM in 1991. In

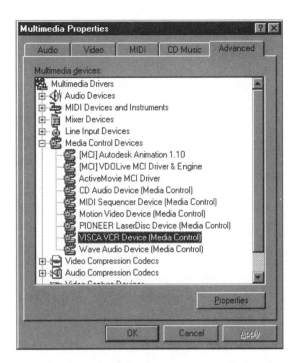

Figure 10.21   Windows 95 Multimedia Properties dialog box showing all
MCI devices installed in the computer.

addition to VFW, the MCI interface controls the playback of analog video
decks like laserdiscs and the playback of digital formats like animation and
WAV audio.

With Windows 3.x, you had to track the drivers down and install them
yourself. With the drivers included in Windows 95, all you have to do is
pick a communications, or COM, port or the internal designation for the
physical port we'll be connecting the laserdisc to in a few moments. You do
this by double-clicking on the device, pressing the "settings" button, which
brings up the screen shown in Figure 10.22.

How do you know which COM port? You try to locate the port associated
with the physical serial port located in the back of your computer. You can
check your System Properties box (Start/Settings/Control Panel/System)
shown in Figure 10.23 to track down the right port. If you have a modem
installed, just make sure you don't choose the same port.

Once you've got the correct port defined, it's time to hook up the cables.

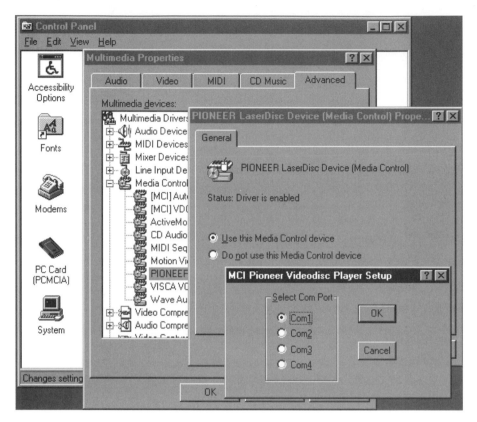

Figure 10.22   Configuring the COM port for your Pioneer laserdisc.

Cables and Connectors   Both devices have specialized cables. The Sony CVD-1000 ships with a VISCA cable, which has an eight-pin Mini-Din connector that connects directly into Macintosh computers but not IBM computers—you'll need an adapter. Which adapter depends on the serial connector that you'll devote to this connection. There are three kinds of serial port connectors, 9-pin (DB9) male (pins sticking out) and 25-pin (DB25) male and female connectors. You'll need the opposite type of connector to the one open on your serial port. For example, if your target port is a DB25-pin male, you'll need a female connector. See birds and bees for details.

The other side of the connector must be the DIN8 connector to hook to the VISCA control. Any of the three connectors should cost under $10. You

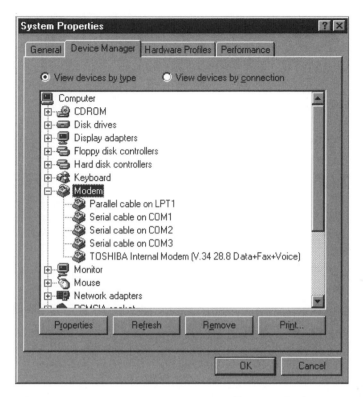

Figure 10.23   Your System Properties screen tells you which COM port to
assign to your laserdisc.

will need this connector if running on an IBM computer, so you should be
sure to pick one up when and where you purchase your deck.

The Pioneer cable costs about $20. A normal serial cable won't work—the
pinouts on the laserdisc end are nonstandard. The cable typically isn't
found in consumer stores like Radio Shack, so if you didn't get a one when
you purchased your laserdisc, you'll have to track one down at your local
A/V store.

You'll also need the video and audio cables. Both decks use S-Video
cables, the 4-pin connector shown in Figure 7.1 (the middle rectangle is a
guide, not a pin). The cable has the same connector at both ends, as does
the 1-pin composite cable.

The CVD-1000 has two main rows of connectors on the back, which look
like the drawing in Figure 10.24. The input side takes input from another

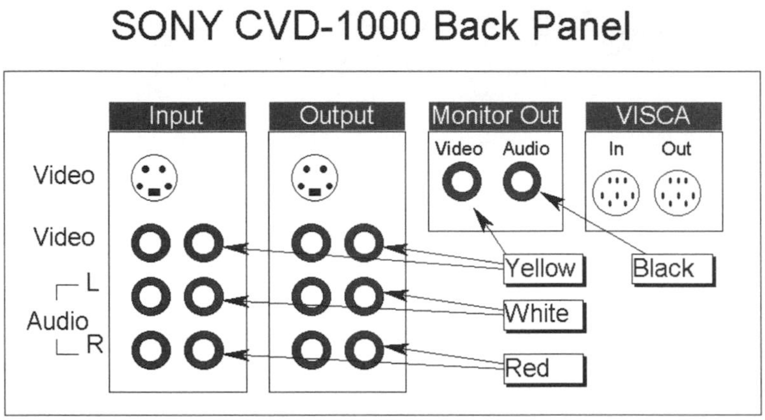

SONY CVD-1000 Back Panel

Figure 10.24 The business end of the Sony CVD-1000, showing analog inputs and outputs and ports for VISCA controls.

deck or computer-generated analog output, used to record the fruits of our nonlinear editing efforts. The output side contains two rows, with one S-Video output, two composite video outputs, and two audio outputs.

To capture video from this deck, connect a cable from the deck's S-Video *output port* into the S-Video *input* connector on your capture card. For nonlinear editing, where you send the video back out to the deck, connect the S-Video *output port* of your capture card to the S-Video *input port* on the deck. While you can flip-flop the cables, it's typically much easier to just buy two.

You can use either audio output. For consumer decks, you'll need a cable that combines the left (white) and right (red) audio feeds into one jack for input into your sound card. For nonlinear editing, you need another identical cable to connect your sound card's audio output port to the deck's audio input ports. Most sound cards include at least one such cable, so you may have to pick up another.

BetaSP and other professional decks have totally different audio connectors called XLR connectors. If you're planning on renting a deck for a couple of days, make sure you've got all the required cables for capture and sending the audio back out to the deck for nonlinear editing. Plan on spending about $100 for the required cables and connectors.

The monitor out outputs go to your NTSC tracking monitor and optional speaker. Most higher end audio cards will output audio simultaneously during capture, so you won't really need the separate speaker. One extra benefit of using the NTSC monitor with the Sony deck is that the monitor out shows time code information, which is essential to identifying start and stop points on the tape. This helps make up for the fact that the Sony doesn't have a liquid-crystal display (LCD) readout of the time code information like the laserdisc and most higher end decks.

Without an NTSC monitor you have to hook the monitor out feed into your capture card to track time codes, which means switching back and forth between the composite and S-Video feeds, which is a real pain. Best advice is, if you use the Sony, get an NTSC monitor.

Although all tape decks will have slightly different configurations, most professional decks and even pro-sumers will have inputs, outputs, and monitor outs. So before you plug into your deck, find the input and output jacks and make sure you use the output.

The laserdisc will be even simpler because it doesn't have video and audio inputs since you can't record on the finished disk. You could confuse the composite video out with the audio outs, but most are pretty well labeled, so if you pay attention you'll have no problem.

Let's summarize our equipment needs:

1. S-Video cable, which typically comes with cameras, capture cards, and professional decks but not consumer decks like the laserdisc.
2. Audio cable, 2 pin to 1 pin, which typically comes with your sound card.
3. Cable hookup between computer and deck. In the case of the Sony, you'll need the VISCA cable, which comes with the V-Deck (remember the adapter). If using the laserdisc, you'll need to pick up the optional Pioneer cable.
4. Composite cable to NTSC monitor. This is typically supplied on consumer decks but not professional ones.
5. Audio cable to audio out (optional).

Still Frame Capture   Press the MCI button shown in Figure 10.17 to bring up the dialog box shown in Figure 10.25. Before loading this dialog box, Windows checks to see which device is attached to the serial port and loads the proper driver, in this instance the laserdisc driver.

Figure 10.25　MCI capture command screen.

If no driver loads in the MCI device box, your installation isn't correct. When this happens:

- Make sure your cables are connected and the deck is turned on. If the deck has a local/remote toggle switch that hands control to and from remote devices (e.g., your computer), make sure this is set to remote.
- If this doesn't work, you've probably selected the wrong COM port and need to go back and select another.
- If you try all four and nothing works, you've probably got a hardware problem, most likely a bad cable.

Once the driver loads, if you select Play video, you'll have real-time, computer-controlled capture. Select Step video to go the step frame route.

Step Frame Capture Averaging　　Here's what VidCap32 has to say about the Step Capture Frame Averaging controls:

> The Step Frame Averaging: The following two options are used with the Step Video capture method to bring out detail and reduce video noise:
>
> 2X Spatial specifies whether to expand the frame size during capture to bring out more detail in the image. VidCap doubles the frame size captured and then uses spatial averaging to reduce

aliasing effects. This technique enhances fine lines in the sequence, at the cost of some fuzziness.

n Frame(s) Temporal specifies whether to reduce video noise by repeatedly capturing frames and averaging out the noise from the captured images. Specify how many images to capture and average per frame. Note: Some capture boards provide hardware routines for performing these enhancements. If your capture board includes such a feature, you should not select any of the step frame averaging options provided by VidCap.

As shown in Figure 10.7, the interpolation and filtering done by most hardware cards are superior to those performed by Video for Windows. We tested 2X spatial averaging and found virtually no difference between the nonaveraged and 2X averaged. Two raw frames from these files are included in the chap_10 subdirectory under zoomby1.avi and zoomby2.avi. Load them into VCS, compare at various zoom ratios, and see if you can tell the difference.

This could be, as Microsoft says, because our capture card is zooming anyway. You might test for yourself, but in the absence of proof that it does improve your video, I'd recommend against 2X spatial averaging.

The n frame averaging is a more interesting question. In concept, this is a great idea. Remember that during digitization, your capture board has to assign each pixel one color out of 16.7 million possible colors. The sheer number and closeness of choices virtually ensure that the captured value will differ from the real value to some degree. N frame averaging lets you digitize the same frame a number of times and average the pixel values to derive one averaged value, which should more accurately represent the real color.

When you select three, for example, the capture board digitizes each frame three times and averages the values. In theory, this should help interframe compression, since there would be more interframe redundancy, and intraframe compression, which would benefit from internal redundancy. Alas, a panacea it's not, and in application we saw very little difference between files that were averaged upon capture and not averaged.

We tested two kinds of files, high- and low-motion sequences (see Table 10.7). The control file was captured without averaging, and the test file was captured with three-frame averaging. In the low-motion videos, there was no perceptible difference. In the high-motion sequences, when there was a

Table 10.7   Frame averaging test files.

Video Type	Averaged File	Nonaveraged
Low motion	tlkstep3.avi (1,949,950 bytes)	tlkstep1.avi (1,942,988 bytes)
High motion	actstep3.avi (3,019,716 bytes)	actstep1.avi (2,953,666 bytes)

difference, it typically manifested as an artifact in the averaged file that wasn't in the nonaveraged file. Translation: Averaging produced artifacts in laboratory rats ... er, videos.

On the other hand, I recently received a facsimile from a product manager of a leading capture board manufacturer stating that they found that 3X averaging "cleaned the video up" and "marginally improved visual integrity and helped compression." As you can see from Table 10.7, we found that the averaging increased the average compressed frame size of the action file by 197 bytes and the size of the talking head file by 97 bytes. The difference isn't statistically significant but certainly is counterintuitive to the product manager's claim.

Once again, this may relate to your capture board, so you may want to try one or two short files yourself to see if you can spot a difference. If you don't see a clear improvement, don't do it, since averaging caused artifacts in some videos and increased the file size in all of our tests.

Capture Start and Stop

Laserdisc: When working with the laserdisc life gets really simple. Use the remote control unit to move the laserdisc reader to the desired start frame and then press the Set Start button. VidCap32 checks the location of the reader and enters the proper time code. Then move the reader to the desired stop frame and press the Set Stop button to enter the proper stop time. Dutifully record either the frame numbers or time code information in your trusty notebook and you're ready to capture. Press OK to return to the Capture Video Sequence screen.

If your laserdisc has an LCD counter, it's pretty simple to track your start and stop points. If not, you'll have to use the display control to show the frame number in the screen itself. Remember to shut off the display control before you start to capture, because what you see is what you get, and if the frame number is visible it will appear in your video.

Remember also that laserdisc step frame capture requires a CAV disk. Most commercial laserdiscs are *not* CAV, so if you're capturing from a commercial laserdisc and having problems, it's probably the format.

Sony CVD-1000:   Setting up the Sony is a bit more difficult. The V-Deck is frame accurate, but there are no step controls that can step you to a precise frame. The easiest way to capture is to estimate time code information by watching the tape on your NTSC monitor. Enter in the values where indicated and press OK to return to the Capture Video Sequence screen shown in Figure 10.17.

If you don't have an NTSC monitor, you'll have to connect both the composite and S-Video cables to your capture board and toggle back and forth between the two signals. Your composite signal will have the time code information and the S-Video signal will be your capture signal. It's not pretty, but it works.

One significant hassle relates to the VISCA control itself. When the VISCA cable is connected and the driver initialized, the deck is under VISCA control, and all other controls are frozen. Exiting the dialog box didn't release the VISCA control.

This means that you can't use manual controls to find start and stop points. Since VidCap32 is a dumb driver designed to capture, not hunt and seek, there's no software to help you seek either. The manual states that VISCA shuts down when you power down the unit, but this wasn't my experience.

This leaves two options. You can find all the start and stop points on the tape and then start capturing, which sounds terribly responsible and almost "Skinner-ish" in that it totally delays gratification, or pull the VISCA cable after every capture, manually find the start and stop points, and then plug the driver back in to capture. Guess which I did?

Working with this deck and others like it really benefits from analog deck controls like those in MediaStudio or Premiere. This is one area where you may be better off abandoning VidCap32 in favor of these other programs.

Sony lists the following points to consider when working with their VISCA drivers in the Install.txt file included with their driver.

1. Be sure to reset your camcorder hms counter at the beginning of the tape; you will not be able to search into negative counter values (either externally or with the mci-string "set vcr counter 0").

2. Time code may not be detectable, even though it is present, on some decks at the very beginning or the very end of a tape. If you are using mplayer, play the VCR for a few seconds and then close and reopen the driver, or issue the "time mode detect" command.
3. Index marking is highly hardware specific. Please refer to your video deck/cameras operation manual.
4. The millisecond time format assumes 30 fps (as opposed to 29.97). This is done for compatibility reasons. SMPTE time formats use the native time format on the tape and should be used whenever possible to avoid rounding errors.

Real-Time Capture Considerations   With either device, when capturing in real time, some boards need a few frames to get rolling and actually start to capture, even when the deck is controlled by the computer. Get in the habit of adding about half a second before the first frame you actually want to capture. When capturing in real time, be sure to check each captured file to make sure that the capture started in time and captured all the frames that you needed. When capturing in step frame mode, you can specify the exact start and stop frame because the capture board starts immediately on the first frame.

Capture at Last   Press OK in the Capture Video Sequence screen (Figure 10.17) and you'll start the step capture process. Now it's time to sit and wait for the capture to finish, which takes about a frame a second. If you're capturing in real time, the dialog box shown in Figure 10.19 comes up, prompting you to press OK to start the capture.

SUMMARY

1. Video capture is very application specific. Each of the four markets, nonlinear editing and conversion to MPEG-1, traditional software codecs, and streaming Internet delivery, has its own unique requirements. Check the tables in the body of this chapter for specific recommendations for capture audio parameters (Table 10.2), video resolution (Table 10.3), display rate (Table 10.4 or 10.5), and format (Table 10.6).

2. Without question, adjusting video input parameters for brightness, contrast, and color information is the primary area where you can improve or degrade video quality. Test early and often on many different computers before arriving at final input settings.

3. Computer-controlled capture is great for accurate real-time captures and non–real-time step captures and is much easier under Windows 95 than Windows 3.x. You'll need drivers and custom cables.

4. Step Frame Capture Averaging produced no tangible benefits in any of our tests and we recommend against it.

Chapter  11

Video Editing

INTRODUCTION

If the playbook for the San Francisco 49ers fell into the hands of the local Pop Warner team, would it make them a better football team? How about the choreography book for the Tolstoy Ballet doing *Swan Lake*—would it improve the performance of your four-year-old's ballet class?

In both instances, the answer is a clear regrettably no. Throw the sophisticated west coast offense at a six-year-old quarterback, and it would rain tears, not touchdowns. Demand pirouettes and grand jetés from your adolescent primas and their demo ballet will falter from divine to disaster. Few things are as worthless as tools too sophisticated for current skill levels.

And so it is with video editors. While most of us struggle to capture and compress good-looking video, the developers of editing software duke it out with features like advanced 3D motion paths, distortion and image warping, and gamma correction. And the inevitable price of added features—regardless of actual functionality to *my* application—is program complexity, making it even harder to perform the basics.

313

In short—give me a break, fellas... I don't wanna be Steven Spielberg, I just want better looking Indeo files. Don't sell me advanced features I won't ever use; convince me that your product will help me achieve this limited, but obviously critical function.

In essence, this is how we approached this review of editing software. Working with three mainstream video editors, Adobe Premiere ($795), Asymetrix Digital Video Producer ($89), and MediaStudio Video Editor from Ulead ($349), we studied the basics, from capture to compression, comparing output quality. Then we looked at common advanced features to identify qualitative differences between the programs, to learn if "parts is parts" or, perhaps more appropriately, if a page curl transition from a program other than Premiere would still look as sweet.

If you received MediaStudio or Digital Video Producer (DVP) bundled with a capture board, you'll learn if and when you'll need to purchase Premiere to produce your best. You'll also learn where Premiere falls short and where DVP or the venerable VidEdit is still your best option. Along the way, we'll pass along some tips learned from working with these complex programs to help speed up your journey on the learning curve.

As always, our focus is on CD-ROM publishing, so we're more concerned with compression-oriented features than whether you can export edit decision lists (EDLs) in the Grass Valley format. So if you've got some time scheduled in the virtual editing room, hop aboard.

WHAT EDITORS DO

In the beginning, there were VidCap and VidEdit, the capture and editing tools supplied by Microsoft with its original Video for Windows release in 1991. While these programs lacked the advanced features of second- and third-generation editors, they excelled at the simple tasks they were designed for.

VidEdit is still the standard for compression performance by which other programs are judged. Due to Microsoft's poorly documented application programming interfaces (APIs), most video editors had or still have problems matching VidEdit's compressed video quality and ability to produce files that play back smoothly from CD-ROMs.

In fact, for a surprising number of simple functions like clipping un-wanted frames from a captured file, reinterleaving audio and video files, computing an optimal palette, and compressing to final output, VidEdit is still the program of choice. If you've got a copy, archive the disk for eternity, 'cause you'll always want to be able to reinstall it. If you don't, praise the Lord and surf on over to ftp.microsoft.com with your ftp software. Microsoft has made VidEdit available free of charge. Download it at /developr/drg/multimedi/jumpstart/vfwlle/winvideo. Download into a subdirectory on your computer and run setup. The primary benefit of the download is VidEdit. VidCap is a 16-bit version that won't work with most capture boards, and the 16-bit version of CapScreen crashes on Windows 95.

When it comes to video captured for digital playback, the first measure of an editing program is still how it stacks up to VidEdit and VidCap. For that reason, we'll be referring to these classics frequently.

THE VIDEO CREATION PROCESS

Video creation involves four discrete steps: capture, editing, garnishing, and compression. Since each step can affect output quality, comparing the editors involves taking a close look at each stage.

Briefly, the first step, video capture, is when you capture the video from your analog source. Critical here is the comparative ability to capture at high bandwidths without dropping frames, as well as the availability of advanced features such as batch capture.

Next is editing the captured video to its final length and collecting other assets like bitmapped images and audio onto the program time line. Most editors can perform the basics; the difference here is in tools that enhance precision and overall ease of use.

The third and most time-consuming step is garnishing, or enhancing video appearance with transitions, special effects, overlays, and titles. We analyzed all four processes in detail, looking at the nature and extent of program options and also qualitative differences that make one program's output look better than another.

The last step is rendering, or combining the whole enchilada into one compressed video file. Here we compared compressed output to VidEdit, analyzing both data rate and playback speed. Intuitively, if a program can't produce a file that plays back smoothly from a CD-ROM, exceptional performance in the other areas becomes much less valuable. We also looked at some advanced features, like the ability to compute an optimal palette and concatenate multiple compressed video files into one without recompression.

Video Capture

We analyzed capture in two areas: features and performance. From a feature perspective, it's important to remember that most basic functionality comes from your capture board, not the software. The latter simply accesses onboard options like capture format, resolution, and adjustment of incoming color and brightness. This means that all editing programs should be able to access the same capture board features. For this reason, we focused on program- rather than capture board–related features.

From an architectural standpoint, DVP and MediaStudio capture via a separate program, while Premiere's capture is integrated. Both approaches had their good and bad sides. Working with the two separate capture programs was relatively intuitive, especially for someone used to VidCap, since all controls were capture related.

In contrast, Premiere's capture controls were scattered across several menu items and relatively difficult to find. For example, you couldn't set the capture file from the movie capture menu, you set it from the general preferences window. Ditto for selecting machine control. On the other hand, once you captured a file with Premiere, you were in the editing program, instantly trimming the file and placing it on the time line. In most instances, this felt like a preferred approach.

Premiere also lets you save most capture settings into a .PCS capture settings file. Curiously, however, Premiere doesn't save perhaps the most critical pieces of information—the incoming color and brightness adjustments. These are preserved in the premiere.ini file and are restored to their most recent setting every time you load the program.

Capture Features

In terms of common features, all programs enabled both real-time and step capture via machine control over our test bed laserdisc. Note that the level of machine control differed by program. While Premiere and MediaStudio provide videocassette recorder (VCR)–like controls over the laserdisc that let you play, stop, start, and rewind from within the program (see Figure 11.1), DVP doesn't, forcing you to use external controls.

This is a problem with VISCA devices that don't enable external control once program control is engaged. Without software-based controls, you need to sever the link by disconnecting the cable from the deck to unfreeze the hardware controls, then manually set the location for the next capture—a tedious process that outweighs many of the benefits of computer control.

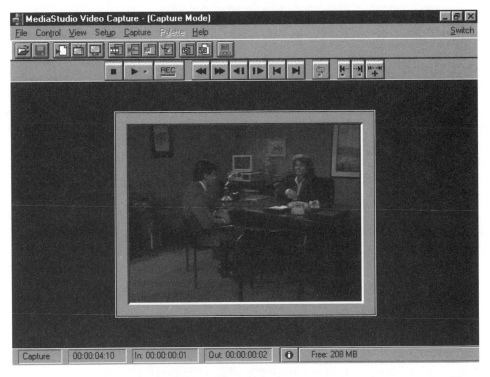

Figure 11.1 MediaStudio provides control over the analog source via VCR-like controls above the video window, streamlining the capture process.

While DVP and MediaStudio were limited to MCI devices, Premiere went much further, supporting V-LAN and ARTI protocols within the program and RS-422 and others through third-party plug-ins. This can be helpful when working with BetaSP and other advanced decks but probably is most critical in nonlinear rather than capture for compression applications.

One of VidCap's major faults was that it overwrote previously captured files without a warning, destroying the fruits of your previous capture. All programs except DVP avoid this problem.

Finally, video capture cards drop frames during capture when capture rates are set too high. When this happens, most developers prefer to reduce the capture data rate until the card captures all frames successfully. Virtually all capture programs display dropped frame data in real time, so you can stop the capture and reduce the data rate, if necessary, before the capture is complete. Strangely, MediaStudio doesn't, or at least we couldn't find where it did.

Capture Performance

Video capture boards are rated by their ability to capture at high data rates without dropping frames. This is important because higher data rates translate to better video quality, essential to both nonlinear editing and capture for compression. The board itself, however, isn't the only factor affecting performance; also contributing is the overhead imposed by the capture software, with more efficient programs enabling capture at higher rates without dropped frames.

We tested relative capture performance on a Pentium 133 running Windows 95 with 16 MB for RAM using a miroVIDEO DC30 capture card. Our capture disk was a ProMax Small Computer Systems Interface (SCSI) drive connected to an Adaptec 2940W controller. We captured video at 640×480 resolution at 60 fields, and CD-ROM audio quality (44 kHz, stereo, 16 bits). We set graphic mode to 800×600×8 bits, disabling preview during capture, and defragmented the disk between tests.

We started testing at 5800 KB/s, at which VidCap 32 dropped no frames. Then we tested each capture program, noting the number of dropped frames and the actual data rate of the video captured. If substantial frames were dropped, we reduced the data rate to 5600 KB/s, then 5400 KB/s. The results are presented in Table 11.1.

Overall, the tests revealed why many capture cards ship VidCap 32 with their products—the boards simply can't achieve optimum performance

Table 11.1 Video capture features and performance.

Video Capture	Adobe Premiere	Asymetrix DVP	Ulead MediaStudio
Architecture	integrated	separate	separate
Presets	yes	no	no
Machine control	MCI, V-LAN, ARTI, third-party plug-ins for RS-422, RS-232, Control L, M	MCI (laserdisc/VISCA)	MCI (laserdisc/VISCA)
VCR controls	yes	no	yes
Step capture	yes	yes	yes
Batch capture	yes	yes	yes
Warning before over-writing previous file	yes	no	yes
Display drop frame data during capture	yes	yes	no
Capture Tests: 5800 KB/s			
Frames dropped	36	27	36
Actual data rate (combined)	6012 KB/s	5969 KB/s	5957 KB/s
Capture Tests: 5600 KB/s			
Frames dropped	18	3	15
Actual data rate (combined)	5614 KB/s	5879 KB/s	5624 KB/s
Capture Tests: 5400 KB/s			
Frames dropped	11	n.a.	6
Actual data rate (combined)	5478 KB/s		5498 KB/s

with either Premiere or MediaStudio, although DVP is slightly better. This means that developers seeking advanced features like batch processing and VCR-like controls may be forced to reduce their capture data rate by 10% or more to obtain them.

CD-ROM publishers shouldn't panic, however. We tested capture at 320×240 resolution, 30 frames per second, at the highest data rate the DC30 could generate, and capture performance improved significantly. Both DVP and Premiere dropped no frames, while MediaStudio dropped only three. For CD-ROM publishing, as opposed to nonlinear editing, all three programs should be fine.

VIDEO EDITING 101

After capture comes editing. If you've captured without machine control, the first task is usually clipping the extra frames from the beginning and end of the clip, the so-called heads and tails. In many applications, the next stage would be compression to final output. However, for more sophisticated applications, you may want to combine two or more clips, perhaps adding titles, transitions between clips, or special effects.

To facilitate this activity, all editors use a "time line" paradigm that typically shares the following elements, illustrated in Figure 11.2 from DVP. In the upper left-hand corner is the Media window, which collects all assets integrated into the final video. On the right is the Player window, which serves as DVP's clip editor, used for trimming heads and tails from the captured video. DVP has two Player windows, though only one is shown.

Along the bottom is the time line, showing the two videos contained in the Media window. The time line has four component tracks: video, audio, trans(ition), and overlay, in this instance used for a title. The video tracks contain all visual footage, including animation and bitmaps. The transition track contains all transitions between videos A and B, selected from the floating Transition window shown in Figure 11.2. The audio tracks contain audio from the videos and can accept discrete audio clips from other sources, as well. Finally, the overlay track, often called the S track (for superimposition), contains titles, graphics, and video superimposed over the main A and/or B video tracks via chroma keying and similar techniques. More on this in a moment.

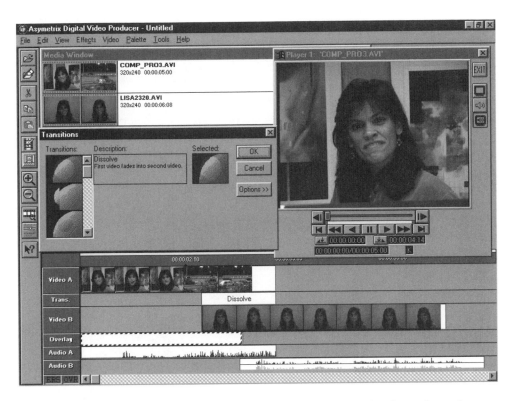

Figure 11.2   DVP's interface shows the classic components of a video editor: Media window, Player window, and time line.

Gathering Your Assets

Captured video clips are typically only one component of the final video. Most projects also contain bitmapped images, perhaps animations and other audio files. As shown in Table 11.2, all three programs accept AVI and WAV files, Autodesk Animator FLC/FLI files, and sufficient bitmapped formats for most applications. Probably most significant is MediaStudio's ability to work with audio files embedded in AVI and MOV files, which saves a step when reusing audio already interleaved with another video file. Heavy Mac users will also appreciate Premiere's ability to work with Macintosh filmstrip (FLM) files.

The next few lines deal with creature comfort issues, or features that make working with the respective programs easier. MediaStudio can't input multiple files at one time, a minor hassle when working with directories of

Table 11.2 File input functions.

File Input	Adobe Premiere	Asymetrix DVP	Ulead MediaStudio
Video formats	AVI, MOV, and FLM	AVI	AVI/MOV
Audio formats	WAV/AIF	WAV	WAV/AVI/MOV
Bitmapped formats	BMP, DIB, RLE, JPG, PCX, PIC, PCT, PSD, TIF, and TGA	GIF, PCX, TIF, TGA, DIB, BMP	BMP, CGM, CLP, CUR, DRW, EPS, GIF, HGL, ICO, IFF, IMG, JPG, PCD, PCT, PCX, PIC, PLT, PNG, PSD, PXR, RAS, RLE, SCT, XHG, TGA, TIF, WMF, WPG
Other formats	FLC/FLI	FLC/FLI	FLC/FLI
Input multiple files	yes	yes	no
Preview before opening	audio/video	AVI/WAV	all
Info before opening	no	no	yes
Double-click to file/ open screen	no	no	yes

files bound for the same video. On the other hand, MediaStudio can preview all files before opening, including animations, and provides file details before actually opening the file, useful when trying to identify the correct file. Finally, MediaStudio lets you double-click on an audio or video track to load the file/open screen, a time-saver that quickly feels essential.

Editing on the Time Line

The time line is the digital cutting room where assets are input, edited, and finally rendered. A number of features affect a program's ability to perform comprehensive tasks and ability to make these features easily accessible to the user.

All programs let you save "projects," which include all assets and editing characteristics like transitions and special effects. This lets you spread the editing task over several periods. Only MediaStudio, however, stores the project file name in the file/open screen, like most word processors and spreadsheets, so you don't have to search for the project when you're ready to start working on it again.

One of Premiere's greatest strengths is project presets, which let the user specify time base, compression options, and preview options (see Table 11.3). Premiere ships with about 15 presets which can't be altered and allows users to build their own (Figure 11.3). Selected when loading the program, presets let you forget about setting discrete output options each time you render a file, saving time and helping you avoid mistakes. This is especially useful when you work with a number of different types of projects, such as nonlinear editing and capture for compression.

Although MediaStudio doesn't offer presets, it does save output and compression options in its .INI file each time you exit the program. This helps when you consistently work on the same type of project but obviously doesn't if your projects vary.

Table 11.3 File input functions.

File Input	Adobe Premiere	Asymetrix DVP	Ulead MediaStudio
Save projects	yes	yes	yes
Saves projects in file menu	no	no	yes
Project presets	yes	no	no
Retains previous settings	no	no	yes
Number of audio/video tracks	99	2	99
SMPTE/frames	yes	yes	no
Zoom viewing window	yes	yes	yes
Fit project in window	no	no	yes
Bitmaps on/off	yes	yes	yes
Snap edges	yes	yes	yes
Edit guides	yes	no	yes
"Sticky" mouse	yes	no	no
Levels of "undo"	1	1	up to 99
File load time (min:sec)	0:05	5:17	00:16
Reset zoom level	0:03	crash	0:05

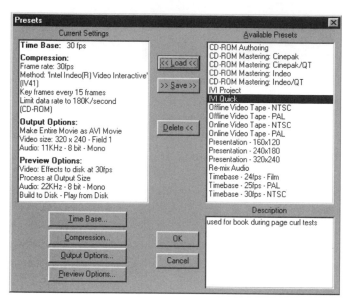

Figure 11.3   Premiere's presets let you set output settings once and then never worry about them again.

The number of video and audio tracks controls basic editing capabilities. Although 99 doesn't practically help the average CD-ROM developer, two is unnecessarily restricting. DVP, for example, can't overlay a video and place a title at the same time, since the same track is used for both purposes.

Whereas most analog video editors work in SMPTE time code, their lingua franca, most CD-ROM developers prefer to work in frames. Premiere and DVP support both metrics, MediaStudio only the former.

When moving assets on the time line, you often need to place the media at a point defined by another asset on the time line. For example, when adding audio to an animation file, you need to drag the audio file to the precise starting point of the animation. Premiere and MediaStudio provide edit guides, or vertical lines that frame a clip on all other time line tracks whenever it's moved, providing a guide for aligning the clip with other assets. With DVP you're on your own, which complicates file synchronization.

Premiere enhances its edit guides with a "sticky" mouse that tends to stop the asset at each possible editing point along the way, hanging for just a brief moment before moving along to the next point. This lets you easily align the assets with precision.

Finally, taking its lead from the image editing world, MediaStudio offers 99 levels of undo. This is extremely helpful, since you don't always find your mistakes before making another edit decision.

Editing Essentials

The next four line items in Table 11.3 describe features that are common to most editors and are basic creature comforts that simplify the editing process. Whatever program you use, locate how to enable/disable these in a hurry, because they'll save you a lot of time and hassle.

All video editors enable viewing from various perspectives, from low-level views that display each frame to high-level views in which each frame on the time line represents a minute or more. Premiere's controls are located on the bottom of the time line, MediaStudio's on the top right, and DVP's plus and minus buttons are on the left-hand side. Locate these controls immediately, because you'll use them frequently. In addition to providing discrete values, MediaStudio has an automatic option to fit the entire project in the time line, a fast lane to the big picture.

All three editors let you customize how the audio and video tracks are represented on the time line, which affects system responsiveness. For example, when displaying a bitmapped representation of the video, the program first scans through the audio and video files to approximate the content and then paints the screen. This can take anywhere from several seconds to several minutes, depending on the file length and video resolution. All programs offer an alternate view that displays only thumbnails of the first and last frames and the file name in between (Figure 11.4).

How much difference does it make? With a 17-second video file in Premiere, you can scroll from one end to the other instantaneously when bitmaps are off. When both audio and video are represented as audio, it takes six seconds. Loading the same file in MediaStudio with bitmaps off takes less than half a second. With bitmaps enabled, it takes about 16 seconds.

Common editing functions like moving an asset on the time line or changing the zoom factor also take much longer when bitmaps are displayed. For this reason, it's usually fastest to edit with bitmaps disabled.

The final feature to be aware of is "snap to edges." This feature ensures that when you move two clips together on the time line they actually concatenate. With snap to edges disabled, there's always a risk that one or two open frames will lodge between the two videos, especially when you're

Figure 11.4   MediaStudio's Display Mode dialog box lets you customize how the audio and video tracks are displayed on the time line.

working in big picture views. Usually, you won't notice the open frames until you spend a couple of hours compressing the project and then play the clip back—black gaps between video clips are usually pretty hard to miss. To prevent this, keep snap to edges enabled.

Editing Creature Comforts

In most instances, it's best to edit video in the clipping or player window offered by all programs, but sometimes it's more convenient to edit after placing the asset on the time line. These situations really start to highlight DVP's deficiencies (Table 11.4).

Drag duration edits are accomplished by grabbing the bitmap, animation, or video file with the mouse and dragging it to the proper size. Drag edits are especially helpful when working with background bitmaps, because you can easily drag the bitmap to the required length, rather than entering duration via menu commands. MediaStudio and Premiere offer drag duration edits, DVP doesn't. Premiere takes this one step further by offering in and out flags to set physical beginning and end points on the time line.

Table 11.4 Editing creature comforts.

File Input	Adobe Premiere	Asymetrix DVP	Ulead MediaStudio
Drag duration edits	yes	no	yes
Set in/out flags	yes	no	no
Trim windows	yes	no	yes
Razor	yes	no	yes
Ripple edits	yes	no	no
Project trimmer	yes	no	yes
Lock/unlock audio	yes	no	yes
Hand audio control	yes	yes	yes
Right mouse button	yes	no	no
Speed: Load file 480 MB, 640×480×60 field file, one-second view (min:sec:msec)	0:04:49	05:17:03	00:16:29
Change to frame-by-frame view	0:02:94	crash	00:04:62
Load 105 MB, 320×240×30 fps raw file, one-second view	00:01:48	1:24:62	00:05:81
Change to frame-by-frame view	00:00:60	00:44:9	00:00:80

Both Premiere and MediaStudio offer trimming windows that let you see up to five frames before and after the edit point to adjust frames precisely where two clips abut (Figure 11.5). This feature dates back to the old "measure twice, cut once" film editing days, when razors cut celluloid tape and an accurate trim mechanism was critical to smooth transitions. Although it's undoubtedly beneficial in nonlinear editing applications, most CD-ROM publishers can obtain sufficient precision without using the trimming window.

Speaking of razors, this is one tool as valuable in the digital domain as it was in the analog. Razors cut a video into two segments, leaving both on the time line, which is incredibly useful when applying special effects like fades to black that affect only the initial or final few seconds of video in a clip. In DVP, which doesn't have a razor, you have to split the video into two segments in the player window, which is cumbersome and time consuming.

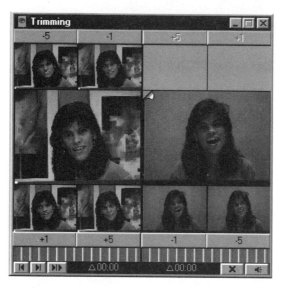

Figure 11.5   Premiere's trimming window, one high-profile option that may sound better than it really is.

Advanced Features

Ripple edits become important when adding assets to the beginning of the time line after laying out much of the video. For example, suppose you decided to add a 15-second title to the start of your three-minute clip comprising 10 discrete videos and nine transitions. Ripple edits, available only in Premiere, let you add the title and then automatically *ripple* the other clips back to their proper position, preserving their relative spacing and transition placement. MediaStudio lets you get close to the same effect by grabbing all assets on the time line and moving them back 15 seconds. However, this is neither as convenient nor as accurate.

Another unique Premiere feature is the project trimmer, which lets you reclaim valuable space on your hard disk after editing. Note that when you trim a video in an editing program, you don't change the actual video file on the disk. For example, say you were capturing a 30-second clip and ended up with 45 seconds, the 15 extra representing heads and tails.

In the clip window you cut the heads and tails and send your 30-second file to the time line. But the disk file still contains an extra 15 seconds of video, at up to 6 MB a second. In our 10-video example above, this means up to 900 MB of extra video, enough to strain even the largest disk systems. The project trimmer provides the mechanism to delete unwanted video files from the files on disk, reclaiming the wasted space.

Synchronization between audio and video is key to final appearance, and Premiere and MediaStudio preserve this by locking audio and video tracks copied from the same video file and treating them as one file during all subsequent edits. DVP doesn't, forcing you to move the audio file separately and carefully to exactly the same location as the video file each time you move the video. MediaStudio and Premiere also let you adjust audio volume manually on the time line with finger controls, a nice convenience.

Video editing is a very hands-on task, and it's nice to have the controls instantly available via right mouse clicks. Both Premiere and MediaStudio make this so.

One of the most important creature comforts is, of course, program speed—never has an off day, never has a slump, and pays dividends every edit you make. We tested this by loading a 17-second, 640×480 raw file into each editor with the zoom ratio set to one second and the bitmaps on. Then we shifted the zoom factor to one frame and timed how long it took for the program to return editing control.

For the most part, Premiere proved faster than both other programs, usually only slightly faster than MediaStudio and much faster than DVP. DVP's times indicate that it's not really designed for real-world nonlinear editing, which involves very large files. Even with 320×240 files, the program was much, much slower than the other two.

While you can reduce the wait by working with bitmaps off, sometimes you have to go low on the video with bitmaps on. Unless you're working with extremely small files, count on a wait with DVP.

Editing Summary

In terms of pure functionality, DVP's two audio/video tracks can prevent developers from completing even moderately complicated projects or force them to build the product in stages, adding layers along the way. Otherwise, the three programs offer similar functionality but vary greatly in ease of use. You can "get there from here" from each editor; the ride is just much more pleasant with Premiere and MediaStudio. This changes in the next few sections, where we see both qualitative and quantitative differences between the editing programs.

GARNISHING

Once your assets are captured and on the time line, it's time to garnish your video with transitions, special effects, and titles. Here's how the programs stack up in these categories.

Transitions

Transitions are mechanisms for moving smoothly from one clip to the next. The simplest transition is none at all, a "cut" where the first frame of the second video immediately follows the last frame of the first. Other simple transitions include fades, where the first video fades out, to either white or black, while the next fades in, from white or black, and wipes, where a line moves across the screen, "wiping" off the first video and "wiping" on the second.

Contrary to popular opinion, the number of available transitions isn't the most important program feature. Most professional video editors will tell you that the best transitions are those that go unnoticed and that simpler is usually better. This is especially true when editing for compression, since garish transitions typically create additional motion, limiting interframe compression and degrading compressed quality (see the Compression-Friendly Transitions sidebar at the end of the chapter).

No, the sheer number of available transitions isn't key—it's the quality of the implementation, the ability to customize, and ease of access to the features. This is what truly sets programs apart.

Basics   While the sheer number of transitions isn't critical, we'd be ejected from the Video Writers Association if we failed to note them, so there they are in Table 11.5. All programs store available transitions in a dialog box, allowing the user to scan through and drag or otherwise select the desired transition to the time line.

MediaStudio organizes its 103 transitions into 12 discrete categories, like rolls, wipes, and 3D transitions, and lets you build your own custom groupings. The other two programs pack their transitions into one big dialog box, which makes the right transition a bit tougher to both select and find, especially if you have to work through Premiere's alphabetized list of 75.

All three editors let you preview the transitions with the actual source videos, which helps select the best looking transition (Figure 11.6). Media-

Table 11.5 Transition details.

Transitions	Adobe Premiere	Asymetrix DVP	Ulead MediaStudio
Basics			
Number of transitions	75	15	103
Organization	none	none	transition type
Preview with sources	yes	yes	yes
Set duration	yes	no	yes
Drag and replace	no	kind of	yes
Customize			
Set direction	yes	yes	yes
Set orientation	yes	yes	yes
Set border/size/color	yes	no	yes
Soft edges	no	no	yes
Set multiples	limited	one transition only	yes
Customized antialiasing	yes	no	no

Figure 11.6 MediaStudio's transition editor lets you preview with the actual source video files and select from a host of options.

Studio and Premiere also let you set transition duration, simplifying the editing process. With DVP, for example, to create a one-second transition, you have to move the clips so that they overlap by precisely one second, which often requires that you change to a low-level time line view. With the other two programs, you simply drag the transition into place, set the one-second duration, and then move the two clips to the required locations.

Finally, drag and replace lets you sample new transitions simply by dragging a new transition from the dialog box and replacing the old. MediaStudio is the only program offering this option. DVP is similar in that once you select a new transition and close the dialog box, the time line automatically updates. In contrast, Premiere forces you to delete the old transition first, which tends to be a pain, since the transition window moves behind the construction window when deleting the transition, forcing more than a few extra mouse clicks.

Customization   Transition customization options fall into two categories: creative and qualitative, with the first allowing the producer more creative choices and the latter affecting transition quality. We'll deal with both categories in turn.

Common creative options include direction, where one wipe transition lets the producer wipe from right to left, left to right, top to bottom, and vice versa. Orientation is a similar option, letting the producer rotate a clock-wipe transition either clockwise or counterclockwise. Both Media-Studio and Premiere let the developer place a border on the transition effect, set its width, and choose a color. MediaStudio also enables a "soft" edge, which blurs the hard lines of the transition.

Multiples is the ability to divide the transition into a number of smaller windows, all accomplishing the same basic transition. For example, applying a vertical multiple of two to a wipe creates two wipe effects, the first starting at the left edge and working through to the middle of the video and the second working simultaneously, starting at the middle and working through to the right edge. Applying a horizontal multiple divides the transition window north/south, creating four simultaneous wipes.

MediaStudio leads the pack here, offering multiples on virtually all transitions. Premiere has one or two multiple transitions, and DVP has one.

Premiere is the only editor with quality-related options, specifically its customized antialiasing. One constant problem with computer graphics is aliasing, also known as the "jaggies," which occurs most frequently on hard diagonal edges. Since many transitions use hard diagonals, aliasing is often a problem.

As shown in Figure 11.7, Premiere's antialiasing, available in three levels, blurs this aliasing, reducing the starkness of the jagged edges. When transitions feature diagonal lines, this feature makes Premiere's smoother than the other two editors, though only slightly.

Artistic Transitions   During our review, we also scanned through the various transition files, looking for standout effects worth noting. Our favorite was MediaStudio's killer "Burn" transition, reminiscent of the final transition in the introduction to *Bonanza*, where they burn the map of the Ponderosa in an expanding ring, then transition to Dad, Hoss, and Little Joe, together on horseback (Figure 11.8). It's probably worth the product purchase price for anyone working with cowboy videos.

We also noticed that parts isn't parts, or in English, that not all transitions are created equal, at least when 3D effects like page curls are involved. Figure 11.9 shows two page curl transitions from MediaStudio and Premiere. Compare the aliasing on the perpendicular line at the root of the page curl in the two clips—the angle of attack chosen by Adobe really limited the jaggies. On the other hand, Adobe's other edges showed more jaggies, though somewhat smoothed by the antialiasing filter.

What really stands out on the attention-to-detail scale, however, is this: All of Adobe's page curl transitions have shadows beneath the curved edge, just where they would be in real life. MediaStudio's don't.

What's the net/net on transitions? For simple cuts and wipes, DVP is probably sufficient. As you move up on the creative scale, MediaStudio offers more transitions and the most options, although Premiere's antialiasing filter adds a touch of professional quality not available in the other two programs. But just a touch.

Figure 11.7   Premiere's antialiasing blurs the jaggies, creating better looking transitions when diagonal lines are involved.

Figure 11.8 MediaStudio's artistic "Burn" transition, reminiscent of the burning map of the Ponderosa in the introduction to *Bonanza*.

Figure 11.9 A page curl isn't a page curl isn't a page curl. Compare the two page curls from Premiere and MediaStudio. What's missing in the latter?

Filters

Filters also break down into two categories, corrective filters and special effects. Once again, the sheer number of filters matters little so long as the necessary filters are present. Still, for the sake of completeness (and my union card), they're listed in Table 11.6.

Corrective filters fix problems in the video itself, while special effects change the basic look of the video for artistic effect. We'll discuss them in order.

Corrective Filters Corrective filters fall into two categories: color/brightness and clipping/scaling. Many times after capturing video, you'll find that the color is a bit too dark or perhaps tinted incorrectly. It's always, always, always preferable to resolve these issues during capture, but sometimes you can't. All three editors provide both brightness/contrast and

Table 11.6 Filters/special effects.

Audio/Video Filters	Adobe Premiere	Asymetrix DVP	Ulead MediaStudio
Number of filters	63	30	15
Preview with sources	some	yes	all
Corrective			
Color	yes	yes	yes
Clipping/scale	yes	yes	yes
One-pass clip/scale	yes	no	no
Artistic			
Fade to/from black/white	yes	yes	yes
Vary filters over time	some	no	all
Apply to frame regions	no	no	yes
Copy filter attributes	yes	no	yes
Audio special effects	6	levels only	13
Rubber band volume	yes	yes	yes
Automatic cross-fade	yes	yes	no

either red/green/blue or hue/saturation/brightness color controls, allowing you both color and brightness levels.

Both Premiere and MediaStudio let you customize settings at both the start and finish of the clip, adding a level of precision and an exceptionally simple way to fade the video to or from black or white. DVP doesn't allow customization of its brightness/color filters but has dedicated fade video filters, a nice convenience for beginners.

Premiere starts to break away with clipping and scaling. You clip unwanted pixels from the video either to address capture card equalization problems that can produce rows of black pixels on one of the video edges or simply to cut the video to the desired resolution. You scale to adjust the entire video to a new resolution, say to reduce a 320×240 video down to 176×144 resolution for streaming over the Internet. All three programs can clip, and all can scale. However, they vary in terms of how they implement these features, which affects usability.

Here's a scenario. Say you've designed your application for 320×240 video files, but your capture card caused a row of four black pixels on the video bottom. What you'd like to do is crop the unwanted pixels, then scale back to 320×240 so the video fits your application, preferably in one step. We had this problem with one of our test videos, captured from Sony's DCR VX700 digital camera with their DVBK still-image capture board, which had no equalization controls. This is the video shown in Figure 11.10.

Premiere handles this best with two separate filters: clipping, which removes the pixels and leaves the video at its new resolution, and cropping, which clips the pixels and then stretches back to the original resolution. Premiere also enables *compression time* cropping and scaling (they call it clipping), allowing the user to adjust all component clips at one time (Figure 11.10). The "better resize" option shown in Figure 11.10 is a resizing algorithm from sister product Adobe After Effects that helps avoid scaling artifacts that can occur when adjusting video resolution.

MediaStudio's approach is more awkward. While you can crop unwanted pixels from any video edge (in the compression options screen, rather than as a filter), you can't resize back to the original resolution in one step—you have to crop, then reload the video and expand it back to the original size. In addition, since all cropping is performed at compression time, rather than as a filter on the time line applied to arbitrary clips, you have to crop *all* videos, not just those that need it. This also makes for additional steps.

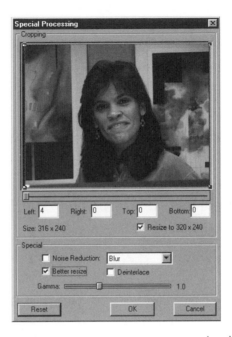

Figure 11.10 Premiere's compression time cropping/scaling lets you modify all component videos at one time.

Similarly, DVP can clip unwanted pixels, or scale to a different output size, but not both in one step. Those working with the program should note that cropping and scaling are not implemented as filters, but as a separate menu command (file/scaling). Unlike those of the other two programs, DVP's clipping control doesn't show the actual video when clipping, making it tougher to produce accurate results.

Artistic Filters Artistic filters are most commonly used for fading to and from white or black at the start or end of clip. All three programs let you modify your clips in these fashions, though once again using different techniques.

DVP works most simply with dedicated fade to/from black and white filters which ratably apply over the duration of the clip. With Premiere and MediaStudio, you work with the standard brightness/contrast filter, which lets you adjust the values at the start and end points (see Figure 11.11). This is the "vary filters over time" line item in Table 11.6.

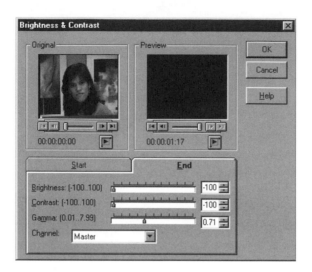

Figure 11.11   MediaStudio's filter editor setting starting and ending values
for brightness and contrast to fade clip to black.

This, once again, is why it's so important to be able to cut a video clip
into two segments on the time line. To fade to black in the last three seconds
of a 30-second clip, you use a razor tool to cut or separate the final three
seconds of the clip from the other 27 seconds and apply the brightness/con-
trast filter to the stub clip. If you can't cut on the time line you have to use
the clipping window to create two clips, which is much less efficient.

In general, MediaStudio is more customizable than either of the other
two programs. For example, Premiere offers blur, blur more, and Gaussian
blur filters, all without any user options or the ability to preview the filter
over the source video in the filter selection screen. In contrast, MediaStudio
offers blur and Gaussian blur, both completely adjustable for start and
ending values and both with preview over source footage. In general,
advanced users may find themselves getting frustrated with some of these
limitations in Premiere.

MediaStudio is unique in its ability to apply a filter to a clip region,
allowing you, for example, to blur a subject's face without blurring the
entire frame. Both Premiere and MediaStudio let you paste filter attributes
from one clip to another, a nice timesaving option.

Audio Filters   The most commonly used audio filters are fades, used to fade
in from silence at the start of a clip and fade out at the end. All three

programs let you increase or decrease audio volume by grabbing an audio volume line beneath the audio wave form and moving it upward or downward (see Figure 11.12). Premiere and MediaStudio offer their controls conveniently on the time line, while DVP opens a separate window.

Unlike video fades, which force you to cut a clip into two components to fade to black at the end, you can start your audio fade from any point in both Premiere and MediaStudio. You simply anchor the clip by touching the audio volume line at the point where you want to begin your fade and then drag the stub downward. Anchors are the small black dots on the audio volume line in Figure 11.12 that represent the point of change between level volume and the fade out of the first clip and fade in of the second.

A cross-fade occurs during transitions when the first clip's audio fades to silence while second clip's audio fades in from silence. Both Premiere and DVP offer automatic cross-fade tools that build the cross-fade shown in Figure 11.12, a nice convenience, while MediaStudio makes you apply the cross fade by hand.

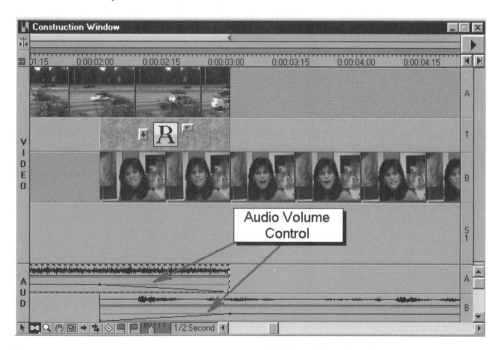

Figure 11.12 Premiere's automatic cross-fade tool works during transitions to fade out the first clip's audio and fade in the second.

MediaStudio offers the widest range of audio filters, no doubt pinched from its sister audio editor. Unfortunately, in both Premiere and MediaStudio, you can't sample the filters when you select them; you have to apply the filter and then preview. This makes audio filters somewhat more difficult to access than the video filters. For example, in MediaStudio, you can't test the amplitude filter without selecting a value and previewing the entire clip, an unnecessary step.

Filter Summary   Nothing really striking in this category from a qualitative standpoint. DVP offers all the basics, but little else. MediaStudio tends to offer greater flexibility with its filters, which advanced users will appreciate, while Premiere handled cropping and scaling with aplomb.

Don't underestimate the value of this last feature. None of the five video capture cards we reviewed have equalization controls, making it highly likely that fastidious video developers will be cropping pixels and, if working in Premiere, glad they could do it in one step.

Keying: The Basics

The overlay process is used to combine elements of two or more clips into a single video. Overlay works through "keying" techniques that "tell" the editor which part of the video to ignore and which to "overlay" onto the final rendered video.

The most common overlay technique is called chroma keying or color keying, shown in Figure 11.13. Here the model hawking cookies was filmed

Table 11.7   Keying techniques.

Keying	Adobe Premiere	Asymetrix DVP	Ulead MediaStudio
Number of techniques	14	2	5
Layers	99	1	99
Color picking	yes	yes	yes
Tolerance controls	yes	yes	yes
Preview	yes	yes	yes
Zoom preview	yes	no	no
Variable keying	yes	no	yes
Smoothing controls	yes	no	no

Figure 11.13 Overlay 101: Our model and a title chroma keyed over a background globe.

against a blue screen (lisablue.avi on the middle time line). Using chroma keying, we defined blue as the transparent color, overlaying the model against the globe video background. The lowest track, in black, is the title track, which also was superimposed over the globe.

Editing programs implement a number of keying techniques that are variations on the same theme—they all allow the developer to describe which portion of the video to ignore and which to include in the final rendered sequence. Once again, for most developers, the sheer number of keying options isn't critical—just be sure to film using a technique supported by your editor, and in most instances chroma keying is just fine.

As we discussed earlier, the sheer number of layers is important, as DVP, with one superimposition line, can't place a title and chroma key at the same time. The 99 layers offered by Premiere and MediaStudio are both more than adequate.

Figure 11.14 is MediaStudio's Overlay Options screen, which illustrates the basic components of the keying system. On the left is the clip being overlaid, on the right is the preview screen. For this test we overlaid the video onto a white screen, which naturally highlighted any keying artifacts.

Figure 11.14   MediaStudio's Overlay Options screen, showing the lovely star "Eraser Turnabout" in a somewhat compromising position.

We used chroma key as the key type and then selected the color blue as the color to be ignored by using an eyedropper tool that appears above the overlay clip when the mouse cursor passes over it. In most instances, you'll have to adjust the tolerance of the chroma key, increasing or narrowing the definition of the keying value to completely eliminate the key color. As we'll see, tolerance adjustments are critical to achieving good results, and the different programs handle keying with varying levels of success.

All three programs offer these basics and the ability to preview over the actual video, obviously essential to getting good results. Premiere takes preview an extra step by letting you zoom the video in the preview window and move the video around to examine closely the edges where keying typically breaks down. With MediaStudio and DVP, you really have to preview in the time line to gauge your results.

Both MediaStudio and Premiere let you adjust similarity at both the start and end points, useful when the subject matter of the video changes. These are the controls shown on the bottom left-hand side of Figure 11.14.

Variable keying is an advanced control that adjusts the intensity of the overlaid videos, especially when more than one overlay is active. This is how producers fade multiple video components in and out of a scene, as in the movie *Ghost*, when Patrick Swayze appeared ghostlike when appearing on-screen after his untimely death. More common applications might be fading text and graphics into a video, rather than placing them on-screen at 100% strength.

In Figure 11.14, initial transparency is set to 0, meaning that the entire video will show through in full force. However, at its final setting of 100, the video will be completely gone, fading out slowly over the life of the clip. Premiere has similar variable keying capabilities, but DVP, with only one superimposition track, doesn't.

Smoothing

So far so good; for simple, one-track overlay the editors are running neck and neck. But Premiere offers smoothing, not offered by either MediaStudio or DVP, which enhances final appearance significantly (see Figure 11.15). In addition, while not obvious in this example, other tests showed that the mere ability to select a tolerance level doesn't mean you wipe out all the blue, and Premiere and MediaStudio generally did better than DVP in this regard.

In the end, after overlaying the videos over the background and compressing with Indeo 3.2, Premiere's smoothing capabilities made a small but noticeable difference. Comparative files are included in the chap_11\key subdirectory as key_dvp.avi, key_ms.avi, and key_pre.avi. See "The Making of 'Eraser Turnabout'" at the endof the chapter for details about the actual blue screen process.

Figure 11.15   Note the jaggies in MediaStudio and DVP and the smooth output in Premiere.

In summary, keying appears to be one area where Premiere produces more polished results than either of the other two products. If you're developing content with lots of overlays, Premiere may be your best choice.

Motion Paths: The Basics

Most motion controls probably fall into the most hyped, least useful variety, especially for CD-ROM publishers, because as we all know, motion makes video more difficult to compress, degrading overall quality. For this reason, this section will be brief.

Two-dimensional motion is movement across the X and/or Y axis of the video. Common examples are scrolling credits, which start at the bottom and end at the top, or spinning logos or other graphics that rotate around a fixed axis. These types of motion are well within the capacity of all three video editors (see Table 11.8), as is resizing an object to make it appear as if it's getting closer or farther away, a faux 3D effect.

Three-dimensional effects range from spinning on a Z axis, like those old rotating gas station signs, to simulated views around a circle or cylinder. These artistic, complicated effects are fun, but probably best left to true artistic professionals.

Table 11.8   Two- and three-dimensional motion.

Motion	Adobe Premiere	Asymetrix DVP	Ulead MediaStudio
2D motion			
Move along X/Y axis (right/left or up/down)	yes	yes	yes
Spin X/Y axis (rotate like a wheel)	yes	yes	yes
3D motion			
Scale or resize	yes	yes	yes
3D spin (horizontal spin along Z axis)	camera view filter	no	yes
Subpixel rendering	yes	no	yes

Figure 11.16 shows Premiere's motion control screen. The big window in the upper right-hand corner, marked "motion path," shows the essence of the process—motion is the movement of a video or graphic into, around, and out of the visible area. The tiny small square in the upper left-hand corner is the starting point, the small square in the lower right-hand corner the finishing point, and the motion consists of the graphic moving across the frame along the faint line with the small squares.

The visible area itself is represented by the "visible area" window in the upper left-hand corner, showing the right edge of the Doceo logo. The time line in the middle of the screen represents clip duration. At any given point on the time line, you can create a "key" frame with unique X,Y placement coordinates as well as the rotation, zoom, and delay levels. Key frames are the small cross-bars on the time line and the small squares in the big window. In essence, the clip's motion is its journey from key frame to key frame, adjusting ratably during the move from the coordinates of the first to the coordinates of the second.

For example, to scroll a text title from top to bottom, you would move the start square to the top of the visible area and the end square to the bottom, leaving the other controls alone. To add a 360 spin, you would change the final rotation coordinate to 360, and the title would spin one full turn ratably over the duration of the move.

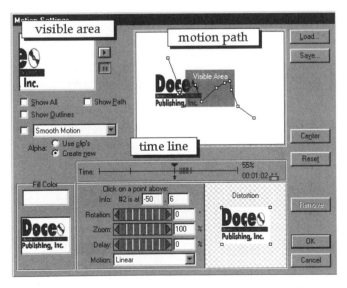

Figure 11.16 Elements of motion: Premiere's motion control screen.

To build a stationary, spinning logo, you would place the logo in the same position on the screen at the start and finish but change the rotation. In Figure 11.17, MediaStudio's 2D motion screen, for example, setting the end rotation value at 360 spins the graphic once during the three-second clip.

Premiere's zoom control and MediaStudio's sizing control let you zoom the image closer to or farther from the viewer, creating the appearance of 3D motion. Both products also let you warp or distort the clip, again over time.

Qualitative Aspects

Other than these basics, we limited our inquiry to the qualitative aspects of motion filters, specifically whether the subpixel rendering claimed by Premiere and MediaStudio delivered cleaner, antialiased lines. To test this, we built the same spinning Doceo logo in all three editors and then examined the results, presented in Figure 11.18 (files are in chap_11\motion).

As you can see, subpixel rendering is more than just a buzzword. While MediaStudio and Premiere were relatively smooth at all angles, DVP showed severe jaggies throughout the rotation, causing noticeable image degradation. The lesson: even when performing relatively simple motion edits, Premiere and MediaStudio will outperform DVP.

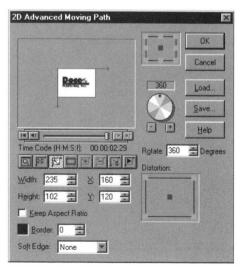

Figure 11.17   MediaStudio's motion control screen.

Premiere   MediaStudio   DVP

Figure 11.18   Even simple motion effects highlight some of DVP's
quality-related weaknesses.

Titling

For the most part, editing programs treat titles like any other bitmapped image—you place the title on a video or overlay track, integrate it with your other videos with keying techniques, and move the title around the screen with motion controls. For this reason, the title generation utilities included in video editors are similar to limited-use graphics editors primarily oriented toward text creation. However, DVP ships with a special 3D title editor for more advanced operation, while the full version of Adobe Premiere ships with Crystal Flying Fonts, which serves the same purpose.

Figure 11.19 shows the typical gamut of title creation features, plus a few features unique to Premiere. Most editors can use all system fonts and modify font size, style, justification, and color. All editors antialias text objects for smooth appearance.

At this point, MediaStudio's and DVP's feature sets start to wane, while Premiere is just getting started (see Table 11.9). Premiere offers kerning, or the ability to adjust the distances between the text letters. In addition to horizontal fonts, Premiere supports vertical titling, a useful creative option. Premiere is the only editor to include drawing tools for boxes, circles, ellipses, and irregular objects and the ability to apply a gradient pattern to any text or graphic object.

Like most graphics editors, Premiere treats text as an object, allowing you to place it manually in the frame. In contrast, there is no WYSIWYG placement in MediaStudio or DVP; you place text using spaces and lines as with an old, DOS word processor and hope for the best. Adobe maximizes the creative potential of these tools by letting you create the title over the actual video frame itself, a unique feature among these programs.

Table 11.9 Title generation utilities.

Titles	Adobe Premiere	Asymetrix DVP	Ulead MediaStudio
Text styles	bold, italic, underline, emboss, shadow	bold, italic	bold, italic, strikeout, underline, 3D shadow, outline
Justification	left, center, right	none	left, center, right
Motion controls	motion filters	title editor	motion filters
Antialiased font	yes	yes	yes
Kerning	yes	no	no
Orientation	horizontal, vertical	horizontal	horizontal
Colors	yes	yes	yes
Drawing tools	yes	no	no
Gradients	yes	no	no
Manual text placement	yes	no	no
Draw over video	yes	no	no
Save title files	yes	yes	no
3D title creation	Crystal Flying Fonts	yes	no

As a result, Premiere offers more options and is much easier to use, providing a significant advantage over the other programs in title-intensive projects. Uniquely, Premiere even lets you save title files for later use in other projects.

3D Titles Which is not to say that DVP doesn't have its own charms. A separate program, Asymetrix's Titling Specialist, creates three-dimensional titles that can be rendered as AVI files and added to video presentations. As with most titling programs, you can specify font, size, and attributes. In addition, the Titling Specialist lets you create three-dimensional titles with varying thickness, colors, and surface materials.

You control the motion across the X,Y axes with key frames, selecting from canned motion paths or creating your own. In addition to motion across the X and Y axes, you can spin and rotate the title and move it closer

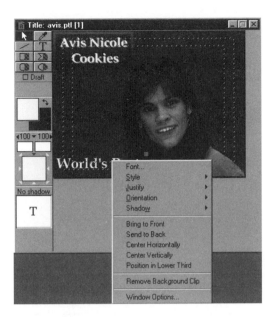

Figure 11.19   Premiere's Title Editor outfeatures the other two editors
                    significantly.

to and farther from the viewer. You can also change the lighting implemented, choosing between back and front lighting, a flashlight, and many other effects.

An educated guess is that the Titling Specialist is a derivative of Asymetrix's highly regarded 3D FX program, a general-purpose 3D creation program. Either way, this function alone might justify DVP's $79 purchase price.

Preview

Although many edits are mechanical in nature, an equal number involve subjective, creative decisions that benefit from immediate feedback (see Table 11.10). All editors provide a preview function to provide this feedback.

To prepare the preview, the editor assembles all assets; implements transitions, filters, special effects, and motion controls; and draws all titles, presenting the user with a composite clip of the final video.

Table 11.10   Preview options.

Motion	Adobe Premiere	Asymetrix DVP	Ulead MediaStudio
Display while rendering	no	yes	yes
Real-time preview	yes (after first preview)	no	yes (after first preview)
Playback controls postrendering	no	yes	no
Partial preview	yes	not really	yes
Instant preview	yes (but no special effects until full preview)	no	yes
Preview with compression effects	yes	no	no
Preview time (min:sec)	00:20	1:05	00:38

The three programs use different preview schemes. Premiere displays the preview in a stand-alone window that launches when processing is complete. Previewed video plays back in real time, and you can see the file again by pressing enter after the first preview playback. Unfortunately, Adobe doesn't provide a slider bar or other playback control to navigate to particular frames, and your only option is to play the preview back from start to finish in real time.

MediaStudio has a similar scheme but, unlike Premiere, displays the clip during preview, providing instant feedback, and then launches a playback window with a slider bar. You can play the file back in near real time or work through the file slowly, examining the individual frames.

DVP uses still a third option, opening up a preview window with a slider bar which you can drag to any frame. Unlike the other two programs, DVP doesn't process first and then preview, it simply walks through the video frame by frame, slowly applying all effects and then moving to the following frame. Also unlike MediaStudio and Premiere, DVP doesn't save the resulting preview file into a temporary file that would enable real-time playback. All previews are non–real time.

That said, DVP provides virtually instant access to all frames, since you can move the slider bar to any video location. Premiere and MediaStudio provide roughly similar functionality by letting you preview only a region.

Both Premiere and MediaStudio let you instantly preview any particular frame by clicking on the time line above their respective construction windows. The value of Premiere's instant "preview" is eroded by the fact that it doesn't incorporate most filters, transitions, keying, or special effects, so often you end up looking at a background matte and a big red X advising you certain effects were unrendered. Running a complete preview ameliorates this situation, allowing you to go back and examine individual frames in all their rendered glory. In contrast, MediaStudio takes a bit longer to display a frame but incorporates all time line elements in its instant preview.

Since compression can degrade video quality, previews that comprehend the deteriorating effects of compression are most accurate and therefore most useful. Only Premiere takes this extra step. Strangely, MediaStudio requests the compression technology in the preview options box, but not the data rate, which usually has more impact on quality.

Because preview is a frequent step, we thought we would time the respective programs when compiling a two-second preview of two clips joined via a wipe transition. Time is displayed in seconds, and as you can see, Premiere was almost twice as fast as MediaStudio and over three times faster than DVP. This first performance test was an accurate harbinger, as Premiere proved substantially faster than both programs in virtually all similar tests.

Garnish Summary

Overall, Premiere ranks at or near the top in all garnishing functions, most clearly in cropping/scaling, keying, and overall program speed. The only significant qualitative advantage over MediaStudio is in keying, however; otherwise Ulead's editor generally performs the same functions. Both programs offer several qualitative advantages over DVP and many artistic ones, and DVP proved much slower in most critical functions.

COMPRESSION AND OUTPUT

Compression performance has two factors, the ability to compress a file correctly, and extra features that improve output quality or performance. We'll deal with them in that order.

Most video captured and edited for digital playback is destined for compression into Video for Windows' AVI format. As we mentioned earlier, the standard for compression performance was, is, and apparently may always be Microsoft's VidEdit. In theory, writing compression routines that match VidEdit's results shouldn't have been difficult for programmers, since all codecs fit into the prescribed Video for Windows architecture. However, the initial compression APIs Microsoft supplied were poorly documented and incomplete and apparently didn't improve with Windows 95.

As a result, most first-generation video editors compressed incorrectly, resulting in files that failed to achieve the target data rate or suffered from defective audio/video synchronization or incorrectly computed CD-ROM padding. For this reason, many CD-ROM developers to this day process their videos with another editing program but then compress the raw file with VidEdit.

If a video editor can't match VidEdit's performance with your target codec, you have to render the finished file in a raw format and compress with another tool, preferably VidEdit. At the very least, this means another administrative step, complete with pretty stiff disk space requirements.

Basic Compression Performance

We tested three codecs (Table 11.11), Indeo 3.2, Indeo video interactive, and Cinepak, with a five-second, real-world clip comprising talking head and action footage, with a wipe transition in between. We compressed with all codecs to 150 KB/s, using a key frame setting of 15, CD-ROM padding engaged, and quality set to the codec's default value.

We tested the same clip and a short animation sequence with Video 1, where we also tested the editor's palette management skills. Video 1 is still used for real-world videos targeted toward the 8-bit display environment and is the best VFW codec for compressing FLC/FLI animations to add audio and enable streaming from CD-ROMs.

Indeo video interactive   We compressed with IVI's advanced features, scalability, and bidirectional encoding enabled. Both Premiere and DVP closely matched VidEdit in both data rate and appearance. MediaStudio's data rate was substantially higher than VidEdit's, but appearance was very similar. We compressed several other IVI files with MediaStudio without similar data rate spikes, but this issue bears watching if you're working with close tolerances.

Table 11.11 Basic compression performance.

Compression	VidEdit	Adobe Premiere	Asymetrix DVP	Ulead MediaStudio
IVI: bandwidth	150 KB/s	150 KB/s	148 KB/s	179 KB/s
Visual quality		same	same	same
Compression time five-second clip (min:sec)	8:12	8:23	5:27	3:23
Indeo 3.2: bandwidth	156 KB/s	157 KB/s	155 KB/s	122 KB/s
Visual quality		same	same	much worse
Cinepak	163 KB/s	173 KB/s	163 KB/s	163 KB/s
Visual quality		OK	OK	unacceptable
Compression time (min:sec)	1:34	1:43	1:37	1:29
Palette capabilities		load (BMP, PAL, AVI), compute	load (PAL), compute, save	load (BMP/PAL), compute
Video 1: video	168 KB/s	145 KB/s	167 KB/s	822 KB/s
Visual quality		better	worse	n.a.
Video 1: animation (640×480)	188 KB/s	49 KB/s	169 KB/s	49 KB/s
Visual quality		worse	worse	same
Time: compute optimal palette and compress animation sequence (min:sec)		3:13	1:45:70	0:56

IVI's bidirectional prediction feature creates a file that starts with three identical frames unless the editor makes corrections during compression. VidEdit doesn't, while the other three editors do. Compare ivi_vide.avi to ivi_dvp.avi, ivi_pre.avi, and ivi_ms.avi in the chap_11\compress subdirectory.

Indeo 3.2 Once again, both Premiere and DVP closely matched VidEdit's performance in both data rate and appearance. However, MediaStudio's video data rate was inexplicably about 32% lower than VidEdit's (93 versus 138 KB/s), resulting in the gauzy-looking video shown in Figure 11.20. We compressed several other clips with Indeo 3.2 with similar results. If you're compressing with Indeo 3.2, MediaStudio is probably not your best option. (Files are in chap_11\compress, as 132_pre, 132_vide, 132_ms, 132_dvp.)

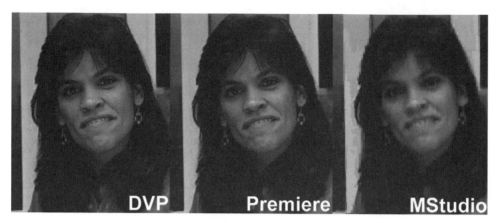

Figure 11.20   For Indeo 3.2, MediaStudio's data rate was inexplicably 30% less than other encoders with a very noticeable drop in quality.

Cinepak   Premiere's data rate was about 10 KB/s higher than VidEdit's, primarily due to excess CD-ROM padding in the Premiere file (12 KB/s as compared to 9 KB/s). On other clips, Premiere generally duplicated Vid-Edit's CD-ROM padding numbers, so this appears to be an isolated problem. Premiere's visual quality was virtually identical to VidEdit's.

With Cinepak, DVP did Premiere one better, matching VidEdit's data rate and visual quality almost exactly. Although MediaStudio produced acceptable data rates, visual quality was suboptimal on our test clip and several other clips compressed on several different computers to verify our results. The program produced ugly blotches on key frames, rendering the compressed footage unusable (Figure 11.21). (Files are in chap_11\compress\ cp_pre, cp_vide, cp_ms, cp_dvp.)

Video 1

Palette Management: Most Windows video graphics cards display in 8-bit, 16-bit, or 24-bit color depth with 8-bit systems predominating. When a computer is in 8-bit graphics mode, display is limited to 256 colors. This collection of 256 colors is called the palette, and all screen elements must be painted with colors contained in the palette. The 256-color combination is not fixed—palettes can and do frequently change. But at any one point, only 256 colors can be used to describe all the objects on the screen.

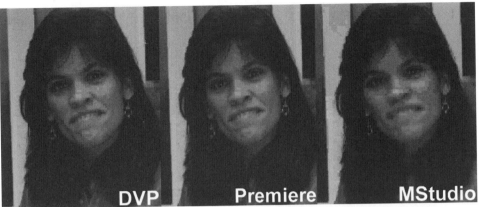

Figure 11.21 MediaStudio produced ugly blotches on key frames when compressing with Cinepak, rendering the video unusable.

All graphic objects, including animations, video, and bitmapped images, have their own palette. When a graphic object displays, Windows makes certain that its palette is installed. If it isn't, Windows automatically changes the palette to that of the new object by momentarily blanking out and "realizing" the colors of the new palette. Known in the trade as "palette flashing," this effect can be quite distracting.

Cinepak and both Indeos are native 24-bit codecs that use over 16 million colors to describe their compressed video. When displaying in 8-bit mode, Cinepak and Indeo have to drop from 16 million to 256 colors. To conserve file size and preserve display rate, neither codec stores palette information in its file—they simply decompress to the same fixed palette for all videos. To minimize the potential for distortion, 24-bit codecs "dither" or draw minute geometric pixel patterns of various sizes to simulate colors not contained in the palette.

Because these codecs decompress to their own palette each time a video plays, developers need to use one of several techniques discussed in the next chapter to avoid palette flashing. Even then, however, the video is dithered, which degrades appearance.

The two 8-bit codecs, Video 1 and RLE, don't have either problem. They don't have to dither because the video is already described in 256 colors or less. In addition, 8-bit codecs can "hold a palette," which allows developers to select one palette for a screen or presentation and compress all videos and other graphics to that palette.

For this reason, many developers consider Video 1 for mass market multimedia products that will probably play on lower end machines with 8-bit displays. As we've seen, however, Video 1 simply doesn't have the horsepower for action footage. On the other hand, for low-motion videos and certain animations, Video 1 does a great job.

To compress video to a fixed palette, editing programs must be capable of two tasks at which VidEdit excels—calculating an optimal palette for the graphics elements in the presentation and applying a previously calculated optimal palette. (Actually, I should say *excelled*. VidEdit crashes regularly now when asked to compute a palette.) It also helps if they can save the palette as a separate PAL file for subsequent use.

Editor Performance: Only DVP can perform import, compute, and save a palette file, although its import capabilities are limited to Windows palette files with the PAL extension. DVP can also compute a palette from a partial file, which can be a huge time-saver when working with large animation files.

In addition to PAL files, MediaStudio can grab a palette from a BMP file, while Premiere works with PAL, BMP, and AVI files, at least in theory. We tried loading a palette from a number of AVI files without success, each time getting the message "error reading file," even from files compressed by Premiere that loaded normally into the time line.

When computing an optimal palette for a video file, MediaStudio and DVP matched VidEdit's palette very closely on both the animation and real-world video. Premiere performed well on the real-world video but faltered strangely on our 640×480 animated sequence, missing virtually all primary colors. We tested a smaller 320×200 animation, and Premiere computed an appropriate palette.

Animation: MediaStudio was the star when compressing the full-screen animation, equaling VidEdit's quality at a substantially lower data rate (49 KB/s versus 188 KB/s). Premiere mangled the first few frames with excessive blockiness, and DVP alternated between smooth and blocky frames. With the 320×240 animation file, the programs produced files of similar quality.

Real-World Video: Premiere bettered VidEdit's visual quality at a lower data rate, an impressive feat. While DVP matched VidEdit's data rate, visual quality was noticeably worse than with VidEdit and accordingly was rated suboptimal. MediaStudio had problems with Video 1 when compressing difficult footage that stressed the target data rate, producing a data rate of 822 KB/s.

Advanced Compression Options

This is the time when the chapter starts to sound like a Premiere brochure, because Adobe is clearly one generation ahead in terms of creature comforts, codec support, and compression enhancements (Table 11.12). I'll try to keep it brief.

What's the first thing you want to do after compressing a file? You want to play it and you want as much relevant information as possible about data rate and other file statistics. Premiere excels here by loading the file into its clip window, which enables a movie analysis providing comprehensive audio and video file statistics, including a histogram showing streaming data rate. Neither DVP nor MediaStudio offers anything like it; of course, you're in great shape, since you have VCS installed already, which does all this and more.

Another unique Premiere feature is batch compression of Premiere projects. This allows developers to edit a number of captured clips, cutting

Table 11.12 Advanced compression options/performance.

Compression	Adobe Premiere	Asymetrix DVP	Ulead MediaStudio
Creature Comforts			
Histogram	yes	no	no
Batch compress	yes	no	no
Compression Time			
Filtering	yes	no	no
Cropping	yes	no	yes
Scaling	yes	no	no
Compression time gamma correction	yes	no	no
IVI Features			
Key frame location	yes	no	no
Key frame at edits	yes	no	no
Abut without recompression	CP/IVI/IV3.2	CP/IVI/IV3.2/ Video 1	CP/IV3.2

Figure 11.22   Studio models prefer Premiere when compressing with Video 1, which looked better than VidEdit at a lower data rate. MediaStudio is not shown because it couldn't meet the data rate requirements. (Files are in chap_11\compress\vi_vide, vi_pre, vi_ms, vi_dvp.)

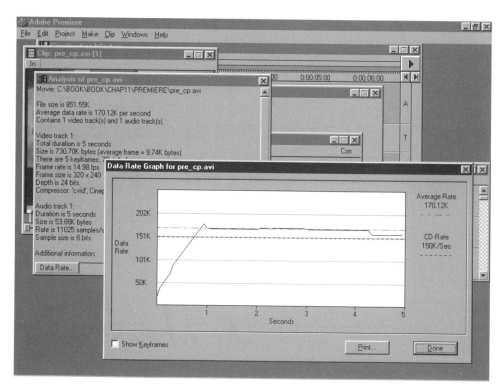

Figure 11.23   Premiere's excellent data rate graph and movie analysis screen.

heads and tails, adding filters, titles, and other effects, selecting output options, and then saving the project. When it's time to go home, you can queue up the projects for overnight or weekend processing, a big time-saver. (We demonstrate how to use this feature in Chapter 12.) Again, neither DVP nor MediaStudio offers a similar feature.

Compression Time Options   Premiere was also the first to focus on filtering as a way to improve video quality and to place a number of options in its compression menu, saving time for those who perform very little time line editing. Figure 11.24 shows both the compression settings and special processing screens, which house the new options.

At compression time, you can select either a blur, Gaussian, or median filter to assist compression performance (see the Noise Reduction Filtering at the end of the chapter) and change project gamma levels, affecting video

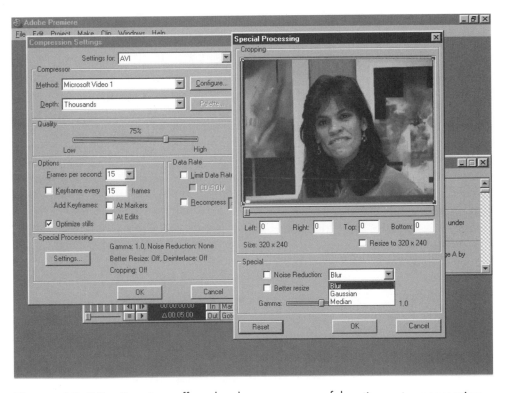

Figure 11.24   Premiere offers developers some useful options at compression time.

brightness. For the record, note that DVP offers a blur filter, while MediaStudio offers blur, Gaussian blur, noise reduction, and an average filter that should offer the same benefits, but none are offered at compression time. Note also that both DVP and MediaStudio allow the user to customize filter settings on the time line; Premiere doesn't, either at compression time or on the time line.

Both Premiere and MediaStudio offer compression time clipping, but only Premiere can scale the video back to the original resolution. As we discussed, Premiere uses a scaling algorithm from PhotoShop to avoid scaling artifacts.

Key Frame Placement   Most compression formats use two types of frames, key and delta frames. Key frames, or I frames in Moving Pictures Experts Group (MPEG) lingo, stand alone and are compressed without reference to any other frame. Delta frames, or B and P frames in MPEG speak, are compressed on the basis of their differences from other frames.

Key frames serve several purposes in the compressed bitstream. First, since they are compressed without reference to any other frame, they can be decompressed very simply and therefore act as an entry point when randomly accessing the video stream. That is, to seek a delta frame, you typically decompress the immediately previous key frame and then scan forward. For this reason, interactivity, or the ability to move quickly to random points in the clip, is optimized when entry points are key frames.

Second, key frames are larger than delta frames and able to produce a high-quality frame, even at scene changes, which can dramatically degrade delta frame quality. Placing a key frame at scene changes therefore optimizes quality for both the key frame and all delta frames that reference the key frame.

For these two reasons, the ability to place a key frame at desired locations can improve both quality and performance. However, until Premiere 4.2, publishers were forced to select one key frame interval that was applied uniformly throughout the video.

New in version 4.2 is the ability to place key frames at edit points, which automatically addresses many scene changes, and also at random markers on the time line, providing completely random placement. A new dialog, accessible from the compression options screen, enables these functions.

We tested this feature by compressing clips with several markers and edit points using Indeo 3.2, Video 1, Cinepak, and Indeo video interactive. With all codecs except for Indeo 3.2, the feature worked as advertised, placing key frames at the appropriate frames and then returning to the regular key frame interval. Indeo 3.2 blithely ignored Premiere's commands, placing key frames at the specified key frame interval. (We test and show the benefits of this feature in Chapter 12.)

Concatenation   In certain, limited situations, you'll need to abut several previously compressed video files *without recompressing them*. This technique is used to join files that need different key frame intervals, for joining together files developed at different times or animation or screen capture files that need key frames placed at irregular intervals.

To abut files without recompressing, the files have to have exactly the same resolution and be compressed with the same codec. If compressed with Video 1 in 8-bit mode, both files must use identical palettes. Key frame intervals and data rates can be different, however.

Interestingly, the different editors have different capabilities in this regard. DVP was the best performer overall, combining files compressed with Indeo 3.2, Indeo video interactive, Cinepak, and Video 1. Premiere was next, combining all formats save Video 1. MediaStudio brought up the rear, successful at combining only Cinepak and Indeo 3.2.

Compression Conclusions

As the jazzmen used to say back in the roaring '20s, "it don't mean a thing if it ain't got that swing." For us publishers, this roughly translates to "if you can't compress accurately, you can't place it on a CD!" I won't quit my day job, but you get my point.

Overall, MediaStudio was generally neck and neck with Premiere until the endgame. At compression time, however, MediaStudio faltered with Indeo 3.2, Cinepak, and Video 1 with real-world videos. The lack of a histogram or other data analysis tool makes these problems difficult to address. If you plan on using MediaStudio for CD-ROM publishing, you better have a copy of VidEdit or another program handy.

Noise Reduction Filtering

Even the cleanest videos contain noise, or random changes within and between frames. For example, study your TV from close range during the evening news and you'll see a constant shifting in the back wall behind the talking head. This type of noise, present in all videos to a greater or lesser degree, isn't really a problem in the analog domain.

Unfortunately, noise is deadly in the bandwidth-limited digital world. When compressing videos for digital publishing, codecs can't distinguish noise from real motion and allocate precious bandwidth to preserve the background motion you wish wasn't there in the first place. This steals bandwidth from real motion and video details, creating blockiness and artifacts.

Noise filtering is a technique used by high-end MPEG encoders to reduce noise and increase video quality. Most noise filters work by averaging values of pixels within a predefined region, say the target pixel and the four pixels to the east, west, north, and south. Averaging minimizes the differences between pixels within a frame and between frames, increasing both inter- and intraframe compression, which typically minimizes compression artifacts.

Premiere 4.2's noise reduction filtering available at compression time raises some obvious and interesting questions. First, of course, is when does filtering help improve compressed video quality? With three options presented, blur, Gaussian, and median filters, the second question becomes which filter for which type of video?

Adobe placed three filters, blur, Gaussian, and median, in the Special Processing screen. In general, blur filters are typically the least complicated, simply averaging the values within the range. According to Adobe's documentation, Premiere's blur filter is a bit more complex, "smoothing significant color transitions by averaging the pixels next to the hard edges of defined lines and shaded areas."

Gaussian filters are stronger than blur filters, giving more weight to pixels proximate to the target pixel to preserve edges. Median filters operate like blur filters but use the median, rather than average values, which helps eliminate data spikes from the image.

Talking Head   We tested Premiere's filtering with two clips. We captured both clips at 15 fps using FAST AV/Master at a compression ratio of about 1.3:1 and compressed all clips to 150 KB/s using Indeo video interactive. We created a control clip without filtering and three other clips using the three filtering methods. We then compared the various clips by studying individual frames and then real-time playback.

The first clip was a talking head clip from an old laserdisc exhibiting lots of dropouts, or random spots and streaks in the video. The clip was professionally shot, however, with good lighting and good contrast between the subject and the back wall.

The control clip was marred by significant dropout, and the general noise within the clip created a shimmering around the subject's head and frequent minor compression artifacts like blockiness.

In terms of still image quality, all of the filters reduced artifacting but also blurred the image. The blur filter produced the best result, with only a slight, uniform blurring across the entire image. The Gaussian filter was next, producing blurring that reduced the contrast between facial features, making them all less distinct. The median filter was most noticeable, blurring most minor details and at times virtually eliminating the contrast between the nose and face.

The median filter really shone in real-time playback, however, eliminating most of the minor dropouts. Although facial quality was superior using the blur and Gaussian filters, neither reduced analog background noise to any significant degree.

In general, if your talking head videos are fairly clean and compress to your target data rate without artifacting, you probably shouldn't filter. If you need a bit more space on the disk, filtering will reduce your data rate without creating artifacts at the cost of some blurriness. The blur filter appears to be the best choice of the three for this purpose.

If your video is generally noisy but without data spikes, the blur filter should improve quality noticeably. The median filter is the best choice for videos with significant high-contrast noise like analog dropout, but many viewers might find the facial blurriness more distracting than the analog noise.

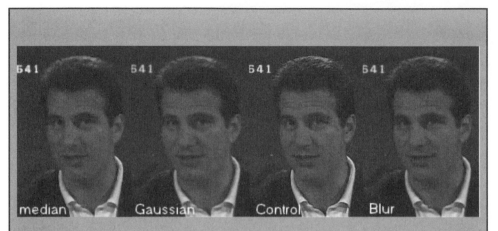

Figure 11.25   The effects of filtering on noisy video.

Action Sequence   The second test clip was an action sequence captured without compression. Capture quality was excellent, but motion was constant throughout the clip. All clips were compressed to under 100 KB/s.

The control clip exhibited frequent blockiness and artifacts. All three filters reduced gross blockiness, but the median filter obscured significant detail and created its own brand of artifacts. The blur filter obscured detail but created no artifacts, while the Gaussian filter proved the best of both worlds, decreasing blockiness without obscuring details.

Since high-motion clips have few clear reference points, the blurriness created by all the filters was barely noticeable. For this reason, if your high-motion clips exhibit any artifacts or blockiness, you should try the Gaussian filter.

Producers working with sequences containing both high and low motion should apply these filters on the Construction window rather than the Special Processing screen, which applies the selected filter uniformly over the duration of the clip.

Premiere LE

Does your copy of Premiere taste less filling than the version we're discussing? Well, it could be that you have Premiere light, or Premiere LE as it's officially called. This is a feature-defoliated version of Premiere that Adobe put together to serve the needs of low-end capture cards. We spoke with Joyce Chung, Premiere product manager, to get the skinny on the features lost in LE. Here's what she identified as the major differences.

1. LE is limited to three audio/video tracks.
2. LE has no 2D/3D motion capabilities.
3. LE has fewer effects, transitions, and filters, and won't accept third-party plug-ins.
4. LE's titler has no gradients or shadows and has limited drawing capabilities.
5. LE has no ability to export an edit decision list.

Of the differences, CD-ROM publishers are likely to find the track limitation most burdensome. Cost to upgrade to the full version is $149. Details at www.adobe.com.

Compression-Friendly Transitions

We've mentioned that most professional producers tend to minimize the use of transitions, pursuing the creative attitude that the best transitions are those that are barely noticed. Here's another reason to use "low-octane" transitions.

From a compression perspective, transitions are "motion," which, like other video noise, degrades overall quality. Usually, the more exotic the transition, like tumbling videos or 3D page curls, the more motion it creates and the more image degradation.

How much degradation? We tested a number of transitions by compressing a short clip with the Video 1 codec to 150 KB/s. Of course, Video 1 isn't the most industrial strength codec, but all lossy codecs will respond similarly, albeit not to the same degree.

Hide/Reveal Versus Push   Hide/reveal transitions are those that keep both images stable, clip A on top of clip B, and then use some mechanism to hide clip A while revealing clip B. Common hide/reveal transitions are wipes, clocks, irises, diamonds, and other transitions that maintain both videos in the same visual plane.

Push transitions are those that use clip A to push clip B from the visual area, almost simulating two simultaneous pans in the video window. Common push transitions are the push, slide, barn doors, and others.

Note the major quality differences between the two frames shown in Figure 11.26. On the right is a wipe, a hide/reveal transition that maintains good fidelity throughout the transition. On the left is a push, showing much more pronounced degradation. It's interesting to note that from the viewer's perspective, quality differences notwithstanding, these transitions are almost indistinguishable. Thus you can increase quality significantly with minimal impact on creativity.

Simple Is Better   Whether you decide to use a hide/reveal or not, in all instances simpler transitions are better than more exotic ones. Examples?

The common dissolve isn't a hide/reveal transition, but the amount of motion perceived by the codec is surprisingly small. On the other hand, dissolves come in many flavors, including the fizzle shown in Figure 11.27. While this transition may look beautiful in the analog domain, it ... well, fizzles in the digital.

Figure 11.26   The same frame from a wipe transition and a push.

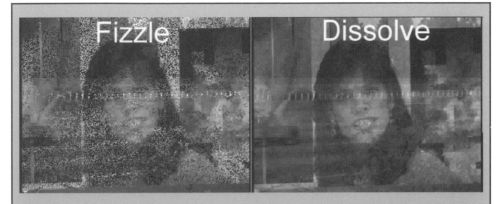

Figure 11.27 Simpler is definitely better when it comes to transitions.

3D Is Out Figure 11.28 shows three 3D transitions available in both Premiere and MediaStudio. The motion transition on the left spins the new video in over the old, creating extreme artifacting. The page curl maintains surprisingly well but shows blockiness in the page back and also in the video. Finally, the barn door transition, where the first track swings away like a barn door, is perceived as significant motion by the codec, producing blockiness that degrades image quality.

Fade-In/Fade-Out How about fading in from black at the beginning of the sequence and fading out to black at the end? Thinking about it for a moment, you might conclude that a fade involves what the codec might see as a heck of a lot of motion, and if you did you'd be right.

Figure 11.28 Three-dimensional transitions translate to lots of motion that stresses out most codecs.

Figure 11.29 shows original and compressed frames from a fade-from-black sequence. The original frame is pristine, but note the blockiness marring the compressed frame, once again the degrading effects of motion.

The lesson on fades? If you have to use them, make them quick. A long, slow fade to black may look artistic, but not at 150 KB/s.

Probably the best advice for both transitions and fades is to test them all at your final compressed data rate before you become too attached to them. We hate to limit creative artistry, but compression artifacts are a real-world factor that must be comprehended in the creative process.

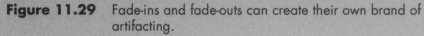

Figure 11.29   Fade-ins and fade-outs can create their own brand of artifacting.

The Making of "Eraser Turnabout"

By Jyotsna Murthy

In its continued efforts to push the envelope in new gaming technologies, Chicago-based Imagination Pilots Entertainment has developed a proprietary software engine to run its latest CD-ROM game, "Eraser Turnabout." Based on the Warner Bros. blockbuster *Eraser*, starring Arnold Schwarzenegger and Vanessa Williams, the game utilizes variable video sequences to establish game environments and character interaction. Game designer Howard A. Tullman has conceived several personality-driven scenarios that the player can define at the outset of the plot, which allow for randomized combinations of characters and alternative environments in the final outcome of the game.

Market considerations necessitated the release of the game on the PC platform, so after a series of tests with various video compression schemes, Imagination Pilots settled on Intel's new Indeo video interactive (IVI) codec. IVI allows superior video quality at data rates as high as 300 KB/s and compression ratios of nearly 1:20, crucial considerations since approximately 90% of the game design is exclusively video-based. Impressed with the extent to which Imagination Pilots was able to stretch the capabilities of the IVI codec without compromising on video quality, Intel extended complete support to "Eraser Turnabout" by putting their extensive technical expertise and problem-solving resources at the project's disposal.

Imagination Pilots primarily used Adobe Premiere versions 4.0 and 4.2 for the digitization and finishing of the video footage. Operating on a Macintosh platform, video editors Eli Brown and Jyotsna Murthy used the Radius Telecast Board with Adobe Premiere version 4.0 for video capture from BetaCAM SP at a 320×240 frame size and a full frame rate of 30 fps. The complex permutations involved in the game's scenarios required that several primary characters be shot and composited over a variety of background environments. To this end, much of this footage had been shot against a green screen. However, on digitization it was found that Premiere responded better to compositing with Ultimatte blue, outputting a cleaner, sharper edge and less pixel break-up along fuzzy outlines. Therefore, it became necessary to key out the green-screen background with the program's Transparency tool and replace it with a blue-screen background. This footage was rendered out as uncompressed QuickTime movies, converted to AVIs for the PC platform, and finally compressed with IVI.

The quality of most blue/green screen video is commensurate with the manner in which the subject and the background have been lit. In video that is well-lit for the purposes of compositing (flat, even, diffused lighting with clear separation between the subject and the background), one might intuitively select Premiere's Blue Screen key type (or Green Screen, as the case may be) for transparency. However, such perfect lighting conditions are hard to come by, so a little bit of experimentation with the key type options is well in order. In the case of "Eraser Turnabout," the editors found that the chroma key, with its accompanying blending and smoothing options, offered the clearest key separation and maximum flexibility. Overall, Adobe Premiere ably stood up to the task of compositing live-action video onto full-screen bitmap backgrounds, and allowed for a good deal of experimentation with the numerous keying techniques it offers.

Chapter

Video for Windows Compression Controls

IN THIS CHAPTER

Now that our video is captured, preprocessed, and ready for output, it's time to select the codec and compression parameters and create, make, build, or otherwise render the final video file, depending on the nomenclature used by your editing program. This chapter will outline selection criteria and alternatives.

The bulk of the chapter is focused on compression controls for software encoders like Indeo video interactive and Cinepak. Although it is much less complicated, we'll also cover the output parameters for creating a video file for input into a third-party program for encoding to Moving Pictures Experts Group 1 (MPEG-1) or streaming Internet format.

The final stage of nonlinear editing is a similar rendering process, where you create a finished file to transfer back out to tape. We'll discuss the output parameters for these activities as well.

To make this chapter as self-contained as possible, we'll review some findings from previous chapters. We'll do our best to minimize redundancy.

Author's Note   Late in the writing process I discovered that Microsoft had made the original Video for Windows 1.1 kit available for download on their FTP site, ftp.microsoft.com. The location is /developr/drg/mul-timedi/jumpstart/vfw11e/winvideo. Download all the files into a subdirectory on your development machine and run setup.

The primary benefit of the download is VidEdit, still extremely efficient for many day-to-day editing tasks as described throughout the book. You'll also get VidCap, but this 16-bit version won't work with most new capture cards, and the 16-bit version of CapScrn invariably crashes on Windows 95.

Still, VidEdit and *free!* Download today and you'll send silent blessings toward Redmond every time you have to clip a few frames or reinterleave audio.

MEET THE ENEMY

Figure 12.1 is Premiere's Compression Settings screen, which we'll use as a road map for walking through the various compression options. Other editors like MediaStudio, VidEdit, and DVP have the same basic options, and later in the chapter we include screen cams illustrating the location of the various compression screens for the respective programs.

In addition to the generic settings scattered about Figure 12.1, you'll notice that the "configure" button located next to the selected codec, Intel Indeo video interactive, is live. This means that IVI has unique compression options. We'll describe each codec's unique options in codec-specific sections at the end of the chapter.

If you haven't done so already, you should scan through the compression section of Chapter 11, specifically around Table 11.11. As we discovered in Chapter 11, although all editors have the same basic controls, they don't compress with the same level of accuracy, and you definitely need to be

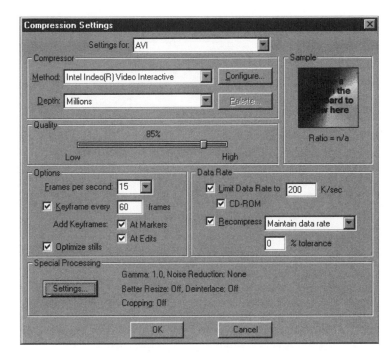

Figure 12.1   Premiere's Compression Settings screen shows all generic compression options.

aware of the potential problems this can cause during the very important rendering stage.

Finally, since Smacker isn't a Video for Windows codec, you have to use its own proprietary interface to encode your audio and video files. We'll describe how to work with Smacker in the codec section as well.

CODEC SELECTION

Introduction

Figure 12.2 is a close-up of Premiere's compression method selection screen. A couple of quick notes.

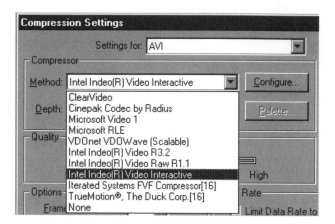

Figure 12.2   Premiere's compression method screen showing all the codecs available to compress the edited video.

First, Premiere and most other editors don't show codecs that aren't available for the type of video being compressed. For example, TrueMotionS requires 24-bit video, so it won't show up when 8-bit animations are being compressed. In addition, if the resolution of the image is too large for the codec, it won't show up.

You can tell when a codec is installed by looking through the Advanced screen in your Multimedia Properties dialog box: Start (me up)/Control Panel/Multimedia Properties icon/Advanced tab (Figure 12.3 and Fig12_3.avi). If the codec is listed here but not available in your compression screen, it's probably a video configuration issue, either color depth or resolution. Check your codec's documentation.

No Recompression   Users familiar with VidEdit will quickly note the absence of a No Recompression option (see Figure 12.4), a key option used in a variety of settings. For example, when reinterleaving audio, a task at which VidEdit excels, you would always select No Recompression before saving the file to ensure that VidEdit didn't recompress the file.

You were never quite sure when No Recompression would remain available and which editing actions would make it go away. Deleting frames from a newly captured file was fine, for example, and you could save the file without recompression. Delete frames from the start of a compressed file and No Recompression disappeared, unless, of course, you deleted frames up to a key frame, which was OK.

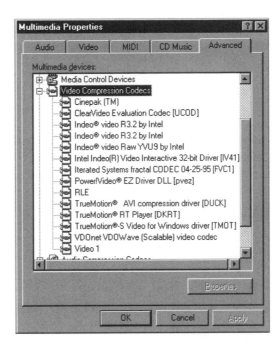

Figure 12.3   The Advanced screen in your Multimedia Properties dialog box shows all codecs installed in the system.

Despite the somewhat elusive flavor, when No Recompression was there you knew you could save the file without recompression, and when it was gone, you knew you couldn't. However, since video editors do much more to video than VidEdit ever dreamed of, including titling, filtering, special

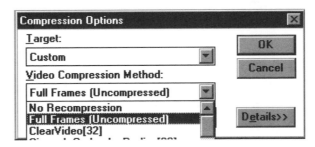

Figure 12.4   VidEdit's No Recompression option provided certainty in an uncertain world. This binary approach was simply inadequate for today's nonlinear editors, which perform a bevy of much more complicated functions.

effects, and transitions, VidEdit's binary recompression/no recompression approach was inadequate. For example, applying filters to fade in at the start of the clip and fade out at the end, the editor should be smart enough to recompress only the frames involved in the fades and leave the rest alone.

For this reason, all video editors, including Premiere, take a different approach. Here's what Adobe says regarding this issue in their help files:

> By default, Adobe Premiere will not recompress a clip if the project's compression options and output options are set to the same values as those of the source clip and if no special effects have been applied to the clips. To prevent recompression, the project and the source clip must have the same settings for all of the following options:
>
> - frame size
> - frame rate
> - key frame rate
> - codec
> - color depth
>
> New material, such as effects, will be always recompressed, as will any clips whose settings are not the same as the project output and preview settings.

DVP has a routine called "SmartEdit" that lets you select whether to recompress or not. We'll cover how to access this option below.

> *All* Compresses all frames on the timeline, no matter what compression method has previously been applied. When unchecked, DVP only re-compresses frames that have changed. (Changes include edits such as resizing or cropping frames or applying filters and other special effects.) Because SmartEdit (partial recompression) is not available when using Indeo interactive's bi-directional prediction, full compression is required when using this compressor. Consequently, when Indeo interactive is the selected compressor, Compress All is checked and dimmed.
>
> *Note* Compressing only changed frames helps speed compression and can improve image quality. However, if you make global changes to a video, such as changing the frame rate, you should check Compress All.

I couldn't locate any discussion of this issue in MediaStudio's help file, although this program also saves without recompression in a number of instances.

In addition to the normal clipping and editing functions, processing without recompressing is important in many scenarios. Probably the most important advanced technique that it enables is file concatenation, which we discussed in Chapter 11 and will demonstrate in the case studies presented below.

Raw Video   Note that the Full Frames (Uncompressed) option also visible in Figure 12.4 corresponds to the "none" setting in Premiere. Both options convert the compressed file back to a raw file, expanding your tightly compacted 150 KB/s file back its original 3.5 MB/s.

I use Premiere's none option a lot, generally to resize videos that I've captured for recompression (I know, not advisable but often necessary). For example, when scaling 320×240 video to 176×144 for low-bandwidth streaming Internet tests I used Premiere's better resizing option to avoid scaling artifacts and convert the image to raw format.

Note here that you can convert to any color depth, including millions+ (Figure 12.5), which I believe is 32-bit color depth, including an alpha channel. Several times I've run into problems with the millions+ option, where codecs wouldn't recognize the file or proprietary compression interfaces like Xing's MPEG Encoder or Vivo's streaming video encoder would distort the file. For this reason, whenever I convert to raw format, I make sure to convert to millions of colors, which is a standard 24-bit image that everyone recognizes, rather than millions+.

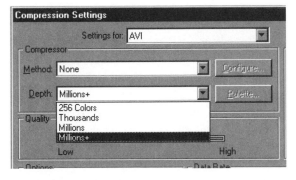

Figure 12.5   When converting a file to raw format, use the millions rather than millions+ option, which creates a 32-bit file that some programs don't recognize.

Codec Selection: "Software-Only"

This is a full-blown, "sit down here beside me and let's have a talk" discussion about something you've probably already done—choosing a codec. If you're beyond this stage, this section will be of little value. On the other hand, if you're still wavering...

Display Rate   We covered codec quality and performance in Chapter 6, but we'll review quickly here. Codec selection is a complicated, tricky subject that involves a number of parameters, including target platform (processor, storage mechanism, and graphics card) and content type. Our view is that performance on your target system should be, if not the single most important consideration, certainly afforded great weight. In English, that means if the codec won't play at or near its frame rate on most computers in your target market, you shouldn't use that codec.

A talking head, for example, captured and compressed at 15 frames per second needs to play faster than 12–13 frames per second to appear synchronized. Sequences involving even moderate motion need to play at that rate to appear smooth. Table 12.1, pinched from Chapter 6, shows the performance of the respective codecs on a broad base of target computers.

Table 12.2 converts this data into a more cohesive recommendation chart, using traffic light lingo—go, caution, stop—to describe recommended usage. Basically, at P133 speeds and faster, you have your choice of codec, which narrows pretty much at every processor level. Even for 486/33 computers, you still have two choices, Cinepak and Smacker, and two other codecs you could use in a pinch.

Comparative Quality: Real-World Videos   After understanding performance on your target computer, we move to content type. Here we say, "OK, we're targeting 486/66 computers and faster, which disqualifies IVI and MPEG-1, but leaves Cinepak, Smacker, Video 1, and Indeo 3.2 as valid options. Let's look at the motion content of our footage and its original origin, either video or animation."

I know it's slightly Pollyannaish to believe that all projects fall neatly into the categories that we've listed, but many do. Note that while you can use different codecs for different types of footage, it can complicate palette planning for working in 8-bit environments. More on that later in this chapter. In the meantime, here's a quick rundown on how the codecs fared with the various footage types, with Tables 12.3 and 12.4 summarizing data

Table 12.1 Display rate by computer and codec.

Display rate	486/66		P60		P90		P133		P166	
Quality by codec	15 fps	30 fps	15 fps	30 fps	15 fps	30 fps	15 fps	30 fps	15 fps	30 fps
Cinepak	15	30	15	29	15	29	15	29	15	30
Indeo video interactive										
Bidirectional	5	4	9	4	15	24	15	28	15	30
No bidirectional	7.5	5	10	4	15	26	14	29	15	30
No bidirectional, good compression	5	n.a.	11	n.a.	15	n.a.	15	n.a.	15	n.a.
Quick compressor	9	n.a.	10	n.a.	15	n.a.	14	n.a.	15	n.a.
Indeo 3.2	15	6	15	26	15	27	15	29	15	30
Power!Video Pro	14	n.a.	15	n.a.	15	n.a.	15	n.a.	15	n.a.
TrueMotionS	9	n.a.	14	n.a.	15	n.a.	15	n.a.	15	n.a.
Smacker	15	30	15	24	15	25	15	30	15	30
MPEG-1	n.a.	3.7	n.a.	9	n.a.	19	n.a.	23	n.a.	28
Video 1	15	n.a.	15	n.a.	15	n.a.	15	n.a.	15	n.a.

Table 12.2 Codec usage guide.

	486/33	486/66	P60	P90	P133 +
Cinepak	Go	Go	Go	Go	Go
Smacker	Go	Go	Go	Go	Go
Video 1	Caution	Go	Go	Go	Go
Indeo 3.2	Caution	Go	Go	Go	Go
TrueMotionS	STOP	Caution	Go	Go	Go
Indeo video interactive (150 kb/s)	STOP	STOP	Caution	Go	Go
Software MPEG-1	STOP	STOP	STOP	STOP	Go

Table 12.3 Still frame and moving quality for low-motion videos. Ratings on a scale of 1–5 with 5 being the highest.

Quality by Codec	Still Quality, LMV	Moving Quality, LMV	Total, LMV	Still Quality, HMV	Moving Quality, HMV	Total, HMV
Cinepak	2	3	5	2	3	5
IVI, bidirectional	5	5	10	5	5	10
IVI, no bidirectional	4.5	5	9.5	4	3	7
IVI, no bidirectional, good compression	5	5	10	3	3	6
IVI, quick	4	4	8	3	3	6
Indeo 3.2	3	2	5	2	2	4
Power!Video Pro	1	1	2	2	2	4
Duck TrueMotionS	2.5	3	5.5	4	2	6
Smacker	3	3	6	1	1	2
MPEG-1	4	5	9	4	5	9
Video 1	2	2	4	n.a.	n.a.	n.a.

Table 12.4 Appearance when displayed in 8-bit environment.

Quality by Codec	Color Matching	Dither Pattern	Total
Cinepak	2	4	6
IVI	4	4	8
Indeo 3.2	3	4	7
Power!Video Pro	1	1	2
TrueMotionS	2	2	4
MPEG-1	5+	5+	10

from Chapter 6 (please note that LMV denotes low-motion video, and HMV denotes high-motion video).

Low-Motion Videos: Overall, all IVI flavors were quite impressive, with bidirectional encoding apparently worth the wait, but only barely for these easy to compress, low-motion videos. Without careful scrutiny, however, the differences between the Quick compressor and full bidirectional encoding was fairly small, and you should feel comfortable using the codec for all but the final, final compression. Even at double the frame rate, MPEG-1 was also impressive, particularly in moving quality.

If your target systems can't play videos compressed with these codecs back at close to full frame rate, you'll have to consider second-tier codecs. TrueMotionS won in this tier by half a point, but royalties apply. Cinepak and Indeo 3.2 were next, followed by Video 1. As we've seen in all of our tests, Power!Video really wasn't meant to play at these data rates and performs poorly at 200 KB/s.

High-Motion Videos: Indeo video interactive clearly carries the day with high-motion videos. Unlike the talking head video, where we saw very little difference between videos compressed with the various options enabled and/or disabled, here bidirectional encoding and compressing using the "best" setting created significant differences. If your target platform can play back full-bore IVI, these options will pay real quality dividends.

Developers courting the installed base of 486/66 computers will have to settle for artifact-ridden videos, since neither Cinepak nor Indeo 3.2 can handle high-motion files without visibly dropping quality. TrueMotionS does a great job with still frame quality, but the dropped frames used to maintain the target data rate kill playback smoothness. Power!Video Pro is also outmatched by the high-motion sequence, with low scores in both still frame and real-time playback tests.

Finally, even MPEG-1 had difficulty maintaining still frame quality in this sequence, with slight blockiness marring our test frame. Moving quality was still outstanding, however.

8-Bit Appearance   As we explain in Chapter 6, displaying in 8-bit environments is challenging for 24-bit codecs, which have to dither from 16 million plus colors to 256. Table 12.4 illustrates the wide performance disparity in both color matching, or how bizarre the video looks after dropping so much color information, and dither pattern, which can either be unobtrusive or downright distracting.

As 8-bit codecs, both Video 1 and Smacker look better than 24-bit codecs in 8-bit mode because they don't have to color reduce and because you can assign a custom palette to the video rather than using a standard palette. When compressing low-motion video content for display in the 8-bit environment, both are excellent options.

Animation Performance   Converting animations from FLC format to AVI pays dividends when trying to synchronize audio and video or when pulling the interleaved video from CD-ROM. Not all codecs handle these specialized files with equal adroitness. Table 12.5 represents our findings from Chapter 6.

Table 12.5 Moving and still image quality for quarter-screen animation compressed to under 150 KB/s and full-screen animation compressed to under 250 KB/s. Display rate tests on a Pentium 133 from CD-ROM.

Animation Quality by Codec	Cinepak	IVI (all flavors)	Indeo 3.2	TMS (1)	Power!-Video	Smacker	Video 1
Still Image Quality							
Quarter screen	4	1	1	3	n.a.	5	5
Full screen	3	1	1	4	n.a.	5	4
Moving Quality							
Quarter screen	4	2	2	4	n.a.	5	5
Full screen	2	1	1	5	n.a.	5	3
Display Rates—P133							
Quarter screen	14	14	14	14	n.a.	15	14
Full screen	2	2	2	14	n.a.	15	12
File Size							
Quarter screen	936	1.7 MB	895 KB	745 KB	3 MB	372 MB	1 MB
Full screen	2.23 MB	3.97 MB	3.05 MB	1.8 MB	n.a.	449 KB	2.6 MB

Finally, Table 12.6 summarizes all these findings into some hopefully coherent recommendations, subject, as always, to being able to perform well on your target computer platform.

Codec Selection: Nonlinear Editing

This is a simple one. Since you're capturing for nonlinear editing, your capture card almost certainly uses a Motion Joint Photographic Experts Group (JPEG) codec. In order to send the video back out to the card, you have to render in that Motion JPEG format. End of story.

Codec Selection: MPEG-1

If you captured in a raw format with a card like the Intel Smart Video Recorder III, by all means render the video in raw format. Take note of our earlier discussion about color depth. Although most programs can deal with the 24-bit color output by Premiere when you select millions of colors, several hiccup at the millions+ formats. For this reason, I always use 24-bit (millions) as my output format when working in Premiere.

If you captured in a compressed format, your decision is a touch more complicated and involves a judgment call. Here's why: As we know, the lossy compression used by most capture cards degrades quality. You compressed during capture to get the video to disk and would prefer not to recompress if at all possible. If your editing was extremely limited, like clipping heads and tails from the start and finish of the video, you can render the file in the Motion JPEG format and the editor won't recompress;

Table 12.6 Codec usage guide by content type.

	Cinepak	Indeo 3.2	Video 1	TMotion	IVI	Smacker	MPEG-1
Low motion	Caution	Go	Go	Go	Go	Go	Go
Moderate motion	Go	Caution	STOP	STOP	Go	Go	Go
High motion	Go	Caution	STOP	STOP	Go	Caution	Go
Small animation	Go	STOP	Go	STOP	STOP	Go	STOP
Large animation	STOP	STOP	Go	STOP	STOP	Go	STOP

it will simply save the file in its original format. No double compression takes place.

On the other hand, if you edited extensively, inserting transitions, perhaps some filters or titles, you definitely don't want to store the video in the Motion JPEG format, since much of your video file will be recompressed. Even at the highest possible quality setting, this double compression degrades video quality. In these instances, it's best to render in a raw format.

Why not just render raw all the time and leave it at that? You should always leave the video in its original format as long as possible, because this limits the number of color conversions and other modifications that can distort video appearance.

When you convert to raw format, a color conversion takes place, as Video for Windows converts the compressed Motion JPEG data to 24-bit raw video. When you input the file into a third-party program for compression to MPEG-1 format, another conversion takes place, from AVI file to some intermediate format, which may involve another color conversion.

Every color conversion is an interpolation, or judgment call, which may or may not distort your video colors. If editing is limited and double compression is not a significant issue, you would just as soon avoid the intermediate step of converting to raw format. On the other hand, if editing is significant, you would output in raw format to avoid double compression.

Codec Selection: Streaming Internet Format

Same deal as with MPEG-1, with one caveat. If you had to resize your video after capture, recompression is assured, so output in raw format to avoid double compression. For example, if you used the miro DC30 to capture at 320×240 and want to output at 176×144 for encoding to VivoActive format, select a raw format. On the other hand, if your Motion JPEG card let you capture directly to 176×144, you would render raw only if other editing changes were significant.

Table 12.7 summarizes our output recommendations by application.

Table 12.7 Summary of recommended output format by application.

Capturing for:	Recommendation
Compression with traditional software codec	Choose your codec on the basis of display rate first, quality second.
Software MPEG-1 compression	If raw capture format, output raw. If compressed capture format, output raw if significant editing; output in compressed format if editing minimal.
Streaming Internet delivery	If raw capture format, output raw. If compressed capture format, output raw if significant editing (note the resolution change is significant editing); or output in compressed format if editing minimal.
Nonlinear editing	Output in capture format, usually Motion JPEG.

DATA RATE

Software-Only Codecs

Factors in Data Rate Selection   All relevant codecs are lossy in nature, so as data rates decrease, so does video quality. This makes data rate selection a key decision, since it will ultimately affect video quality, the duration of video you can place on a CD-ROM, and, surprisingly, the display rate at which that video will play on marginal computers.

CD-ROM Publishers   In these days of 6, 8, 10, and 12X drives, the concept of 200 KB/s video seems almost quaint. Why bother with this anemic video, you might ask, when we can easily stream close to six times as much without breaking a sweat?

Well, here's why. First, although you can't find a new computer with slower than a 4X drive, a substantial number of low-end machines (e.g., 486/66, Pentium 60) still have only 2X drives. Exceed 250–280 KB/s video data rates and your video won't play on these machines.

In addition, higher data rates mean less video on the CD-ROM, which holds about 650 MB of data. Pack 12X video on your CD-ROM, and you get a whopping nine minutes of video on your disk.

Higher data rates also mean that the poor CPU is left with more work to do. Retrieving 2X data is roughly twice as hard as retrieving 1X data and retrieving 4X data is . . . well, you get the point. In the tenuous world of software-only video playback, if your target computers are "on the edge," when it comes to playing 15 fps, the extra bandwidth might knock them over.

We ran some tests on our resident 486/66 computer, which used to run our business but now sits over there in the corner, waiting to be dusted off for tests like these. Using Microsoft's VidTest, we measured the percentage of CPU cycles required to pull data off the disk at 150, 200, and 250 KB/s and then played back Indeo video interactive files compressed at those bandwidths. Table 12.8 contains the results.

As you can see, IVI almost becomes viable on this platform at 150 KB/s, since the CPU has to do relatively little work to retrieve the data. At 250 KB/s, the poor CPU is working so hard to retrieve the video that it has very little left to decompress and display the video frames. For this reason, the display rate drops, and IVI becomes completely useless on this computer.

When using IVI, there's another consideration related to the codec's Achilles' heel, start-up latency, or a delay in the start of smooth playback. Generally, files with higher bandwidths take longer to start playing smoothly than lower bandwidth files. This came to my attention when I reviewed Intel's announcement CD-ROM, which featured videos of luminaries saying wonderful things about the codec (you bet I'm bitter—they didn't ask me).

Table 12.8   CPU horsepower required to pull different bandwidth files from CD-ROM and resultant frame rate (Indeo video interactive) and CD capacity.

	CPU Required	Frame Rate	CD Capacity (video minutes)
150 KB/s	37%	10	72
200 KB/s	47%	5	54
250 KB/s	60%	3	43

When fooling around with Intel's CD-ROM, I noticed that their videos tended to start running smoothly much faster than ours. A quick frame profile in VCS revealed that Intel had compressed their videos to 150 KB/s while we compressed ours to 200 KB/s. At lower data rates, our videos performed identically to theirs.

One final consideration. All codecs have bandwidth "sweet spots" after which the benefit of high data rates starts to drop. In all but the most high motion videos, Cinepak seems to stop gaining quality after about 200–220 KB/s, and the extra bandwidth is manifest as an increase in background noise, which, of course, is counterproductive. Compare cp_tk150.avi with cp_tk250.avi in the chap_12 subdirectory. On the other hand, the 250 KB/s high-motion file looks substantially better than the 150 KB/s file, as shown in Figure 12.6 (cp_ac150.avi versus cp_ac250.avi).

Table 12.9 summarizes the sweet spots for the most common codecs by content but does *not* consider the display rate implications of these data rates. For CD-ROM publication, try to keep your data rate within the sweet spot.

If you're low on real estate, or selling into an extremely marginal class of machine for the codec, the minimum data rate is the lowest bandwidth at which the codec produces acceptable results. Go lower, and quality noticeably starts to head south. At the other extreme, the maximum data rate is where diminishing returns really start to kick in. Go higher, and the perceptible benefit will be very slight.

Figure 12.6   For high-motion videos, Cinepak looks much better at 250 KB/s than 150 KB/s. The same can't be said for low-motion videos, which often look noisier at higher data rates.

Table 12.9 Recommended minimum, sweet spot, and maximum data rates for low- and high-motion videos by content.

	Talking Head			*Action*		
	Min data rate	*Sweet spot*	*Max data rate*	*Min data rate*	*Sweet spot*	*Max data rate*
Cinepak	150	180–200	200	180–190	210–250	285
Smacker	100	120–150	200	200	220–250	380
Video 1	150	180–220	220	n.a.	n.a.	n.a.
Indeo 3.2	100	100–150	150	180	200–250	250
TrueMotionS	275	300–350	400	300	350–450	600+
Indeo video interactive (150 KB/s)	100	150–180	190	150	180–200	220

Overall, if you're using a codec that's marginal in terms of display rate on your target platform, bumping the data rate for quality isn't a grand idea. On the other hand, if you've got the CD-ROM real estate and display rate is assured, bump up to the codec's maximum but not beyond.

In any event, never encode to within 5–10% of the CD-ROM's rated transfer capacity. If targeting single-spin drives, don't exceed an average data rate of 140–145 KB/s, or roughly 270–285 KB/s on 2X drives. In this way, you'll have no trouble with the poorer performing drives in the class.

Always, always, always check your streaming bandwidth with VCS's frame profile or a similar tool before calling it a keeper. If *any sustained portion of the file* exceeds the drive's rated capacity, your users will suffer the heartbreak of severe frame drops and maybe even the dreaded audio breaks.

Hard Drive Video   If you're playing your video back from your hard drive, tolerances become much less critical, and you can generally compress for quality rather than display rate or bandwidth. You also have the option to use different codecs like Power!Video from Horizons, which looks great at 400 KB/s and even better at 600 KB/s. Still, for the most part, higher bandwidth videos can slow display rates, so test, test, test before concluding that bigger is always better.

Operation   Let's quickly rehash information covered in Chapter 6. Job number one for all codecs is to *achieve* and *maintain* the data rate target over the duration of the clip. These are two very separate tasks, since *averaging* below target data rate doesn't prevent data spikes from interrupting smooth CD-ROM playback, a significant issue for CD-ROM title developers.

There are two basic compression control paradigms (Table 12.10). The first and best is the *data rate* paradigm, which lets the developer set a target data rate that the codec achieves and maintains by lowering video quality. The other paradigm is *control oriented*, in which the developer sets certain compression controls that maintain uniform quality over the duration of the video by adjusting data rate upward and downward according to scene complexity.

Table 12.10   Compression details by codec.

Compression	Cinepak	IVI	Indeo 3.2	Power!-Video Pro	True MotionS	Video 1	Smacker
Compression paradigm	Data rate	Data rate	Data rate	Control	Data rate (with drop frames)	Data rate	Data rate or control
Quality setting	Ignored	Ignored when data rate checked	Ignored	Grayed out	Grayed out	Comprehended	n.a. (proprietary interface)
Other controls	None	Quick, bi-direction, scalability target platform	None	Compress (high/low), color resolution, detail slider, others	Intra-frame, inter-frame options, with temporal quality and filtering	None	Key frame trigger

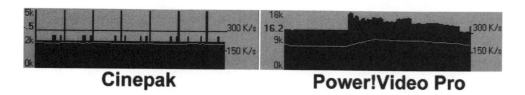

Figure 12.7   Data rate–oriented codecs like Cinepak meet and maintain the data rate target. Control-oriented codecs like Power!Video Pro adjust frame size upward and downward to deliver consistent quality over a range of video scenes.

Figure 12.7 uses VCS's frame profile to illustrate the two approaches. On the left is Cinepak, a staunch and exacting data rate codec with a penchant for maintaining precise key and delta frame sizes. Note that the wavy line hovers uniformly just above the 150 KB/s line. On the right is Power!Video Pro, a control-oriented codec. Note how frame size varies over the clip with resultant increases and decreases in streaming data rate.

For the most part, CD-ROM developers prefer *data rate*–oriented codecs, since they ensure that the video will stream successfully from your target CD-ROM drive. At the end of the day, uniform quality does you no good if your customer can't play the video. On the other hand, developers working on kiosks and similar hard drive–oriented projects may prefer control–oriented codecs that deliver uniform quality irrespective of scene complexity.

Note that data rate–oriented codecs often have an apparent conflict between the data rate and quality setting (see Figure 12.8). After all, you can't meet 100% quality at any data rate, so something has to give. All codecs handle this differently, as described in Table 12.9, some ignoring quality, some comprehending it, and some simply graying out the control. We cover specific codec controls later, but all codecs save Power!Video Pro follow the data rate paradigm and struggle to produce the requested data rate by either reducing quality or dropping frames.

Figure 12.9 shows Premiere's data rate control, a control found on all encoders. On the left, shown as Step 1, is the screen where you chose between maintaining the data rate and "Always" recompressing. Note that Premiere will automatically compress or recompress all frames that must be recompressed and that by selecting Always you will probably recompress frames that probably don't need it. I can't think of any situations in which I would use this, so use it carefully.

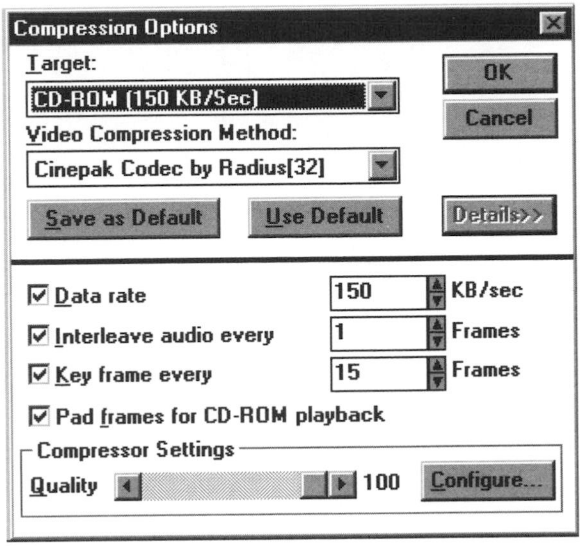

Figure 12.8 When both quality and data rate settings are engaged, which does the compressor ignore? Cinepak unabashedly ignores the quality setting and meets the data rate. We like that in a codec!

Once you've told the program to maintain data rate, you've got to select it (Step 2, on the right). To achieve your actual target, you often have to choose a data rate of 5–8 KB/s *less* than your target to ensure achieving the requested data rate.

Premiere's data rate tolerance control, while unique, tends to have little impact on actually achieving the target in my experience. Nonetheless, we always compress at zero percent tolerance. Hey, we run a tight ship at

Figure 12.9 Premiere's data rate control, which also includes a box for selecting CD-ROM padding, discussed later.

Doceo, and if you let one thing slip . . . well, you never know what's going to happen.

Note also the CD-ROM padding control found in Figure 12.9, which we'll discuss in a moment.

It goes without saying that you should test all compressed files for both appearance and data rate achievement and maintenance before considering them keepers. All encoders stumble occasionally, and who knows, maybe you or I might slip up now and again and input the wrong compression parameter. Or sometimes, simply, gremlins strike.

Whatever the cause, play the entire file back, make sure the audio is clear and unbroken, and use VCS to test the display rate and measure the data rate. It's always better to find anomalies sooner than later.

Data Rate: Nonlinear Editing

With nonlinear editing, you're always pushing the envelope, boosting data rates as high as possible without dropping frames during capture or when writing the video to tape. For the most part, the least demanding side of the equation is capture, meaning that most boards can capture at higher data rates than they can write to tape without dropping frames.

For example, the miro DC30 could capture at close to 5.3 MB/s in our tests but couldn't write more than 4.8 MB/s back to tape without dropping frames. If you captured at 5.3 MB/s, you would have to compress the video down to 4.8 to stream it back out to tape, which involves the heartbreak of double compression. Obviously, it's preferable to capture at 4.8 MB/s and avoid the heartbreak.

Although we didn't quantify this, we also found that some capture cards had a harder time working with video that had been edited and rendered than with the original captured video file. Often we had to drop the data rate during compression another 200–300 KB/s to write to tape successfully after editing.

Early in your experience with your capture card, you'll isolate the data rate at which you can successfully write edited and rendered video back to tape. This is the data rate you should use when capturing and rendering. You should also instruct the encoder to recompress when necessary to maintain the data rate, since data spikes can cause dropped frames when writing back out to tape. The relevant control in Premiere is shown in Figure 12.9.

Data Rate: MPEG-1/Streaming Internet Formats

If you're saving the file in raw format, don't sweat, there is no data rate control. If you're saving it in Motion JPEG format, check the actual captured data rate in VCS and set the data rate somewhere north of that figure. Or simply uncheck the data rate box, which in theory should produce the highest data rate allowed by the encoder.

Watch the editor while it's building the file to get a sense of whether it's recompressing or simply saving the original video file. If it zips through completion like nobody's business, you've probably saved without recompression. If it chugs along like the little train that couldn't, you're probably recompressing.

When the latter happens, check all your output options and deselect anything that looks as if it might constrict the data rate. If all else fails, punt and use a raw output format.

Audio

Software-Only Codecs

From our perspective, audio bandwidth is a "capture" parameter, or one best set during capture. See Chapter 10 to review factors involved in selecting audio bandwidth. After capture, you can always modify your audio parameters, using controls like Premiere's Project Output Options shown in Figure 12.10. Also shown in Figure 12.10 is the ability to compress the audio using Microsoft's ADPCM compression, available in the Video for Window run time and on all Windows 95 computers.

Let's deal with the three issues in turn: first, choosing the optimal audio data rate, then the operational aspects of creating a file with that data rate. Finally, we'll experiment a bit with audio compression.

Choosing the Right Audio Parameters   From a compression perspective, audio bandwidth is a component of total video bandwidth. Since data rate is another zero-sum game, the higher the audio data rate, the lower the video data rate.

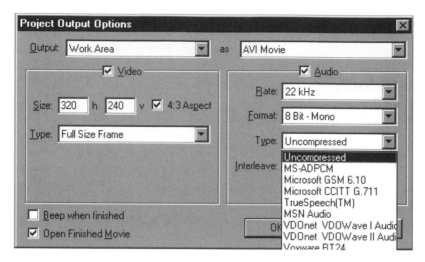

Figure 12.10   You can always change the audio parameters after capture and even compress with Microsoft ADPCM.

Table 12.11, duplicated from Chapter 10, illustrates the data rates at the various audio parameters. As you can see, at the higher quality sound settings, the results are somewhat alarming, especially if you're working with CD-ROM products. Choosing the right combination relates primarily to the sound system on the target computer. Obviously, if you can't hear the difference, the additional quality isn't worth the bandwidth.

Table 12.11   Audio data rates at specified audio parameters.

	11.025 kHz	22.05 kHz	44.1 kHz
Mono Audio			
8-bit	11 KB/s	22 KB/s	44 KB/s
16-bit	22 KB/s	44 KB/s	88 KB/s
Stereo Audio			
8-bit	22 KB/s	44 KB/s	88 KB/s
16-bit	44 KB/s	88 KB/s	176 KB/s

Whatever combination you choose, make sure you test on a computer with a very low-end sound board, which often yields some interesting results. For example, I've experienced a fuzzy sound called "white noise" when playing 16-bit audio on an 8-bit sound system. Other developers have reported audio distortion when high-quality audio is played on lower quality sound systems.

For these reasons, and to save bandwidth, most CD-ROM publishers seem to use either 22- or 11-kHz, 8-bit mono audio. All of the videos on the CD-ROM use 8-bit, 11-kHz mono audio.

Achieving the Optimal Parameters   One frequently discussed topic among multimedia folks is how to create a file with the optimal parameters. Assuming, for example, that you selected 11-kHz, 8-bit mono audio as your target, what's the best way to actually create the audio file with those data parameters? As is usually the case in multimedia, there are two schools.

The first school says capture pristine quality and then use your audio software to convert the 44-kHz, 16-bit stereo audio down to 11-kHz, 8-bit mono. The other school, to which I (mostly) adhere, is to capture directly at your target rate. If you want 11/8/mono, capture 11/8/mono.

The first approach assumes that your sound card does the best job at full CD audio quality and that your sound software is adept at converting to lower formats. The second assumes that your sound card is wonderful at capturing at any configuration, why bother with the software?

The problem is, of course, that neither approach is universally true. In developing a screen capture file for VCS 2.0, our target was 22-kHz, 8-bit mono. When we captured at that configuration, however, we consistently heard a slight but annoying background hiss. To avoid this, we ended up capturing at CD audio quality and letting the software subsample down, which eliminated the noise. Other developers have described scenarios in which the reverse was true.

The key lesson is to be aware of both approaches. Whichever you adopt, if you can't create consistently high audio quality using one approach, try the other before trashing your sound card.

Audio Compression   Audio compression has been around for a couple of years now but doesn't seem to have caught on in the publishing community. In part, the realities of the computer audio playback environment contribute to this lack of interest, because 11, 8-bit mono sounds pretty much the same as 44, 16-bit stereo on $15 speakers.

One of our goals for this edition of the book was to focus on audio compression, trying to understand its strong and weak points. But as we started our tests, we noticed that Premiere started doing some pretty funky things during compression, like distorting our talking head files until they resembled scenes from *Poltergeist*. More important, when playing the audio back on our somewhat more expensive sound system, we couldn't tell the difference between the higher quality compressed audio and the low-quality uncompressed audio. So, in the interest of time, space, and a continuing fruitful relationship with our publisher, we (once again) punted on audio compression.

If you decide to experiment, focus on these areas. First, on marginal computers (e.g., Pentium 90s with IVI), does audio compression slow the video display rate and, if so, how much? Second, on a somewhat broader-than-normal test of your target audience, does the audio play well on all sound systems? Finally, what are the implications of distributing compressed videos in the Windows 3.x and Macintosh environments (if you care)? Sorry we couldn't help you answer these questions, but if you do the work, please let us know.

Nonlinear Editing/MPEG-1/Streaming Internet

Once again, audio parameters are a "capture" option for these applications, which means you want to capture at your intended parameters and not mess with them during rendering. In the case of nonlinear editing, you generally capture and render at 16-bit, 44 kHz stereo, or CD-ROM quality audio. Ditto for MPEG-1, since the MPEG-1 specification includes compression for CD-ROM quality audio.

Most streaming video technologies have precise input requirements for audio. Check your documentation to make sure you capture and render according to these requirements. Table 12.12 summarizes the requirements for each application.

Audio Interleave

Finally, a simple category for all applications. You select audio interleave using the control shown in Figure 12.11. Note that this is part of Premiere's Project Output screen rather than a compression option.

Table 12.12   Summary of recommended audio rendering parameters.

Capturing for:	Recommendation
Compression with traditional software codec	Capture at planned publishing parameters, generally not to exceed 22 KB/s, whether 16-bit, 11-kHz mono or 8-bit, 22 kHz mono
Software MPEG-1 compression	16-bit, 44-kHz stereo
Streaming Internet delivery	Check codec's documentation
Nonlinear editing	16-bit, 44-kHz stereo

The audio interleave control dictates how frequently audio chunks are divided for storage within individual video frames. In a video compressed at 15 frames per second, for example, a setting of "1" will interleave 1/15 of a second of audio with every video frame. A setting of "15" will interleave one second of audio with every 15th frame.

A one-to-one interleave promotes a smooth file without data spikes, which is essential to smooth CD-ROM playback. You can use larger settings for files destined for other storage media as long as the interval isn't the same as the key frame setting. On the other hand, I've never heard any reason to use any value other than one, so we use one all the time.

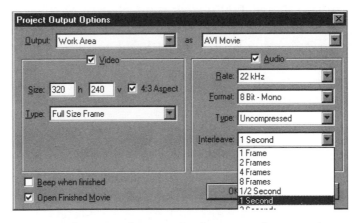

Figure 12.11   Finally, a simple control. Always interleave audio into each frame, using an audio interleave interval of one, or 1 frame.

KEY FRAME SETTING

Nonlinear Editing/MPEG-1/Streaming Internet

Simple answer for all three applications: use a key frame interval of "1" that makes every frame a key frame.

Software Codecs

Quick Answer　Key frame settings are one of those subjects that you could spend just shy of forever experimenting with and writing about but still end up in roughly the same place. Some of you may be in a hurry, so we provided the quick answers in Table 12.13. For those interested in the gory details, read on.

Key Frame Description　The key frame interval, selectable in Figure 12.1, controls the interval between key frames. An interval of 15 means that every 15th frame is a key frame.

For discussion purposes, a *low* key frame interval, say of 7, means *more frequent* key frames. A *high* key frame interval of 60 means *less frequent* key frames and fewer key frames in the video as a whole. This can get confusing, so I'll try to be clear throughout.

As you may recall from our compression primer, a key frame is a frame compressed solely with reference to itself using only *inter*frame compression. Delta frames are compressed using *inter*frame compression that defines some portion of the video frame with reference to another frame or frames.

Key frames are generally larger than delta frames, both naturally and by design. They're naturally larger because intraframe compression is gener-

Table 12.13　Recommended key frame setting by content.

	Low Motion	High Motion	Animation	Screen Shots
Minimum	30	15	One per	One per
Maximum	60	30	scene change	scene change

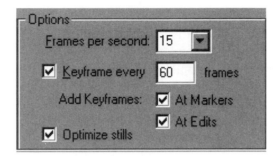

Figure 12.12   Premiere's key frame control, showing some of Premiere's innovative options, including the ability to place a key frame at a marker or edit point.

ally less efficient than interframe compression, requiring a larger frame for quality equivalent to that of a delta frame. They're also larger by design, since a high-quality key frame improves the quality of all delta frames that refer back to it, making key frames especially useful at the start of a scene change. Preserving quality is the first function of the key frame.

The second function is as a point of access into the video. Since delta frames have to borrow information from another frame to display, you can't directly seek to a delta frame. Instead, you have to seek to a key frame and then decompress forward to the desired delta frame. Having frequent key frames speeds random access to specific frames within a video file.

Some sources, most notably Intel, also claim that key frames limit dropped frames. Specifically, in *Compression Techniques for Great-Looking Indeo ® Video*, Intel states:

> In addition to affecting video quality, data rate control and user access, the key frame also affects playback performance. When a video is being played on a system with a slow CPU or CD-ROM drive, video decode and display can lag behind audio playback. When this occurs, Video for Windows tries to speed up the video by either decoding some video frames but not displaying them, or by not decoding them at all. If a frame is neither decoded nor displayed, it is *dropped*.
>
> The effect of dropping a frame depends on:
>
> - the type of frame, and
> - the key frame interval.

If a key frame is dropped, then every subsequent delta frame must be dropped until the next key frame. Files with higher key frame intervals drop more frames.

If a delta frame is dropped, the effect varies. Some delta frames can be dropped without impacting the decode of any subsequent delta frames. However, some delta frames contain information about other delta frames, and if one such delta frame is dropped then the other delta frames must be dropped as well.

Delta Frames   Delta frames, of course, supply the bulk of the actual compression, although in some instances they actually preserve quality compared to a key frame. Thus to select the proper key frame interval you have to consider video content, the degree of required interactivity, and to a lesser extent the target data rate.

A video file composed solely of key frames would look great, drop fewer frames, and be extremely responsive, but it would have a fat data rate. A video file composed of one key frame and the rest deltas would drop frames like mad, suffer on the quality side, but would be extremely skinny. Finding a balance between the two is the essence of the key frame interval.

For our purposes, we strove to understand first the relationship of key frames to quality, then interactivity. Finally, we looked at whether we could confirm Intel's findings that high key frame intervals have a negative effect on dropped frames.

Content

High-Motion Sequences: In high-motion sequences, interframe redundancy *decreases*, which makes interframe compression *less* efficient. For extremely high motion videos, key frames can add quality and let the compressed video stream "catch up" with the analog video. This is illustrated in Figure 12.13, showing a delta frame and the next frame in the sequence, a key frame, which is significantly more clear.

Of course, the additional quality comes at a price, since the delta frame weighs in at 8.15 KB, and the key frame at 14.2 KB. Although not every key frame will look this much better than the surrounding delta frames, in general, in high-motion sequences, key frames add quality. Thus, for high-motion videos, more frequent key frames are better.

Low-Motion Sequences: In low-motion sequences, the situation tends to reverse, and frequent key frames tend to detract from video quality. In

Figure 12.13   Although key frames aren't always this effective, they generally add quality to higher motion sequences. See Fig12_13.avi for the Cinepak file from which this was derived.

low-motion videos, delta frames are extremely efficient because interframe changes are small. In contrast, key frames can "stress" the video, as shown in Figure 12.14, derived from a 100 KB/s Video 1 file.

Although the comparative frame sizes were roughly the same, 14.2 for the key frame and 8.15 for the delta, here the key frame detracts from quality. This is because the interframe changes are so small that they're simpler to compress than the entire frame. Note that once a key frame goes bad, the checkerboard effect is carried over to the next four or five subsequent frames before going away.

Figure 12.14   Note the checkerboard effect on the key frame, while the delta frame looks great. Check out fig12_14.avi to experiment further.

For low-motion videos, then, key frames clearly detract from quality, making higher key frame intervals and fewer key frames a better option. All other things being equal, of course.

Scene Changes   Later in the chapter we'll learn how to place key frames with Premiere. Once again, placing a key frame at a scene change concentrates extra bandwidth on this frame, which should produce higher quality than is obtained with a delta frame. To test this theory, we found a short clip with several hard cut scene changes and compressed with and without a key frame placed on the scene change.

As you may be able to see in Figure 12.15, the key frame looks substantially better than the delta frame. For your information, this frame is frame 59 in keyplace.avi and nokyplac.avi, located in the Chapter 12 subdirectory.

Degree of Interactivity   As we discussed, frequent key frames accelerate "seeking" to random spots in the video file. This is because codecs can't seek directly to a delta frame, they have to go to the immediately preceding key frame and decompress forward from there. For example, if a video file had a key frame interval of 60 and the user wanted to seek to frame 118, the decompressor would seek to key frame 60 and then decompress frames 61–117 to build 118. Although this is faster than actually playing the video, because the frames are not displayed, it can create a noticeable delay. For this reason, if users will frequently page through the video file, shorter key frames are recommended.

Figure 12.15   Major scene changes look better from the start when the initial frame is a key frame, just one of several unique compression-oriented features from Premiere.

Table 12.14 The effect of key frames on interactivity, display rate, audio breaks, and data rate.

	Seek Time	*Frame Rate*	*Audio Breaks*	*Data Rate*
Low Motion				
Key frame 60 (iv_tk515.avi)	22 seconds	12	0	159 KB/s
Key frame 300 (iv_tkhky.avi)	59 seconds	12	0	143 KB/s
High Motion				
Key frame 15 (iv_ac515.avi)	12 seconds	11	0	155 KB/s
Key frame 300 (iv_achky.avi)	62 seconds	10	1	153 KB/s

How much difference does this make? Using Indeo video interactive, we compressed files to a number of key frame intervals, all compressed to the same target data rate. Then, using VCS, we timed how long it took to page through from start to finish and then back to the start in 10% increments on a Pentium 60. The results are presented in Table 12.14 in the column labeled "Seek Time."

As you can see, files with a key frame interval of 300 were substantially less responsive than files with lower key frame intervals. If random access to your video file is important, lower key frame intervals can make a difference.

Of course, as we'll see in a moment, if you don't need *random* access but rather need fast access to a number of specific frames, you can use Premiere to place key frames on those frames and maintain a high key frame interval elsewhere in the file. Assuming, of course, that high key frame intervals don't create additional problems like those raised in Intel's compression white paper. Let's see what else our little experiment showed in this regard.

Although our tests weren't exhaustive, they didn't produce the wholesale frame drop scenario discussed by Intel. In fact, display rate was relatively the same between the files irrespective of key frame interval.

We did, however, experience consistent audio breaks with the higher motion file at the higher key frame interval, although the talking head played fine. For this reason, we wouldn't recommend going beyond a key frame interval of 60 for any video.

Also, Intel's warning in perspective reflects the company's decision to reverse its previous stance of making the maximum key frame interval 15; that is, with Indeo 3.2 and before, the codec inserted a key frame every 15 frames, even if you selected 16 or higher. IVI provides complete flexibility, like all other codecs. The default key frame interval of 4 used by Indeo 3.2 also jumped to a default of 15 in IVI.

All that said, Intel makes no recommendation regarding key frame interval beyond:

> The default key frame interval usually provides a good balance between video quality, data rate control and CD-ROM playback performance. Because different types of video material present special challenges and work well at different key frame intervals, experiment with other settings to maximize video quality and playback performance for your video clip.

Special Situations

Animations: As we've discussed, many producers convert animated sequences to AVI files to synchronize audio with the animation. We'll look at this process later in the chapter.

Most animations bound for conversion are or should be relatively low motion, and key frames can significantly degrade compressed quality. For this reason, I tend to use one key frame for the entire animation unless there is a scene change that requires a key frame. More on this later.

Screen Captures: One of Video for Windows key tools was Microsoft's ScreenCap application, which enables the capture of both still and moving screen images. For Windows 95, Microsoft licensed the technology to a couple of companies, including Blue Sky Software, the Robohelp folks.

We used Blue Sky's version to make all the screen captures scattered throughout the book. Their version, called the Software Video Camera, uses RLE to capture the screen shot. I've had bad luck with RLE and typically convert to Video 1 for final publishing. Either way, the best key frame interval is also one per video, unless you have a major transition, in which case you should place a key frame at that interval.

PAD FOR CD-ROM PLAYBACK

Quick Answer

You select CD-ROM padding in Premiere via the checkbox captured in Figure 12.9. All other editors have a similar function.

Most major CD-ROM publishers, including Microsoft, pad video files destined for playback on CD-ROM. All of the video editors advise you to pad. On the other hand, Intel advises very strongly *not* to pad with Indeo video interactive.

So. Pad with all codecs except for IVI.

Discussion

CD-ROMs are divided into 2-kilobyte sectors. When CD-ROM drives read data, they must start at the beginning of a sector. This is called a "seek." Each seek can take from 100–500 milliseconds (as compared to 10–15 ms for fast hard drives). While seeking, the video flow to the computer stops, which endangers smooth video playback.

CD-ROM padding theory states that to allow the drive to "stream" and avoid seeking, all frames must begin and end on consecutive sector boundaries. If a new frame started in the middle of the sector, the drive would have to stop, seek to the beginning of the sector, and start reading again.

When you enable padding, the compressor hands the compressed frame back to your editor, which "pads" the frame with garbage bits to bring the frame to a multiple of 2 KB. In theory, this should allow the video to flow more smoothly.

Arguing against CD-ROM padding is the fact that it takes up anywhere from 1 to 5% of the entire video bandwidth, depending on codec and video content. In the context of a lossy compression algorithm, this drops quality by 5–10%. Fortunately, this is down from the 5–15% characteristic of older versions of codecs before they started optimizing for CD-ROM padding and reducing the waste.

In addition, all CD-ROMs provide some onboard buffering, and MSCDEX, Microsoft's CD-ROM driver, also buffers. This buffering should smooth out the interruptions caused by multiple seeks. Moreover, in-house testing failed to prove that CD-ROM padding helped performance or that failing to pad hurt performance. Admittedly, however, our sample was very small.

Nonetheless, if you scan the documentation for DVP, Premiere, and MediaStudio, you'll see that they all advise you to pad. Given the relatively modest cost these days, who are we to buck the trend? Just make sure you don't pad Indeo video interactive.

QUALITY SETTING

Software Codecs

Quick Answer   Once you check the data rate box and input a desired data rate, the quality setting is ignored by every codec except Video 1. Note that Power!Video Pro grays out the data rate setting and compresses exclusively on the basis of quality settings, all defined in the following.

Discussion   Table 12.10 describes how each codec handles the quality versus file size trade-off. In general, Power!Video Pro is the only codec that compresses to a fixed quality without the option to achieve a target data rate, a disadvantage for CD-ROM publishing. Indeo video interactive adopts a similar approach, but only when the data rate box is unchecked or set to zero, at which time the encoder compresses according to the quality settings. Intel's documentation expressly states, however, that this approach optimizes neither quality nor data rate and recommends against it.

Through some unexplained mechanism, Video 1 also uses the quality slider to improve video quality, though taking much longer to compress at high quality settings. This time differential, even on very fast Pentiums, is often significant enough to convince you to give back some quality to get the project compressed. We'll cover this in a case study later in the chapter.

Nonlinear Editing/MPEG-1/Internet Streaming

Most, if not all, Motion JPEG codecs are data rate driven, not quality driven. If rendering in Motion JPEG format for any of these applications, worry about the data rate, not the quality setting.

Raw formats have no concept of data rate or quality. For this reason, expect the quality setting to be grayed out whenever you render to a raw format.

CASE STUDIES: PUTTING IT ALL TOGETHER

Now that the basics are behind us, let's pull it altogether and actually compress some files. We'll look at several scenarios, starting with a low-motion sequence to be compressed with Indeo video interactive, just to get the flow of pushing all the right buttons to create a perfectly compressed file. We'll use Premiere as our pro forma, then discuss the highlights of MediaStudio, DVP, and VidEdit along with some screen cams to tie it all together.

Low Motion: Indeo video interactive

Encoding Options When compressing video, you need to get into a rhythm with your encoding software, working through the various screens to make sure that all the output and compression options are in the required setting. Compression is often very slow, so if you err, you won't find out about it for a while, and usually there's no quick fix—you have to perform the entire compression again. As we go through Premiere's compression and output settings, we'll identify all the items you need to consider before starting your compression.

You access Premiere's Make Movie screen (Figure 12.16) from the Make menu option. After naming the file, you progress through the Output Options and Compression screens to access all the controls discussed above. After completing all options and happily compressing our file, we'll learn how to create Premiere Preset so you don't have to worry about setting most of the options ever again. Not much going on here, so let's move to the Output Options screen (Figure 12.17).

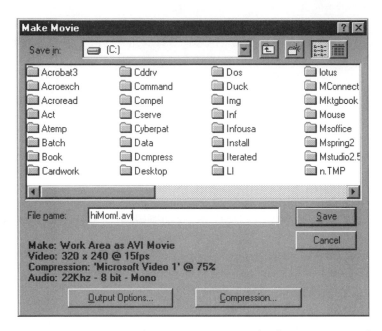

Figure 12.16 Premiere's Make Movie screen is the first stop toward compressing your edited video.

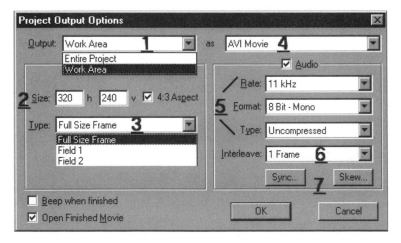

Figure 12.17 Premiere's Output Options screen, the first stop in our compression by numbers tour. It's as easy as 1, 2, 3!

Here are the various stops you need to make in the Output Options screen:

1. *Output Work Area versus Entire Project.* This is the single largest reason to make a preset, since you'll get burned here more than any other place. If you choose to output your work area, which is the *default* setting, you'll output the work area defined by the yellow bar that sits above the Premiere time line, defaulting to two seconds when you create a new project. If you select Entire Project, of course, you'll output the entire project.

   Note, however, once again, that the *default* is output work area, which is probably appropriate for nonlinear editing but not for capture for compression. If you want to compress the *entire file*, you'll need to change this to Entire Project.

2. *Size.* We consider size a "capture" option, so in most instances all you want to do here is make sure the capture resolution is correctly input into the dialog box. You must change the resolution in two instances. First, if your capture card doesn't support your ultimate target resolution, which occurs frequently with streaming Internet video files, adjust resolution to your target here. For example, if you captured at 320×240 but really wanted 176×144, change the 320×240 to 176×144 here. You also need to adjust the resolution if you selected a preset with an output size different from your target.

   The 4:3 aspect ratio preserves the ratio of four horizontal pixels to three vertical pixels. To input a nonconformist resolution like 176×144, you'll need to deselect this box before entering any numbers; otherwise Premiere will modify the input values in real time to preserve the 4:3 ratio.

3. *Fields versus Frames.* When compressing for CD-ROM or hard drive playback, always select frames, which combines the two fields captured by some capture cards into one frame. We're outputting a compressed AVI file that is frame based, so we select frames here.

4. *Output As.* If you're creating a file for playback on the Windows platform, you want this set to AVI Movie, as we do. This setting also allows you to output the video as an Apple MOV or FLM (filmstrip) file, an animated FLC file, or a sequence of bitmapped, Targa, or TIFF files.

5. *Audio Options.* This is where you select your audio options. This is also a capture decision, unless you opt to compress the audio,

which you would do here. Note the Audio checkbox above the Rate option, deselect this and you'll create a silent movie. We select 11 kHz, 8-bit mono.

6. *Interleave.* Audio interleave is so critical we thought we would address it separately. Whenever compressing for CD-ROM publishing, this must be set to 1, as shown in Figure 12.17. Note that several Premiere presets set this interval to one second, but none oriented toward CD-ROM publishing. This would be important if you captured for nonlinear editing and then wanted to compress a section to play from disk.

7. *Sync and Skew.* These are two controls unique to Premiere that I'll bet the Premiere designers wish you would never touch.

   Audio sync relates to the amount of audio packed with video in the video file, enabling developers to configure Premiere precisely for their system. Adobe finishes their description with this warning: "WARNING: change this setting at your own risk. Using this setting incorrectly will produce badly synched movies."

   Ouch! Sounds like a bad risk. Let's look at skew.

   Skew relates to the amount of audio placed in the front of the video file for AVI playback purposes. Premiere finishes their description with this warning: "Setting this value to a non-default value could result in movies that will play back badly or not at all on some systems."

   Same deal. I don't mess with either of these values, and you probably shouldn't either.

   That's it on the Output Options screen; now it's time to head back to the Compression Settings screen, where we continue our session of compression by numbers. Check out Figure 12.18.

8. *Settings.* This reflects the output decision made in step 4. Check to make sure this says AVI if you want AVI.

9. *Codec.* This is where you select your codec. It's a drop-down box triggered by the downward arrow on the right, bringing up the additional information shown in Figure 12.2. We're going IVI for this compression.

10. *Codec Configuration.* Depending on the codec you chose, the configure button will either stay grayed out or become active. Press the Configure button with IVI loaded and you bring up the screen shown in Figure 12.19. Note that this screen is specific to IVI, not to Premiere. All programs that enable compression, including

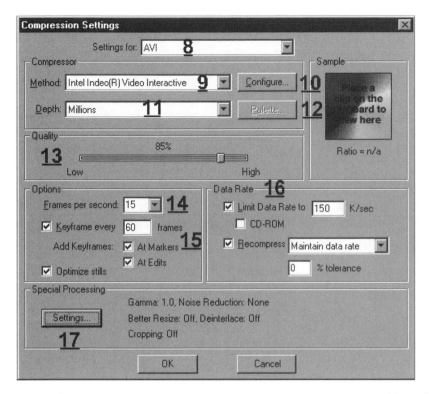

Figure 12.18   Premiere's Compression Settings screen. Sure seems like a lot more steps. Thank goodness that Premiere's presets make most of them unnecessary—once you build a custom preset, of course. That's our next stop. But first, compression by numbers screen two.

VidEdit, will provide you access to this specific screen from somewhere in their interface.

Let's assume our target computer is Pentium 200, so we blow out the stops on IVI's compression options, including scalability, bidirectional prediction, and the absolute best quality. Press OK and we're back at Figure 12.18.

11. *Depth.* Generally, you have to worry about this screen only when compressing with an 8-bit codec like Video 1 or RLE. The 24-bit codecs like Indeo and Cinepak let you select only millions in this category.

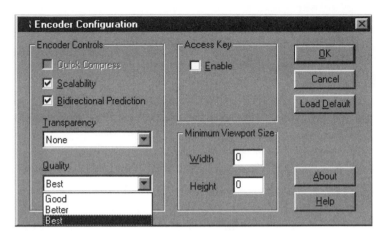

Figure 12.19 Indeo video interactive's encoder configuration screen.

12. *Palette.* When using an 8-bit codec, you have certain palette options that must be exercised. We'll cover these in the Video 1 case study later.

13. *Quality.* This is where you input a quality value, important primarily for the Video 1 codec. As we described earlier, most other codecs ignore this setting after you select a data rate. We leave it at IVI's default setting of 85.

14. *Frames per Second.* Once again, this is a capture option, not a compression option, which means that you shouldn't have to change frame rate come compression time. Nonetheless, if you need to change the frame rate, here's where you do it. We're encoding at 15 fps, so we make no changes here.

15. *Key Frame Setting.* All encoders let you select the key frame interval, or the number of frames between key frames. If you enter a number and don't check the box, you'll probably end up with every frame being a key frame, which makes no sense but there it is. Always make sure the box is checked. Premiere also gives you the option to place key frames at markers and/or edit points. We'll review how to do this in a few moments.

The Optimize stills option helps preserve the compressed quality of still images that are stretched over more than one frame but has no effect when compressing real-world videos. The default option is to check it, and I leave it checked irrespective of video content.

We have a low-motion video, and we're going with a key frame every 60 frames. Since we have some edit points with scene changes, we're telling Premiere to place key frames there. Note that Premiere will then restart the 60-frame interval.

16. *Data Rate.* Here's where you select data rate, enable or disable CD-ROM padding, and choose whether to maintain the data rate or recompress the entire video.

   We're going for a data rate of 150 KB/s because it's Indeo video interactive and we want to limit start-up jitters. We didn't select CD-ROM padding because Intel recommends against it. Finally, we told the encoder to maintain the data rate at 0% tolerance.

17. *Special Processing.* These are Premiere's compression time Special Processing options, shown in Figure 12.20. For completeness, a brief summary of their functions follows.

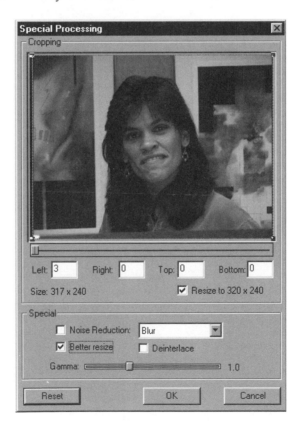

Figure 12.20   Premiere's compression time Special Processing options.

18. *Scaling/Resizing.* As you may notice, there's a small row of black pixels on the left-hand border of the video caused by our inability to equalize the incoming video during capture. To "crop" these pixels out and then "resize" the video to 320×240 for compression, we either enter the number 3 into the left box, representing the three rows of black pixels, or grab the little holders on the inside of the video window and drag them to the proper location.

Then we select resize to 320×240 to scale the video back to full quarter screen, making sure to select the "better resize" option below. This tells Premiere to use special algorithms from Adobe After Effects to scale the video, rather than letting the codec do the work. We found this option beneficial whenever scaling video.

19. *Noise Reduction Filtering.* Video noise degrades quality, because the encoder, not being able to distinguish between noise and real motion, has to allocate bandwidth to both rather than focus solely on real motion. Premiere enables three compression time filters, median, Gaussian, and blur filters, that can reduce noise and improve video quality, depending on the content of the source video.

At a high level, all filters work by averaging values of adjacent pixels, which can cause blurriness, especially in talking heads. Filtering is generally desirable when the incident blurriness is less distracting than the quality degradation caused by noise. In Chapter 11 we focused on several types of video, and Table 12.15 summarizes our findings.

When working within Premiere, remember that if your content varies among several categories, you can apply the recommended filter on the time line rather than at compression time. In addition, note that you can access most of these filters in MediaStudio and DVP, you just can't access them at compression time.

Since our video is extremely clean, we don't filter.

20. *Deinterlacing.* When you capture video at 60 fields per second, your video is stored in interlaced mode. This is fine when writing the video back out to tape, but it can cause artifacts when compressing smaller resolution video footage. The deinterlacing option helps minimize these artifacts.

We captured our video at 15 frames per second, so deinterlacing isn't required.

21. *Gamma Correction.* Last chance to brighten or darken your video footage. Note that all editors, including DVP and MediaStudio, let you adjust brightness on the time line. We like our color the way it is, so will keep the gamma at 1.0.

Press OK to get back to Figure 12.18, then OK again for Figure 12.21. Note the text underneath the file name. This is my final opportunity to check for configuration errors, like selecting only the work area rather than the entire movie. Although the information is admittedly incomplete, it's useful to review this screen for errors. Press Save and compression begins.

Building a Compression Preset   Whew! I'm beat. Let's build a compression preset so that we never have to go through that lengthy process again. Wait for the file to finish compressing, of course.

Once it's done, go to Make/Presets in Premiere's main menu, which brings up the Presets screen shown in Figure 12.22. Note that our current configuration shows up on the left-hand side in the Current Settings screen, while the right-hand side lists the Available Presets.

Press Save to generate the screen shown in Figure 12.23. Press OK and the preset magically appears on the right-hand side. Next time you start a

Table 12.15 Recommended filter settings by video type.

Content	Recommended Filter	Rationale
Talking head, high quality	None	When noise is limited, blurriness is more apparent than noise artifacts.
Talking head, general noise	Blur	Blur filter smoothes general noise and creates a uniform look without obscuring any details.
Talking head, analog dropout and other spikes	Median	The median filter removes small data spikes with minimal blurriness.
Action footage	Gaussian	The Gaussian filter reduced noise artifacts without obscuring detail or creating any other artifacts.

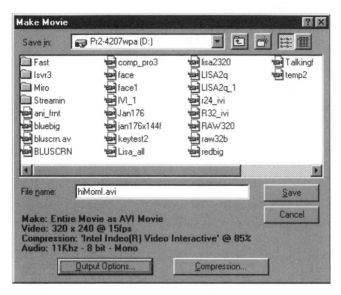

Figure 12.21   Back to the Make Movie screen. Note the brief description of the output options below the file name, your last chance to see if you're compressing the entire movie or just the work are. Gosh I wish Adobe would change this preset!

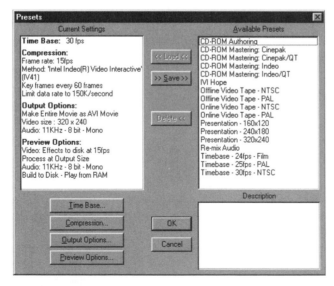

Figure 12.22   Premiere's Presets screen, where you can save your custom output parameters once and never have to mess with them again.

Figure 12.23   Saving the Preset Name for posterity.

project, select that preset, and all the options shown in Figure 12.22 will be restored. Although it's still a good idea to run through options 1–21 shown earlier, you probably won't have to make any changes.

Just for the record, we've had problems creating and reusing Indeo video interactive presets, for some reason unknown to Intel. Specifically, when we've created an IVI preset and then selected that preset when starting a new project, Premiere consistently crashed. We've never had this problem with any other codec, so if you're using IVI and create a preset, don't be surprised if you run into this problem, which unfortunately at this time has no resolution.

Other Encoders   We promised to run through the same options with the other encoders, not in text, but in moving pictures. Run ms_com.avi to see MediaStudio's screens, dvp_com.avi to see DVP's, and VidE_com.avi to see VidEdit.

Low-Motion: 8-Bit Environment, Video 1

Suppose this video was destined for an 8-bit display and after reading the Tour de Codec you decide to use Video 1 because it can hold a palette. Outstanding choice! Let's walk through the steps necessary to make this happen, first in VidEdit to get the theory down and then in MediaStudio.

Converting to 8-Bit Format   Video 1 can compress in 8- and 16-bit modes, but you have to compress in 8-bit mode to achieve the benefits that we're seeking. The first step is converting the source video to 8-bit mode.

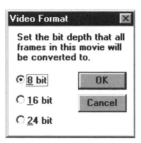

Figure 12.24   The wrong control for converting your videos from 24-bit to 8-bit unless you're trying to create a gray-scale video.

There's two ways to do this, the wrong way, which pretty much everybody tries six or seven times until they read the manual, and the right way. The wrong way is to use the Video Format control accessed from VidEdit's Video menu. This control is shown in Figure 12.24. It's a pretty natural mistake, given the subheading, but all you'll accomplish with this control is to convert your video to gray scale—a success of a sorts, since it is 8-bit gray scale, but a step backward nonetheless.

After staring at a gray-scale video seven or eight times, you'd start to feel like there's something you don't know, so you might check VidEdit's context-sensitive Help file from the Video Format dialog box. This is what you'd see.

When converting a 16- or 24-bit sequence to 8-bit format, VidEdit remaps all colors to a gray-scale palette. To retain accurate colors, you should not use the Video Format dialog box to perform the conversion. Instead, build an 8-bit palette (for more information, see Creating a Palette), then apply the palette to the entire sequence (for more information, see Pasting a Palette).

This makes sense, because the whole purpose of the exercise is to compress to a standard palette, and we haven't told VidEdit which palette to use. In essence, the way Video for Windows converts from 24-bit to 8-bit video is to create an 8-bit palette and then paste the palette to the video.

Creating a Palette: Video   Creating a palette from the video itself is fairly simple. Use the Create Palette control shown in Figure 12.25 to create a palette for the individual frame, the entire video, or any number of contiguous frames. The maximum number of colors that a palette can contain is 256, which includes 20 colors reserved by Windows. When you select 256

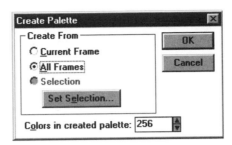

Figure 12.25   Control for creating a palette used to convert 16- and 24-bit videos to 8-bit video.

colors in your palette, you really get only 236, plus the 20 colors reserved by Windows. When you select a number below 256, VidEdit creates a palette containing the 20 Windows colors and the number you selected, up to a total of 256.

If the video is essentially one sequence without significant scene changes, it's fastest just to compute the palette from the Current Frame. It there are many different scenes, you should compute the palette from All Frames. This can take a few moments when your video is on a hard drive and seemingly hours when the video is on a CD-ROM. Once the process starts, there's no stopping it except by shutting your computer off or giving the three-finger salute.

You can create an unlimited number of palettes for any video sequence, but during compression VidEdit will limit the total number of colors to 256. In operation, it's usually easiest to let VidEdit select the optimum palette for the entire video, then paste the palette to the entire video.

Your alternative is to separate the various sequences that require different palettes and ask VidEdit to compute a custom palette for that sequence. Overall, however, the total number of colors must be less than 256. For example, if your target video has three completely different color sequences, you would have to compute a palette composed of about 78 colors per sequence, so that the three custom palettes, plus Window's 20 colors, don't exceed 256 colors.

Author's Note   VidEdit's create palette function may not work under Windows 95, in which case you may still want to use VidEdit to compress since it still does a better job with Video 1 files than MediaStudio or DVP. You would need another tool like Photoshop to create the palette and load it

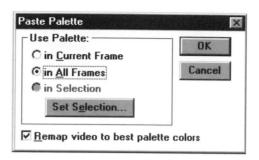

Figure 12.26   Pasting a palette into a video file.

into memory, however, or perhaps use MediaStudio to create a palletized 8-bit file to load into VidEdit.

Pasting a Palette   The Paste Palette control shown in Figure 12.26 lets you paste the palette into one frame, all frames, or a selected number of continuous frames. Frames that the palette isn't pasted into will become gray-scale frames, although the color information can be regained by computing a palette as shown above.

Always "Remap video to best palette colors," which arranges the new palette to match the colors in the old palette as closely as possible. Otherwise, the new palette is blindly mapped over the old palette, which typically causes apparent color distortion.

Once you've pasted the palette, the video is in 8-bit mode. When you compress this 8-bit file with Video 1, the final video will always decompress back into the palette used to create it.

Since you'll probably use Video 1 only for low-motion sequences, use a fairly high key frame setting unless the video will be used interactively. This will optimize quality over the length of the video and eliminate background "pulsing" often caused by key frames. Start with one key frame for the entire video. If you notice blurriness in the motion segments, drop the interval to around 60 and try again. The default key frame interval of 15 should be used only as a last resort.

The best data rate/quality strategy for Video 1 is to select about 5 KB/s below the actual desired data rate and use a quality setting of 100. This will lengthen your compression time but provide the highest possible quality video for the selected bandwidth. Using the default setting of 75 will definitely lower the data rate and detract from overall quality.

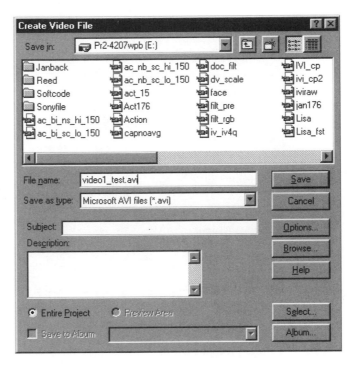

Figure 12.27   MediaStudio's Create Video File screen, step one of their
compression by numbers.

MediaStudio: Streamlined Approach   With MediaStudio the approach is much
more streamlined: you simply load the file into the program, select Video 1
as your codec, and then choose a palette option. Then you're on your way.

Select File/Create/Video file to open the screen shown in Figure 12.27.
Pressing Options brings up the four-tabbed screen shown in Figure 12.28,
which is MediaStudio's main compression interface.

Here we note that both audio and video are to be comprehended in the
file, which will have a frame rate of 15 fps and a resolution of 320×240. So
far, so good.

Press the Compression tab to access the compression options screen,
shown in Figure 12.29. Once you select Video 1, the data type options enable
both 8-bit and 16-bit, and we choose the former for this compression. Video
1 is really the only codec that delivers better quality at higher compression
settings, so we choose 100. Since this is a low-motion video, we choose a
key frame setting of 60.

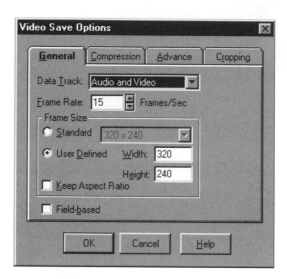

Figure 12.28   This four-tabbed panel contains all MediaStudio compression options. Note the options on the front screen.

Figure 12.29   This is the compression screen, where we select codec and relevant options.

Figure 12.30   The Advance tab contains a number of fairly prosaic
parameters, but also palette handling for 8-bit files.

Note that you can access audio options from this screen as well, and we
select the familiar 11, 8-bit mono. Now we're off to find the palette handling
options, available via the next screen (Figure 12.30).

The Advance screen would clearly be mislabeled if not for the palette
handling capabilities. After all, data rate, audio interleave, and CD-ROM
padding options are far from advanced.

On the palette handling side, if you care about this issue, you probably
have an image editor with palette capabilities, and you've probably already
created a common palette for all your assets. If so, now would be a good
time to load that palette. If not, you've got to choose how to compute your
palette.

MediaStudio enables four different options, with the following advice
found in their help files:

> **Use Common Palette** specifies the palette to create, (only if an 8-bit
> data type is selected). For some video sequences 6-6-6 levels or 6-7-6
> levels are good enough and the saving process is much faster.

Hhhmmm. I'm confused, too. What about optimum and 3-3-2? Our
experiments produced best results with the optimum setting, but that's just
a starting point. If that doesn't work for you, try the other options.

Figure 12.31   MediaStudio's compression time cropping can't scale you back to full resolution, a significant disadvantage compared with Premiere.

One more MediaStudio screen before we go away. Press the Cropping tab and Figure 12.31 shows up. Note that MediaStudio crops but doesn't scale back to 320×240, a serious disadvantage compared to Premiere.

Press OK and the compression starts.

Note that if you were using MediaStudio or Premiere to convert animations to Video 1 format, rather than a talking head, the procedure would be exactly the same.

CODEC-SPECIFIC INSTRUCTIONS

Working with the various codecs is a challenge, without question. Here are our views on how best to work with the various technologies.

IVI reference chart.

At a Glance: Indeo video interactive	
In a nutshell	Intel zigged when everyone else zagged, creating a new codec paradigm by combining absolute top quality with innovative game-oriented features. Horsepower requirements and compression time are the only real limitations.
	IVI's quick compression mode delivers high-quality compression in almost real time, making it a godsend for prototyping and other fast turn encoding.
Peculiarities	Intel says don't enable CD-ROM padding when compressing with IVI.
Compression paradigm	Data rate when data rate checked; otherwise control
Target platform range	Pentium 90 and above
Bandwidth sweet spot	150 KB/s (for CD-ROM based display rate, not quality)
Appropriate content	All real-world videos
Inappropriate content	Animations
When to use	Limited only by target platform
When to avoid	Pentium 60 and below
Key strengths	Video quality, interactive features
Key weaknesses	Compression time, decompression horsepower
User guidelines	1. *Filming*: IVI can suffer some start-up latency on low-power machines, manifested by up to two seconds of jumpy video. Minimize this effect whenever possible with 1 or 2 seconds of little or no movement before the shot actually starts.
	2. *Capture*:
	a. IVI may accentuate blues and reds during compression, so capture accordingly.
	b. With low-motion video footage, IVI can mangle the first few frames. Capture one key frame interval in front of your actual video file (e.g., if your key frame interval is 30, capture 30 extra frames) so you can clip any mangled frames from the start of the video.

(continued)

IVI reference chart. *(continued)*

3. *Encoding:*

    a. The quality produced by IVI's higher end features, bidirectional prediction and compressing for the "best" platform, was substantial for some videos and the display rate penalty minimal or nonexistent. So, compress with bidirectional prediction enabled and select the best compression option.

    b. Scalability is supposed to enhance playback rate at a minor quality cost. We saw no quality cost and minimal improvement in display rate. Still, we'll go with Intel and recommend scalability.

    c. Compress to no higher than single-spin rates to minimize start-up latency.

    d. IVI's quick compressor does an outstanding job with low-motion videos but falters somewhat with action clips. It is wonderful as a prototype codec, but you should plan on using the higher level features for your final clips.

Indeo video interactive

Introduction   Before Indeo video interactive, lossy compression theory was simple. The more you compressed, the worse the video looked. The fundamental compression trade-off has always been quality for file size. With IVI, Intel added three new compression parameters, bidirectional prediction, scalability, and target platform settings, which, in theory, let developers trade video quality for display rate, *at the same data rate* (Figure 12.19). Their latest release also added a quick compressor that delivers very high quality in a fraction of the normal compression time.

Compression Controls   Our quality tests found significant differences between files produced by the various settings, particularly with high-motion footage. In these videos, files compressed with bidirectional prediction and scalability enabled at the best quality setting looked noticeably better. The only question was, how much slower did they play back on low-power computers?

As shown in Table 12.1, the differences on the playback side were nominal. So what's our advice on IVI? Well, all in all, the options designed to increase the display rate on low-power machines had only a marginal effect. At the same time, the quality-related options had a significant effect on video quality, albeit only for higher motion videos.

You're probably best advised to stay away from IVI altogether if a significant portion of your target market falls under the Pentium 60 range. If you choose IVI, however, go full bore, and compress using bidirectional interpolation, scalability, and the best quality setting. Dropping to lower power parameters will make your video look noticeably worse and probably won't make it play significantly faster.

Considerations   Like most advanced technologies, IVI has a couple of "gotchas" that can bite you in the rear if you don't look out for them.

Start-Up Latency: The first IVI video that plays on the computer may have a tendency to play irregularly for a few seconds before playing smoothly. You can minimize the effect by:

- Playing a short IVI clip while loading the program
- Planning your shots to minimize motion during the first one or two seconds
- Compressing to single-spin rates

Figure 12.32   IVI sometimes mangles the first frame of low-motion videos. You can crop these frames, but you have to make sure you don't recompress the entire file or you defeat the purpose.

- Remembering not to enable CD-ROM padding, even if shipping on a CD-ROM

Mangled First Frames: In some instances, IVI mangles the first few frames of low-motion videos, creating artifacts and other anomalies and generally not looking its best. The encoder generally settles down after a few frames, almost always after one key frame interval.

For example, Figure 12.32 shows the first and eleventh frames of an IVI video. The first frame, on the left, shows mosquito artifacts around the face and collar, and what looks like Gibbs effect around the frame numbers. Frame 11 is clear, the IVI that we know and love.

Video for Windows lets you delete file segments at the start of a clip without recompressing if the first frame left in the video is a key frame. Accordingly, if you used a key frame interval of 30, you can delete frames 1–29 and then save the file without recompressing, since frame 30 will be a key frame.

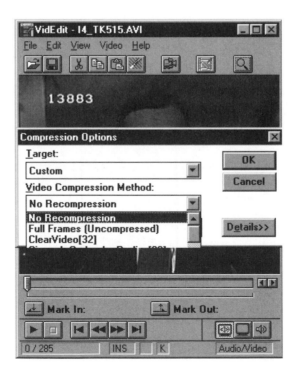

Figure 12.33　Yet another task best accomplished in VidEdit: clipping unwanted frames and avoiding recompression.

If your IVI videos suffer from this initial image degradation, capture one key frame interval in front of the video, compress normally, and then clip the first frames up to the second key frame. You should be able to save the file without recompression.

This is yet another task most easily accomplished in VidEdit, not only because it tells you which frames are key frames (note the small K in the bottom status line of Figure 12.33) but also because it uses that lovely No Recompression option to let you know you can save without recompressing.

With Premiere, MediaStudio, and DVP there's a bit more guesswork involved. Essentially, you have to count the number of frames to the second key frame and use the editing program's respective clipping windows to cut out the first key frame interval. It's probably easiest to rely on counting frames as opposed to the frame number nomenclature used by the editors, since some consider the first frame frame 0 (zero) and some consider it frame 1.

Simply use VCS to step through the file counting the number of frames until the first key frame, then do the same thing in the editor's clip window (Figure 12.34). One critical issue is whether the editor includes the frame in the window when you press out. I ran some quick tests, and it appears

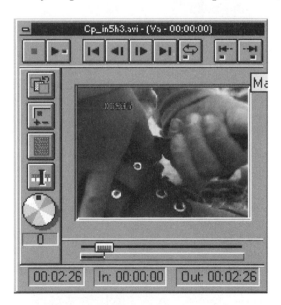

Figure 12.34   MediaStudio's clip window doesn't place the mark out frame on the time line, but Premiere's does. Important data to know when you have to be exact.

that MediaStudio does not include the clip on the time line, whereas Premiere does. This means that in Premiere you would step over to the frame immediately *before* the key frame and then press mark out, and with MediaStudio you would mark out with the key frame in the window. Then you build, save, or make the file, depending on the editor's operating scheme.

If the encoder quickly saves the file, you know you've hit your mark. On the other hand, if it starts to chug along and look like it's compressing the video, rather than just saving it, you've missed your mark and need to try another frame. Either way, step through the first couple of frames—if you have the same problem you miscounted and should try again.

All this sounds incredibly anal as I write, but it can make the difference between a great looking first frame and a mangled one. Since the first frame is the one that usually stays on screen the longest, well, you know how it goes with first impressions. Best advice? Do it with VidEdit.

Bidirectional Prediction   You can also run into problems compressing with bidirectional prediction enabled in an editor that isn't IVI aware. Here's Intel on the subject, from their Web site (http://www.intel.com/pc-supp/multimed/indeo/compress.htm), with figure references added by the author:

> During the encoding process, bidirectional prediction requires that the Indeo video interactive codec look three frames ahead as it compresses the file. Therefore, the Video for Windows editing application starts to send source frames to the codec for compression, but the codec doesn't compress a frame until it has retained the three frames required for bidirectional prediction. Once it has the required three-frame lead over Video for Windows, the codec starts compressing frames.
>
> This poses a challenge, however, because (as previously mentioned) Video for Windows requires that each time a source frame is sent to a codec, a compressed frame must immediately be returned. Therefore, for each source frame it receives, the Indeo video interactive codec must return a compressed frame, even when it isn't ready to do so. The Indeo video interactive codec establishes its required three-frame lead at the beginning of each compression session by returning repeated copies of the first frame to Video for Windows. It then remains three frames behind throughout compressing the rest of the file. When the editing application sends the last frame to the codec, the codec returns the fourth-from-the-last frame. The editing

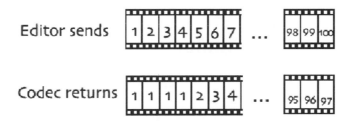

Figure 12.35   Compression with bidirectional prediction.

application, having sent the last frame and received a compressed frame in return, exits without receiving the last three frames.

Assuming a 100-frame example file, the result is as shown in Figure 12.35:

An editing application that doesn't support bidirectional prediction is unable to compensate for this three-frame latency when pairing video frames with audio data. Instead, it simply pairs each video frame returned by the codec with the next available audio chunk, and writes the audio and video data as an .AVI frame. Because the first frame was returned three extra times, however, the audio and video in the resulting .AVI file is out of sync by three frames.

The resulting compressed file displays three unusual characteristics:

- It has three extra video frames at the beginning, duplicates of the first frame, which must be deleted.
- Because of these duplicate frames, the audio and video are out of sync by three frames.
- The file has all hundred frames of audio but only 97 frames of video; the last three frames of video from the source file are missing because the editing application exited after sending the last frame to the codec for compression and receiving a compressed frame in return.

In order to avoid this situation and ensure that the editor receives the last three compressed frames, you must prepare a source file that appends three dummy frames. When the last three dummy frames are sent to the codec, the codec returns the last three frames of compressed video from the source file, and the three dummy frames

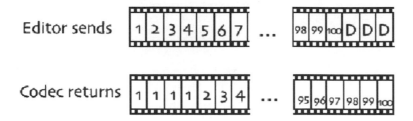

Figure 12.36   Example file with dummy frames after bidirectional compression.

are the ones that the editor inadvertently omits. In this case, the files appear as shown in Figure 12.36, with the dummy frames marked with a D:

The resulting compressed file contains all of its audio and video data. However, extra video data remains in the beginning of the file. Correct this by the same method described in the section entitled "Transparency":

1. After compressing, reopen the file in the editing application.
2. Trim the first three frames of video but not audio.
3. Save the file without recompression.

After deleting the extra frames, the file still starts with a key frame—the true first frame of the video—and can therefore be saved with causing recompression.

Fortunately, Premiere, MediaStudio, and DVP are all bidirectional prediction savvy, so you should have no problem encoding with these products. If you're a VidEdit bigot like I am, you will experience this problem, but since you have VidEdit you can fix it easily.

- To add the frames to the end of the file, go to the last visible frame, select video only from the bottom time line and then Edit/Copy, and paste the frame three times. Compress as normal.
- After compression is completed, select video only and delete the first three frames. Go into video compression options and select No Recompression as your codec, and then save the file. Mission accomplished.

Figure 12.37   Intel's Kplay is the only way to tell which IVI options were used to compress the clip.

Indeo 3.2

Indeo 3.2 reference chart.

At a Glance: Indeo 3.2	
In a nutshell	Not made obsolete by its younger sibling, Indeo 3.2 is still appropriate for a range of applications.
Compression paradigm	Data rate–oriented codec that ignores quality setting. No special configuration options.
Target platform range	486/66 (8-bit) and higher
Bandwidth sweet spot	100 (very low motion) to 250 (high motion)
Appropriate content	Very crisp talking head and other low-motion clips. Adequate on higher motion, but not as fast as Cinepak.
Inappropriate content	Extremely high motion, animations
When to use	Good all around CD-ROM codec, especially for the 8-bit environment
When to avoid	Very high motion
Key strengths	Indeo's characteristic good 8-bit palette handling

(continued)

Indeo 3.2 reference chart. *(continued)*

Key weaknesses	Can distort faces in motion, but individual frames typically look great
User guidelines	1. *Capture:* Some developers say that Indeo boosts color values during compression, which can result in a somewhat garish appearance. This wasn't our experience, but you definitely don't want oversaturated videos during capture.
	2. *Compression:*
	a. Maximum key frame interval is 15, so don't bother to set higher.
	b. For low-motion videos, especially those that are filtered, data rates can go extremely low, like under 100 KB/s for 320×240×15 fps file. Don't bother trying to compress to a higher data rate; once it reaches maximum quality it just won't go any higher.

Cinepak

Cinepak reference chart.

At a Glance: Cinepak	
In a nutshell	"Could have been a contenda" (raspy voice), but why should Supermac, now Radius, invest the dough when Intel is giving Indeo away free? Still very useful, especially on low-power platforms and for high-motion videos.
Compression paradigm	Data rate, baby, all the way. Ignores quality slider once data rate set. No custom compression controls except option to create black-and-white video.
Target platform range	If you're still using it for Windows, Cinepak can play video on it. During testing for the first book, Cinepak actually came close to 15 fps on a 386/33.
Bandwidth sweet spot	Over 200 on talking head clips increases background and foreground noise. Action clips can go as high as 285.
Appropriate content	Better on high-motion sequences

Cinepak reference chart. *(continued)*

Inappropriate content	Tends to muddle up talking heads, in both color and consistency. You don't want to compress your boss with Cinepak.
When to use	Low-power computers, high-motion videos
When to avoid	Talking head, whenever you can use IVI, 8-bit environment
Key strengths	Display rate on low-power computers
Key weaknesses	Muddles up the face, looks bad in 8-bit mode

User guidelines	1. *Capture:* low-motion color fidelity was quite good. In high-motion sequences, colors became washed out and the video appeared greenish in tint. When capturing high-motion video sequences, experiment with bumping up color saturation values to counteract this effect.
	
	2. Compression:
	
	  a. Cinepak can tend to "pulse" with low-motion videos at the key frames. It's not a bad strategy to use high key frame intervals, up to and perhaps beyond 60, to avoid this effect.
	
	  b. With this of all the codecs, don't be afraid to goose the data rate on high-motion videos up to the sweet spot max. Cinepak will play all your frames and more.

Working with Indeo video interactive   Intel was kind enough to allow us to include two of their utilities with the book. The first, IndeoApp, is discussed in Chapter 6.

The second, Kplay (Figure 12.37), included in the chap_12 subdirectory, is the only tool that can open an IVI compressed file and tell you which IVI options were enabled and which settings used. Hopefully, in the future we'll be able to add these features to VCS, but Intel's demanding development schedule prevented them from supplying the required data in time for this version.

We've also included some articles from Intel's IVI developer CD-ROM that describe how to optimize IVI in different settings. Updates and new information can also be found on Intel's well-maintained Web site, at, you guessed it, www.intel.com.

Power!Video Pro reference chart.

At a Glance: Power!Video Pro	
Description	Control-oriented, intraframe-only compression algorithm based on technology licensed from Duck Corporation. Very similar technology to TrueMotionS.
Target platform range	486/66 (with DCI graphics) and up
Bandwidth sweet spot	275 KB/s and higher
Appropriate content	Low-motion, small animation files
Inappropriate content	High-motion, big animation files
When to use	Quality-oriented, high-bandwidth videos like presentations and kiosks, prototyping
When to avoid	When CD-ROM real estate is dear, 8-bit displays
Key strengths	High quality at high bandwidths, very interactive due to intraframe-only implementation, excellent low-end scaling algorithm, very fast compressor
Key weaknesses	Clunky compression interface, doesn't normalize data rate over clip duration, causing data rate spikes. Eight-bit quality is very poor. Low-bandwidth performance is very poor.
User guidelines	1. It's very important to minimize detail in the shot. Use very soft backgrounds and/or shoot with the background slightly out of focus.
	2. Compress at 312×224 resolution to access Power!Video's 2:3 scaling. Either capture at 312×224 or "crop" captured video to the smaller size, since scaling to 312×224 may introduce artifacts and distortion.
	3. Power!Video clips tend to darken, so bump up brightness and contrast values before compression. For example, Horizon's least setting bumps brightness up to 140 and saturation up to 150. These figures were too high for our clips, however, which did well with lower values.
	4. Different types of clips will compress to different data rates using identical controls. Test with smaller clips until you find the correct compression configuration and then save the configuration. One easy way to do this is in Premiere, which allows you to compress a partial file, say 2 seconds. Once settings are optimized, go ahead and compress the entire file.

Power!Video Pro reference chart. *(continued)*

5. Power!Video clips are especially susceptible to bandwidth overages in high-motion segments. Always check file bandwidth graphically with a tool like VCS Play or Movie Analysis in Premiere to ensure that all sections are under the target bandwidth.

Power!Video Compression Controls		
Control	*Effect on Data Rate*	*Effect on Quality*
Compression (normal/high)	High reduces data rate by two thirds (requires horizontal resolution evenly divided by 12—normally 312×224 resolution).	Minimal
Color Resolution Vertical/Horizontal	Normal/normal reduces data rate by up to 50 KB/s. High/normal or normal/high reduces by about 25 KB/s.	High/high produces least background noise, normal/normal produces the most.
Detail (0–100)	Reduces between 10 and 25 KB/s.	Dramatically reduces quality of edges and other detail.

Power!Video Pro

Introduction   Power!Video Pro is a proprietary technology licensed from Duck Corporation in New York City. Horizons is fairly close mouthed about the algorithm, describing it a "transformless algorithm" that works with differences between RBG (red, green, blue) values of tight groups of pixels. Horizons attributes the codec's decompression speed to the fact that decompression requires many simple addition functions but few processor-consuming multiplications. After working with the codec for several days and reading between the lines of the manual, it's clear that Duck also performs some vertical scaling and pixel averaging to achieve lower data rates.

Power!Video Pro stores color information in 24-bit mode, dithering to a standard 8-bit palette during decompression. Unlike all other reviewed codecs, Power!Video Pro is an intraframe-only technology that performs no interframe compression. This improves the ability to page directly to a random frame but typically prevents the algorithm from achieving single-spin data rates with the benchmark 15 fps, 320×240 video file.

Operation: Horizons sells both Macintosh and Video for Windows versions of the Power!Video Pro compressor. We tested the latter, using Microsoft's VidEdit utility as the compression interface.

When you select the Power!Video Pro compressor, the data rate and key frame options gray out, and you press the configuration button to reveal the codec's proprietary controls. As a control-oriented codec, Power!Video Pro doesn't offer a direct data rate control and doesn't normalize data rate over the duration of a file. Instead, you regulate data rate via the controls shown in Figure 12.38. During compression, the codec encodes each frame according to the control settings with the data rate rising and falling throughout the video in relation to the complexity of the individual frame. This technique makes it extremely difficult to select and regulate data rate for clips containing different sequences.

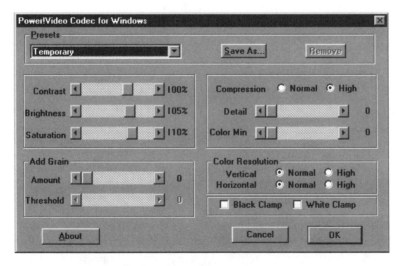

Figure 12.38   Power!Video Pro's control-oriented compression screen makes compressing for 2X CD-ROMs somewhat of an adventure.

By experimenting with small extracts of our main test clips, we quickly found the optimal compression settings, which we saved as a separate preset. Fortunately, Power!Video Pro is an extremely fast compressor, burning through our 45-frame clip in just over one minute and 21 seconds.

Compression Controls Horizons offers five compression presets, ranging from Least (least quality/least data rate) to Most (most quality/most data rate). Since the presets produce different data rates for different types of clips, their primary value is to illustrate how the various controls affect data rate.

The largest single data rate determinant is compression scaling, toggled on and off with the Compression (normal and high) control. This control subsamples information horizontally at a ratio of 2:3, essentially reducing data rate to two thirds of the original without significant quality degradation. However, to access this compression feature, the video's horizontal vertical resolution must be a multiple of 12, which is why most Power!Video Pro clips tend to have a resolution of 312×224.

The second largest factor in reducing quality is Vertical and Horizontal Color Resolution, which sets pixel block sizes for color averaging. At the high-high resolution, color is sampled in 2×2 pixel blocks, which are usually too small to discern during normal playback. At normal-normal resolution, the codec samples color with 4×4 pixel blocks, producing significant bandwidth savings (approximately 50 KB/s in a 312×224×15 fps clip) but creating more background noise.

The Detail slider controlled data rate by between 11 and 24 KB/s (312×224×15 fps clip) depending on clip content, but significantly affected the quality of sharp lines and edges. The Contrast, Brightness, and Saturation controls only slightly affected data rate but conveniently helped correct the Power!Video Pro tendency to darken and fade colors during extreme compression. We briefly tested other compression controls but found that they had a limited effect on compressed video quality or data rate.

Overall, Power!Video Pro has dramatically improved in both quality and playback performance since the early versions that surfaced in late 1994. Now that Horizons has made decompression free, publishers seeking high-quality, high-data-rate video may also want to take a look.

ADVANCED TECHNIQUES

File Concatenation

Now the moment you've been waiting for, the act where the magical man joins two files born apart with disparate key frame intervals and data rates into one cohesive whole. Read on and learn a trick that will amaze your friends, win you free drinks in bars, and cause you to become friends of the rich and famous.

Here's the problem. For some reason you've got two compressed video files that you have to join together. Perhaps you got them from different sources; perhaps disk space limitations forced you to create two smaller files instead of one longer one.

Maybe you're trying to optimize the compression of an animation file that has scene changes that require a key frame and you don't have Premiere. Perhaps you have Premiere and found, like me, that key frame placement works fine on quarter-screen AVI files but not on full-screen converted animations. Maybe you're trying to join two screen shots compressed in Video 1 format and want a key frame at the beginning of each sequence and no others.

Obviously, you don't want to recompress both files in the process, since this double compression would degrade video quality. You simply want to join the two files together like peas in a pod and make the resultant file act forevermore as if it had been created in one fell swoop rather than by the belated merger of two previously independent files.

Let's deal with the animation issue. As we discussed before, you generally want one key frame at the start, then key frames at every major transition and no others, since they degrade the quality of this low-motion video. This means key frames at irregular intervals, which you can accomplish only in Premiere. Unfortunately, although Premiere worked fine with quarter-screen, real-world videos, it kept misplacing the key frames on our animation, as well has crunching the first couple of frames beyond recognition. So we had to find a better way.

Let's have a quick look at our test animation file, which has a sharp transition between the title frame, shown in Figure 12.39 and the animation body, which is Mikey pumping some data from a CD-ROM in Figure 12.41. Without a key frame at the transition point, you produce the results shown

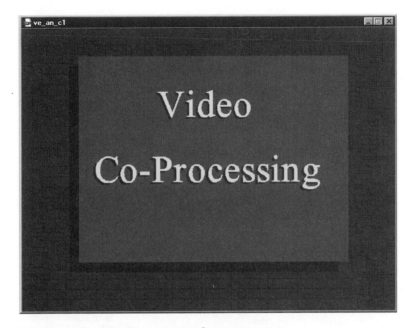

Figure 12.39 The initial sequence of an animation.

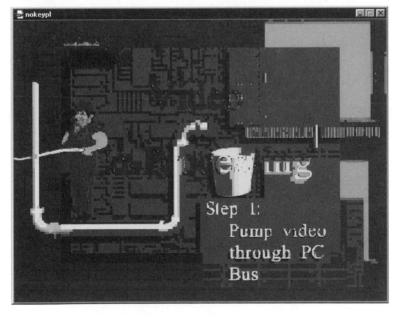

Figure 12.40 How not to do a transition between Figures 12.32 and 12.34.

Figure 12.41   A transition optimized by compressing two files separately and concatenating them in DVP.

in Figure 12.40, a delta frame with tons of blue detritus from the opening screen.

Figure 12.41 (fig12_41.avi) is what you get when the transition happens on a key frame, a much better result. You'll note that this video file has 81 frames and that the transition happens on frame 25. Figure 12.42 is a frame profile of fig12_34.avi, showing two key frames, one on frame 1, the other

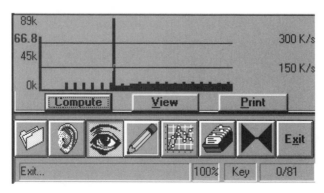

Figure 12.42   A frame profile of fig12_41.avi, showing an irregular key frame interval.

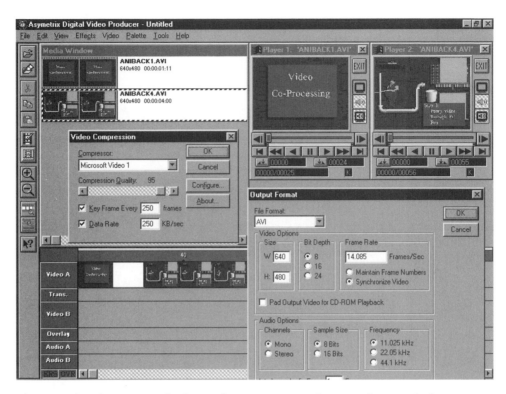

Figure 12.43 DVP is the king of concatenation, here working with the two halves of our full-screen animation file.

on frame 25. This irregular key frame interval proves that the file was created from two separate files, one a short file of 24 frames, the other a longer file with 56.

Here's how we did it. First we compressed the two stub files in Media-Studio, using the techniques discussed above. But MediaStudio won't concatenate Video 1 files, so we loaded DVP to try there.

Figure 12.43 shows the two files loaded on DVP's time line and DVP's Video Compression options and Output Format screens. Here's where it starts to get a bit fuzzy, changing from science to art. For this to work at all, we know that the following file characteristics of the two stub files need to be the same:

- codec
- codec configuration

- frame rate
- resolution
- compressed palette
- bit depth

Key frames and data rates don't have to be the same, but they can't be more constrictive than the stub file settings. If the stub files are 250 KB/s in bandwidth, setting a target bandwidth of 200 KB/s will trigger a recompression. If the key frame interval is set to 15 and the stub files are at 50, you'll recompress. On the other hand, if it's set to 250, you won't.

After setting the options, it's just a question of building the file, and if it works, it works. If it doesn't in DVP, it should, and you've probably got one of the foregoing options different in the two files. Table 11.13 charts which codecs the various editors can abut without recompressing. You'll note that DVP is the most flexible.

Sorry we can't be more precise, but this is one area where you're just gonna have to roll up your sleeves and fiddle. But if you've got two files to join, you'll find it well worth the effort.

Inserting Key Frames in Premiere

As we saw, placing key frames at a scene change can add quality, and key frames at video entry points speed interactivity. In English, this means that if you want to jump quickly to frame 462 when the user clicks on the sorceress' phone number, make frame 462 a key frame (hey, I can dream, can't I?).

We tested this feature by compressing clips with several markers and edit points using Video 1, Cinepak, and Indeo video interactive. The feature worked as advertised, placing key frames at the appropriate frames and then returning to the regular key frame interval. However, for some reason, we couldn't get this feature to work with Indeo 3.2, or with Video 1 for the animation concatenation discussed earlier. Don't know why, but there it is.

Although placing key frames at edit points is a pretty simple concept, it took me more than a few minutes to figure out how to set a marker in Premiere. So here's a couple of tips that will help you through this process.

First, you'll have to set the time line to show every frame when placing key frames on specific frames. You do this by adjusting the slider bar on the bottom left-hand side of the time line, shifting it to the left until you get to one frame.

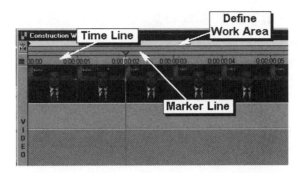

Figure 12.44   The top line in Premiere's Construction window is feature packed but a touch confusing.

Obviously, you have to have the video bitmaps turned on, rather than using the file name option—otherwise you couldn't see which frame to adjust. These controls are in the Construction window options box, accessed by touching the black-and-blue box in the upper left-hand corner of the Construction window.

To mark a frame, you have to position the mouse cursor in precisely the right location on top of the time line, shown in Figure 12.44. The very top bar, which is either yellow or gray, defines the work area, used for partial compressions or previews.

The bar immediately below this does nothing, and the next line below is the marking line. Positioning is important; you'll know you're correct when the cursor becomes a little black triangle within the gray time line. If the cursor is the normal pointer, you're too high. If an arrow pointing downward, you're too low.

In my experience, the arrow tends to default to the start of whatever frame you're in when you click the mouse, which often ends up one frame early for me. At this point you can move the marker by going to another spot and clicking again.

When you've got the triangle located on the correct frame, press the shift key and a select a number from 0 to 9, which will create a numbered green marker within the time ruler. If you have more than 10 desired key frame points, don't worry, simply start over at number 1 after number 9. To delete a place marker in the time ruler, position the hairline in the time ruler over the marker and press C.

Batch Processing in Premiere

Batch processing is one of Premiere's most effective features, allowing you to queue up multiple projects, complete with titling, special effects—the whole megillah—and compress overnight or during the weekend. We've used this feature many times while writing this book.

Once you arrive at a set of standard output and compression parameters, the process is fairly simple. The first step is creating the various project files. As we discussed in Chapter 11, Premiere stores works in process as "project" files and the batch feature works by outputting multiple project files in sequence.

Say you just captured 10 files and needed to trim, add titles, and compress with Indeo video interactive. We've already talked about building a preset. Once you have preset, you open your file, trim the header and footer, and add the title.

When you're ready to roll, select File>New>Project and Premiere will ask you if you want to save the file. Save it as clip1.ppj. Note that during compression, by default Premiere will apply the project name to the compressed output file, compressing clip1.ppj as clip1.avi. You can change both later, but naming the project and saving the project name in the correct location save steps. Make sure you select the correct preset for the new file and repeat the process for all 10 files.

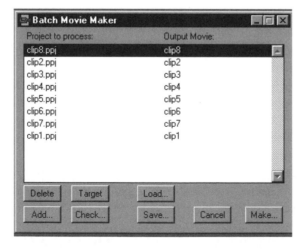

Figure 12.45   Premiere's Batch Movie Maker helps preserve your nights and weekends.

After saving the last project file, select File>Tools>Batch Movie Maker, which spawns the screen shown Figure 12.45. Press Add to add projects to the batch or Load to load a previous batch file. Checking the files before pressing Make makes sure that all of your assets are present, though Premiere checks all files before starting the batch anyway. Press Make to start the process, shut off the monitor to avoid monitor burn, and it's Miller time.

Chapter

MPEG-1: Overview

THE MPEG STANDARDS

MPEG-1

MPEG is a video compression technology formulated by the Moving Pictures Experts Group, a joint committee of the International Organization for Standardization (ISO). The first MPEG standard, known as MPEG-1, was formalized by the MPEG committee in January 1992.

MPEG-1 incorporates both audio and video. For NTSC video (United States and Japan) MPEG-1 uses the Standard Image Format (SIF) of 352×240 at 30 frames per second. Audio is 16-bit, stereo sampled at 44 kHz. MPEG data rates are variable, although MPEG-1 was designed to provide VHS video quality and CD-ROM audio quality at a combined data rate of 1.2 megabits per second, or 150 KB/s.

MPEG-2

By resolution and data rate MPEG-1 is targeted primarily at the computer and games markets. In contrast, MPEG-2, adopted in the spring of 1994, is a broadcast standard specifying 720×480 playback at 60 fields per second at data rates ranging from two to 10 megabits per second. MPEG-2 is the core compression technology for DVD, the high-density CD-ROM standard that many feel will replace VHS tapes as the standard for consumer video.

Where today's average new computer is capable of playing back MPEG-1 video without special hardware, MPEG-2 playback requires either a hardware coprocessor or an MMX-enabled Pentium 200 class computer. For this reason, MPEG-2's short-term impact on the general computer market is more likely to be in vertical markets like kiosks and training than in general markets like CD-ROM publishing.

Note that MPEG-2 is backward compatible. This lets extremely advanced devices like IBM's 760CD, equipped with a hardware MPEG-2 player, play back MPEG-1 files as well.

MPEG-3/4

MPEG-3 was the designated HDTV codec, designed for dimensions of up to 1920×1080 with bit rates from 20 to 40 Mbit per second. However, after some experimentation, the committee learned that high-bandwidth MPEG-2 worked well in these applications, so MPEG-3 was dropped.

MPEG-4 is a very low-bit-rate codec targeted toward videoconferencing, Internet, and other low-bandwidth applications that should have little short-term impact on traditional CD-ROM publishing markets.

MPEG-1 TECHNOLOGY

The MPEG-1 Codec

MPEG-1 is a codec, or en*cod*er/*dec*oder, which means that MPEG-1 technology is involved during development and playback. MPEG-1 encoders create MPEG-1 files that are played back with an MPEG-1 decoder or player. Since MPEG-1 includes both audio and video, all MPEG-1 decoders must address both formats.

In addition to general MPEG-1 files, designated with the .MPG extension, MPEG is the underlying compression technology for CD-i and VideoCD, two vertical market derivatives. Hereinafter, when we refer to MPEG, we mean lowest common denominator MPEG-1 format.

The MPEG-1 Algorithm

MPEG uses two techniques during encoding, interframe and intraframe compression. Interframe compression eliminates redundant information between frames, a powerful form of compression with minimal impact on video quality.

Intraframe compression focuses on compressing data within a frame, without reference to other video frames. MPEG uses the discrete cosign transform (DCT) algorithm as its intraframe compression engine. DCT is a "lossy" compressor, which means that information is lost during compression, causing image degradation, usually in the form of artifacts or blockiness.

Here's how it works mechanically. MPEG uses three kinds of frames during the compression process: intra or I frames, predicted or P frames, and bidirectionally interpolated, or B frames. Most MPEG encoding schemes use a 12- to 15-frame sequence called a group of pictures, or GOP, as shown in Figure 13.1.

All GOPs start with an I frame, which serves as a reference for subsequent frames in the GOP and also as an entry point for random access into the MPEG file. For these reasons, only intraframe compression is applied to I

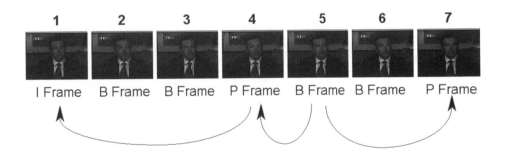

Figure 13.1   The first seven frames of a GOP.

frames, not interframe compression. Since the quality of the P and B frames referencing the I frame is related to the quality of the I frame itself, most MPEG encoders perform only limited compression on the I frame, making it the largest individual frame in the GOP (see Figure 13.2).

In contrast, encoders apply both forms of compression to P and B frames. First the frames are divided into 16×16 pixel blocks called macro blocks. During interframe compression, the encoder searches for exact or near matches between the compressed frame and its reference frame or frames.

When the encoder can't find a match, it compresses the macro block with MPEG's intraframe compression algorithm, DCT. When a match is found, the encoder records the location of the reference block for use during decompression, which is much more efficient than DCT or any other form of intraframe compression. In English, this means that interframe compression is more efficient than interframe compression, producing high compression ratios with minimal image degradation.

When compressing P frames, the encoder searches for redundancies in the closest previous I or P frame (see Figure 13.1). With the bidirectional B frames, the encoder first eliminates redundancies in the closest previous and future I or P frames and then compresses the balance with DCT (Figure 13.1). The ability to look forward and backward generates maximum redundancy, making B frames the most compact of all three frame types.

Figure 13.2 is a graphical representation of an MPEG-1 profile showing three frame sizes. The largest spikes, of course, are I frames, averaging approximately 15 KB in size in this 150 KB/s file. The next largest frames are P frames, about 8 KB in size, while the efficient B frame weighs in at about 3 KB per frame.

Interestingly, MPEG's I, B, P sequence forces a unique frame order in the compressed file, shown in Figure 13.3. Since B frame 3 can refer to both I frame 1 and P frame 4 during decompression, frames 1 and 3 must be

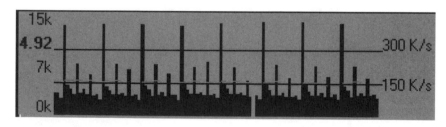

Figure 13.2   MPEG-1 frame profile. The highest frames are I frames, the next P frames, and the most compact are B frames.

packed in the file and decompressed before either of the two intermediate B frames, 2 and 3. In the same vein, both frames 1 and 4 must be available in RAM while decoding frames 2 and 3, as shown in Figure 13.4.

MPEG Decoders

What Is an MPEG Decoder?

An MPEG-1 decoder is any hardware device or software program capable of decoding an MPEG-1 stream. MPEG-1 decoders were initially hardware based because the computational requirements for playing back MPEG-1 are very intense. As computers advanced from 386 to Pentium, however, CPUs became powerful enough to decode MPEG-1 without hardware, and software-only MPEG-1 players arrived.

All MPEG decoders—hardware and software—decode both MPEG-1 audio and video. Hardware-based decoders decompress video back to its original resolution at 30 fps, with the usual ability to scale the video to higher resolutions. In contrast, software-based decoders decompress according to the abilities of their host computer, generally producing close to 30 fps on Pentium 133 computers and beyond.

All MPEG-1 decoders also decode audio. Once again, whereas hardware-based decoders typically reproduce CD-ROM–quality audio, software-based MPEG-1 decoders generally cut corners, producing 22 rather than 44 kHz, saving bandwidth and improving video performance.

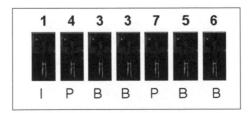

Figure 13.3 MPEG packed file order. The MPEG interframe compression sequence requires a unique packing order in the compressed file.

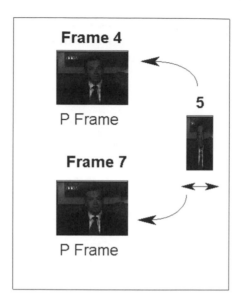

Figure 13.4   MPEG decoders. An inside view of an MPEG decoder, showing that two reference frames must be available to decode a B frame.

Playback APIs—Ties that Bind (Mostly)   All MPEG playback devices have one or more Application Programming Interfaces, or APIs, which provide the link between MPEG applications and MPEG playback devices, theoretically ensuring widespread compatibility. The first nonproprietary MPEG API was Microsoft's MCI-MPEG specification, released in June 1994. This spec garnered widespread support and soon made the transition to an industry group called the Open MPEG-1 (OM-1) Foundation.

Unfortunately, the OM-1 specification contains 29 separate calls, some with as many as 10 options. The sheer complexity of the specification, combined with inadequate documentation, resulted in inconsistent implementations among playback vendors, especially offshore clones, creating an unstable playback environment. The potential technical support issues this created prevented many title developers from shipping retail MPEG titles.

Two things should happen in 1996 to end this API logjam. First, in March 1996, the OM Foundation released more comprehensive documentation that should enable tighter adherence to the specification. Hopefully, this will resolve many incompatibilities prior to the 1996 Christmas season.

Second is Microsoft's ActiveMovie, a media-streaming architecture for Windows 95/NT introduced in March 1996. In addition to a complete revamping of the video playback architecture, ActiveMovie incorporates a software MPEG decoder, licensed from MediaMatics, that will be available free to all Windows 95/NT developers. The free decoder will dramatically increase the installed base of MPEG players and, more important, provide the industry with a stable API target.

Released in final form in the fourth quarter of 1996, it's unclear how much effect ActiveMovie will have in 1996. However, it should be widely disseminated in 1997, setting a stable standard that should solidify the MPEG specification in 1997 and beyond.

MPEG-1 Derivatives (CD-i/Video CD)   Depending on the application, MPEG players should also decode the various higher level MPEG formats in addition to the lowest common denominator ISO 9660 format, which all decoders handle. These include CD-i (Green Book), Video CD (White Book), and karaoke. Although most decoders support these formats, they do so with various levels of sophistication.

For example, as MCI devices, all MPEG decoders are accessible through Media Player, the basic Windows Media Playback application and OLE engine. However, not all decoders support track selection, a valuable feature for flipping through videos on a CD-i title. Decoders without track support treat all videos on the CD-ROM as one video, making it difficult to find precise starting points for the individual video tracks.

Decoder Designs

Overlay   The first approach taken by hardware developers was video overlay, where a decoder board, containing dedicated MPEG audio and video decoder chips, connects to and displays graphics sent via the internal VESA feature connector (VFC) from the computer's graphics adapter (Figure 13.5). Most early MPEG playback boards, including Sigma Design's RealMagic, were overlay cards.

Unfortunately, because the VFC is an 8-bit serial connection, it can't handle the data flow necessary to support high color modes at the fast refresh rates necessary for flicker-free display. Consequently, the graphics

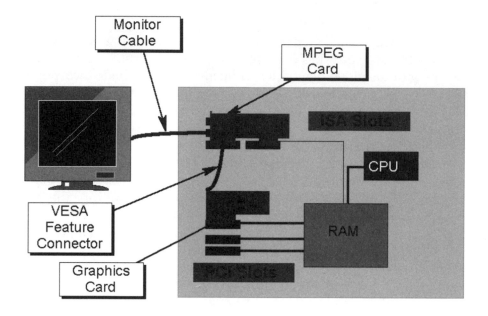

Figure 13.5   MPEG playback via the VESA feature connector, a short-lived
approach with numerous technical problems.

card you purchased for rock solid 1280×1024 display or blazing 24-bit
graphics speed was forced into low color, low resolution, or low refresh
mode, just to play MPEG files. Because all graphics were pumped through
the VFC, you were forced into lower performance modes even when not
running MPEG applications.

For example, back in June 1994, the original RealMagic software was
incompatible with an ATI Mach 32 graphics adapter in all modes higher
than 4-bit graphics, useless for playing back AVI files or image editing. By
June 1995, Sigma's new drivers enabled operation in 8-bit mode, which was
better but still unacceptable for those working with graphics-intensive
applications.

Playback board manufacturers attacked these problems on two fronts.
To improve overlay compatibility they invested in compatibility testing and
additional software development to stabilize their drivers. More important,

they introduced combo boards that combined the two functions and avoided the problem altogether.

Combo Boards   Rather than attaching to video cards, combo boards replace them, containing graphic accelerator chips along with the dedicated MPEG audio and video decompression hardware. This integrated design reduced the compatibility headaches but was an expensive solution for the installed base, especially for users with relatively new graphics cards.

In addition, combo boards were pursued primarily by MPEG vendors like Sigma and Jazz Multimedia, rather than graphics giants like Matrox, Diamond, ATI, and Number 9 Visual Technologies. For this reason, combo boards tended to lag the market leaders in pure graphics performance, which generally deterred most volume buyers from committing to the combo architecture.

A related approach is an MPEG daughtercard, which attaches to the main graphics card via proprietary connectors without the bandwidth limitations of the VFC (Figure 13.6). This approach lets graphics cards provide

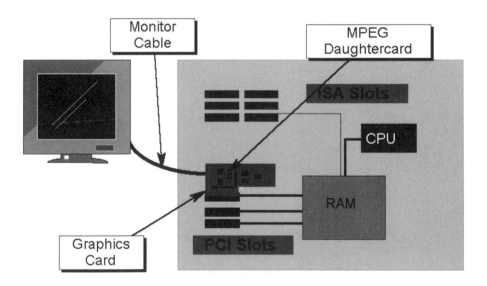

Figure 13.6   An MPEG daughtercard, an approach favored by graphics companies like Diamond and Matrox.

hardware MPEG functionality without burdening the cost of the basic graphics card with onboard MPEG decoder chips.

For example, Diamond's Stealth 3D 2000 and Matrox's new Mystique both have daughtercard connectors and daughtercards. When attached to the main graphics card, this daughtercard creates a combo-like product with all the advantages of a combo board and lightning fast graphics.

Loopback Cable   Another common architecture involves the VGA loopback connector, an external cable between the graphics card's monitor port and the MPEG card, with the monitor connecting to the MPEG card (Figure 13.7). Since the external loopback cable isn't bandwidth limited like the VESA Feature Connector, this approach doesn't place artificial limits on graphics performance and is better suited for users requiring access to high-performance graphics.

Unfortunately, the VGA loopback connector isn't without its limitations. Like the VFC approach, MPEG video is overlaid on top of the analog graphics during transmission to the monitor. Unfortunately, the lack of video overlay standards makes it difficult for MPEG applications to conform to common Windows display protocols like yielding foreground screen display when boxes or other applications are placed over the MPEG video window. Although this may not be a problem for gamers or in dedicated applications like kiosks, it can be a pain for training, presentation, and other business-oriented, interactive uses.

One design that avoids many of these limitations is Sigma Designs' RealMagic Ultra, which features an analog overlay technology that virtually eliminates the compatibility problems associated with many MPEG-1 playback cards.

PCI Decoders   Another new wrinkle in the MPEG add-on decoder market is PCI-based MPEG decoders that transfer decompressed MPEG video to the video card via the PCI bus rather than a feature connector or loopback cable (Figure 13.8). Since the MPEG is sent to the graphics card, rather than vice versa, there are no limitations on graphics performance.

Under this approach, MPEG playback is architecturally similar to playing other formats like Video for Windows or QuickTime. Rather than maintaining two distinct video streams—one graphics and one MPEG—combined via overlay, the decompressed MPEG transfers to the video card just like other formats, making it easier to conform to Windows display protocols. Using the PCI bus rather than a direct MPEG-graphics connec-

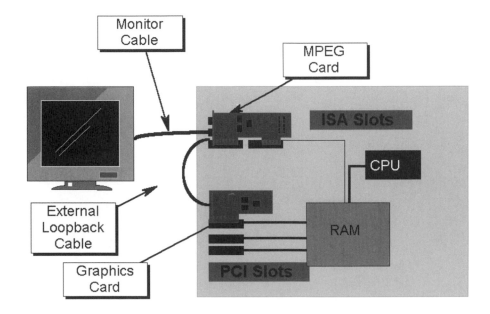

Figure 13.7 MPEG playback via an external loopback cable, the architecture used by Sigma Design's RealMagic Ultra.

tion also avoids most compatibility issues between MPEG decoder and graphics card.

Although newer hardware MPEG decoders overcome most technical problems associated with older designs, they haven't overcome the objections of potential buyers. Overall, sales of hardware MPEG decoders, in all forms, have been disappointing. At the same time, advances in processors and graphics subsystems rapidly accelerated the performance of software-only MPEG decompression.

Although hardware players provide the utmost in responsiveness and performance, the general retrofit market for hardware players simply never materialized, and most new graphics cards ship with a software MPEG player. The installed base of software players will get a further boost when Microsoft ships ActiveMovie to games developers later in 1996. For these reasons, most analysts predict that hardware MPEG-1 playback will be relegated to vertical markets, while software MPEG will rapidly become ubiquitous.

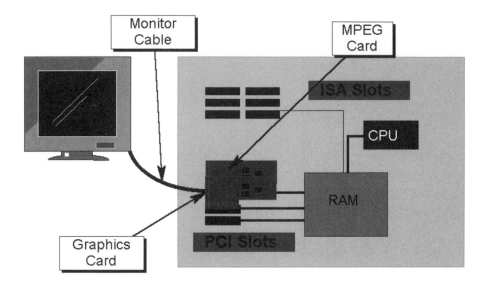

Figure 13.8   PCI MPEG decoders make MPEG look like just another video
stream to the computer, which eases integration woes.

Software-Only Decoders   Four companies actively market software MPEG
decoders, although IBM distributes their proprietary decoder solely on
their branded computers. The other three companies, CompCore Multimedia, MediaMatics, Inc., and Xing Technologies, sell primarily to graphics
card developers and CPU manufacturers.

Playback performance improves almost daily as the three companies
jockey for marketing leverage and Microsoft releases video enhancements
to Windows 95 like Direct Draw and Direct Video. As mentioned previously, all three players can produce close to 30 fps on optimized Pentium
133 computers and above, sufficient for all but the most interactive applications.

To achieve this impressive performance, software MPEG players sacri-
fice audio quality, producing 22 kHz, 16-bit stereo audio or less rather than
the true CD-ROM quality 44 kHz, 16-bit stereo. However, this difference is
apparent only to audiophiles working on high-fidelity computer speakers.

Software playback performance varies dramatically by CPU, graphics card, and CD-ROM, and it's unusually important to have the latest drivers, especially for Windows 95 computers. In-house developers should ensure that all Windows 95 machines have been updated for Direct Draw and Direct Video, which usually must be obtained from the graphics card manufacturer. Title developers should include drivers for these new specifications and as many graphics cards as possible with their titles.

MPEG-1 COMPARED TO OTHER CODECS

Competitive Strengths

MPEG's complex interframe algorithms produce the best-quality video of any computer-based codec. That is, when compressed to any common set of compression parameters (e.g., data rate, resolution, frame rate), the visual quality of the MPEG stream will be higher than that of Cinepak, Indeo, or other similar codecs. In addition, since the MPEG compression algorithm also delivers CD-ROM quality audio (44 kHz/16-bit/stereo), MPEG sounds better than other codecs, which typically don't compress audio and consequently use 22 kHz/8-bit/mono audio.

As mentioned above, however, MPEG-1 initially required specialized hardware for playback, which limited MPEG's acceptance. In the development community, MPEG was considered a "hardware" codec, while codecs like Indeo and Cinepak, which played back without specialized hardware, were "software" codecs. Seeking the largest possible target audience, most title developers used software codecs that delivered much less quality to a much broader market.

As computers got faster and graphics subsystems become more video capable, software-only MPEG players appeared. As we've seen, software MPEG-1 players deliver close to 30 fps on an increasingly relevant class of machines. Moreover, software MPEG-1 players are quickly becoming ubiquitous, the combined effect of MPEG support becoming a checklist item for graphics cards and being required by the MPC-3 standard. Once Microsoft ships ActiveMovie with its software MPEG-1 player, any application developer can supply software MPEG with their titles at no cost.

Essentially, this means that software MPEG is close to becoming a free, software codec, shedding its hardware roots. While many applications, such as high-performance games, full-screen presentations, and kiosks will still benefit from hardware support, software playback will suffice for the mass market, and the installed base is rapidly increasing.

Competitive Weaknesses

Although MPEG excels at pure compression performance, it does have several limitations. First, as a lossy codec, it tends to create serious artifacts in 8-bit animations, and its 352×240 maximum resolution can't handle full-screen animations. In these instances, 8-bit codecs like RAD Software's Smacker and the ancient Video 1 to do a better job.

In addition, as a committee-driven standard, MPEG can't match innovative new features like those found in Intel's Indeo video interactive (IVI). Introduced in late 1995, IVI debuted key game and interactivity features like:

> *Transparency support:* enabling video sprites and other overlays that can be interactively controlled during playback.
>
> *Local window decode:* allowing the developer to decode regions within the compressed video rather than the entire video during run time.
>
> *Random key frame access*: enabling the developer to insert key frames randomly into the video to maximize quality and interactivity.
>
> *Saturation/contrast/brightness controls:* letting users customize video characteristics for their graphics card and monitor.
>
> *Password protection:* preventing video editing and alteration.

These features will make IVI indispensable for many developers. Nonetheless, in terms of pure linear playback quality, MPEG beats IVI hands down, and on many titles linear play quality is the most important criterion.

Conclusion

Quality Centric, Limited Distribution   MPEG should be strongly considered for all applications in which pure linear quality is key, like training, kiosks, and sales presentations. Since the distribution of content in these applications is generally limited, the MPEG consumer can either purchase MPEG hardware players or high-end computers that can drive software players to full 30 fps.

If your application requires full-screen video, consider investing in MPEG hardware, which typically provides somewhat higher quality. Note also that a Pentium 133 laptop typically won't play MPEG video using a software player as adroitly as a Pentium 133 desktop computer, the result of the lower power graphics chipsets used in laptops.

If your portable application requires high-quality MPEG-1 playback, you should purchase a computer like IBM's 760 CD, with MPEG-2 hardware. Another option is Toshiba's new Tecra line of computers with the advanced Zoomed Video (ZV) port, which makes PC Card (PCMCIA) MPEG playback devices a practical reality.

Mass Market Titles   If you're pursuing mass market nirvana, your decision becomes a bit tougher, because you can't control the playback configuration used by your customers. Most publishers I've spoken to err on the conservative side, assuming that their mass market customers are one or two generations behind the latest hardware.

For example, for holiday season 1995 (December 1995), most title developers targeted 486 computers and above, using Indeo 3.2 and Cinepak for most linear playback video needs and shying away from MPEG and Indeo video interactive. Christmas 1996 will mark the real beginning of Pentium-only titles, but most developers will work with Indeo/Cinepak and perhaps MPEG, especially if they've closed a bundling deal with an MPEG hardware developer.

For the purpose of deciding when to cut over to exclusively MPEG-1 titles, here are the hardware and software requirements for high performance software MPEG playback.

1. *Software MPEG Players:* should be able to ship a free player with your Windows 95 title by December 1996.
2. *Pentium 133 and above:* an entry-level machine today, but how many of your target customers still have slower computers?
3. *Graphics card with Direct Video support:* a surprising number of relatively new boards don't have Direct Video drivers, and some may never have as graphics card developers focus on their newer products. Without Direct Video support, playback performance will likely be inadequate.
4. *Direct Video Drivers:* If the board has a direct video driver, supplying it to your users also shouldn't be a problem, since most companies are supplying these to Microsoft for inclusion in the Direct Video SDK. Just be sure to budget real estate for these drivers on your CD-ROM.

Unless your target customer meets all four of these criteria, you're probably best off sticking with a traditional software-only technology like Indeo and/or Cinepak. Said another way, unless you're selling only to users who have purchased new computers in 1996 and beyond, stick with the older stuff.

SUMMARY

1. MPEG-1 compression incorporates both audio and video. In the NTSC world (United States and Japan) MPEG-1 video is 352×240 at 30 frames per second, and audio is 16-bit, stereo sampled at 44 kHz. MPEG-1 was designed to provide VHS video quality and CD-ROM audio quality at a combined data rate of 1.2 megabits per second, or 150 KB/s.
2. MPEG-2 is full-screen, high-bandwidth video, targeted at broadcast, DVD, and similar applications. MPEG-2 probably won't significantly affect the computer desktop for some time, although it should storm through the home beginning in 1997. MPEG-3 was dropped, and MPEG-4 is very bit rate codec targeted toward videoconferencing, Internet, and other low-bandwidth applications.

3. MPEG uses I, B, and P frames to implement both interframe and intraframe compression. The discrete cosign transform (DCT) algorithm is MPEG's intraframe technology.

4. MPEG decoders decode audio and video and typically work with CD-I, Video CD, and other MPEG derivatives. As of the time of this writing, the installed base of MPEG playback APIs was generally considered too unstable for mass market titles. Microsoft's ActiveMovie, which includes a software player, should establish a firm API by December 1996.

5. MPEG decoders come in five basic flavors:

    (a) Overlay using the VESA Feature Connector: due to the technical problems associated with this approach, most overlay products were superseded by more compatible designs.

    (b) Combo cards/daughtercards: these boards combine graphics and MPEG on one board, a more stable design. The latter approach is favored by the graphics card industry because they can provide hardware MPEG options with little additional cost on the baseboard.

    (c) Loopback cables: uses an external cable between the MPEG card and graphics card to avoid the bandwidth limitations of the VFC. Still used by Sigma for their Real-Magic Ultra products.

    (d) PCI decoder: PCI decoders use the PCI bus rather than cables to communicate between the MPEG card and graphics card. This design is architecturally easier to implement, which promotes graphics card compatibility.

    (e) Software decoders: software-only decoders use the power of the CPU and graphics card to decode MPEG-1 video and audio at close to 30 frames per second on Pentium 133 computers and higher. The only trade-off is audio quality, which doesn't equal that produced by hardware cards but still exceeds that of Video for Windows codecs.

In general, hardware decoder sales have been consistently disappointing and with the advent of software decoders is probably relegated to niche status. Those seeking the ultimate in both quality and responsiveness should consider hardware MPEG decoders.

Owners of high-performance systems seeking just average playback performance should find software-only adequate.

6. For strict linear play video, MPEG currently produces better quality video at lower data rates than any other codec, and better audio quality. MPEG stumbles somewhat on animations and can't match Indeo video interactive's game-oriented features like overlay, local window decode, and variable frame rates.

7. Consider MPEG strongly for quality centric, limited distribution applications like training, sales, and kiosks. Mass market titles are probably better served by waiting until holiday season 1997 before jumping exclusively into MPEG.

Chapter

Low-End MPEG Compression Tools

Introduction

Question: When is an $89 MPEG-1 encoder better than a $75,000 MPEG-1 encoder?

Answer: When you don't have $75,000.

Now the big question: What do you give up when you go the $89 route, or the $125 or even $1000 route as compared to real-time MPEG encoders that cost from $8000 to $40,000, or Sony's $75,000 RTE-3000B?

Answer: Not as much as you might think.

Let's face it. Even if you've got the 75 large, it's tempting to at least take a look at the systems that even an average Joe or Jo-ette could afford. So, that's exactly what we did.

This chapter reviews six MPEG-1 encoders that cost under $1000. To be fair, four of the products are software-only encoders that require a separate capture card, but if you've already got the card the incremental cost starts at $89. Products in this category include CeQuadrat's PixelShrink ($199), Ulead's MPEG Converter ($249), Vitec's MPEG Maker ($125), and Xing Technologies XingMPEG Encoder ($89).

Where these software options have been around for a while, we're pleased to take the wraps off two brand-new hardware encoders bound to make waves in their respective categories. Darim's MPEGator may have a name that's tough to swallow, but the price goes down real easy. This $995 *real-time* MPEG-1 encoder costs literally 12% of the price of its nearest competitor.

Finally, Data Translations thinks their $995 two-pass encoder, Broadway, is just the ticket for CD-ROM title developers hoping to hit the big screen. Will Broadway's price motivate title developers to create MPEG titles as Data Translations claims? Tough to tell, but Broadway, and the rest of the reviewed products, sure takes the sticker shock away from MPEG encoding.

OVERVIEW

Briefly, software-only encoders input previously digitized video and spit out MPEG-1–encoded files. Xing Technologies created this category in 1994 with XingCD, a breakthrough product introduced at $995 at a time when the next cheapest MPEG-1 encoder cost about $20,000. Although cheap, software encoders are extremely slow, with some products taking as long as 60 minutes to encode one minute of MPEG on a Pentium 133.

Broadway, our two-pass encoder, first captures the video to disk in a format called "editable MPEG," which is comprised solely of I frames and actually more similar to Motion-JPEG format than MPEG. Either way, because the file is an AVI file under the Video for Windows specification, you can use AVI video editors like the bundled MediaStudio to add titling, transitions, and special effects. Broadway then compresses the final edited file using the onboard C-Cube RISC processor, which takes about five minutes for each minute of video rather than the 60:1 compression time of pure software-only encoders.

Darim's MPEGator is a genuine, real-time MPEG-1 encoder, inputting analog video and producing fully formatted MPEG files using the I, B, and P frame sequence. Unlike Broadway, which relies on the computer's sound card for audio capture, MPEGator includes both audio and video, impressive specifications for a product so affordable.

EVALUATION CRITERIA

We reviewed these systems from three perspectives. First and foremost was video quality, how the systems compared on the 12 test clips we compressed to identical MPEG-1 parameters. We compared still frame quality by clipping frames from the various compressed files and looking for artifacts like blockiness and color distortion. Then we played the files back at full speed, hunting for motion artifacts like mosquitoes, flickering, and background noise.

We ranked the systems from first to last, and after picking a winner, compared quality to MPEG-1 video produced by a top MPEG service bureau. We'll show you how well these low-end encoders stack up against the world's best and, to a certain degree, whether they're usable within the context of a commercial or in-house title.

Second—but equally foremost—was compatibility, because even the best-looking video is worthless if it won't play on your target system. We tested each system with Microsoft's ActiveMovie decoder, licensed from MediaMatics, with CompCore's and Xing's software players and also with the RealMagic Ultra, the hot new decoder from Sigma Designs. Here we judged each system either satisfactory or unsatisfactory, with any incompatibility producing an unsatisfactory rating.

Then we then looked at usability, clearly a distant third in importance but certainly a valid, distinguishing factor between systems tied in the first two categories. We broke this metric down into two categories, feature set and ease of use, to assess whether the respective products had the requisite features and how difficult it was to use them.

QUALITY-RELATED FEATURES

By way of background, MPEG-1 encoding is essentially a three-step process. *Capture* converts the information acquired during filming into information the encoder can compress. Capture used to be synonymous with analog-to-digital conversion, or digitization. As we'll see in a moment, however, the emergence of digital videotape formats makes capture a digital-to-digital conversion in many instances.

The second step is *preprocessing*, in which the video is filtered and otherwise prepared to maximize compression efficiency and quality. *Compression* to MPEG-1 format sequence is the final stage.

As you would expect, each stage plays a big role in the ultimate video quality. We'll deal with the three stages in sequence, focusing on how the products compare and also how their capabilities as a class match up against more expensive real-time encoding systems and the high-end supercomputers used by service bureaus. This will illuminate the respective performance of our reviewed products and help answer the $75,000 question—exactly what do you give up with a low-end encoder?

Capture

As we discussed in Chapter 7, one of the most radical shifts in the video creation and editing world is the movement from traditional analog tape formats to digital tape formats like Digital BetaCAM and D-1. While expensive, these systems avoid the generational loss experienced with traditional analog systems, enabling cleaner video output and much more complex editing and special effects without degradation.

High-end encoding systems accept digital information from these decks, simply storing the data to disk like any other file transfer. Any format conversions are similar to converting QuickTime video files to Video for Windows format, which, if performed correctly, doesn't introduce loss or noise into the video.

Low-End Systems   Our testing involved three different capture systems, which we tested using the same source tape and the same BetaSP deck. Both Broadway and MPEGator are self-contained products that capture and compress to MPEG format, Broadway in two steps, MPEGator in one. We used FAST's AV/Master (reviewed in Chapter 7) to capture video for the software encoders. We'll deal with the individual characteristics of their respective capture systems in a moment.

In contrast to the digital conversions performed by high-end systems, all three capture systems perform the more traditional "digitization," inputting the analog video into a frame buffer and assigning a digital value to each pixel in each frame. This necessarily introduces error into the captured video. Here's why.

The process of assigning a value to each pixel is an approximation rather than a direct conversion. When you have over 16 million colors to choose from, the odds of picking the correct value are minimal. The odds of assigning adjacent pixels in a single frame the correct values are almost nil, even if the colors were identical in the real world.

We look at MPEG encoding techniques in detail below. Briefly, however, the approximations used during digitization reduce intraframe redundancies that fuel MPEG's intraframe compression algorithms. Similarly, the odds of assigning the same pixel in consecutive frames the same value are also fairly small, which limits interframe redundancies that fuel MPEG's interframe algorithm.

Said another way, traditional digitization techniques create noise which is manifest as "changes" that the encoder must preserve. For example, when pixel values randomly change between frames, the encoder sees this as motion that must be represented in the final compressed bitstream. The encoder sees intraframe noise as additional frame detail that must also be preserved. This noise makes it tougher for the encoder to perform its real job, which is preserving the *real* frame detail and the *real* motion.

Double Jeopardy Broadway and the software encoders also suffered another loss when compressing the video data for storage to disk. Like most Motion JPEG cards designed for nonlinear video editing, the AV/Master can't capture raw video and compresses all video in motion JPEG format. Though our PCI Bus Gateway system and ProMax hard drive could have handled more throughput, the AV/Master maxed out at about 2.6 MB/s at the 320×240 capture resolution, a compression ratio of around 2.6 to 1.

At its native capture resolution of 352×240, Broadway maxed out at about 1.1 MB/s, a compression ratio of around 7:1. While the captured video may appear visually lossless to the eye, once again, any deviation from the original information creates noise that hinders MPEG's compression algorithms.

Note that MPEGator doesn't suffer from this double compression loss. Like all real-time MPEG-1 encoders, the Darim product outputs a 150 KB/s bitstream that can be easily be stored to disk without additional compression.

And Another Thing   One characteristic of all the reviewed capture systems is the inability to handle component analog input, the highest quality format output from the BetaSP deck used during the review. Like most $1000 capture cards, the FAST AV/Master we used to capture video for the software encoders and Broadway and MPEGator all support S-Video input, still fairly high quality, but not as clean as component.

Let's review. High-end systems directly convert and store the output of digital decks in a fundamentally loss-free transaction. Our low-end products input S-Video rather than component, digitize the old-fashioned way complete with approximation error, and two of the three types of systems use a lossy compression algorithm to shrink the video for storage to disk.

Hmmmm. Bet you can't wait to see how it all turned out.

Capture—The Subjective   Since MPEGator compressed to final MPEG format, it was difficult to isolate capture performance from the other two processes in the compression food chain. Not so with the FAST AV/Master or Broadway.

We reviewed raw footage from both sources, concentrating on our final comparison clips. In both instances, we were surprised at the amount of color distortion and loss, but not artifacts, in the original captured video.

For example, in a sky sequence showing an amusement park parachute ride, we noted slight blotchy patches of pink and yellow bleeding from the parachutes, while cabling was slightly blurry and indistinct. In a high-quality studio sequence we noticed faint pinkish tinges in the background gray wall. Uncompressed text over water showed extreme text degradation.

Since much of this didn't show up in tests of higher quality input systems, we can only presume that they relate to the S-Video format used during capture. In truth, given the often challenging quality submitted to the encoder, we were impressed by the final results. For this reason, where appropriate, we included the raw captured video with the compressed clips to show how well the encoders dealt with this flawed video.

Another consideration is a system's ability to adjust video offset, or the placement of the video within the capture board's fixed capture window. Sometimes the analog source doesn't precisely match up with the capture window, pushing the video slightly off center and usually creating a band of black pixels along one of the video edges. Darim's MPEGator provides a video offset control, but Broadway doesn't, resulting in a three- or four-pixel band around the bottom of all video sequences.

Finally, both systems provide hue, saturation, brightness, and contrast slider bars but no precise digital values. This makes it extremely difficult to reproduce settings that had worked previously.

Preprocessing

In essence, preprocessing techniques make video more "compressible." In contrast to the numerous techniques used by service bureaus, like antialiasing, interframe noise filters, and intraframe blur filters, only one reviewed product, Broadway, preprocessed at all, applying a slight median filter during capture.

Median filters average the values of surrounding pixels, in many ways reversing noise created during capture and increasing both interframe and intraframe redundancy. On high-motion shots, filtering is very effective, since it homogenizes the fast-moving frames, making them easier to compress. The downside is that filtering can also smooth edges, making high-contrast video like talking heads look blurry (see Figure 14.1). Even on these shots, however, filtering smooths the background walls, minimizing artifacts and noise.

Compression

The basic building block of an MPEG file is called the Group of Pictures, or GOP, comprising of three kinds of frames: intra or I frames, predicted or P frames, and bidirectionally interpolated, or B frames. Most MPEG encoders work with GOPs of between 12 and 30 frames.

Interframe Compression Management   MPEG uses two techniques during encoding: interframe and intraframe compression. *Inter*frame compression eliminates redundant information *between* frames, working with regions that don't change significantly in a GOP sequence.

*Intra*frame compression is performed entirely within an individual frame, without reference to others. Like the still image standard JPEG, MPEG uses the discrete cosign transform (DCT) algorithm for interframe compression. DCT is a "lossy" compressor that discards information dur-

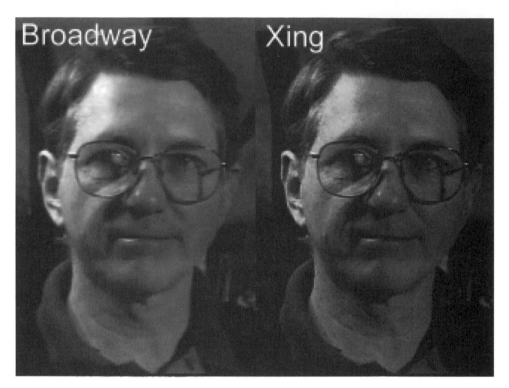

Figure 14.1   Broadway's filtering during capture creates a fuzzy, gauzy
talking head that looked better on Hedy Lamarr than Ken
Santucci, president of Four Palms Video, who supplied several
test clips. Xing, which compressed without filtering, is much
sharper.

ing compression, degrading image quality, usually in the form of artifacts
or blockiness.

All GOPs start with an I frame, which serves as a reference for all
subsequent frames in the GOP and also as an entry point for random access
into the MPEG file. For these reasons, only intraframe compression is
applied to I frames, not interframe compression.

In contrast, encoders apply both forms of compression to P and B frames,
eliminating redundant regions in the frame with interframe compression
first, then using intraframe compression to compress the balance. While
compressing P frames, the encoder searches for redundancies in the closest

previous I or P frame. With the bidirectional B frames, the encoder searches for redundancies in the closest previous and future I or P frame. Figure 14.2 illustrates how it works mechanically.

All MPEG frames are divided into 16×16 pixel blocks called macro blocks. During interframe compression, the encoder searches for exact or near matches between the frame being compressed and its reference frame or frames. Blocks that don't change are essentially ignored. Blocks that change are compressed using intraframe compression.

MPEG encoders seek to maximize interframe compression because it creates less image degradation than intraframe compression. In one commonly used technique, called motion compensation, the encoder starts searching at the original block location and then expands the search pattern to other macro blocks. If the encoder finds the identical block in another location in the reference frame, which happens frequently in panning and other motion sequences, it stores the block location, allowing the decoder to refer to that block during decompression.

Real-time encoders are often forced to use limited search patterns to operate in real time. In contrast, software encoders and even two-pass systems operate in non-real time and can extend the search to all macro blocks in the reference frame(s), which should improve comparative quality.

GOP Management   High-end MPEG encoders have great flexibility regarding GOP management. The most basic level is the number of frames in the GOP, known as the "N" value, and the interval between P frames, usually

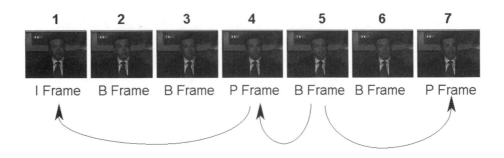

Figure 14.2   All MPEG encoders, low and high end, compress the finished video to the now familiar I, B, P sequence.

expressed as the "M" value. High-end systems often change the frame order or duration, or input I frames at scene changes or where necessary to maximize quality.

In contrast, as shown in Tables 14.4 and 14.5, most low-end encoders use fixed GOP sizes and M intervals, and only one, Broadway, had the ability to input I frames at scene changes.

We tested the various systems' abilities to handle rapid scene changes by encoding a video file with hard cuts every 28 frames. Figure 14.3 shows partial results. On the extreme left-hand side is Vitec, our worst performer, showing extreme blockiness. Broadway, in the middle, should have won going away with automatic scene detection, but placed third. MPEGator, which as a real-time system should have had the toughest job, won hands down.

No system can avoid artifacts all the time, they're a simple fact of life in high motion video. This is especially true in high motion sequences of multiframe duration and interframe changes that are significant, but not dramatic enough to qualify as a scene change. We tested overall GOP management by measuring how long it took for the system to "clean up" artifacts in high motion video, stepping through a high motion video frame by frame and counting the number of frames that exhibited artifacts after a major scene change.

 Figure 14.3 The good, the bad, and the ugly. How the different encoding systems compressed the initial frame after a hard cut.

Figure 14.4 is the third frame after a dramatic scene change with the original included to show detail. Xing, in a rare bad performance, rated at the bottom on this image, while Broadway, more because of filtering (see below) than GOP control, exhibited the least blockiness. Overall, however, this is one area where the service bureaus clearly outperformed the low-end entries, with none of the encoders returning to good quality inside seven or eight frames.

Other Tests

While the tests listed above tended to be related to the various characteristics under discussion, several tests measured overall performance.

Noise/Artifacts We compared overall quality of two scenes, a studio shot against a gray background and an action sequence, focusing on both background noise and artifacts. Figure 14.5 shows the best and the worst

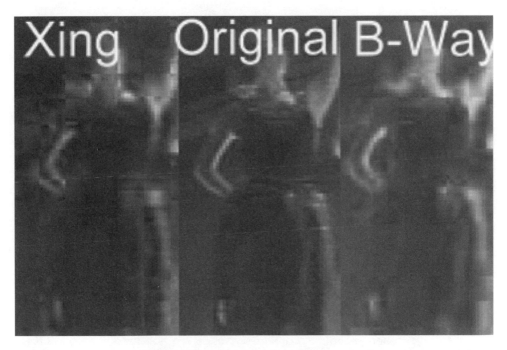

 Figure 14.4 Cleaning up after a major transition was a chore that none of our low-end encoders performed particularly well.

of artifacts and blockiness found in the action sequence. Rather than comparing identical frames in this test, we compared the *most* artifacted frame in the sequence.

We compared the videos by stepping through frame by frame using the ActiveMovie player and also at full speed, full screen using Sigma Design's RealMagic Ultra.

Text against Noisy Background   Measured text applied against the ocean. Best and worst are shown in Figure 14.6, in addition to the original frame showing the poor quality of the source materials used by the software encoders. Table 14.1 summarizes the results of all quality-related tests.

As you can see, Xing was the clear quality winner, beating the pack in both still frame and moving quality. Broadway and MPEGator flip-flopped, with MPEGator winning the still image competition and Broadway winning the motion. Since motion is obviously more important, we gave the No. 2 position to Broadway.

Figure 14.5   Speed kills. Interframe compression, that is. Here we see the best and the worst on this water slide sequence. Xing was absolutely phenomenal through this sequence; we had to look hard to find this bad frame. In contrast, Vitec and most others were blocky and distorted all the way through.

Table 14.1 Quality rankings by encoder.

Company	CeQuad	Darim (M-Gator)	Data Trans	Ulead	Vitec	Xing
Still Image Tests						
Face (Figure 14.1)	4	3	2	5	6	1
Hard Cut (Figure 14.3)	5	1	3	4	6	2
Water (Figure 14.5)	5	3	2	4	6	1
Text (Figure 14.6)	2	1	6	4	6	3
Total Score	**16**	**8**	**13**	**17**	**24**	**7**
Ranking	**4**	**2**	**3**	**5**	**6**	**1**
Real Time - MediaMatics Player						
Action	4	3	2	5	5	1
Talking head	2 (tie)	2 (tie)	2 (tie)	6	5	1
Subtotal	**6**	**5**	**4**	**11**	**10**	**2**
Real Time - RealMagic Ultra						
Action	3	4	2	6	5	1
Talking head	4	3	2	6	5	1
Subtotal	**7**	**7**	**4**	**12**	**10**	**2**
Total Score	**13**	**12**	**8**	**23**	**20**	**4**
Ranking	**4**	**3**	**2**	**6**	**5**	**1**
Overall Rank	**4**	**3**	**2**	**6**	**5**	**1**

CeQuadrat ranked fourth in both still and motion quality, placing fourth overall. Vitec placed fifth, but its still image quality was so far behind the pack that it is difficult to recommend. Bringing up the rear was Ulead, primarily because of playback incompatibilities with both ActiveMovie and RealMagic Ultra.

Figure 14.6   It's easy to see why none of the software encoders performed well in this test, since even the original footage captured by the FAST AV/Master was distorted. The MPEGator performed remarkably well on this sequence, showing the benefits of avoiding double compression. Vitec, once again, trailed the pack.

Service Bureau Comparisons

On the talking head sequences, the differences between Xing's MPEG encoder and the higher quality service bureaus were surprisingly small. On both the still image and real-time playback tests, Xing actually scored higher than the Sony RTE-3000B, a $75,000 real time MPEG-1 encoding system popular among service bureaus (Figure 14.7).

As you would expect, Xing's bubble burst when higher motion, tougher-to-compress clips entered the equation. Through judicious use of filtering, GTE made it through the same sequence with nary a blocky artifact (Figure 14.8). Motion tests revealed many discrete sections where most service bureaus outperformed Xing, but the differences were subtle and limited in duration. While you may not want to encode your million dollar title with Xing, it certainly is acceptable for virtually all in-house encoding and commercial encoding of nonchallenging footage. Time permitting, of course.

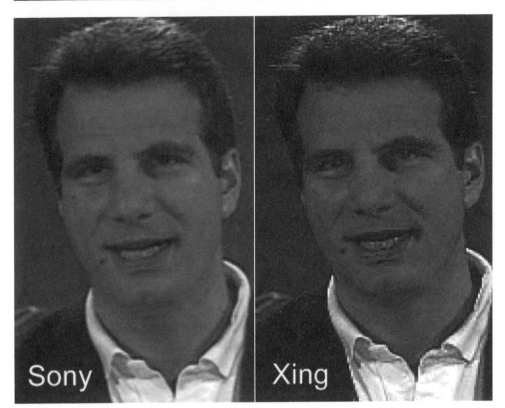

Figure 14.7   Our quality winner, Xing, compared to Sony's $75,000 RTE-3000B real-timed encoder. Xing performs well on this easy-to-impress clip.

COMPATIBILITY

Using the Diamond Stealth 3D 2000, we tested compatibility with CompCore's SoftPEG software MPEG player, MediaMatics' MPEG Arcade player, and Microsoft's ActiveMovie, which uses technology licensed from MediaMatics. We then tested playback compatibility with Sigma Design's RealMagic Ultra hardware MPEG decoder. We noted the following irregularities:

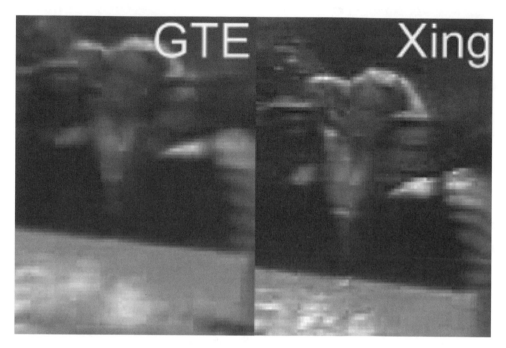

Figure 14.8   The stuff hits the fan on this higher motion clip, where service bureaus output higher quality than Xing, especially in real-time playback tests.

Ulead

- *ActiveMovie:* First 100 (approximate) frames played smoothly, then video froze and audio continued without problem. Problem occurred with *all tested videos.*
- *MediaMatics/RealMagic Ultra:* Distorted playback from the start. Movies played very quickly for short bursts and then stopped to wait for the music to catch up.

Darim MPEGator

- *MediaMatics, ActiveMovie:* First few frames played back very quickly and then video started playing normally. Where most other technologies dropped frames smoothly, Darim's dropped frames created a pulsing effect.

- *MediaMatics:* Three tests would not open, generating the following error: "MMSYSTEM277 A problem occurred in initializing MCI. Try restarting Windows." Restarting Windows didn't help, and files played normally with the other decoders.

CeQuadrat, Data Translations, Vitec, Xing

No exceptions noted.

Table 14.2 Playback tests from the hard drive of a Gateway Pentium 133 equipped with Diamond's Stealth 3D 2000.

Company	CeQuad	Darim (M-Gator)	Data Trans	Ulead	Vitec	Xing
CompCore	30	30	30	30	30	30
ActiveMovie	29.7	27.1	28.5	3	29.7	29.2
MediaMatics Arcade Player	29.7	28.8	29	2.9	29.7	29.4
Compatibility rating	satisfactory	unsatisfactory	satisfactory	unsatisfactory	satisfactory	satisfactory

OPERATIONAL CONSIDERATIONS

System usability closely follows video quality as a critical prepurchase consideration. The individual reviews describe program operation in detail. Here are some highlights from the features table that illuminate the respective capabilities of the reviewed products.

Batch Processing

Batch processing is the ability to queue multiple files for overnight or weekend compression. You would think that the lengthy compression times characteristic of the software encoders would make batch processing a necessity, and thankfully, three of four software developers felt the same way. Vitec was the only product without batch processing.

You would also think that the various encoders would make it fairly simple to select one compression template or group of settings and then select all your files at once and compress them. Not so. Only one program, Ulead, enabled batch loading, shown in Figure 14.9. After setting all compression parameters, it took Ulead four keystrokes to load all files for compression. It took other programs over 80. How's that for a difference in usability?

Encoding Functions

The basic encoding function is AVI to MPEG, using the AVI file's audio and video components as the source for the same two MPEG streams. Also

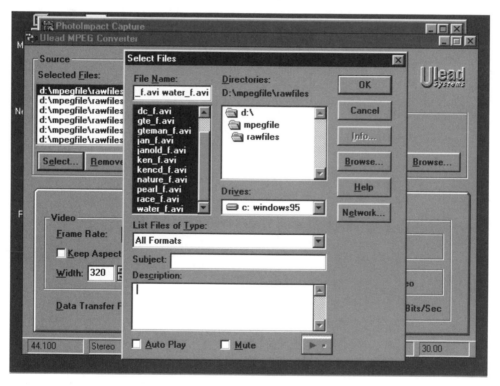

Figure 14.9   You wouldn't think that in 1997 we'd be bragging about a product's ability to load multiple files in one step. Nonetheless, here we are, bragging about Ulead, since it's the only product that does it.

useful is the ability to separately encode audio and video from two different sources and then multiplex the audio/video content into one MPEG system stream.

Ulead's MPEG Converter is unique in its ability to convert MPEG-encoded assets back to AVI or WAV files. Although it's never optimal to use such highly compressed materials as a source file for AVI compression, sometimes you don't have a choice, and this feature has come in handy on several occasions.

Video Input Adjustments (Broadway/Darim only)

Both Darim and Broadway provide controls for adjusting incoming analog video, which is *good*. Unfortunately, neither provides precise digital values, which is *bad*. Adjustments to brightness, contrast, saturation, and hue are among the most sensitive we make in our relentless pursuit of top-quality video, and it's really hard to duplicate a location on the slider bar (Figure 14.10).

On the other hand, Darim did include video offset controls with precise values that allowed us to center the video within the capture screen and avoid those messy black pixel blocks you get when your video is off center. Pity that Broadway didn't.

Inputs

As we've noted, AVI files are the basic building blocks for the software encoders. CeQuadrat takes this a step further by accepting FLI and FLC animation files, IFF, BMP, TGA, and JPEG files. On the audio front, CeQuadrat also accepts AIF, IFF, and WAV formats.

If you decide against CeQuadrat, you can duplicate these functions in most video editing programs, which generally also accept multiple video and audio input formats. You would assemble your assets in the editing program and then output a raw AVI file to input into the MPEG encoder.

On the hardware front, the focus switches to the type of signal input into the capture card. As mentioned previously, all three boards accept S-Video signals as well as composite, ideal for working with lower end formats like S-Video and Hi-8.

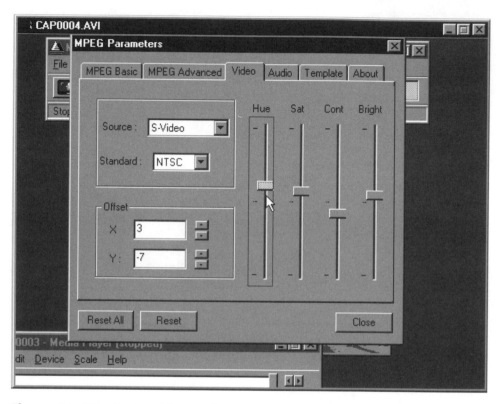

Figure 14.10   Darim video configuration screen with incoming brightness and color control, sans digital values, and video offset.

Outputs

Perhaps the most significant output option is square pixel format, which addresses the fundamental aspect ratio differences between NTSC and computer-based video. The "official" NTSC video resolution is defined by CCIR 601 resolution to be 720×480 pixels, while computers use the familiar 640×480 full screen.

When developing the MPEG standard, the MPEG committee members chose 352×240 as the Standard Image Format (SIF) resolution, meaning that the *entire NTSC video image* is subsampled down to that resolution for compression. When playing the image back on an NTSC monitor, the image looks normal. However, when playing the 352×240 image on a VGA monitor, it looks stretched by about 10 percent—because it is stretched by about 10 percent (see Figure 14.11).

For this reason, the MPEG committee defined a "square pixel" mode for squeezing the video during playback to achieve the proper aspect ratio, leaving a slot in the MPEG file header to tell the decoder. The problem is that squeezing video in real time can dramatically affect the display rate of software-only decoders.

Darim handles this with an optional "square pixel" output that actually produces a properly formatted 320×240 file. If you capture at 320×240 and encode from there, you should have no problems with any of the software encoders. This leaves Broadway, which doesn't support square pixel mode in its current release but plans to in an upgrade scheduled to ship by early 1997.

Figure 14.11   Ken looks happier on the left, but the wider smile is strictly courtesy of the stretching effect of mapping NTSC video to VGA screens. Using square pixel mode, on the right, corrects the aspect ratio.

Compression Controls

The abilities to input I frames and change the GOP sequence are some of the chief weapons of service bureau compressionists and standard features on higher end products. We would like to see more low-end encoders provide these capabilities as well, but only if well hidden from the average user.

Presets/Templates

Most publishers interested in low-end encoders probably want to output plain-Jane MPEG files in a configuration most likely to play back successfully on their target system. Presets are standard configurations provided by the developer that enable one-button compression to a predetermined format. For example, if you select CeQuadrat's Single Spin NTSC preset you should feel pretty safe that your video will play on most single-spin systems.

Templates are similar to presets in concept, but typically let you create custom capture and compression configurations for your own specialized requirements and then save the template for later use. For example, the MPEGator provide a template feature which we used to customize capture sequences for high and low motion videos (Figure 14.12).

Table 14.3 contains our ranking for feature set, ease of use, and compression times for Broadway and the software-only encoders.

Table 14.3 Feature and ease of use rankings, and compression time for 13-second file on a Pentium 133.

Company	CeQuad	Darim (M-Gator)	Data Trans	Ulead	Vitec	Xing
Feature Set	good	good	limited	limited	good	limited
Ease of Use	poor	average	good	outstanding	poor	average
Compression time	11:58	real time	1:08	16:42	12:15	9:30

Conclusion

Overall, if you've got the time, Xing's got your encoder from a price and video quality standpoint. If you need real time, Darim is your only option,

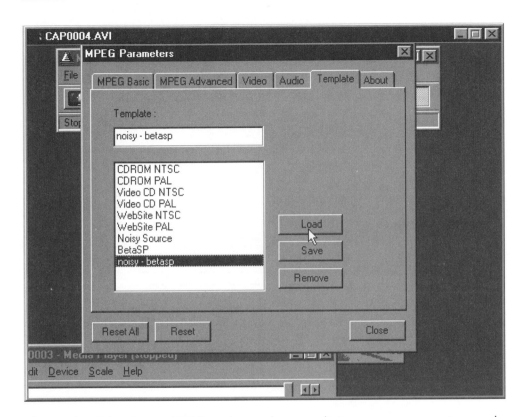

Figure 14.12 Darim MPEGator's templates made it easy to save capture and compression settings for later use with the same or similar material.

but the slight incompatibilities and irregularities we noticed during playback tests are a bit scary for commercial titles. Broadway performed well on all tests; we just wish they had made filtering an option rather than a requirement and addressed the square pixel issue.

Beyond these three the pickings get slim. CeQuadrat placed fourth in quality, rated poorly on ease of use, and costs $100 more than Xing. Ulead needs to address its compatibility problems before MPEG Converter is ready for all but the most restricted use, and despite the wealth of options, we could never get Vitec's quality to match up to the others.

Oh well. Given the handicaps these products face—the rigors of digitization, double compression, and low-end analog formats—we were impressed to find three that produced better than acceptable MPEG quality.

Table 14.4 Hardware Reviews.

Company	Darim	Data Translations
Product name	MPEGator $995 without audio ($1495 as tested)	Broadway $995
Phone/fax	508-481-3700 fax 508-624-6782	ph 800-432-8905 ph 213-637-1700 fax 213-637-1705
Address	100 Locke Drive Marlboro, MA 01752	Korea
Web page	www.b-way.com	www.darvision.com
Basics		
Inputs, Video		
S-Video	yes	yes
Composite Input	no	yes
NTSC/PAL/SECAM	NTSC/PAL	NTSC/PAL
Audio		
Audio in	yes	no
Audio out	yes	no
Outputs, Form Factor		
352×240 (NTSC SIF)	yes	yes
352×288 (PAL SIF)	yes	yes
320×240 square pixel (NTSC)	yes	by 6/97
176×144 (PAL QSIF)	yes	yes
160×120 (NTSC QSIF)	yes	yes
160×120 square pixel	yes	by 6/97
Output streams	Video only, system layer with video, muxed audio/video and video CD	Video CD (by September)
Bandwidths	Up to around 400 KB/s	1, 2, 4XCD, hard disk, video CD and Internet format

Table 14.4   *(continued)*

Company	Darim	Data Translations
Frame rates	29.97 (NTSC)/25 (PAL)	29.97 (NTSC)/25 (PAL)
Features		
Ships with decoder	no	no
Batch operation	no	no
Machine control	no	no
Capture Adjustments		
Hue, sat, bright, contrast	yes	yes
digital values	no	no
Bit rate control	yes	yes
Video offset	yes	no
Templates/user configurable	yes/yes	no
Filtering		
Does filtering include:		
Interframe (temporal) filter	no	no
Low-pass filter (spatial)	no	yes
Softening filter (spatial)	no	yes
Antialiasing	no	yes
Filtering optional or hardcoded	n.a.	currently hard coded, optional by 12/96
Compression		
Compression speed	real time	5:1
Default GOP (e.g., 12, 15, 30)	GOP, P	15
Default B Interval (e.g. 1, 2)	no	2
Automatic I frame insertion?	no	yes
User Available settings		
Set GOP size	yes	no
Set B frame Interval	yes	no
Place I frames	no	no

Broadway: $995, Data Translations

Author's Note   Just prior to the completion of the book, Data Translations released new software that allows filtering to be disabled upon capture. While we had time to capture additional files included on the CD-ROM, we didn't have time to redo our comparisons or change the review.

The only video file affected by the new software is Figure 14.1, where the sample files, like all in this chapter, are included in their own subdirectory. In the \chap14\fig14_1 subdirectory, the filtered file is named broadfil.mpg, while the nonfiltered file is named broadnfl.mpg. Sorry for any inconvenience.

Affordably priced at $995, Data Translations' two-pass encoder, Broadway, combines an engaging interface with the latest C-Cube compression engine to produce better than average quality that sailed through all compatibility testing. A comprehensive manual, quick start guide, and tutorial round out a package ideal for the beginner but without some of the advanced controls an experienced compressionist might like.

Configuration   Broadway is a PCI bus master half card with S-Video and composite video inputs, but no audio inputs, relying upon the system sound card for this task. Broadway is the first product using C-Cube's CLM4110 VideoRISC processor for capture and MPEG encoding. A third-generation chipset, the CLM4110 contains C-Cube's most advanced MPEG compression algorithms, as well as features like automatic scene detection and filtering. Broadway ships with composite video and stereo audio cables, but no S-Video cable, so you'll need to purchase one if you're using S-Video.

By way of software, Broadway ships with a simple capture/encoding interface developed by Data Translations and Ulead's MediaStudio 2.5, Video Edition, for more comprehensive editing. Broadway is a true 32-bit codec and won't work with 16-bit programs like VidEdit.

Note that while you can edit video captured by Broadway in MediaStudio, you can't compress to final MPEG format from there. You have to save the edited video into I-frame-only format and compress using Broadway's utility, adding another compression generation to all frames edited in MediaStudio.

Painless Installation   Broadway could be the "poster child" for plug 'n play, installing on our loaded test bed without a hitch. A look at the required system resources revealed why—Broadway requires only one memory address and no DMA channels or interrupts, a nice departure from the I/O-hungry boards of yesteryear.

Seeking a mass market audience, Data Translation designed their capture and encoding utility to optimize simplicity, at the cost of some functionality. They also designed in some thorns characteristic of a first-generation product.

The capture/encoding utility is an easy-to-use program built around a preview window, so you won't need an external NTSC monitor for capture. The software also lets you adjust incoming video hue, saturation, intensity, and contrast, always a nice feature, but the controls were slider bars only, without precise digital values, making it difficult to experiment with small changes.

We also noted that all captured video attained a slight greenish tinge when played back from the Broadway utility, which Data Translations attributes to a proprietary color space converter. Whatever the reason, when adjusting these parameters to achieve perfect capture fidelity, compress to final MPEG before assessing the results—don't rely on the initial captured video.

Broadway doesn't provide capture templates or presets, so you can't save the values it takes so long to perfect. If you're working varying source videos that each require customization, consider taking screen captures of the optimal settings to help duplicate them in the future.

Changing capture drives is a bit of a pain, because the default is to capture to the drive where you installed the software. For example, if you install on C drive and want to capture to SCSI drive D, the manual tells you to reinstall the software on D, a bizarre result. Data Translations had already developed a workaround when we called—simply load an AVI file into the Broadway utility from the drive you want to capture to, and the software will capture future files to that drive.

Other capture controls include data rate, which captures up to a maximum of 70 MB/minute, or roughly 1.1 MB/s. Compared to the FAST AV/Master's 2.6 MB/s, this relatively low rate raised our eyebrows, but didn't appear to adversely effect capture or compressed video quality.

Broadway captures only at SIF resolution, 352×240, so you can't use Broadway to capture for compression to other formats, like Indeo or Cinepak, without scaling the video down to 320×240. More important, this, combined with Broadway's lack of a square pixel option, prevents the board from outputting perspective-corrected 320×240 files.

Two chips digitize and compress the video. The Philips SAA 7111 analog-to-digital converter is a popular part that digitizes the analog source, while the CLM4010 performs the I frame compression. One feature of the CLM4010 is spatial filtering and antialiasing, which Data Translations enables for all captures. In English, this means that Broadway filters all incoming video, whether it needs it or not, which affected some of our quality ratings.

Broadway doesn't provide video offset controls, so all compressed files had a four or five pixel black boundary on the bottom. Broadway also provides no control over the analog source, not even the laserdisc and/or VISCA controls provided in Windows 95, so you capture the old-fashioned way—roll tape, press start at the appropriate moment, and escape to stop

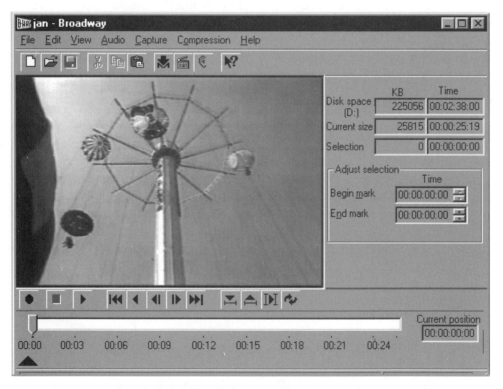

Figure 14.13   Broadway's capture and editing screen provides real-time status messages during capture (upper right) and basic cut-and-paste editing via the controls and timeline on the bottom.

the capture. During capture, the screen updates in near real time and the program posts useful capture statistics like the size and time of the current capture and remaining disk space (Figure 14.13).

As a two-pass system, Broadway captures video as an AVI file in I frame only, "editable MPEG." This means you can edit the file in any true 32-bit Video for Windows editor. MediaStudio worked like a charm, though we experienced some minor anomalies in Adobe Premiere 4.2 that didn't affect program operation.

Editing/Compression Broadway atones for the lack of machine control by making it exceptionally simple to trim "heads" and "tails," or unwanted frames at the start and end of the video. The utility also provides simple file inserts and fade to and fade from black transitions, but you'll have to use MediaStudio for more advanced transitions, titling, and special effects.

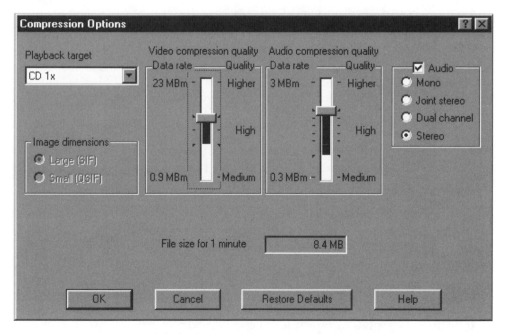

Figure 14.14   Broadway provides minimal compression controls, which may frustrate advanced users but prevents novices from producing videos that won't play on their target platforms.

On the compression front, Broadway provides six presets for 1, 2, and 4X CD-ROM drives, hard disk, Video CD, and an Internet format that scales the video down to QSIF resolution (176×120). There is no option for square pixel output, probably Broadway's most significant feature gap. See Figure 14.14.

Audio presets include mono, stereo, dual channel, and joint stereo. Broadway also provides an audio gain control that lets you adjust postcapture audio levels, a nice feature that saves having to recapture.

After selecting a preset, slider bars let you adjust both video and audio data rates, with a window updating the combined data rate per minute. Data rates range from 100 kbps to 3 mbps, or approximately 12.5 KB/s to 375 KB/s.

Broadway defaults to a GOP size of 15 and an N interval of two, placing two B frames between each P frame. You can't change either setting, though the CLM4010 can automatically detect and place I frames at scene changes.

We compressed many files with Broadway but were unable to duplicate the claimed 3X conversion rate on our Pentium 133. Still, the 5X rate felt supersonic compared to the 60:1 ratios characteristic of the software-only products.

Output Quality   Broadway's capture fidelity was generally very good, roughly matching the FAST AV/Master. As with the AV/Master, sky sequences showed hints of yellow, and the gray background in the talking head shot showed slight hints of pink.

The filtering performed by the CLM-4010 definitely paid dividends in the action sequences, making the high motion frames much simpler to compress. This manifested as fewer blocky regions and less artifacts than most other encoders, with Broadway placing second to Xing.

On the talking head clip, however, filtering created a soft, gauzy effect reminiscent of close-ups of the female leads in movies from the '40s and '50s. While that worked for Garbo, it may not be appropriate for your CEO—male or female. This effect definitely detracted from talking head quality, with Xing besting Broadway because of image sharpness. We found ourselves wondering how Broadway would have performed with filtering disabled and capture data rate bumped up to FAST AV/Master levels.

Filtering also totally obliterated the detail on the text over water shot. If you have some high-contrast detail that must be preserved in the final MPEG file, tough to do in the best of cases, Broadway may not be a good option.

Broadway placed third in the hard cut quality tests, surprising given the CLM-4010's ability to identify scene changes and automatically insert I frames. Using FutureTel's MPEG Analyzer, we verified that I frames were inserted, but saw that at an average size of about 9 KB, inserted I frames were much smaller than normal sequenced I frames, which ranged from 15 to 20 KB. Apparently, inserted I frame size was limited to maintain the data rate, resulting in a frame too small to describe the scene without degrading quality.

Compatibility We experienced no problems playing back Broadway files on any of our test bed decoders, which was an expected ancillary benefit of having the CLM-4010 chip perform the compression. While not fastest on the decode side, Broadway was certainly respectable, and publishers should have no qualms about distributing the video this board produced.

Since Broadway doesn't have onboard audio, sound synchronization could have been a problem. To test this, we captured and compressed an 18-minute clip which ended with a talking head sequence. We played the clip on several decoders and synchronization was perfect.

Conclusion Several upgrades were in the works while we were testing and writing this review. By the time you read this review, filtering will be a user-selectable option, square pixel output should be available, and, via an upgraded C-Cube chip, Broadway may be capable of real-time MPEG encoding.

Even without these improvements, however, Broadway is an excellent first cut at a product designed for the mass market. If you don't need absolute real time and can't wait for Xing's compression times, Broadway is probably your best option.

Broadway: $995
Data Translations, Inc.
Commercial Products Group
100 Locke Drive
Marlboro, MA 01752
Ph 508-481-3700/fax 508-624-6782
www.b-way.com

MPEGator: $995 and $1495, Darim Vision Co., Ltd.

The only real-time MPEG-1 encoder in this review, Darim's $1495 MPEGator ($995 without audio hardware) produced credible quality video but stumbled slightly in usability and especially compatibility tests. While this may rule out use for commercial titles, MPEGator is exceptionally well suited for prototyping and similar in-house uses.

Physically, MPEGator is a half slot PCI Busmaster board with an MPEG encoder daughtercard equipped with two-chip MPEG encoder from Samsung. A fan and heat exchanger glued to the Samsung Chips add breadth to the profile, making the board difficult to install in narrow PCI slots.

Unlike Broadway, MPEGator handles both audio and video onboard, with S-Video and composite video inputs and 3.5 stereo minijacks for audio input and output. While unclear from the manual, MPEGator works with your sound card and doesn't replace it. MPEGator also provides no MPEG playback functions, and the interface calls the installed MCI-compatible decoder to preview the video.

MPEGator ships with its own capture and compression utility, essentially consisting of a menu/icon bar and detached preview and playback windows. Unlike more expensive real-time MPEG encoders, MPEGator doesn't provide machine control, not even access to the laserdisc VISCA drivers featured in Windows 95. A manual, stereo audio cable, and composite video cable round out the bundle.

In terms of outputs, MPEGator can produce MPEG system streams (audio/video), MPEG video streams, and VideoCD streams directly, with the latter fixed in terms of bit rate and resolution. Resolutions include 352×240 and 176×120, and 320×240 and 160×120 square pixel mode, which minimizes file distortion. Maximum compressed data rate is about 400 Mbytes per second.

Installation was completely painless, courtesy of plug 'n play. We installed the board, turned on the computer, and were capturing video within five minutes.

Program Operation   MPEGator provides NTSC and PAL compression templates for VideoCD, CD-ROM, WebSites, and Noisy Source video. You can also add your own templates, which is the simplest way to coordinate all program controls.

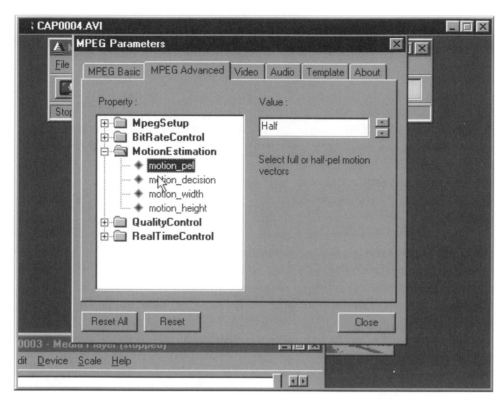

Figure 14.15 Darim offered almost complete access to chip-based compression options but little documentation and not enough templates demonstrating how to optimize quality for different types of sequences. This made these features inaccessible to all but the most experienced MPEG compressionists.

In addition to bit rate and resolution controls, Darim provides virtually complete access to all chip-based compression parameters, including inputs controlling motion estimation and the allocation of GOP bandwidth to I, B, and P frames. Unfortunately, Darim doesn't explain how to manipulate the parameters for noisy, high motion, low motion, or other video types, leaving the user to experiment potentially ad nauseam. All but the most adventuresome are better off starting with an individual template and working toward a new composite suited for their video.

Since there was no machine control, it was impossible to automatically insert I frames at scene changes. We parsed through several MPEGator files containing hard cuts and found no evidence of scene change detection or I frame insertion.

Darim provides slider bars for adjusting the hue, saturation, contrast, and brightness of incoming video but no digital readouts, making it difficult to experiment with the minor modifications required to normalize the video. The program also provides incoming audio volume controls, useful for devices like laserdiscs and VCRs that may not have volume controls. Another useful control was the video offset, which we used to center video in the capture window and avoid lines of black pixels like those we experienced with Broadway.

MPEGator can also accelerate the MPEG compression of normal AVI files from video editors like Premiere. We didn't experiment with this technique since we deinstalled the AV/Master prior to installing MPEGator. As with most motion JPEG cards, you can't work with files created by AV/Master without the board being present in the computer.

Capture   Since MPEGator doesn't provide machine control, you capture by rolling tape, watching the preview window and using VCR-like controls to start and stop the capture. While audio didn't play during capture, the video update was quite fast, eliminating the need for an external NTSC monitor. Darim posted elapsed capture time and the number of frames captured and dropped frames in real time, which helped monitor the capture process.

We started capturing using the CDROM NTSC template, but experienced buffer overruns when capturing some of our water sequences, so switched to the Noisy Video template for these videos. We ran into the same problem when we brightening certain videos, which sometimes made it difficult to brighten certain sequences to the appropriate levels.

In addition to the discrete clips, we captured an 18-minute sequence to test synchronization, which was solid. During these tests, however, we noticed that MPEGator had difficulty with deep male voices, which sometimes were distorted during playback. We fixed this easily via the audio gain control, but you could run into problems compressing longer clips containing a range of voices.

Because there is no machine control, you'll probably have two or three seconds of wasted video at the front and back of every clip, which you'll want to trim with an MPEG Video editor. We used Vitec's Video Clip

MPEG-1 SP, included in the MPEG Toolbox ($125), to trim our heads and tails, but the product edits at I frames only so it's accurate only to about half a second. Unless you're willing to shell out another $800 for Vitec's I, B, P frame editor, plan your shoots, edits, and captures to allow for about a second of leeway at the start and stop.

Results, Please   Overall, MPEGator placed second in our still image tests but soundly third in our motion tests behind Xing and Data Translations. This reflects MPEGator's tendency to produce crisp, clear frames laden with significant interframe noise that was evident only during real-time playback.

For example, in the low motion video, the face was clear but marred by frequent mosquitoes during real-time playback. Also apparent at 30 fps was

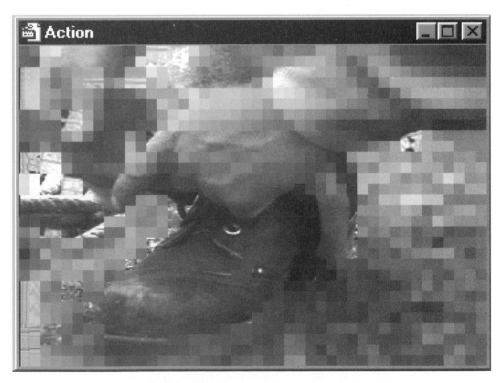

Figure 14.16   While Darim performed well in our hard cut tests, it may have been pure luck, as evidenced by this blocky mess produced by Darim on another video sequence.

a distorted band of 60 or 70 pixels in constant motion in the upper half of the video. Similarly, in the action sequence, MPEGator suffered only minor blockiness in the still frame test, placing third, but dropped to fourth in the motion tests due to high levels of background noise.

One anomaly was Darim's first-place finish in the hard cut still image test, remarkable given that we could find no I frame insertion capabilities. On another video, however, we noticed a somewhat less capable perform-ance at a scene change (Figure 14.16), so don't count on Darim to navigate scene changes with consistent aplomb.

More problematic were minor playback start-up stutters experienced with the MediaMatics and ActiveMovie players. Audio would start and the video would start slowly, then catch up with a quick burst of frames, and then play smoothly. Darim's relatively slow playback rates on these players appear to reflect these problems.

Even at its best, don't think that Darim can replace a $12,000 MPEG encoding system or even an $8000 system from established players like FutureTel. These products offer critical software features like machine control and hardware features like component or serial digital inputs and filtering. While Darim was impressive in this low-end review, quality was clearly degraded when compared to other real-time encoders.

As with a new car, it's tough to get excited about buying a first-generation real time encoder for commercial CD-ROM publishing, especially when it's equipped with a first-generation MPEG chipset. On the other hand, MPEGator is wonderfully appropriate for the vast number of limited distribution or in-house MPEG compression jobs, especially if you need real-time performance on a budget.

MPEGator: $995 (without audio; tested version with audio hardware $1,495)
Darim Vision Co., Ltd.
100 Locke Drive
Marlboro, MA 01752
Ph 800-432-8905/213-637-1700/fax213-637-1705
www.darvision.com

SOFTWARE REVIEWS

Table 14.5 Software Reviews.

Company	Ulead	Xing Technologies	CeQuadrat	Vitec
Product Name	MPEG Converter	XingMPEG Encoder	PixelShrink	MPEG Maker
Price	$249	$89	$199	$125 (component of MPEG Toolbox which also includes VideoClip MPEG SP, and CompCore Player
Phone/fax	800-858-5323 310-523-9399	ph 805-473-0145 fax 805-473-0147	ph 415-843-3780 fax 415-843-3799	941-351-9344 fax 941-351-9423
Address	970 West 190th St. Suite 520, Torrance, CA 90502	1540 West Branch Street, Arroyo Grande, CA 93420	1804 Embarcadero Road, Suite 101, Palo Alto, CA 94303	4366 Independence Ct., Suite C, Sarasota, FL 34234
Web page	www.ulead .com	www.xingtech .com	www.cequadrat .com	http://glimmer .com/vitec
Basics				
CD-ROM/disk install	CD-ROM	CD-ROM	Disk	CD-ROM
Includes player	no	yes	no	yes—compcore
Batch processing	yes	yes	yes	NO!!!!!
Functions				
AVI to MPEG	yes	yes	yes	yes
MPEG to AVI	yes	no	no	no
WAV to MPG	yes	no (yes—in 2.0)	yes	yes
MPEG to WAV	yes	no	no	no
MultiPlex	no	no (yes—in 2.0)	yes	yes

(continued)

Table 14.5 (continued)

Company	Ulead	Xing Technologies	CeQuadrat	Vitec
Program Operation	1	2	4	3
Batch load files	yes	no	no	no
Save batch list	yes	no+D68	yes	no
Edit batch list	no	yes	yes	no
Includes templates/save own template	no	yes/no (yes in 2.0)	yes/no	yes (5)/one user defined
Input file editing	trim	no	no	no
Log files	yes	yes	no	no
Display during compression	yes	optional	yes	optional
Inputs				
Video	AVI/MPEG	AVI	AVI, FLI, FLC, IFF, BMP, TGA, JPG image list	AVI
Audio	WAV/MP2	WAV	WAV, AIF, IFF, AVI	WAV
Outputs				
Frame rate	23.976, 24, 25, 29.97, 30	24, 25, 30 (29.976/23.976 in 2.0)	24, 25, 30	23.976, 24, 25, 29.97, 30, 50, 59.94, 60
Resolution	32×32/480×480	160×120—352×288 (32×32 in 2.0)	48×48/768×512	original only
Data transfer rate	60–200 KB/s	adoptive for 160×120—307,200 Kbytes	1X, 2X, White Book	256–64,000 kbps

Table 14.5 *(continued)*

Company	Ulead	Xing Technologies	CeQuadrat	Vitec
Presets				
Broadcast standard (PAL/NTSC)	no	PAL/NTSC/ Film	PAL/NTSC/ Film	no
Standard (VideoCD, CD-I, White Book)	no	White Book	White Book	no
Bit rate	no	1X, 2X/quarter screen/White Book	1X, 2X	no
Compression Parameters				
Default GOP (e.g., 12, 15, 30)	12	15 (2.0 definable)	15	adjustable
Default B Interval (e.g., 1, 2)	2	2 (2.0 definable)	2	adjustable
Automatic I frame insertion?	no	no	no	no
User-Available Settings				
Set GOP Size	no	no	no	yes
Set B frame Interval	no	no	no	yes
Place I frames	no	no	no	no

PixelShrink: $199, CeQuadrat USA, Inc.

We had high hopes for PixelShrink, CeQuadrat's $199 software MPEG encoder, which contains software written in conjunction with CD-I giant Philips. Unfortunately, the program is behind the curve in both user interface and video quality, leaving no compelling reason to chose PixelShrink over Xing, which costs $110 less.

The 32-bit PixelShrink program runs on Win 3.11 using Microsoft's 32-bit extensions, or Windows 95 or NT without them. Installing from a single floppy, the program opens up into a quarter screen application with menu and icons on top of white area that holds the batch list of processes to be performed.

PixelShrink can compress audio and/or video files to separate MPEG streams, multiplex two previously compressed streams into an MPEG file, and convert audio and video source files into a finished MPEG file in one pass. On the video front, the program accepts a variety of formats, including AVI, FLI, and FLC files and BMP, TGA, and JPG sequences. Or, you can combine all these elements via an image list file. Compatible audio formats include AVI, WAV, RAW, AIF, and IFF files.

CeQuadrat could have gone a long way toward easing the data entry burden on the rushed producer and fails to take more than baby steps. For example, the software could assume that when you input an AVI file as the video segment, you plan to use the AVI audio as well. It doesn't, and you have to enter the audio source file separately, on a separate screen.

The software could assume that when you input an AVI file for left channel audio, you plan on using the same file for the right channel. It doesn't, and you have to enter the same file twice. The software could assume that when compressing multiple files, you wanted the same compression parameters, resolution, and target subdirectory. It doesn't, and you have to enter all these compression parameters separately for each file.

In fact, where our efficiency leader, Ulead, requires only four keystrokes to load and start compressing four MPEG files, PixelShrink requires a criminal 20 keystrokes *per file*, a few less if you use the default compression parameters, but only a few. That's 80 keystrokes for our four files, 80 chances to make an error, four chances to spend 15–20 minutes or longer compressing a file to the wrong compression parameters. Fortunately, PixelShrink does allow you to create and save batch lists containing file names and compression parameters should you need to recompress.

Compression parameters are very spare, reducing flexibility, but also increasing the chances that your files will play on the majority of available players. Bit rate options include Single Speed, White Book, and Double Speed, while frame rate is controlled by the NTSC (30), PAL (25), or Film (24) dialog box. You do have significant flexibility regarding output resolu-

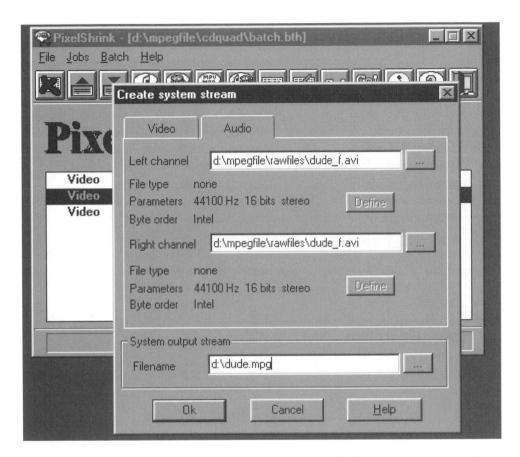

Figure 14.17 CeQuadrat complicated data entry by forcing you to enter the same AVI file in three separate windows and then reset all compression parameters, resulting in a bone-jarring 20 keystrokes for each and every file entered.

tion, which can range from 48×48 to 768×512. PixelShrink is a moderately fast encoder, compressing our 12.7-second test file in 11:58, or about 57:1 asymmetric.

Quality Overall quality was comparatively low, with CeQuadrat scoring fourth in both still image and moving quality tests. After Xing, however, the difference between second and fourth place was not substantial, and the video quality in this range was subjectively fairly good.

In our low motion videos, we noticed frequent distortion at the I and P frames, with occasional blockiness in the back gray wall. During real-time playback, the face remained fairly sharp but background noise was slightly higher than with other encoders.

CeQuadrat maintained very good color fidelity throughout the action sequence, but had real quality problems in the various high motion sequences, often obscuring faces behind pinkish macro blocks. We also noticed mosquitoes buzzing around hard-edged objects in several segments. On a positive note, PixelShrink proved compatible with all test bed decoders, and playback scores tied for fastest with Vitec.

Overall, PixelShrink's usability issues were probably more damning than its relatively low quality scoring, since the video produced was certainly commercial grade. Viewed on its own, PixelShrink does a pretty good job. Compared to Xing, however, which produces better video and is faster, cheaper, and easier to use, PixelShrink is a tough sell.

PixelShrink: $199
CeQuadrat USA, Inc.
1804 Embarcadero Road, Suite 101
Palo Alto, CA 94303
Ph 415-843-3780/fax 414-843-3799

MPEG Converter: $249, Ulead Systems, Inc.

Purely as an MPEG encoder, Ulead's $249 MPEG Converter is a nonstarter. Although clearly the easiest program to use, there were some serious user interface gaps, compression time was by far the slowest, and the compressed clips were definitely not worth the wait—video quality ranked at or near the bottom and the MPEG files were incompatible with three of four tested decoders. That said, the MPEG Converter offers some unique MPEG-to-AVI capabilities that may prove handy for those working with both formats.

MPEG Converter is a native 32-bit application that runs on Windows 3.x systems via Microsoft's 32-bit extensions, which are included on the product CD-ROM. Where all other encoders are solely AVI-to-MPEG encoders, the MPEG Converter goes both ways, converting .AVI files to MPEG format and back to .AVI format again.

If you create your MPEG files with a real-time encoder or service bureau, this feature could be the simplest way to create AVI files, though using previously compressed MPEG source video won't produce the absolute best results. You can also convert Windows audio (.WAV) files to MPEG Audio files (.MP2) and vice versa. Note, however, that you can't multiplex previously encoded MPEG video and audio files, a curious omission given the program's ability to create separate audio/video MPEG streams.

All Dressed Up   Overall, program operation is extremely simple and efficient, a model for all other products. For example, once you set your compression parameters, it takes four keystrokes to load an unlimited number of files located in the same subdirectory, where most other products required 20 or more.

You choose files from the File Select screen. To enter multiple files, you select the top file, hold down the shift key, and select the bottom file. The program assumes that you want to compress audio and video from the same source file, so then you press OK and they're entered. Nothing could be easier or more intuitive. You can also save and edit batch lists, convenient for repetitive tasks.

All basic compression parameters like frame rate (30, 29.97, 25, 24, 23.976 fps), resolution (32×32–480×480) and data rate (60–200 KB/s) were completely user selectable. Ulead was the only software encoder with a "scratch pad" feature, which functions as a minieditor allowing you to select and compress portions of files rather than simply the entire file. Also useful was the AVI File Information Screen, which provides useful file statistics.

MPEG Converter also had some baffling limitations. For example, while you can change the output target directory, you can't change the output file name. The program also lacks templates or presets, making it possible for novices to abuse the program flexibility and create files that are out of spec for their target device.

During compression, Ulead defaults to GOP size 12 and B interval two, which users can't modify. Ulead doesn't insert I frames at scene changes or otherwise customize the compressed video stream for the actual footage. Compression time was extremely slow, taking 16:42 to compress our 13.5-second test file, or about 74:1 compression time.

But Nowhere to Go   Ulead had problems with both still image and motion testing, placing fifth and sixth, respectively. In still image tests, encoding appeared to darken the video and distort smooth areas, like faces and walls, which manifested as slight blockiness and frequent mosquitoes and similar motion artifacts. Action sequences were marred by some of the worst

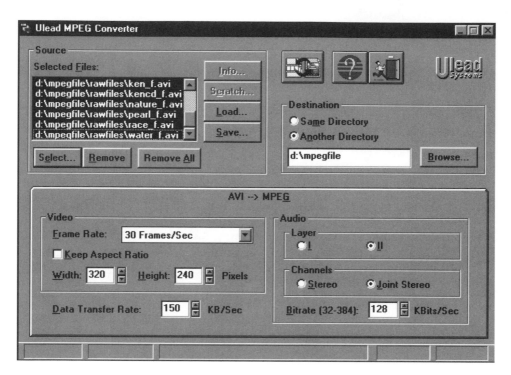

Figure 14.18   Ulead's data input screen is exceptionally easy to use, but
lacks presets and all but the most basic compression controls.

blockiness experienced, though Ulead recovered well in our scene change
testing.

Motion tests were marred by Ulead's incompatibility with our two test
decoders, Microsoft's ActiveMovie, soon to be the most widely distributed
decoder, and Sigma Design's RealMagic Ultra, from the most popular line
of hardware decoders. On both systems, Ulead files would play very
sporadically, stopping, starting, jumping, and dropping tons of frames.

Ulead produced only 3 fps with ActiveMovie and a similar figure with
MediaMatics Arcade Player (2.9), not surprising given that Microsoft licensed
ActiveMovie's MPEG player from MediaMatics. To verify our conclusions,
we tested every file compressed with the Ulead encoder with the Active-
Movie player and got similar results.

To rule out a graphics card problem, we tested the same files with the
ActiveMovie player on another system equipped with the popular Matrox

Millennium graphics card. Once again, the files would play sporadically at first and then the video would jump to the end. On a positive note, Ulead had no problem with CompCore's player on any machine, playing back at 30 fps on our test bed Pentium 133.

Despite the ease of operation, CD-ROM publishers have enough problems without allowing potential incompatibilities into the mix. With cheaper systems outputting better looking, more compatible files, it's difficult to find a scenario where the Ulead product would be your first choice for MPEG encoding. If you need to convert MPEG files to AVI format, however, it's the only game in town.

MPEG Converter: $249
Ulead Systems, Inc.
970 West 190th Street, Suite 520
Torrance, CA 90502
Ph 800-858-5323/310-523-9393/fax 310-523-9399

MPEG Maker: $125, Vitec Multimedia

Vitec Multimedia's MPEG Maker ships as a component of their $125 MPEG Toolbox. While MPEG Maker faired very poorly in all quality-related tests and was the only software encoder without batch capabilities, MPEG Toolbox may be a must buy for MPEG title developers. Not for the MPEG encoding capabilities, mind you, but for bundled MPEG editor, which proved invaluable during our testing.

MPEG Toolbox is a 16-bit program that ships on CD-ROM and includes MPEG Maker, CompCore's software player, and Video Clip MPEG SP, an MPEG editor that enables simple cuts and pastes at I frames. We used the editor extensively to clip frames from files created by MPEGator, our real-time encoder. Vitec also has a full I, B, P editor that retails for $995 that we didn't test.

MPEG Maker can perform all four basic MPEG functions; AVI video to MPEG video, AVI audio to MPEG audio, AVI file to multiplexed MPEG file, and multiplexing of previously compressed audio and video MPEG files. While the program is relatively simple to operate, there are no batch capabilities, a serious competitive disadvantage.

The program itself resembles VidEdit, basically a quarter screen video window with icons and controls above. You start by selecting an AVI file, which the program displays with audio and video file statistics.

There are five compression option presets for Fast Compression, High Quality, High Compression, MPEG Player Hardware, and the Video Maker MPEG Player and one user-definable preset. You can chose between eight frame rates ranging from 23.976 to 60. When choosing a faster frame rate, you have the option to maintain the original duration and audio synchronization or lose synch and keep all the frames.

There is no control for adjusting the original input resolution, but the system correctly recognized the 320×240 resolution and compressed accordingly. Audio options include layer one and two audio from 64 to 384 kbps.

For our comparisons, we chose the High Quality option. If you're feeling adventuresome, MPEG Maker provides an exotic range of compression

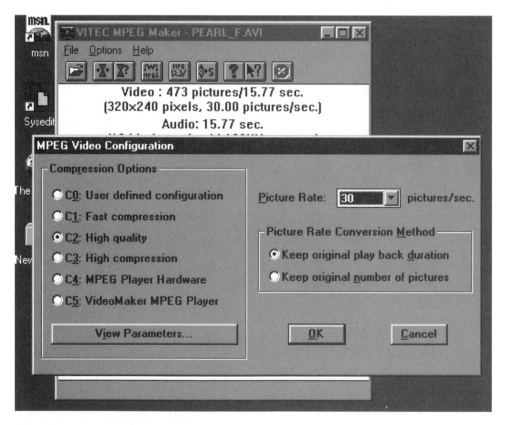

Figure 14.19   Vitec's simple application provides five presets and one user-definable configuration.

options, far more than any other software player. The more mundane (and useful) options include GOP size and B frame interval. Next you choose whether to maintain a constant data rate, useful for CD-ROM publishing, or a constant quality, appropriate for hard disk drive publishing, and the bit rate. You can even set the quantizer scales for each of the I, B, and P frames. Finally, you chose Macro-block Numbers Per Slice (don't ask) and the nature and extent of interframe searching, which, as we'll see, can dramatically affect both time and image quality.

Compression speed varied according to parameters chosen. At the High Quality preset, compression time for our 12.7-second test file was a relatively slow 12:15, or 58:1 asymmetric. To test optimal quality, we compressed a 25-second file with all quality options set to the max. We started the compression on our test bed Pentium 133 at 8:30 one evening, returning at 9:45 the next morning to find the compression run 2 percent complete. At this rate, it would have taken over 662 hours to compress the 25-second clip, or about 95,400 hours to compress an hour of video. Can't say about the quality, because we couldn't wait, but the compression time is probably too slow for most applications.

The Results Unfortunately, the High Quality setting did not live up to its name. Vitec came in dead last in every still image quality test and bested only Ulead, which played at about 3 fps, on real-time tests.

From a pure still image quality perspective, Vitec's clips were probably the only that were truly commercially unusable. On the low motion clip, the face was blocky and artifact ridden, as was the flat gray background. On the action clip, Vitec's sky sequences were blocky and smudged, with distinct artifacts around cables, towers, and other hard edges. While I frames retained their quality in the water sequence, B and P frames suffered badly, with blockiness often totally obscuring two or three characters.

Vitec faired no better in real-time playback. Even at 30 fps, facial artifacts were obvious and distracting in the talking head shot, while the background was the noisiest of all technologies. In the action sequence, the video appeared to flash, the result of quality degradation within a GOP that cleared up slightly at the I frame. Happily for those considering Vitec's video editor, files produced by Vitec were compatible with all players and playback speeds were tied with CeQuadrat for the fastest.

In truth, of all the products, we wished we could have experimented more with MPEG Maker in hopes of finding the magic configuration that produced good video. But slow compression times and the lack of a batch program frustrated our best intentions.

If you work with MPEG files long enough, you'll need a cheap way to clip heads and tails and perhaps merge two files, and Vitec's editor, included in MPEG Toolbox, is a great place to start. As a pure MPEG encoder, however, MPEG Maker is clearly not your best alternative.

MPEG Toolbox: $125
Vitec Multimedia
4366 Independence Ct., Suite C
Sarasota, FL 34234
Ph 941-351-9344/fax 941-351-9423

XingMPEG Encoder: $89, XING Technologies, Inc.

Xing Technologies pioneered software MPEG, and from the looks of their latest product, XingMPEG Encoder, they've put their experience to good use. Our cheapest product at $89, Xing topped our quality charts, was fully compatible with our test bed decoders, performed well in the playback tests, and was our fastest encoder. Although their software could be a bit easier to use, there's no question that Xing is the class of the software-only division and the best low-end encoder if you can afford to wait 42 hours for one hour of MPEG.

Xing was putting the finishing touches on their latest version while we were writing this review. While it was not available for testing, we did note the new feature highlights, especially when they addressed a problem or deficit reported in the review.

XingMPEG ships on a convenient CD-ROM that includes both encoder and player. A 16-bit application, the program was stable and performed well on our Windows 95 test bed. The encoder is a one-trick pony, compressing AVI files to MPEG system files and performing no multiplexing or separate audio conversion. Xing will reportedly provide both in an upcoming version.

Operation   XingMPEG Encoder is a full-screen application with a "jobs" window on the left and an MPEG preview/playback window on the right. You load an AVI file by pressing "new," which spawns another screen where you load the source AVI file, select a target directory and name for the new MPEG file, and choose your compression settings. To use the audio from the AVI file, you simply check a box after loading the file.

All compression settings are template driven—once you select the template, you lock in all video, audio, and system settings parameters. Xing will reportedly open up all parameters in the next version, alleviating the overly restrictive feel of the program.

There are templates for NTSC (352×240 at 30 fps), PAL (352×288 at 25 fps) and Film (352×240 at 24 fps) at single and double speed CD-ROM rates, White Book, quarter screen, and "match source," which matches the frame rate and video resolution of the captured video. This last template is how we matched the 320×240 resolution output by the FAST AV/Master, which didn't have a 352×240 capture option.

Although you can load multiple files into a batch file, you can't load more than one file at a time. The encoder doesn't save the compression parameters from file to file, forcing you to reset audio input and compression template for each file, bumping the number of keystrokes required to load

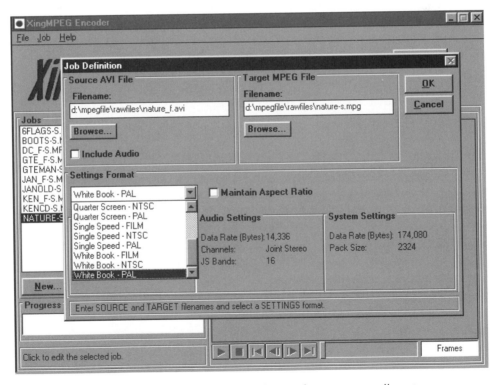

Figure 14.20   Xing's job definition is a bit confining, since all options are controlled by the template setting. Xing plans to fix this in future updates.

four files to about 36 strokes. While the program "remembers" the previous batch file even after exiting, you can't save a batch list and have to remove files manually after compression. Xing also limits the number of files in the batch file to 12.

The MPEG Encoder defaults to a hard-wired GOP size of 15 and B interval of two, but both will be configurable in their new version. Xing doesn't detect scene changes when compressing, but does customize encoding parameters to some degree according to video content.

Pressing "Start" initiates compression, which Xing performed at about a 45:1 ratio, making it the fastest software-only encoder. You can opt to display the file during compression, always a nice way to catch configuration errors.

Quality   When comparing Xing to the original captured video, we noticed that Xing tended to darken the video a bit, so you might consider bumping capture brightness to get an accurate picture.

Other than this, it's tough to find much to criticize about Xing's quality. MPEG Encoder was the overall winner in our still image tests and won every real-time competition outright.

In our low motion studio shot, the talking head was sharp and clear with only minor granularity and a slight hint of mosquitoes around the ears. The background exhibited occasional texturing and slight blockiness, but little of this was apparent at 30 fps playback, where Xing excelled.

In the action video, we had to look hard to find any blocky frame in the water sequence, which was remarkable considering the comparative quality of the other entries. Quality suffered during several hard transitions, but when it really counted, at 30 fps, Xing beat all other competitors with both decoders.

Compatibility   Experience also counts in creating MPEG files compatible with the universe of MPEG players, and Xing's entry sailed through our tests without a problem. Xing also performed well on playback tests, producing 29 fps or higher on all three tested decoders.

Clearly ahead of the pack today, it looks like version 2.0, due in the fourth quarter of 1996, will only lengthen the lead. The new version contains antialiasing and temporal filters and will adapt both interframe and intra-frame bit rate allocation to optimize quality. This means, for example, that highly detailed regions within a frame will get more data to work with than low-contrast regions, which helps maintain detail and eliminate artifacts in flat regions.

As computers get faster, software encoders have almost unlimited ability to stretch the boundaries of the MPEG algorithms to produce the best quality MPEG possible. Xing is well along that road already and appears committed to maintaining their leadership.

XingMPEG Encoder: $89
Xing Technologies, Inc.
1540 West Branch Street
Arroyo Grande, CA 93420-9934
Ph 805-473-0145/fax 805-473-0145

TIPS 'N' TRIX

We spent a lot of time working with these technologies and here's what we learned. Some are general rules about video development, some specific to MPEG compression. We hope you find them helpful.

Capture Station Issues

It's easy to assume that your capture and compression station accurately represents what happens in the real world. Unfortunately, this isn't the case. For this reason, it's important to test your video early and often on other systems representing your average target customer.

Note the emphasis on early. Nothing is worse that preparing half your video only to learn that it's too dark, too light, off synch, or otherwise won't play on your target platform. So as soon as you have a clip that represents your intended final parameters, carry it around and test, test, test. Here are some problems we ran into during our testing.

- *Sound Synchronization:* Several times during the review we swapped back and forth between the FAST AV/Master, which contains on board audio, and another sound card, the Microsoft Sound System. MPEG clips played back with the FAST AV/Master installed were consistently out of synch by one or two seconds, disastrous for talking heads. The same clips, however, were perfectly synchronized on the same computers when using the Microsoft Sound System. We didn't get to the bottom of the problem because we didn't have to, but had we been publishing these clips we would have tested every system in sight.

- *Video Brightness, Contrast and Colors:* We also tend to assume that our graphics cards and monitors represent some form of mass market reality, when they usually don't. Older monitors tend to slowly get darker and darker until all video looks ominous and looming. Different graphics cards can also produce wildly different colors.

Most graphics cards have calibration controls for adjusting video brightness, contrast, hue, and saturation. Some new cards even come with utilities that let you compare your settings to real world equivalents like Pantone colors and adjust your lighting for your workplace conditions. Both can help make sure your system is within normal limits. In any case, however, always test your captured video on several computers, making sure you're in a comfortable range that most graphics subsystems can easily view.

Configuration Issues

- *Use 320×240, not 352×240:* The official MPEG SIF resolution is 352×240, so you feel obligated to use this resolution rather than the more familiar 320×240. However, if your target playback system is a computer with a VGA screen, 352×240 will look stretched, so use 320×240 to produce the correct perspective. Don't worry, virtually all MPEG decoders play back both resolutions, so you're not increasing your incompatibility risks.
- *Don't bump your data rate:* The first time I ever saw a real-time MPEG encoder demonstration, the video looked totally awesome, better than any MPEG I had ever seen before. Then we checked the data rate, which weighed in at about 450 KB/s, and my perspective was corrected, since pretty much any codec looks awesome at 450 KB/s.

Most encoders have 2X options, which may seem reasonable in these days of 8X CD-ROM drives, but chasing the high-bandwidth quality siren will lead to slower playback rates on your software MPEG decoders and greater incompatibilities with hardware decoders. On our test computer, choosing the 2X option slowed playback of Darim-encoded files from 27 frames per second to 19 frames per second, *from the hard drive,* even though the compressed data rate was only about 20% higher. Expect the display rate to drop even further from a CD-ROM drive.

Process Issues

- *Don't batch process until you perfect the process.* As with all video development, assume that whatever can go wrong will go wrong. Don't capture 12 files, load them into Xing's encoder, and expect everything to be perfect the next morning. Capture one file, test for audio content and dropped frames, then compress it and make sure that Xing correctly recognizes the file and doesn't darken it too much for your target system. Then start batching.
- As with all video processing, time spent perfecting incoming video parameters like brightness, contrast, and color values is time exceptionally well spent. If you're working with a software encoder, you won't have time to fix it later, so get it done right the first time.

SUMMARY

1. All that glitters is not gold. Not all the inexpensive MPEG encoders are safe to use if you're concerned about issues like compatibility and real-world performance.
2. Our field of six yielded three clear winners based on quality, usability, and compatibility. These are:
    (a) Xing: best software-only encoder by far and best quality overall. If you've got the time, Xing produces the best quality of this bunch, certainly suitable for many commercial titles. A steal at $89.
    (b) Broadway: two-pass system produces video at 5:1 compression times. By the time you read this, Broadway will have square pixel output and the ability to turn filtering off for low motion videos. Interesting to compare quality with Xing then.
    (c) MPEGator: real time for under $995! Even if you're not from Florida you have to like this product, which produced surprisingly good video. Probably best used inhouse until some minor incompatibilities are worked out.

Chapter 15

MPEG-2 Technology

If there was a god of software publishing, it would almost certainly be Janus, the Roman god of new beginnings, always shown with two faces, one looking left, the other right. To be successful, software publishers must maintain a similar dual focus, one toward maximizing sales of current products, the other looking forward toward tools and technologies critical to future products.

Lately, all of our technology radar screens have been full. That bright greenish mass at the center is the Internet, now or very soon to be integral to even the most arcane software products. Right behind it is 3D, for three-dimensional graphics, now standard on most new graphics cards. Way out on the horizon, but approaching at warp speed, is Moving Pictures Experts Group 2 (MPEG-2), a digital video technology that represents the next quantum quality leap.

We know from our MPEG-1 experience that MPEG-2 encoder and de-coder vendors will soon be making the public relations rounds, generating mass quantities of editorial coverage with product and partnership an-nouncements. We can expect MPEG-2 advertisements by the bushel, that *Top Gun* will reappear in trade show booths, complete with Cruise close-ups and flybys, and that free seminars about how to profit from MPEG-2 will abound. We also know that, as with any new technology, some money will be made by early adapters and a lot lost.

This chapter seeks to determine whether MPEG-2 is a real blip or, as MPEG-1 was for many title developers, a false positive. We'll study market forecasts and technology projections, hear from MPEG-2 vendors, and explore the wacky, wonderful world of Digital Versatile Disk (DVD), where everyone's counting on Hollywood, but Holly wouldn't—at least not yet. (I'll explain later.) Even chat with a few software publishers. All toward helping you, and I promise this is the last radar metaphor, identify MPEG-2 as friend or foe. We start with a description of MPEG-2 technology.

TECHNOLOGY DISCUSSION

MPEG-2 Defined

MPEG-2 is an audio/video compression technology, or codec, short for en*co*der/*de*coder. As with all codecs, the video must be *encoded* during development with an MPEG-2 encoder and played back through the use of an MPEG-2 *decoder*.

The MPEG-2 standard is actually composed of three standards formu-lated by the Moving Pictures Experts Group, a working group of the International Standards Organization (ISO). ISO standard 13818-1 covers the MPEG-2 system stream, ISO 13818-2 addresses MPEG-2 video, and ISO 13818-3 describes MPEG-2 audio. Work on MPEG-2 started back in 1988, and all three standards were finally approved in November 1994.

MPEG-2 video resolution can range from 720×480 to 1280×720, with the latter targeted at high-definition television (HDTV) applications (Table 15.1). The most common resolution is 720×480, roughly the size of full-screen NTSC (National Television Standards Committee) television. This contrasts with MPEG-1's maximum resolution of 352×240, or quarter-

Table 15.1 Comparison of Video for Windows codecs, MPEG-1, and MPEG-2.

	Video for Windows	*MPEG-1*	*MPEG-2*
Resolution	320×240	352×240	720×480 to 1280×720
Frames per second	30	30	60 fields
Operational data rates	200–300 KB/s	150 KB/s and higher	600 KB/s and higher
Video codec	VQ/wavelet	DCT	DCT
Target quality	As good as possible	VHS	SVHS
Audio codec	None	MPEG-1	MPEG-2 (AC-3 for DVD)
Target quality	n.a.	CD-ROM	Six-channel CD-ROM quality digital surround sound
Target markets	CD-ROM	CD-ROM/CD-I, VideoCD	CD-ROM (DVD), direct broadcast satellite (DBS), cable television (CATV), HDTV

screen TV. Where MPEG-1 is limited to 30 *frames* per second, MPEG-2 can operate at 60 *fields,* the scan rate of NTSC television, enhancing suitability for broadcast applications like HDTV, cable television, and broadcast satellite.

Both MPEG-1 and MPEG-2 use similar interframe compression techniques such as motion compensation and the discrete cosign transform (DCT) intraframe technology. However, technology advances realized during the development process increase MPEG-2 quality to SVHS levels or higher, where MPEG-1 struggled to win VHS comparisons. MPEG-2 audio targets are also higher, enhancing MPEG-1's CD-ROM quality standard with six-channel digital surround sound.

Constant versus Variable Bit Rate   Like most video compression technologies, MPEG-2 uses *lossy* compression to reduce video data rates down to the required bandwidth. This technique makes different scenes more or less difficult to compress, with high-motion sequences with little interframe redundancy being the most difficult. In contrast, talking head sequences are relatively simple to compress.

This dynamic has spawned two compression approaches. Variable bit rate (VBR) encoding holds *quality* constant, increasing or decreasing the bit rate depending on scene complexity. This allows the developer to maintain a similar quality level over an entire title.

In contrast, constant bit rate encoding varies video quality to hold the data rate constant. This ensures that the video will stream smoothly from bandwidth-limited devices, such as 4X CD-ROM drives.

From an encoding standpoint, variable bit rate encoding is more complex, because most encoders must scan the entire movie beforehand to classify the various scenes, making compression at least a two-step process. Constant bit rate encoding is a simpler approach used on most inexpensive real-time encoders. Whereas most VBR-capable MPEG-2 encoders can also encode to a constant bit rate, the reverse is not true.

Since the 600 KB/s average MPEG-2 bandwidth is usually more than sufficient to encode even fast-moving scenery without artifacts, VBR comes in handy primarily when attempting to optimize disk space. For example, Zapex Technologies, manufacturer of the VBR-capable ZX Pro MPEG-2 encoder, claims that it can place up to 30 minutes of MPEG-2 video on a standard CD-ROM with no visual loss in quality.

MPEG-2 Quality   How good is MPEG-2 quality? Ed Heinbockel, president of Tsunami Media, publisher of video-intensive, multi-CD-ROM titles like *Silent Steel* and *Flash Traffic*, was sold on MPEG-2 from the start.

"I was blown away when we got our first samples back from Laser Pacific," Heinbockel gushed, identifying the service bureau that encoded his MPEG-2 footage. "Full screen video, much higher quality than MPEG-1 video—it was gorgeous, and I had to have it."

The inevitable price for this audio/video quality is bandwidth. At 150 KB/s, MPEG-1 targets the single-spin CD-ROM market, enabling about 72 minutes on a single 650-MB CD-ROM. In contrast, MPEG-2's bit rate hovers around 600 KB/s and can go much higher, requiring at least a quad spin drive, but, more important, amounting to at most 18 minutes on standard CD-ROMs.

By way of comparison, today's Video for Windows codecs, like Indeo video interactive and Cinepak, deliver sub-MPEG-1 video quality at quarter-screen resolutions and data rates as high as 300 KB/s. Audio quality is also less than that of either MPEG-1 or MPEG-2, because none of these codecs incorporate audio compression. For this reason, most video publishers typically use 11-kHz, 8-bit, monoaural audio, which is far below that offered by MPEG-1 and MPEG-2.

One final note: By definition, MPEG-2 decoders must also play back MPEG-1 files. As we'll see, this will significantly enhance the adoption of MPEG-2 players in the computer marketplace.

Digital Versatile Disk

For several years, MPEG-2 has played an increasingly important role in both cable television and satellite broadcasting, with nary a whimper in mainstream recognition. Driving MPEG-2 on our technology radar screen is DVD, which used to be Digital Video Disk but now stands for Digital Versatile Disk. Since MPEG-2 is so inexorably tied to this new format, let's discuss what it is and what it isn't.

Back when MPEG-1 was digital video's holy grail, many analysts predicted that VideoCD and CD-I players, which both used MPEG-1 compression, would soon supplant the lowly videocassette recorder (VCR) for home movie playback. Consumer electronics companies favored this motion: since VCRs were nearly ubiquitous, sales were flat, and they needed a new home appliance to boost sales. Eager to replace the relatively expensive and easy to bootleg VHS tape, Hollywood was also on board.

Although VideoCD and CD-I did well overseas, selling over seven million units in Europe and the Far East, according to Richard Doherty, president of Envisioneering Inc., a marketing research firm in Seaford, New York, the United States was the "black hole" for VideoCD. David Taylor, a director at C-Cube, who sold most of the decoder chips that populated the VideoCD units, explained why.

"When VideoCD was introduced into Europe, and especially the Far East," Taylor explained, "VHS and audio CD players were virtually nonexistent. VideoCD caught on because it was a cheap way to play back both audio and video CD-ROM–based formats."

"In addition," he continued, "artifacts in the MPEG-1 video weren't as evident on the small, 13" television screens used overseas. In the States, everyone had VHS and audio CD-ROM players, and 21" screens, which highlighted MPEG-1's deficiencies. For this reason, customers stayed away in droves, and VideoCD withered on the vine in North America."

Enter DVD, a CD-ROM specification formulated by a group of nine consumer electronic, entertainment, and computer companies that includes Sony, Philips, Time Warner, Pioneer, and Toshiba. With a minimum capacity of 4.7 GB, DVD offers seven times the real estate of traditional CD-ROMS, allowing developers to overcome both the quality and capacity issues.

DVD Feature Set   In one sense, DVD is nothing but a giant CD-ROM, capable of holding any kind of computer data, including different audio and video compression schemes whether AVI, MPEG-1, or MPEG-2. In the home, however, the capabilities of the DVD players control the feature set and content of DVD titles, as most developers will create titles that leverage these features.

DVD players will have the capability to:

- Decode MPEG-2 video and AC-3 audio streams with surround stereo.
- Support both wide-screen movies and regular or wide-screen televisions (4:3 and 16:9 aspect ratios).
- Support up to eight tracks of digital audio (for multiple languages), each with up to eight surround channels.
- Support up to 32 subtitle/karaoke tracks.
- Contain menus, icons, and other navigational features for games and other interactive titles.
- Support up to nine viewer-selectable camera angles (if supplied by the developer).
- Support language choice (for audio, subtitle tracks, and menus).
- Have programmability (playback of selected sections in a desired sequence). This would enable the viewer to watch a movie at the desired motion picture rating, cutting out violence and sex to suit the audience.
- Have special effects playback (high speed, frame by frame, and slow motion).
- Support parental lock (to deny playback of disks or scenes with objectionable material).

Even with the higher quality, higher bandwidth MPEG-2 compression, a DVD disk can hold 130 minutes of video, more than enough for most feature films. For most films, one DVD-ROM can hold the movie, with customized scenes for the various movie ratings, audio in different languages and closed captioned, and text tracks for the hearing impaired.

It's unclear whether these features are sufficiently compelling to launch a DVD revolution. What is clear, however, is that these new devices overcome the objections that stifled VideoCD's success in the U.S. marketplace.

DVD Markets   The DVD market segments into two clear branches that will ultimately converge in the middle. Home DVD players have the feature set described above and will launch in early 1997 for around $700 to $800.

DVD playback devices that connect to computers, or DVD-ROMs, are nothing more than storage devices with the greater capacity afforded by the DVD format. Original equipment manufacturer (OEM) prices for these devices dropped below $300 by the end of 1996, adding up to a retail price of $400 to $800 depending on the distribution channel.

Most DVD capabilities are well within the reach of most Pentium-based computers and their Macintosh equivalents. In order to play MPEG-2 movies, however, most computers will need a separate hardware player with MPEG-2/AC-3 audio decoding chips. These devices will initially cost well over $500 but should drop quickly in price if and when demand picks up.

A quick COMDEX survey (Las Vegas, November 1996) reveals that several developers, including Diamond and Panasonic, will offer bundled DVD-ROM/MPEG-2 and AC-3 players in early 1997 for around $1000 or less.

The two different markets for DVD players and DVD-ROMs represent two extremes and some difficult choices. Compared to linear play offered by VHS decks, DVD offers moviemakers and advertisers a wealth of new features.

However, software and CD-ROM title developers will find DVD players sorely lacking in processing power, storage, and graphics capabilities. A Pentium 166 with 16 MB of RAM presents virtually unlimited possibilities, which has spawned the incredible divergence of CD-ROM titles. In contrast, the capabilities of the home DVD player will seem severely restrictive.

For this reason, most computer content developers face a difficult choice. They can either defeature their products to make them compatible with home DVD players or ignore that market and port their products to DVD-ROM. In the latter case, DVD becomes nothing more than a giant CD-ROM, allowing the developer to implement the higher quality MPEG-2/AC-3 formats and pack in plenty of additional data.

For the most part, the success of MPEG-2 in the home will rise and fall on the success of DVD, which depends more on Hollywood content than software titles. As we'll see, most of the issues that could kill MPEG-2 on the computer, like standard application programming interfaces (APIs), won't affect home players.

On the other hand, MPEG-2's short-term success in the computer marketplace is far from assured. Since most software developers will focus on the DVD-ROM market, as opposed to the DVD player, we'll focus the rest of our analysis on DVD-ROM.

MPEG-onomics 101

Let's face it, from a CD-ROM title perspective, MPEG-1 was a flop, at least in the United States. Promises of MPEG Christmases in 1994, 1995, and even 1996 went unfulfilled, even as the installed base of software MPEG-1 decoders swelled into the tens of millions.

Although virtually everyone associated with MPEG-2 and DVD can cite thousands of reasons why MPEG-2 won't go the same route, it's instructive examine why MPEG-1 failed. At a high level, the computer industry works in dreary but predictable cycles, in which similar stimuli bring about similar responses. It always pays to examine the past, if only to make sure that you don't repeat it.

We'll start by debunking some myths about where MPEG-1 went awry. Then we'll move into the real reasons and measure the risk that MPEG-2 will go the same route.

Debunking the Myths

Myth 1: MPEG-1 Quality Wasn't Good Enough While researching for this chapter, we asked every participant why MPEG-1 failed in the CD-ROM title market. The overwhelming response was that pure video quality was insufficient. This sounds reasonable, and even hopeful, because MPEG-2's improved quality could allow it to adroitly avoid the same fate. What the quality myth ignores, however, is the success of the thousands of CD-ROM titles based on Indeo, Cinepak, TrueMotionS, Smacker, Video 1, and the many proprietary codecs written by Lucas Arts and similar publishers. In terms of pure quality per fixed bandwidth, MPEG-1 is superior to all these approaches. This doesn't even factor in the fact that MPEG-1 audio is CD-ROM quality, which far exceeds the 11- or 22-kHz audio used in most successful titles.

No—MPEG-1 looked and sounded better than any other alternative. Still, publishers stayed away in droves.

Myth 2: Encoding Was Too Expensive The second reason cited by most interviewees was encoding cost. In 1994, the cheapest MPEG-1 encoder cost around $20,000, much too expensive for most CD-ROM title developers. However, service bureaus charged under $100 per minute for encoding, which wasn't cheap but was insignificant compared to the seven-figure budgets of many projects.

In 1996, Xing's software MPEG-1 encoder, which delivers commercial quality MPEG-1 video, costs a mere $89, certainly within the budget of any software company. On the service bureaus front, Kent Smithegar, a vice president at Denon Digital, reports that he has dropped prices to as low as $20 per minute to boost production without stimulating new business.

In terms of real-time encoders, C-Cube's Taylor describes the MPEG-1 encoding market as "extremely inelastic," with sales volumes responding sluggishly, if at all, to price decreases. Although Taylor is still hopeful that a mass market for MPEG-1 encoders may yet emerge, clearly some dynamic other than ever-cheaper encoders will drive that market.

The good news is that both service bureaus and real-time encoder manufacturers continue to reduce the cost of MPEG-2 encoding, as we'll cover in detail later. This assures that encoding cost will never be a practical bar to DVD/MPEG-2 titles. The bad news, of course, is that if the lessons learned from MPEG-1 hold true, cheap encoding alone won't make the MPEG-2 market happen.

The law of MPEG-onomics should have been obvious in the first place—you can't force a format on a market simply by making encoders available and inexpensive. Instead, you create demand by showing title developers that converting to MPEG-1/MPEG-2 will increase demand for their products and help them make money.

Thus the chicken-and-egg problem that plagues many new formats. As described by Matrox's Caroline De Bie, "Consumers won't invest in new hardware if there are no titles, and title developers won't ship until they see a stable installed base."

Phil Davis, producer at Chicago-based Imagination Pilots, publisher of the video-intensive titles *Blown Away, Panic in the Park,* and *Eraser,* put it this way: "A new format isn't relevant to us until there's a large, stable market of compatible players that can support our sales volumes. We've stayed with Indeo because it gave us an installed base in the tens of millions."

Davis' comments reveal the two components of an installed base. First, it must be *large*, which hasn't been an issue for MPEG-1 since 1995, when software MPEG-1 players started shipping with most graphics cards and computers. MPEG-2 faces an uphill climb in this arena, since each computer must have two components, a DVD-ROM and an MPEG-2 player.

Second, and more important, the installed base of players must be *stable*, which means that title developers can reasonably expect their titles to be compatible with all players. As we'll see, this is the arena where MPEG-1 fell short and, without some fast intervention, MPEG-2 could fall short as well. But we get ahead of ourselves.

Lessons Learned

Let's look at other lessons learned from the MPEG-1 experience and see how they apply to MPEG-2.

Dual Market: OEM/Retail

From the CD-ROM publisher's perspective, the MPEG-2/DVD market will evolve in two stages. First will be the OEM market, in which vendors sell directly to the DVD-ROM manufacturer to bundle with the drive when sold to the end users. A similar market will probably evolve for titles bundled with MPEG-2 hardware players and for computers shipped with DVD-ROM and MPEG-2 players. The second distinct market will be for retail titles sold through traditional CD-ROM channels—storefront, mail order, or Internet distribution.

The first market is already happening. Tsunami Media has either closed or will soon close bundling agreements for *Silent Steel* with several drive manufacturers, consolidating their four CD-ROM MPEG-1 title into one DVD drive with MPEG-2 video and AC-3 audio. Xiphias Corporation recently announced the *Encyclopedia Electronica*, developed in close collaboration with Toshiba and presumably to be bundled with Toshiba drives. The new encyclopedia delivers 80 minutes of MPEG-2 video and AC-3 audio, 25,000 hyperlinked articles, and 15,000 chronological stories drawn from Xiphias' Timetable of History CD-ROM series.

As with the MPEG-1 market, most bundling agreements will be won by high-profile developers with big-budget titles. If you missed this boat, by timing or pedigree, you'll have to wait for the retail market.

The timing or even the ultimate success of the retail market is still uncertain. Tsunami's Heinbockel feels that the MPEG-2 market will make the transition from OEM to retail in the next 12–18 months. On the other hand, he comments, "the MPEG-1 market never made that transition. While we bundled *Steel* with several OEM products, we never did release a retail version in the MPEG-1 format."

Indeed, whereas most interviewees were ultimately bullish on the DVD market, thoughts on MPEG-2's success were much less sanguine. True, many industry watchers, including Envisioneering's Doherty, felt that the presence of MPEG-2 might retard MPEG-1's adoption. But no one really predicted that MPEG-2 would catch up before MPEG-1 became popular.

Although MPEG-2 has no similar technology waiting in the wings, the CD-ROM industry, voting with its virtual feet, has made it clear that they will adopt no technology that doesn't translate to increased sales. So let's move to the requirements of the MPEG-2 mass market.

Requirements of the Retail Mass Market

The retail mass market for MPEG-2 has three requirements, two described by Imagination Pilots' Davis: quantity and stability. Most industry watchers, like David Guenette, editor of *EMedia Professional* (formerly *CD-ROM Professional*) magazine, also feel that a DVD is necessary for MPEG-2 to succeed. Guenette comments, "MPEG-2 is what—18 minutes on a CD-ROM? It's safe to say that DVD is an absolute prerequisite for MPEG-2 taking off."

DVD-ROMs   Once again, few analysts doubt that DVD will quickly succeed CD-ROM units as the fixed storage medium on computers. Market researcher International Data Corporation, in its excellent report "DVD: Impact Analysis and Forecasts," predicts that DVD-ROM units will ship with 95% of systems with fixed storage by 2001, with DVD-ROM projections of 3.7 million in 1997, 10.8 million in 1998, 36.5 million in 1999, and 95 million in the year 2000. In general, IDC's projections are aggressive, with other analysts predicting about half of these volumes.

Even if IDC is accurate, however, remember that the installed base of traditional CD-ROMs in those years will far outnumber DVD, with projections of 143 million in 1997, 190 million in 1998, 224 million in 1999, and 203 million in the year 2000. Although DVD installed bases will quickly become tantalizing, traditional CD-ROMs still represent far more fertile ground, particularly because DVD players can read traditional CD-ROMs.

It's also important to remember that as of early 1997, the DVD-ROM specification is still not completely final, as the DVD group wrangles over issues like localization and copy protection. This stalls the completion of DVD players and DVD-ROMs as well as the repurposed Hollywood movie titles that ultimately will stimulate sales.

David Jones, group product manager at graphics developer ATI, expresses the frustration shared by many of the companies affected by these delays. "The success of DVD players and ultimately DVD-ROMs," he said, "depends on how quickly the titles come out—the joke is that everyone depends on Hollywood but Holly wouldn't."

"Hollywood wants the whole enchilada," he continued, "interactivity, multiple languages and digital copy protection, all right away, and the DVD specification keeps getting pushed out."

As do the ship dates for DVD players. Both Sony and Pioneer have canceled Christmas 1996 launch plans for their players, delaying their respective launches until 1997. Toshiba and Matshusita still claim that they will ship units in 1996, but as of early 1997, none had shipped.

Early player pricing doesn't point to a frenzy at the storefront either, since the cheapest units cost around $600. This, combined with the early lack of movie content, makes DVD players strictly for the early adapters.

On the business front, early sales of DVD-ROMs will be stifled by their lack of backward compatibility with CD-ROMs burned in CD-recordable devices, an increasingly popular mechanism for corporate mass storage. As DVD can't be a business' all-in-one fixed media reader until this is resolved, many corporations will opt for 10–12X drives for network use. This inability to read CD-R media will also retard title developer's efforts, as well, since they can't test one-off CD-ROMs in DVD-ROMs.

At this point, drive manufacturers are exploring two options: changing CD-R drive media or revving DVD hardware to let it read CD-recordable media. Either way, it's unlikely that a solution will be formulated, agreed upon, and implemented prior to the end of 1997.

All this adds up to a less than rosy forecast for early DVD sales in both the office and the home. Although it's still a "when, not if" scenario, it's tough to assume that market quantities of DVD-ROM drives will exist anytime sooner than 1998.

Even if these problems disappear, however—Hollywood gets a grip, DVD prices plummet, and DVD-ROM readers can magically read CD-R— MPEG-2 players present their own unique issues. And from a CD-ROM title developer's perspective, these problems can make Hollywood squabbling look like a tempest in a teapot.

MPEG-2 Players Like MPEG-1 decoders, MPEG-2 players fall into two categories: printed circuit boards with MPEG-2/AC-3 decoder chips that install in your computer and handle the entire decoding task, and software players that rely on the host CPU's horsepower to decode the two streams. We'll deal with hardware first.

Hardware Players: MPEG-2 add-in cards have existed for several years, courtesy of the companies participating in the broadcast arena. However, players for DVD-ROM will also require AC-3 audio decode, making this a brand-new market.

Graphics card companies, who ultimately ruled the MPEG-1 roost with software-only players, have varying timetables for their market entries. Most conservative is Matrox, which sells primarily to corporate markets. Matrox's Caroline De Bie said, "The momentum is clearly swinging towards MPEG-2, but the pieces haven't all come together. We're not seeing it happen until mid to end of 1997, and are planning accordingly."

ATI Technologies plans to release a hardware-based DVD offering in the first quarter of 1997. ATI's David Jones commented that the company's OEM customers were banking on the convergence of computers and television and needed MPEG-2 to compete with DVD players.

Most aggressive was Diamond Multimedia, which views the DVD/ MPEG-2 player combination as the next great upgrade opportunity, replacing lagging sales of multimedia upgrade kits. Diamond showed an MPEG-2/AC-3 player prototype at the fall COMDEX in 1996. Pricing wasn't set, but product manager Scott Kim stated that it would range between $500 and $1000. Still, he admitted, "until the combined price for DVD-ROMs and MPEG-2 players drops below $800, we'll only be selling to early adopters and enthusiasts."

Fortunately, it shouldn't be long until MPEG-2 decoder prices support Kim's formula for success. C-Cube's Dave Taylor says that by the end of 1996, the complete bill of materials for an MPEG-2/AC-3 decoder board would be less than $150, translating to a end user price of under $300, depending on sales channel. Taylor predicts that pricing will drop slowly but steadily as MPEG-2 catches on in satellite, broadcasting, and DVD markets.

IDC expects early DVD-ROMs to cost OEMs around $275 by the end of 1996, down to under $226 in 1997 and $145 in 1998. Depending on distribution channels, this translates to end user pricing as low as $400 in 1996, dropping to $300 and $200 in 1997 and 1998, respectively. At the fall COMDEX, STB Corporation announced an MPEG-2/AC-3 decoder priced at $200 in OEM quantities, so IDC's numbers may be high. Also at the show, Quadrant International announced a similar product priced at $425 retail.

Combining the numbers, by the end of 1997, consumers should be able to buy a DVD upgrade kit with both DVD-ROM and MPEG-2/AC-3 player for well under $600. A year later, it should easily cost under $400. New computer buyers should be able to upgrade to DVD/MPEG-2 options for about 50% of the upgrade cost.

One caveat on the hardware player side. From a design and interface perspective, most MPEG-2/AC-3 players will be unique and generally proprietary in design. To support the transfer of the high-bandwidth MPEG-1 video from player to graphics card, developers like ATI and Diamond generally eschew the PCI bus in favor of more direct connections to the graphics card.

Since Diamond primarily uses S3 parts, their MPEG-2/AC-3 player will connect to the graphics card's Scenic Highway port, a proprietary S3 connector. Although their MPEG-2/AC-3 player *might* work with other, non-Diamond S3-based boards, it won't work at all with boards based on other chips. Similarly, ATI's approach depends on their own ATI Media Channel, or AMC. This means that ATI's MPEG-2/AC-3 player won't work with *any* non-ATI graphics card.

Not only will these proprietary designs cause confusion in the marketplace, they will also stifle the design and sales of "clone" MPEG-2/AC-3 player cards, which generally help drive prices down. As we'll see, however, even more important is the fact that these proprietary designs make it extremely difficult to achieve a stable playback API, which may create the same dynamic that prevented MPEG-1 from achieving mass-market success.

Software Players: Software players are MPEG-2 decoders that rely on the host CPU for the horsepower to decompress and play MPEG-2 video and AC-3 audio. MPEG-2 software players have been around since early 1996, with CompCore Multimedia showing a software MPEG-2/AC-3 decoder at Intermedia in March 1996. In late October 1996, rival MediaMatics announced a competitive offering.

Estimates vary about the amount of computing power necessary to support an MPEG-2/AC-3 software player, but it is universally agreed that an MMX-powered computer, or the equivalent, is required. Since MMX shipments won't start until early 1997, this means that, at the very least, the entire installed base of computers in December 1996 will never play MPEG-2 in software. Quite a stark concept given that this group of computers must pay all of our bills for at least the next few months.

Still, IDC predicts that over 44 million MMX computers will ship in 1997. Combined with projections of 97 million in 1998 and 112 million in 1999, this adds up to the quite tidy sum of well over 200 million units installed by the new millennium. But this *doesn't* mean that all of these computers can play MPEG-2/AC-3 without hardware assist.

In scarce supply as of the writing of this chapter, we couldn't test MPEG-2 playback on an MMX computer, so we have to rely on anecdotal evidence. Bullish on MPEG-2/AC-3 hardware, Envisioneering's Doherty predicts that the current crop of Pentium-powered computers will never play MPEG-2/AC-3 in software and that the next generation P6 computer, or Klamath, will be required. Diamond's Kim agrees, stating that "MPEG-2 will be a software-only solution way down the road, and doesn't play a factor in our early DVD strategy."

In contrast, Tsunami's Heinbockel reports seeing about "24 frames per second" on an MMX Pentium 166. Both CompCore and MediaMatics expect to ship software players in early 1997, though neither provides playback statistics in their press materials or Web page—perhaps Proposition 211 at work. Intel has also been very close-mouthed about performance numbers, preferring to wait until all computers and software players ship.

In confusing times, it pays to seek answers in the past. Our MPEG-1 experience tells us that early performance numbers will be computed on highly tuned systems that don't represent the real-world norm. For example, both MediaMatics and CompCore consistently demonstrated their early MPEG-1 software on computers equipped with Diamond's highly regarded, but expensive ($700) Viper Pro, with a separate video coprocessing chip. Swap out the graphics card for a consumer model and the same computer produced about 50% *fewer* frames per second.

On a positive note, experience also tells us that the software approach will ultimately bear fruit. On a Pentium 133 with even an average consumer graphics card, software MPEG-1 players produce up to 30 frames per second. Although it's impossible to predict which MMX computer will ultimately suffice, it's clearly a "when, not if" scenario. Sometime soon, certainly by mid-1998 and probably sooner, all new computers will be able to play MPEG-2/AC-3 media without hardware.

As we learned from our MPEG-1 experience, however, the fact that the number of decoders is large doesn't mean it's stable. And in many ways, a large unstable market is worse than no market at all.

API Issues   Application programming interfaces, or APIs, are the glue that holds programs and players together. For example, Diamond's MPEG-2/AC-3 player will have a specific interface that DVD-ROM titles must "call" to make it play, fast forward, rewind, and stop playing MPEG-2 files.

When a body of players has a well-defined API, all titles calling that device play reliably. When customers press play, the video plays in the intended window. When they press stop, it stops.

If there was any single culprit in MPEG-1's failure, it was the lack of a stable playback API that prevented titles from playing reliably over a range of MPEG decoders. As Tsunami's Heinbockel comments, "Standards are good things—unless you have playback standards that are closely adhered to, customers won't buy into a new format, and volume retail sales simply won't happen."

MPEG-1's well-chronicled problems started back in 1994, when Real-Magic developer Sigma Designs tried to force title developers to support its proprietary API. The hardware and software development communities resisted, led by Microsoft, which released the MCI-MPEG API in June 1994. The Microsoft specification garnered widespread support and soon made the transition to an industry group called the Open MPEG-1 (OM-1) Foundation.

Unfortunately, the OM-1 specification contains 29 separate calls, some with as many as 10 options. The sheer complexity of the specification, combined with inadequate documentation, resulted in inconsistent implementations among playback vendors, especially offshore clones, creating the unstable playback environment.

In March 1996, the OM-1 Foundation released more comprehensive documentation that should have enabled tighter adherence to the specification. But the highly fractured market never really responded, and compatibility issues continued.

Many title publishers are pinning their MPEG-1 hopes on the MPEG-1 software player in Microsoft's recently released ActiveMovie. Based on software licensed from MediaMatics, the MPEG-1 player performs well and will be available to all Windows 95 developers at no charge. Essentially, the ActiveMovie player lets each developer ship a known compatible player with its title, ensuring playback stability.

Given the seriousness of the MPEG-1 issues and incident bad publicity, you would expect that Microsoft and the rest of the MPEG-2 community planned ahead to avoid similar issues. Unfortunately, this isn't the case.

It appears that each MPEG-2 player will use a unique, proprietary API. Diamond reports that its MPEG-2 API is "based on Microsoft's MPEG-1 API, as modified by Diamond." ATI will use its own API, as will CompCore and MediaMatics.

While we can assume that the each developer will seek to conform as closely as possible to the OM-1 specification, there is no organization ensuring compatibility. Lessons from MPEG-1 tell us that despite best intentions to stay within a specification, natural entropy causes slight differences between player APIs. In the binary world of computer programming, it doesn't take much for this to make a title designed for one player totally incompatible with another.

Note that this isn't an issue in the DVD player market, an oligopoly characterized by large, established companies with entire departments for maintaining compatibility. Major studios targeting this market can simply purchase most players and test compatibility before release.

In the zero barrier to entry computer market, the $150 MPEG-2/AC-3 decoder cost of materials will likely generate dozens of product entries from the Pacific Rim, reminiscent of the fall COMDEX 1994, when over 50 MPEG-1 hardware decoders were announced and/or on display. Unwary consumers who buy these boards expecting compatibility will be sorely disappointed and perhaps soured on DVD as a format.

Microsoft has committed to releasing an MPEG-2/AC-3 API with the third OEM Service Release (OSR3) of Windows 95, extending their ActiveMovie

API with the help of MediaMatics, scheduled for late second quarter, 1997. If Microsoft is timely and the MPEG-2/AC-3 development community immediately responds, a stable API by Christmas 1997 looks tough but isn't out of the question. If Microsoft slips by even a couple of months, it could delay the DVD mass market for another full season.

Although the MPEG-2/AC-3 specification is certainly of primary importance, it's not the only relevant specification. Today, the API used on DVD players has no analog on the Windows platform. This means that computers have no standardized way to access features like language control and branching, preventing Windows 95 computers from accessing DVD features. Once again, Microsoft has committed to releasing a comprehensive DVD specification with OSR3 during mid-1997.

Analysis: Hardware versus Software   With MPEG-1, many of the same factors conspired to doom the hardware add-in market. Still, hope springs eternal in the computer marketplace, and many developers feel that MPEG-2 will be different.

ATI's Jones admits that ATI's hardware MPEG-1 sales were very small but states that the growing trend toward convergence makes hardware MPEG-2 a significant checklist item of ATI's larger OEMs. "Our OEMs are hoping to move the computer from the back room to the living room," Jones said, "and MPEG-2 is a key ingredient, along with other features like video out and video capture."

Others feel that MPEG-2 hardware will go the way of MPEG-1 hardware, preventing an early retail market from happening. Intuitively, this feels correct. Through the end of 1997 there will be few if any compelling DVD titles, DVD-ROM/MPEG-2 bundles will be priced well over $500, and standards issues will abound. One year later, software MPEG-2/AC-3 decoding on MMX computers will be a reality and essentially free, more titles will be available, and the standards issues (we hope) will be resolved.

EMedia Professional's Guenette flatly states, "If MPEG-1 is any indicator, then hardware MPEG-2 market may never take off." Tsunami's Heinbockel agrees: "One lesson from MPEG-1 is that the hardware market may never happen. We're counting on software MPEG-2 playback on new boxes with MMX technology much more than the upgrade market."

OTHER FACTORS

Also worth considering are other factors that make MPEG-2 more or less attractive than other compression formats. In addition to the always relevant playback platform requirements, these factors range from its full-screen resolution to its lack of interactivity and—gasp!—the specter of per-unit royalties.

Interface Design

As a full-screen video format, MPEG-2 may be somewhat unsuitable for certain interactive software programs, especially in the training arena. Interactive Designs of Wilmington, Delaware, designs and creates training programs for clients as varied as a big six accounting firm and a 2000-unit fast-food chain.

Interactive Design's president, Jan Diamondstone, commented that "full-screen video means non-interactive training, since video is just one element of a good training program. We like quarter-screen video because it lets us incorporate text bullets, animations, or even multiple video windows while keeping all relevant elements on screen at the same time."

Sherry Manning, president of Washington, DC–based Triad Interactive, a title producer whose clients include Richard D. Irwin (subsidiary of McGraw-Hill), feels the same way about retail training titles. Referring to the Multimedia MBA, produced for Irwin, Manning stated, "In our reference products, video is the sizzle, but text-based content is the steak. Our customers like quarter-screen video since it lets them read other screen elements like bullet points and charts that might relate to the video, or quickly decide to move on if the video isn't pertinent to their current research project."

Both Manning and Diamondstone agree that producing for the *installed base of computers* was key to their success. "Our titles have to run on 486 computers installed in up to 1500 stores," Diamondstone explained. "They all have sound cards and CD-ROM drives, and play Indeo files just fine. If you add even $500 for the DVD-ROM and MPEG-2 player, you're adding $750,000 to the cost of deployment, which definitely won't fly."

"Our customer targets the academic market and business users," Manning added, "and their minimum base computer is a 486/66, with 2X CD-ROM running 3.2 or Windows 95. This might increase to a Pentium 133, at the highest, and we might consider MPEG-1 for that edition because the API is stabilizing. But certainly not MPEG-2."

Interactivity

The market has come a long way since adding real-time video to a title guaranteed both editorial and market success. Jill Anderson, CD-ROM editor at *Computer Gaming World*, feels that video is a difficult medium for gaming and is often overused.

"Video is kind of a null format in the game market since it's extremely difficult to make it interactive," Anderson stated. "With 3D graphics and a robust gaming engine, games like Quake and Duke are a unique experience each time you play them. In contrast, video-based games are totally prescripted with usually only two or three branching options."

Imagination Pilots injected a great deal of interactivity in their newest title, *Eraser,* which uses Intel's new Indeo video interactive, with a video maze that simulates 3D action and variability. As users travel through the maze, interactions with other characters are all in real time and randomized, so you never duplicate the same experience. Phil Davis describes how this was accomplished: "We have two engines running simultaneously, one reading the video one second ahead of the player, and one playing," Davis explained. "A table contains all potential branching options and a random number generator jumps the player to various locations in the video file in real time. This gives us 3D-like responsiveness in the video environment."

"We had to get deep into the guts of Video for Windows to make this work," Davis continued, "much deeper than we could get into a software MPEG-1 player."

FREE IS GOOD: MPEG-2 ROYALTIES

One of the basic tenets of software publishing is that free is good, especially when it applies to video compression. With free technologies like Indeo and Cinepak readily available, many codec companies have had difficulty building a successful business model that involved charging and collection per-CD-ROM royalties.

One of the most intriguing but least talked about issues concerning both MPEG-1 and MPEG-2 is royalties. Many companies, including Philips, AT&T, and Compression Laboratories, contributed to the pool of MPEG-1 patents. At some point, one assumes, they would like to be paid for their work.

In a press release dated March 27, 1995, Cable Television Laboratories (CableLabs) announced the results of an MPEG Intellectual Property Rights (IPR) committee meeting held in Switzerland the previous week. The press release states, in relevant part:

> The group arrived at an initial conclusion on a model for paying royalties on MPEG-related products such as digital encoders; digital decoders, including set top boxes; digital videodisk (DVD) players; and pre-recorded storage media such as video CDs, DVDs, and pre-recorded magnetic media.
>
> The group has discussed and has reached consensus on targeting a $3 to $4 (U.S.) royalty on each digital decoder, including MPEG-2 set top boxes, digital videodisk (DVD) players, and decode-for-general-purpose processors. Using that target and based upon the mode discussed below, that would result in a $0.03 to $0.04 (U.S.) royalty on each video CD or DVD that would be purchased. Also, there would be a $0.30 to $0.40 (U.S.) royalty on each video CD or DVD that was for distribution use (i.e., rental market).

The press release did not state whether the royalty would be applied retroactively or prospectively or when the MPEG-IRP group would start calling on MPEG encoder/decoder developers and title developers. However, since the $3 to $4 (U.S.) royalty roughly doubles or triples the licensee fee paid by graphics card developers for software MPEG-1 decoders, it threatens to change the economics of including such decoders with every graphics card.

In late 1995 the rumor mill reported that the MPEG-IRP would attempt to collect a royalty of $0.10 per software decoder, rather than $4. Since the announcement, however, the MPEG-IRP group has remained silent, despite Microsoft's ActiveMovie launch, which will spawn the distribution of tens of millions of additional MPEG-1 decoders. Envisioneering's Doherty expressed surprise, pointing out that "the MPEG-IRP's failure to act could constitute a waiver of their future ability to collect royalties. It may be too late for MPEG-1—unless they act soon, they may miss the boat on MPEG-2 as well."

If DVD takes off in the home, it's almost inconceivable that the MPEG patent holders wouldn't take action to collect royalties. Until we know for sure, however, the potential for royalties is a dark cloud over all facets of the MPEG industry, causing much concern in executive suites about potential royalty obligations on encoders, decoders, and CD-ROM titles.

CONCLUSIONS

Mary Sauer, senior vice president at MPEG-2 manufacturer Sonic Solutions, suggests that software publishers have essentially four options:

1. Do nothing and continue to ship MPEG-1, AVI, or QuickTime-based titles on CD-ROM.
2. Convert to DVD-ROM format using existing assets and program engine, which would cost under $10,000 to get to a master DVD, less if you use a service bureau. Although the resulting title won't play on home DVD players, it will play on DVD-ROMs without MPEG-2/AC-3 decoders.
3. Convert to DVD-ROM format, upgrading the program assets to MPEG-2/AC-3 but using the current program engine. This costs the same as option two, plus conversion costs, which can be considerable. The resulting title still won't play on DVD players

and won't run on DVD-ROMs unless the computer also has an MPEG-2/AC-3 player board.

4. Author a new title, complete with MPEG-2/AC-3, that will run on both DVD-ROMs and DVD players. This provides the broadest possible distribution but severely limits program logic. Note that the new title must be completely reauthored in a DVD authoring system, dramatically increasing total costs.

One other option, which combines options two and three, also comes to mind—shipping dual-media or even trimedia titles containing MPEG-1, MPEG-2, and perhaps Indeo video interactive. Sixty minutes of video in each format adds up to less than 3.7 GB, leaving another GB for programs and other formats. While working with both quarter-and full-screen video poses some challenging interface issues, this alternative maximizes the publishers' target market, for both retail and bundled sales.

Then the issue comes down to when. Certainly publishers chasing bundling dollars are behind the curve, as publishers like Tsunami have obviously been working on DVD/MPEG-2 for a year or more. On the retail front, nothing we've seen indicates that 1997 will end with a large, stable installed base of MPEG-2 players, which probably means that the MPEG-2 market won't hit critical mass before 1998 at the earliest.

Still, Richard Doherty advises, "The average software developer needs to be thinking about DVD and MPEG-2 today." Probably good advice.

MPEG-2 Encoding

Service Bureau   If you're looking to test the MPEG-2 waters, service bureaus represent the least expensive option. Many service bureaus claim MPEG-2 encoding capabilities, but we could track down only two that would quote prices. IBM (770-835-7193) performs MPEG-2 encoding services from their Atlanta office starting at $70 per minute for constant bit rate encoding.

NB Engineering (www.NBENG.com) offers two pricing levels, with constant bit rate encoding starting at $70 per minute, dropping to $30 per minute for large quantities, and VBR encoding starting at $200 per minute, dropping to $100. Both companies offer consulting services to help software developers through the maze of DVD, MPEG-2, and AC-3 issues. Either way, as with MPEG-1, pure encoding costs are so low that even small publishers can convert to MPEG-2.

Stand-alone Encoders If you're looking to purchase, systems start at $40,000 and increase to over $500,000, although the higher priced systems generally include DVD authoring as well. Key options to verify include whether the system performs AC-3 encoding as well as MPEG-2 and whether the encoder does variable bit rate encoding as well as constant. A partial list of encoding systems is presented in Table 15.2.

Table 15.2 MPEG-2 encoding systems.

Company	Product Name	Description	Price	Availability	Contact
NTT Electronics	Reimay	MPEG-2 real-time encoder	$40,000	Shipping	Heuris Pulitzer (314-721-0942)
Vela Research	Centaur	MPEG-2/AC-3	$80,000	Shipping	www.vela.com
Optibase	MPEG Fusion	MPEG-2 (third-party AC-3)	?	Shipping	www.optibase.com
Minerva Systems	Compressionist 250	MPEG-2 (third-party AC-3)	$99,000	Shipping	www.minervasys.com
Optivision	VS40	MPEG-2 only	$45,000	Shipping	800-562-8934
Zapex	ZX Pro	MPEG-2/AC-3	$80–$90,000	Shipping	www.Zapex.com
Sonic Solutions	DVD Creator	MPEG-2/AC-3/ DVD Mastering	Up to $500,000	Shipping	www.sonicsolutions.com

Index

About AP PROFESSIONAL

AP PROFESSIONAL, an imprint of Academic Press, a division of Harcourt Brace & Company, was founded in 1993 to provide high quality, innovative products for the computer community. For over 50 years, Academic Press has been a world leader in documenting scientific and technical research.

AP PROFESSIONAL continues this tradition by providing its readers with exemplary publications that bring new topics to light and offer fresh views on prominent topics. Often, today's computer books are underdeveloped clones, published in haste and promoted in series. Readers tend to be neglected by the lack of commitment from other publishers to produce quality products. It is our business to provide you with clearly written, educational publications that contain valuable information you will find truly useful. AP PROFESSIONAL has grown quickly and has established a reputation for fine products because of this commitment to excellence.

Through our strong reputation at Academic Press, and one of the most experienced editorial boards in computer publishing, AP PROFESSIONAL has also contracted many of the best writers in the computer community. Each book undergoes three stages of editing (technical, developmental, and copyediting) before going through the traditional book publishing production process. These extensive measures ensure clear, informative, and accurate publications.

It is our hope that you will be pleased with your decision to purchase this book, and that it will exceed your expectations. We are committed to making the AP PROFESSIONAL logo a sign of excellence for all computer users and hope that you will come to rely on the quality of our publications.

Enjoy!

Jeffrey M. Pepper
Vice President, Editorial Director

Related Titles from AP PROFESSIONAL

VAUGHAN-NICHOLS, *Intranets*

WATKINS/MARENKA, *The Internet Edge in Business*

WAYNER, *Agents at Large*

WAYNER, *Digital Cash*

WAYNER, *Disappearing Cryptography*

WAYNER, *Java and JavaScript Programming*

Ordering Information

 AP PROFESSIONAL
An imprint of ACADEMIC PRESS
A division of HARCOURT BRACE & COMPANY

ORDERS (USA and Canada): 1-800-3131-APP or APP@acad.com
AP Professional Orders: 6277 Sea Harbor Dr., Orlando, FL 32821-9816

Europe/Middle East/Africa: 0-11-44 (0) 181-300-3322
Orders: AP Professional 24-28 Oval Rd., London NW1 7DX

Japan/Korea: 03-3234-3911-5
Orders: Harcourt Brace Japan, Inc., Ichibancho Central Building 22-1, Ichibancho Chiyoda-Ku, Tokyo 102

Australia: 02-517-8999
Orders: Harcourt Brace & Co., Australia, Locked Bag 16, Marrickville, NSW 2204 Australia

Other International: (407) 345-3800
AP Professional Orders: 6277 Sea Harbor Dr., Orlando, FL 32821-9816

Editorial: 1300 Boylston St., Chestnut Hill, MA 02167 (617) 232-0500

Web: http://www.apnet.com/approfessional

Special Offers for *Publishing Digital Video* Readers

PDV Explorer

We hope to have included a program called PDV Explorer on the CD-ROM to help you navigate through the various chapters, checklists, videos, and other resources. At this time, a few weeks from release, we don't know if the program was completed and tested in time to ship with the book (ain't software development grand?). However, all necessary media is on the CD-ROM, accessible via both Acrobat and VCS Play 32 as described on page xxv, About the CD-ROM.

Check the Readme file on the root of the CD-ROM for status. If PDV Explorer didn't make it, you can upload the file from www.doceo.com\pdv for free *if you are a currently registered user.*

VCS Play 32 $25

The version of VCS Play 32 included with the book loads only when the CD-ROM is in the drive. *Upgrade to a full retail version of VCS Play 32 for $25—a savings of $25 below retail cost.**

VCS 4.0 $75

So many technologies, so little time. VCS is the standard for benchmarking video codecs in the video publishing community. While *Publishing Digital Video* contains a number of sample files from various software and codecs, VCS contains the full test suite for all software codecs, demonstrating performance at all relevant data rates and frame rates. *Purchase VCS 4.0 for $75, a savings of $55 below retail cost.*

VCS MPEG

In a perfect world, before buying an MPEG-1 encoder you'd compress a bunch of footage with competitive systems and carefully compare criteria like low and high motion quality, background noise, and the ability to handle scene changes. Then you'd test the file on a number of target systems to ensure playback compatibility. In your spare time, you'd summarize your findings regarding ease of use and feature set to make sure you were buying the optimally configured system.

Well, the world's not perfect, but you can still buy the best MPEG-1 encoder with VCS MPEG, the MPEG benchmark lab on CD-ROM. We currently ship three versions, VCS MPEG-L for low-end encoders (costing under $2,000), VCS MPEG-H (costing $2,000 and up), and VCS MPEG-S (service bureaus). *As a PDV reader, you're entitled to a $50 discount on any VCS MPEG version.*

Check www.doceo.com for detailed specifications on all products.

*Offer valid only for e-mail upgrades. Readers who want the diskette/CD-ROM must pay $32.50 plus $10 shipping and handling.